D0205722

America's Siberian Expedition, 1918-1920

America's
Siberian Expedition, 1918-1920

A Study of National Policy

BETTY MILLER UNTERBERGER

GREENWOOD PRESS, PUBLISHERS
NEW YORK

Table of Contents

America's Siberian Expedition, 1918-1920

CHAPTER I

Background for Intervention

O N AUGUST 18, 1918, Major General William S. Graves and a contingent of American soldiers sailed from San Francisco, bound for Vladivostok, Siberia. Graves had been informed in a rather unusual manner of the character of his mission. On August 2 he had received a secret code message from Washington, directing him to "take the first and fastest train out of San Francisco and proceed to Kansas City." Upon his arrival, he was to go to the Baltimore Hotel and ask for the Secretary of War. Graves considered this one of the most remarkable communications that had ever come out of the War Department. He left immediately for Kansas City. There he met Newton D. Baker, Secretary of War, who informed him that he was being sent to Siberia. Baker then handed him a sealed envelope, saying, "This contains the policy of the United States in Russia which you are to follow. Watch your step; you will be walking on eggs loaded with dynamite. God bless you and good-bye."[1] Thus began one of the strangest adventures in American military history.

Military intervention in Siberia became the most important phase of American foreign policy in the Far East during and immediately following World War I. Its effects were far-reaching, especially as applied to American relations with two great powers, Russia and Japan. Intervention initiated a trend in America's attitude toward Soviet Russia, and introduced America's greatest offensive against Japanese expansion on the Asiatic continent prior to World War II.

Basically, the decision to send an expedition to Siberia was a continuation of America's traditional foreign policy in the Far East. During the nineteenth and twentieth centuries the keynote of that policy rested upon the principle of equal commercial opportunity for all.

[1] William S. Graves, *America's Siberian Adventure, 1918-1920* (New York, 1931), pp. 2-4.

This principle was supported to a limited degree by interested European powers until after the Sino-Japanese War of 1894-95. China's humiliating defeat introduced a new phase in her history. In 1897-98 Germany and Russia took the lead in carving out naval leaseholds and spheres of influence in China. John Hay, as American Secretary of State, sought to protect American interests by means of the well-known open-door notes in 1899, in which he asked assurances from the powers addressed that equality of commercial opportunity would be maintained within their "spheres of interest." The replies of the powers were in each instance qualified and grudging. Nevertheless, Hay decided to accept them as indicating agreement.[2] Although the American public was heartily in favor of the open-door policy, it had no intention of upholding it by force. Japan, however, was in a different position. She felt that her national security was gravely threatened as Russia continued her politico-economic advance into Manchuria, where she already held important railway concessions and a naval leasehold at Port Arthur in Liaotung. When Russia paid no heed to her protests, Japan launched the Russo-Japanese War.

President Theodore Roosevelt leaned toward Japan during the war in the belief that a limited Japanese victory would safeguard American interests in the Far East. This was in line with America's traditional policy of friendship toward Japan. Having introduced Japan to the modern world in 1854, the United States continued to take a maternal interest in her welfare. Japan fared well in those years. By the end of the century her prestige had grown enormously. Her superior position in the Far East was recognized by Great Britain in the Anglo-Japanese Alliance of 1902, renewed with modifications in 1905 and again in 1911.[3] However, the Russo-Japanese War of 1904-5 marked a turning point in relations between the United States and Japan. Japan's military and naval victories endowed her with a new prestige and contributed to the security problem of the United States in the Philippines. Moreover, the war set Japan well on the road to control in Korea, while by the Treaty of Portsmouth (1905) she secured from Russia the Liaotung leasehold, the southern half of the island of Sakhalin, and control of what later became the vital South Manchuria Railway.[4] This was the beginning of serious friction between the governments of the United States and Japan. Issues more specific in

[2] Paul H. Clyde, The Far East (New York, 1948), pp. 295-296; A. Whitney Griswold, The Far Eastern Policy of the United States (New York, 1938), pp. 36-87.

[3] Griswold, Far Eastern Policy, pp. 88-91, 115-116, 165-169.

[4] Tyler Dennett, Roosevelt and the Russo-Japanese War (New York, 1925), pp. 236-277.

character soon appeared. In 1906 there was the charge by American traders that Japan was closing the open door of equal commercial opportunity in Manchuria.[5] In the same year came the San Francisco School Board incident and demands for Japanese exclusion. Additional racial problems arose to trouble Japanese-American relations during the Wilson administration.[6]

By 1909, despite a multitude of official protestations on Chinese sovereignty and the open door, both Russia and Japan had acquired strong positions in Manchuria. Each controlled a vital railway in that area. Thereupon the American Secretary of State, Philander C. Knox, devised an extraordinary plan for the neutralization of the Manchurian railways and presented it to the interested powers. He privately confessed that he was attempting to "smoke Japan" out of her dominant position. Both Russia and Japan refused to consider his proposal.[7] Realizing their common interests in Manchuria, they had begun to negotiate a series of secret conventions in 1907 which clearly defined their respective spheres of interest.[8] The Knox neutralization scheme only succeeded in hastening the 1910 convention, whereby both powers undertook to respect each other's special interests in Manchuria.[9] Their final treaty, signed in 1916, revealed their attitude toward a possible American intervention in the Far East.[10] The two nations agreed to come to each other's aid in the event of a declaration of war by a third power.

Japan's entry into World War I further increased her prestige and position in the Far East. Early in the war she occupied the German leasehold of Tsingtao, as well as the German islands in the North Pacific. In addition, she took over German interests in Shantung. Then, taking advantage of the world's preoccupation with the war, she presented to China a series of Twenty-One Demands which in

[5] Eleanor Tupper and George E. McReynolds, *Japan in American Public Opinion* (New York, 1937), p. 15.

[6] For a detailed account of these problems, see Thomas A. Bailey, *Theodore Roosevelt and the Japanese-American Crises* (Stanford, 1934).

[7] Paul H. Clyde, *International Rivalries in Manchuria, 1689-1922* (Columbus, 1926), chap. ix; C. Walter Young, *Japan's Special Position in Manchuria* (Baltimore, 1931), chap. v.

[8] Earnest Batson Price, *The Russo-Japanese Treaties of 1907-1916 concerning Manchuria and Mongolia* (Baltimore, 1933), pp. 35-38, 107-108.

[9] Price, *Russo-Japanese Treaties*, pp. 44-46, 113.

[10] Price, *Russo-Japanese Treaties*, pp. 83-90; Foster Rhea Dulles, *The Road to Teheran: The Story of Russia and America, 1781-1943* (Princeton, 1944), pp. 93-94; Gregory Bienstock, *The Struggle for the Pacific* (New York, 1937), pp. 146, 161; Pauline Tompkins, *American-Russian Relations in the Far East* (New York, 1949), pp. 36-40.

effect would make that nation the political and economic vassal of Japan.[11] The American public regarded these demands as an amazing example of Japan's treachery and aggressiveness.[12]

After the United States became a belligerent (1917) its relationship with Japan was made even more difficult. The mere fact that Japan had now become an ally was not sufficient to allay America's suspicions of her. Throughout the war years rumors circulated that Japan was proposing to drop the British for a German alliance.[13] Great Britain suggested that the United States do nothing that might push Japan into German arms.[14] American distrust of Japan was clearly revealed in the secret correspondence carried on between President Woodrow Wilson and Arthur J. Balfour, British Foreign Minister, regarding a proposed naval agreement, which was to be directed against Japanese as well as against German aggression.[15] Since it was vital to the war effort that relations between the two nations assume a friendlier tone, arrangements were made for a Japanese special mission to the United States under the leadership of Viscount Kikujiro Ishii. Discussions between Ishii and Robert Lansing, Secretary of State, resulted in the Lansing-Ishii agreement of November 2, 1917. The agreement acknowledged Japan's "special interests" in China, and reaffirmed the adherence of both powers to the open-door policy.[16] Despite its ambiguity, the Lansing-Ishii agreement was hailed by American newspapers as a great triumph, since Japan had been changed from a

[11] J. V. A. MacMurray, ed., *Treaties and Agreements with and concerning China, 1849-1919* (2 vols.; New York, 1921), II, 1231-1237; Thomas E. LaFargue, *China and the World War* (Stanford, 1937), pp. 49-77; Griswold, *Far Eastern Policy*, pp. 183-193.

[12] Griswold, *Far Eastern Policy*, p. 187.

[13] Roland S. Morris (ambassador to Japan) to Robert Lansing (Secretary of State), Jan. 10, 1918, Woodrow Wilson Papers, series II (collection in Division of Manuscripts, Library of Congress); William G. Sharp (ambassador to France) to Lansing, May 15, 1918, file 861.00/6237, Department of State, National Archives; Memorandum by E. T. Williams, June 13, 1918, file 861.00/2082, Department of State, National Archives. Hereinafter all State Department documents will be identified by file and document numbers and the abbreviation, D.S.N.A.

[14] Sir William Wiseman to Edward M. House, Jan. 30, 1918. William Wiseman Papers (collection in Manuscripts Division, Yale University Library).

[15] Walter Hines Page (ambassador to Great Britain) to Wilson, July 6, 1917; Balfour to House, July 8, 1917, Wilson Papers, series II; Charles Seymour, *The Intimate Papers of Colonel House* (4 vols.; Boston and New York, 1928), III, 67-69.

[16] MacMurray, *Treaties*, II, 1394-1396; Griswold, *Far Eastern Policy*, pp. 216-219. Lansing's views of the agreement are in his *War Memoirs* (Indianapolis, 1935), pp. 301-303; Ishii's views are in his *Diplomatic Commentaries* (Baltimore, 1936), chap. vi. For diplomatic exchanges relating to the agreement, see United States, *Papers Relating to the Foreign Relations of the United States, 1917*, pp. 258-275; hereinafter cited as United States, *Foreign Relations*.

"dangerous rival" to a "trusted ally."[17] The conciliatory attitude of the press was not wholly a reflection of official opinion, for, as Lansing observed, after the visiting Japanese had been shown the United States fleet off the northern shore of Long Island, "I am disposed to think that the motive was not solely to give entertainment to our guests for there was in the minds of some of our officials the thought that it might also give them some idea of the naval power of the United States."[18]

Russian-American relations also assumed a friendlier tone upon America's entry into the war. This was due, not to formal agreement, however, but to the changes which had occurred in Russia's internal situation. In March and November of 1917 Russia was shaken by two successive revolutions. The first overthrew the Romanov dynasty and established a "liberal" Provisional government. This was hailed with delight by the Allies, particularly the United States. American newspaper editors rejoiced that "instead of reluctantly taking the corrupt despotism of the Romanoffs as an ally, we may proudly join hands with the self-governing people of Russia in a war of peoples against kings."[19] Colonel Edward M. House, confidential adviser to the President, suggested recognition of the new Russian government, saying, "I think this country should aid in every way the advancement of democracy in Russia for it will end the peril which a possible alliance between Germany, Russia, and Japan might hold for us."[20] Wilson agreed. He had been loath to enter the war with an autocratic Russia. However, a democratic Russia was a "fit partner for a league of honor."[21] Thus the United States was the first nation to grant formal recognition to the new Russian Provisional government.[22]

Russia's war effort had been steadily declining, and the Allies now hoped for a renewed prosecution of the conflict. To this end they desired to aid her in every way possible. The United States immediately began negotiations to establish credit for Russia in the United States.[23] The United States also sent two missions to Russia. The

---

[17] *Literary Digest,* LV (Oct. 13, 1917), 16-17; *Literary Digest,* LV (Nov. 17, 1917), 15-16.

[18] Lansing, *Memoirs,* p. 279.

[19] *Literary Digest,* LIV (March 31, 1917), 885-887.

[20] House to Wilson, March 17, 1917, Wilson Papers, series II.

[21] Lansing to David R. Francis (ambassador to Russia), April 3, 1917, United States, *Foreign Relations, 1918, Russia,* I, 17.

[22] Francis to Lansing, March 22, 1917, United States, *Foreign Relations, 1918, Russia,* I, 13.

[23] As a result, by May 17, 1917, the United States had agreed to loan $100,000,000 to Russia for war supplies, all of which was to be spent in the United States. For negotiation of the loan, see United States, *Foreign Relations, 1918, Russia,* III, 1-11.

first mission was to aid in the rehabilitation of the Russian railway systems. The second was to extend to Russia the friendship and good will of the United States, and to find the best means of co-operating with her for a successful prosecution of the war. The latter mission, headed by Elihu Root, carried out its formal duties, filed its reports, and then dissolved.[24] Far different was the history of the railway mission headed by John F. Stevens. In effect, it became the forerunner of intervention.[25] Thus, it is important to understand the origin, organization, and activities of the railway advisory mission.

One of the most serious problems which the Provisional government faced, after the March revolution, was the threatened collapse of the Russian railway systems. This collapse was due to inefficient organization, outmoded methods of operation, and lack of equipment. The railways demanded instant attention. The Trans-Siberian Railway, which extended 4,700 miles from Vladivostok to the Ural Mountains, had almost ceased to function. As a result, the supplies purchased by the Russian government in the United States, and shipped across the Pacific, were piling up at Vladivostok. The whole system of rail transportation required reorganization and rehabilitation if these supplies were to reach the Russian armies in Europe. These disheartening conditions were brought to the attention of the American government by Ambassador David R. Francis.[26] The military consequences were further emphasized by Stanley Washburn,[27] correspondent of the London *Times,* and later major in the United States Army.[28] The British, the French, and the Italian governments urged the United States to assist Russia with her railway problems.[29]

Additional credits of $75,000,000, $100,000,000, and $50,000,000 were established on July 17, Aug. 23, and Oct. 12, 1917, respectively (United States, *Foreign Relations, 1918, Russia,* III, 11-25).

[24] Ray Stannard Baker, *Woodrow Wilson, Life and Letters* (8 vols.; New York, 1939), VII, 39. Root later said that Wilson did not want to accomplish anything by the mission; that it was simply a "grand-stand play," an attempt to show American sympathy for the Revolution (Root to Jessup, Sept. 16, 1930; Philip Jessup, *Elihu Root,* 2 vols.; New York, 1938, II, 356).

[25] *Congressional Record,* vol. 58, pt. 3, p. 3140.

[26] Francis to Lansing, April 21, 1917, United States, *Foreign Relations, 1918, Russia,* I, 28.

[27] Washburn was one of the most effective proponents for American control of the Trans-Siberian Railway. He had been in Russia since Sept., 1914, and had covered over eighty battles. He believed the Trans-Siberian Railway was the key to the military situation, and that its efficient operation was imperative to the winning of the war (William Phillips [Assistant Secretary of State], to Lansing, March 30, 1917, file 861.00/7018, D.S.N.A.).

[28] Lansing to Page, Sept. 13, 1918, United States, *Foreign Relations, 1918, Russia,* III, 249-252.

[29] Balfour to Sir Cecil Spring-Rice (British ambassador at Washington), Aug. 21,

After serious and deliberate reflection, President Wilson, with the knowledge and approval of the Russian Provisional government, decided to send a commission of five railway experts to inspect the Trans-Siberian Railway and to offer suggestions for improving its efficiency.[30]

Wilson explained his conception of the railway commission's purpose as follows:

It is not going to ask What can [the] United States do for Russia? but only to say We have been sent here to put ourselves at your disposal to do anything we can to assist in the working out of your transportation problem. They are to report nothing back to us. They are delegated to do nothing but serve Russia on the ground, if she wishes to use them, as I understand she does.[31]

John F. Stevens of New York City was selected to head the mission. He was one of the leading railway engineers in the country, and had acquired a world-wide reputation as the man who had organized the staff for the building of the Panama Canal. Stevens had been recommended by Franklyn K. Lane, the Secretary of the Interior, as being the "best-qualified man for the job in the United States."[32]

The commission arrived at Vladivostok early in June, 1917. It proceeded across Siberia in a special train provided by the Russian railway administration. As soon as it made its survey and placed its recommendations in the hands of the Russian Minister of Ways and Communications, the commission, with the exception of Stevens, returned to the United States. Stevens remained in Russia and was established in the Ministry of Ways and Communications as a special adviser. He was to assist in executing the measures which the commission and the Russian officials had agreed were vital. In addition he was to be given "absolute control of the terminals at Vladivostok."[33]

In September, 1917, the Provisional government asked for the services of a corps of American railway engineers. These engineers were

---

1917, file 861.77/156, D.S.N.A. France and Great Britain later suggested that the United States assume complete control of the Russian railways (Frank L. Polk, counselor to the Department of State, to Daniel Willard, chairman of the Advisory Commission of the Council of National Defense, Oct. 26, 1917, Frank L. Polk Papers, collection in the Division of Manuscripts, Yale University Library).

[30] Lansing to Page, Sept. 13, 1918, United States, *Foreign Relations, 1918, Russia*, III, 251.

[31] Wilson to Lansing, May 17, 1917, Baker, *Woodrow Wilson*, VII, 55.

[32] Lane to Wilson, April 14, 1917, Wilson Papers, series II.

[33] Francis to Lansing, May 15, 1917, United States, *Foreign Relations, 1918, Russia*, III, 190.

to be placed in an advisory capacity along the different sections of the Trans-Siberian line. Russia agreed to meet all expenses involved. Thus it was that three hundred engineers from various American railways were specially commissioned by the Secretary of War as officers of the Russian Railway Service Corps, and placed under the command of Colonel George B. Emerson. They left the United States on November 1, 1917. While the corps was en route, the Bolshevik revolution occurred. As a result, Vladivostok was in turmoil. There were no accommodations available for the railway corps. Moreover, the food shortage was critical. As it was useless to come ashore until some authority was established, the corps returned to Japan to await developments. There it was soon joined by Stevens, whose efforts had also been interrupted by the revolution.[34] Stevens had little patience with the revolution and advocated that "we should all go back shortly with man-of-war and 5,000 troops. Time is coming to put the fear of God into these people."[35]

The Bolshevik program demanded an immediate, general, and democratic peace with the Central Powers. On November 29, 1917, Ambassador Francis reported that military operations on the Russian front had ceased and that preliminary peace negotiations between Russia and Germany would begin on December 2.[36] All the Allies were invited by Russia to participate. None accepted.

Quite apart from whatever relationship it might bear to the war was the character of the new Russian government, which did not commend itself to the Allies. They were naturally suspicious of a revolutionary government which claimed to rule in the name of the proletariat and advocated class war, world revolution, and the overthrow of capitalism. The Soviet decree of February 3, 1918, which repudiated all foreign state loans, scarcely increased Bolshevik popularity with the Allies.[37] Furthermore, rumors were increasing that the Bolshevik leaders, Lenin and Trotsky, were German agents who had returned to Russia with the assistance of the German General Staff for the

[34] Willard to Lansing, Oct. 8, 1917, file 861.77/187, D.S.N.A.; Lansing to Wilson, Feb. 14, 1918, file 861.77/291, D.S.N.A.; Stevens to Lansing, Dec. 20, 1917, United States, *Foreign Relations, 1918, Russia,* III, 213; John K. Caldwell (consul at Vladivostok) to Lansing, Jan. 9, 1918, United States, *Foreign Relations, 1918, Russia,* III, 216.

[35] Stevens to Lansing, Dec. 20, 1917, United States, *Foreign Relations, 1918, Russia,* III, 213.

[36] Francis to Lansing, Nov. 29, 1917, United States, *Foreign Relations, 1918, Russia,* I, 253.

[37] United States, *Foreign Relations, 1918, Russia,* I, 29-32.

purpose of inciting civil war and demoralizing the Russian armies.[38] In these circumstances there arose among Western statesmen the natural hope that somehow a great Russian leader would arise, around whom the "sane" elements would rally in relief of the stricken nation. The Allies placed great faith in this idea, especially since the consequences of Russia's withdrawal from the conflict were terrifying to contemplate. Thus none of the Allies extended recognition to the new Russian government, but continued to recognize the diplomatic representatives of the defunct Provisional government. There were, however, differences of opinion as to how Bolshevik Russia should be treated. Naturally, the immediate policy of the Allies was to keep her in the war. This objective was sought by two rather antagonistic means. Some Allied representatives encouraged revolutionary groups to overthrow the Bolsheviks and re-establish the Eastern Front, while others conferred with Bolshevik leaders and intimated a promise of Allied support if Russia continued in the war against Germany.[39] Ambassador Francis himself was opposed to any thought of intervention as long as there was a possibility of keeping Russia in the war. He was "willing to swallow pride, sacrifice dignity, and with discretion do all that is necessary to prevent Russia's becoming [an] ally of Germany."[40] Balfour, the British Foreign Minister, also thought it would be wise to avoid an open breach with the Russians:

> Russia, however incapable of fighting, is not easily overrun. Except with the active good will of the Russians themselves, German troops . . . are not going to penetrate many hundreds of miles into that vast country. A mere Armistice between Russia and Germany may not for very many months promote in any important fashion the supply of German needs from Russian sources. It must be our business to make that period last as long as possible by every means in our power, and no policy would be more fatal than to give the Russians a motive for welcoming into their midst German officials and German soldiers as friends and deliverers.[41]

[38] Francis to Lansing, June 23, 1917, United States, *Foreign Relations, 1918, Russia*, I, 98; David R. Francis, *Russia from the American Embassy* (New York, 1921), p. 226; Pitirim Sorokin, *Leaves From a Russian Diary* (New York, 1924), pp. 41, 71; E. A. Ross, *The Russian Soviet Republic* (New York, 1923), pp. 140-141; George Stewart, *The White Armies of Russia: A Chronicle of Counter-Revolution and Allied Intervention* (New York, 1933), p. 84; Great Britain, *Parliamentary Debates, House of Commons* (Hansard), 5th series, CI, 954-956.

[39] James Bunyan, *Intervention, Civil War, and Communism in Russia, April-December, 1918* (Baltimore, 1936), p. 61.

[40] Francis to Lansing, Dec. 24, 1917, United States, *Foreign Relations, 1918, Russia*, I, 325.

[41] David Lloyd George, *War Memoirs* (6 vols.; Boston, 1933-37), V, 114. Colonel House shared this viewpoint and suggested to Lansing that American newspapers re-

The British Foreign Office soon decided to open negotiations with the Bolsheviks.[42] Bruce Lockhart, former acting consul at Moscow, was sent to Petrograd to establish unofficial relations with Lenin and Trotsky, while Downing Street recognized Maxim Litvinov as the representative of the *de facto* Russian government in London.[43] Lieutenant Colonel Raymond Robins, head of the American Red Cross in Russia, and General William V. Judson, American military attaché in Russia, served as go-betweens for the American Embassy, while Jacques Sadoul was the personal representative of Albert Thomas, French Assistant Minister of War. It is significant that all of these men, who had personal contact with Lenin and Trotsky, advocated that the Allies enter into some kind of a working agreement with the Bolsheviks for the purpose of keeping Russia in the war.[44]

On January 8, 1918, President Wilson made a powerful appeal to the Russian people with a memorable statement of American war aims. Referring directly to the negotiations at Brest-Litovsk, he praised the Russian representatives for their insistence on full publicity for the proceedings. He also expressed his desire to assist "the people of Russia to attain their utmost hope of liberty and ordered peace." The President then enunciated his historic Fourteen Points.[45] The sixth point, relating to Russia, was of special interest as it represented the official attitude of the American government toward Russia:

> The evacuation of all Russian territory and such settlement of all questions affecting Russia as will secure the best and freest cooperation of the other nations of the world in obtaining for her an unhampered and unembarrassed opportunity for the independent determination of her own political development and national policy and assure her of a sincere welcome into the society of free nations under institutions of her own choosing; and, more than a welcome, assistance also of every kind that she may need and may herself desire. *The treatment accorded to Russia by her*

---

frain from criticizing Russia as an enemy. He feared that this would "throw Russia into the lap of Germany" (Seymour, *Intimate Papers*, III, 281).

[42] Bruce Lockhart, *Memoirs of a British Agent* (New York and London, 1933), p. 199.

[43] Spring-Rice to Lansing, Jan. 9, 1918, United States, *Foreign Relations, 1918, Russia*, I, 337.

[44] Bunyan, *Intervention*, pp. 61-65; James Bunyan and H. H. Fisher, *The Bolshevik Revolution* (Stanford, 1934), p. 515; Herman Hagedorn, *The Magnate: William Boyce Thompson and His Times, 1867-1930* (New York, 1935), chaps. xii-xvi; William Hard, *Raymond Robins' Own Story* (New York, 1920), pp. 70-71, 110; Francis to Lansing, Dec. 2, 1917, United States, *Foreign Relations, 1918*, Russia, I, 282.

[45] See Edgar Sisson, *One Hundred Red Days* (New Haven, 1931), pp. 209, 211, and *Literary Digest*, LVI (March 2, 1918), 17, for an account of how the Fourteen Points were used in Russia.

Reprinted from *The Testimony of Kolchak and Other Siberian Materials*, edited by Elena Varneck and H. H. Fisher (Stanford University Press)

SIBERIA AND THE RUSSIAN FAR EAST

sister nations in the months to come will be the acid test of their good will, of their comprehension of her needs as distinguished from their own interests, and of their intelligent and unselfish sympathy.[46]

The next months were to indicate how this policy would be carried out.

Toward the close of 1917 while the Allies were conducting their unofficial negotiations at Petrograd, the Bolshevik revolution was spreading to Eastern Siberia. There the longest frontier in political history separated China from Siberia. This area soon became the scene of recurrent border disturbances. Thousands of Russians fleeing from the Bolsheviks sought a haven in the cities of North China and Manchuria, particularly along the line of the Chinese Eastern Railway. There in relative safety some of them plotted and intrigued against the Bolshevik regime.

The Chinese Eastern Railway formed a part of the great Trans-Siberian line which linked Asia with Europe. Completed in 1904, it measured 1,073 miles in length from Manchouli on the western border of Manchuria to Pogranichnaia on the southeast border near Vladivostok. The railroad and the zone through which it ran were in reality, if not legally, a Russian semicolony stretching across Manchu territory. This extraordinary state of affairs had come about in an unusual way. When the Trans-Siberian Railway proper was nearing the Chinese frontier (1896), the Russian government discovered that three hundred and fifty miles of construction could be eliminated if the line were run through Central Manchuria, rather than through the Russian provinces to the north. Furthermore, the former route would practically guarantee Russian control of Manchurian commerce.[47] By the terms of the Chinese Eastern Railway Agreement of 1896 China agreed to give Russia construction privileges across Manchuria in return for a defensive military alliance.[48] Through a liberal interpretation of the agreement the Russian imperial government gradually assumed complete authority within the railway zone. Thus, by 1917 the railway zone had in effect become a Russian crown colony in China, despite the fact that Chinese authority had never been renounced within the railway area.[49]

[46] Italics inserted. Ray Stannard Baker and William E. Dodd, *The Public Papers of Woodrow Wilson* (3 vols.; New York, 1927), III, 159-160.
[47] *The China Yearbook* (1923), pp. 613-614; Tsao Lien-en, *The Chinese Eastern Railway—An Analytic Study* (Shanghai, 1930), pp. 1-3; Clyde, *The Far East*, pp. 262-263.
[48] MacMurray, *Treaties*, I, 74-82.
[49] Tsao, *Chinese Eastern Railway*, p. 29; LaFargue, *China and the World War*, p. 160.

The Bolshevik revolution introduced a period of lawlessness in the zone of the Chinese Eastern Railway, particularly in the cities of Harbin and Changchun. At Harbin the Bolsheviks attempted to secure control of the railway from General Dmitri L. Horvat, Russian governor and general manager, who maintained the pretense of representing the defunct Provisional government.[50] Unable to resist the pressure, "General Horvat [was] ready to conduct joint administration with the Bolsheviks." At this point the Allied ministers asked the Chinese government to send troops to support Horvat against the Bolsheviks.[51] The Chinese government complied and by December 15 had sent three thousand troops to insure order and to support General Horvat. Shortly thereafter Chinese troops disarmed two regiments of Bolshevik troops, deported them across the borders of Manchuria, and took over the Russian barracks along the line of the Chinese Eastern Railway, presumably at General Horvat's request.[52] Within the next few months the railway zone became a center of counterrevolutionary activity against the Bolsheviks.

England, France, and Japan soon extended financial aid to these anti-Bolshevik groups.[53] Throughout the early months of 1918 agents of the Japanese government offered assistance to General Horvat in return for commercial concessions and the dismantling of the Vladivostok fortifications. Horvat preferred Allied support.[54] As soon as he secured promises of assistance from the Allied diplomats at Peking, with the exception of the American minister, Horvat began to organize and support various anti-Bolshevik armed detachments in the railway zone.

In March, 1918, the Japanese government urged General Horvat to organize an anti-Bolshevik government in the Far East.[55] The

---

[50] Charles K. Moser (consul at Harbin) to Paul S. Reinsch (minister in China) Nov. 17, 1917, United States, *Foreign Relations, 1918, Russia*, II, 2-4. John F. Stevens later pointed out that he believed that Horvat was always loyal to the Provisional government, despite the intrigues of the Japanese, Chinese, and Bolsheviks at Harbin (Stevens to H. H. Fisher, Jan. 28, 1931, Railway Service Corps Papers, collection in Hoover War Library, Stanford University).

[51] Reinsch to Lansing, Dec. 6, 1917, United States, *Foreign Relations, 1918, Russia*, II, 5.

[52] Reinsch to Lansing, Dec. 8, 1917, United States, *Foreign Relations, 1918, Russia*, II, 8; New York *Times*, Dec. 15, 1917.

[53] Griswold, *Far Eastern Policy*, pp. 227-288; Ludovic H. Grondijs, *La Guerre en Russie et en Siberie* (Paris, 1922), p. 513.

[54] Reinsch to Lansing, Feb. 21, 1918, United States, *Foreign Relations, 1918, Russia*, II, 53.

[55] Moser to Lansing, March 15, 1918, United States, *Foreign Relations, 1918, Russia*, II, 79.

Allied representatives in Harbin, including the American consul, supported this proposal.[56] General Horvat, however, hesitated to follow Japan, particularly when he learned that in return for her support, Japan would probably ask for the dismantling of all the fortifications at Vladivostok, fishing rights in Siberia, open navigation of the Amur River, and forest and mining concessions. Horvat feared to act on such a proposal "lest he be charged with selling his country to Japan."[57]

While Horvat organized his cabinet, a rival government, headed by Petr Derber, established itself in railway cars in Harbin. Organized in Western Siberia in February, 1918, the anti-Bolshevik Derber government had been forced to retreat to the safety of the Chinese Eastern Railway zone to escape the Bolsheviks. An attempt to unite the Horvat and Derber movements failed.[58] The Derber government appealed directly to the American government for aid.[59] President Wilson was interested in these independent Siberian movements. He told Lansing that it would give him "a great deal of satisfaction to get behind the most nearly representative of them. . . ."[60] However, the Russian Division of the State Department reported that "none of them could make any claim to be representative of any large body of Russian opinion."[61] Therefore, despite the appeals of the American consul at Harbin, the American government refused to commit itself toward the Harbin movements.[62]

In the meantime Great Britain, France, and Japan were supporting the independent operations of Captain Grigorii Semenov, who was attempting to wrest control of the Trans-Baikal province from the Bolsheviks.[63] Although later evidence revealed that Semenov was a villain capable of the most infamous crimes, nevertheless, at the height

[56] Willing Spencer (secretary of Legation in China) to Lansing, March 29, 1918, United States, *Foreign Relations, 1918, Russia*, II, 93.

[57] Moser to Lansing, April 4, 1918, United States, *Foreign Relations, 1918, Russia*, II, 97-99.

[58] Moser to Lansing, April 12, 1918, United States, *Foreign Relations, 1918, Russia*, II, 119-121.

[59] United States, *Foreign Relations, 1918, Russia*, II, 101-102.

[60] April 18, 1918, United States, *Foreign Relations, Lansing Papers* (2 vols.; Washington, 1939-1940), II, 360, hereinafter referred to as *Lansing Papers*.

[61] Memorandum by Basil Miles (acting chief of Russian Division), April 22, 1918, file 861.00/1664½, D.S.N.A.

[62] Lansing to Reinsch, May 1, 1918, Phillips to Reinsch, May 4, 1918, Lansing to Reinsch, May 8, 1918, United States, *Foreign Relations, 1918, Russia*, II, 150, 152, 157.

[63] Colville Barclay (British chargé) to Lansing, Feb. 6, 1918, United States, *Foreign Relations, 1918, Russia*, II, 38-41; LaFargue, *China and the World War*, p. 163; Elena Varneck and H. H. Fisher, *The Testimony of Kolchak and Other Siberian Materials* (Stanford, 1935), pp. 114-115; British ambassador at Tokyo to Lord Reading (Rufus Daniel Isaacs), March 28, 1918, file 861.00/1437½, D.S.N.A.

of his campaign he succeeded in arousing considerable enthusiasm for his cause among certain American representatives in the Far East.[64] The American consul at Harbin spoke glowingly of Semonov's attempts to bring law and order to Trans-Baikal, while the American ambassador in Tokyo believed that supporting Semenov would "be the most direct way to take issue with the Bolshevik movement in Siberia."[65] In contrast, both Paul S. Reinsch, the American minister at Peking, and John F. Stevens regarded Semenov as a "military autocrat of the old order."[66] When Stevens informed the State Department of Semenov's attempts to use the Chinese Eastern Railway to aid his military efforts, he was told that the corps of American engineers should not "be drawn in to take sides in a movement which partakes of civil war, consequently their work on the Chinese Eastern Railway must not have any semblance of supporting Semenov or contributing to the success of his military operations. If this can only be accomplished by their withdrawal then they should be withdrawn. . . ."[67]

At the beginning of May Admiral Alexsander V. Kolchak, former Russian commander of the Black Sea Fleet, appeared in the zone of the Chinese Eastern Railway.[68] He reported to Prince Kudashev, Russian minister at Peking, who was planning to organize an armed force in the Chinese Eastern Railway zone under the guise of a railway guard. As soon as the troops were prepared, Prince Kudashev planned to move them across the Chinese Eastern to Vladivostok or elsewhere.[69] In order to implement this plan, Prince Kudashev organized a new board of directors for the Chinese Eastern Railway to replace the one that remained in Petrograd. General Horvat was

[64] For an urgent plea for intervention to aid Semenov, see George Kennan, "Can We Help Russia?" *Outlook*, CXIX (May 22, 1918), 141. Lansing considered Kennan to be the highest authority on Russia in America, and he paid careful attention to his views. Kennan frequently wrote letters to Lansing, who placed them before the President (Lansing to Kennan, May 28, 1918, Lansing Papers, collection in Division of Manuscripts, Library of Congress). Lansing was not so sure as was Kennan of the wisdom of aiding Semenov.

[65] United States, *Foreign Relations, 1918, Russia*, II, 48, 53, 134; Morris to Lansing, May 16, 1918, United States, *Foreign Relations, 1918, Russia*, II, 163. Thomas Garrigue Masaryk, *The Making of a State* (New York, 1927), p. 183, states: "I thought the Allied support of anti-Bolshevik movements a mistake, especially when it was given to out-and-out adventurers like Semyenoff and others."

[66] United States, *Foreign Relations, 1918, Russia*, II, 54, 133, 138.

[67] Lansing to Reinsch, May 2, 1918, United States, *Foreign Relations, 1918, Russia*, III, 233.

[68] Varneck and Fisher, *Testimony of Kolchak*, pp. 108-109, 236, note 150; United States, *Foreign Relations, 1918, Russia*, II, 169, 191.

[69] Varneck and Fisher, *Testimony of Kolchak*, p. 110; M. I. Smirnov, "Admiral Kolchak," *Slavonic and East European Review* (London), XI (Jan., 1933), 385.

made chairman of the board, while Admiral Kolchak was appointed commander-in-chief of the railway guards in the zone. The Japanese government immediately promised assistance to the new board in return for exclusive mining rights in Eastern Siberia and free navigation of the Amur River.[70] Horvat was forced to accept Japanese support, since Britain and France were absorbed in Semenov's efforts and the United States had already declared its neutrality toward the rival anti-Bolshevik factions.[71] The American government was "disturbed" by reports that Chinese soil was being used for conferences "looking toward the establishment in Russian territory of a government opposed to those in control, and as a base for possible military operations to effectuate such a government." It urged the Chinese government to consider carefully the possible results of such activities.[72] The State Department also advised its minister in Peking that "strict neutrality" was "desirable and must be observed" toward contending factions in Russia. Although the United States and the Allied governments had not recognized the Soviet, they were "interested in stimulating its opposition to the Central Powers."[73]

Kolchak's appearance in the railway zone was viewed unfavorably by the Russian leaders already operating in the area. Shortly after his arrival, Kolchak attempted to secure Captain Semenov's co-operation for joint action in the Far East. He discovered that Semenov preferred to operate alone, supported by Japanese financial assistance.[74] Despite the lack of co-operation between Kolchak and Semenov, the Japanese government supported both factions.[75] Although Kolchak soon learned that Semonov's independent attitude was the direct result of Japanese handiwork, he continued to organize railway guards and even attempted to launch an offensive in the direction of Pogranichnaia and Vladivostok.[76] His efforts met with little success, for he was op-

[70] Reinsch to Lansing, April 25, 27, 30 and May 7, 1918; Moser to Lansing, May 8, 1918, United States, *Foreign Relations, 1918, Russia*, II, 137-138, 140-141, 147, 154-155, 155-156.

[71] The Japanese were also supporting Captain Ivan Kalmikov at Pogranichnaia, at the eastern end of the Chinese Eastern Railway zone (Bunyan, *Intervention*, pp. 314-316).

[72] Lansing to Reinsch, May 6, 1918, file 861.00/1763a, D.S.N.A.

[73] Lansing to Reinsch, May 6, 1918, file 861.00/1736, D.S.N.A.

[74] Varneck and Fisher, *Testimony of Kolchak*, pp. 121-122; Grondijs, *La Guerre en Russie*, pp. 513-514; Smirnov, "Admiral Kolchak," *The Slavonic and East European Review*, XI, 385.

[75] Moser to Lansing, May 23, 1918, United States, *Foreign Relations, 1918, Russia*, II, 169.

[76] Varneck and Fisher, *Testimony of Kolchak*, pp. 123-124, 127, 316; Moser to Lansing, June 6, 1918, United States, *Foreign Relations, 1918, Russia*, II, 190.

posed constantly by the activities of the Japanese. Thereupon Kolchak decided to go to Japan to plead his cause before the Japanese General Staff.[77] Shortly after his arrival in Japan, Kolchak resigned as commander-in-chief of the railway guards.[78]

In the meantime Semenov had not been idle. Between March and June he made no less than three attempts to secure control of Trans-Baikal. In each case he was repulsed. After Semenov's first attack, the Bolshevik authorities began arming some of the German prisoners of war in Siberia to defend the territory against further intrusions.[79] When Semenov began his third offensive, his forces included Japanese volunteers.[80] The failure of his third attempt forced him to cross into Manchuria, where he became the center of Japanese intrigue, and a source of constant irritation to China.[81]

The chaos bordering on semianarchy created by the November revolution had its repercussions in Siberia as well as Manchuria. The Allies feared that once the Bolsheviks secured control of Siberia, the war supplies which had piled up in Vladivostok for the Russian prosecution of the war would fall into the hands of the Germans. As Siberia seemed to be the ideal spot for mobilizing the anti-German elements in Russia, the Allies early considered the possibility of sending an expeditionary force to Siberia to aid these elements in the rehabilitation of the Eastern Front.

The idea of sending a military expedition to Russia was by no means a result of the Bolshevik revolution alone. Throughout 1917 Allied statesmen considered such a possibility. During January and February, General S. Inagaki, the Japanese military attaché in London, and Colonel Charles à Court Repington of the British Foreign Office discussed informally the possibility of using Japanese troops on the Russian front. The number of troops mentioned was ten divisions, or 250,000 men.[82] General Inagaki personally believed that in return for this assistance Japan desired "control of the railway to Kharbin

[77] Grondijs, La Guerre en Russie, p. 154; Varneck and Fisher, Testimony of Kolchak, p. 127.

[78] Varneck and Fisher, Testimony of Kolchak, p. 154.

[79] Reinsch to Lansing, April 2, 1918, United States, Foreign Relations, 1918, Russia, II, 95.

[80] Moser to Lansing, June 6, 1918, United States, Foreign Relations, 1918, Russia, II, 191.

[81] Moser to Lansing, June 19, 1918, United States, Foreign Relations, 1918, Russia, II, 216; Reinsch to Lansing, June 26, 1918, United States, Foreign Relations, 1918, Russia, II, 231-232.

[82] Charles à Court Repington, The First World War, 1914-1918; Personal Experiences (2 vols.; Boston and New York, 1920), I, 432, 437-440, 442-443, 469.

[Harbin] and the dismantlement of Vladivostok and the Russian naval base at this port. . . ."[83] Colonel Repington was left "with the impression that Japan would act if the concessions named were granted."[84] Nothing, however, came from these informal feelers, probably because of the outbreak of the first Russian revolution.[85] Later, in the summer of 1917, Constantin Nabokov, the Russian ambassador in London, suggested to the Russian High Command that 200,000 Japanese troops be sent to the Russian front to fight against the Germans. The suggestion was rejected as being impracticable.[86]

When the French began to urge the use of Japanese troops to rehabilitate the Russian front in June of 1917, President Wilson wrote Ambasador Sharp: "There are very many reasons why it would be unwise even if it were practicable."[87] Later, in the fall of 1917, when Russian soldiers were abandoning the Eastern Front, the French ambassador in Petrograd was instructed to suggest to the Provisional government the possibility of using Japanese troops. Both the Premier, A. F. Kerensky, and the Foreign Minister, M. I. Tereschenko, refused to consider the suggestion. Apparently the Provisional government was completely opposed to having its territory traversed by its "old enemy of 1905."[88]

In late 1917 the French became quite vigorous in their demands for military intervention in Siberia. At an inter-Allied conference at Paris, Premier Clemenceau discussed with Colonel House the possibility of sending a Japanese expeditionary force to Russia. House was completely opposed to the idea. He believed the Bolsheviks had come to power, not through German intrigue, but because they satisfied the real demands of the Russian peasants. He was convinced that any effort at intervention except at the request of the Russian government would be a mistake. He so advised the President on his return to the United States.[89] In the meantime the American press had been

[83] Repington, *First World War*, I, 470.
[84] Repington, *First World War*, I, 471.
[85] Repington, *First World War*, I, 477, 491.
[86] Constantin Nabokov, *The Ordeal of a Diplomat* (London, 1921), pp. 244-245. Certain authorities have written that the Japanese initiated proposals for intervention in the summer of 1917. See Thomas F. Millard, *Democracy and the Eastern Question* (New York, 1919), p. 283; Foster Rhea Dulles, *Forty Years of Japanese-American Relations* (New York, 1937), p. 134; John Spargo, *Russia as an American Problem* (New York, 1920), pp. 236-237.
[87] Baker, *Woodrow Wilson*, VII, 214; William G. Sharp to Wilson, June 30, 1917, Wilson Papers, series II.
[88] Joseph Noulens, *Mon ambassade en Russie soviétique, 1917-1919* (2 vols.; Paris, 1933), II, 46.
[89] Seymour, *Intimate Papers*, III, 386-388. Across the top of one of his letters to

speculating on the possibility of American or Japanese aid to Russia by means of the Trans-Siberian Railway.[90] The American Naval Intelligence in Russia presented a report which advised sending to Siberia an American corps of 80,000 men strengthened by a Japanese force.[91] The British government also suggested that the United States consider the possibility of sending troops if Russia were agreeable.[92] Ambassador Francis had a similar idea:

What would you think of our sending two or more army divisions via Vladivostok or Sweden to her [Russia's] aid if I could get consent of Russian Government therefor or even induce Government to make such a request? Moral effect of American troops on Russian front [would] be more beneficial than the material assistance so rendered as millions of sensible Russians only need encouragement to organize.[93]

None of these suggestions was followed. By the end of 1917 the State Department appeared firm in its decision to follow a policy of nonintervention in regard to Russia and Siberia.[94]

Lansing is the following notation: "This was the beginning of outside interference in Russia's internal affairs—an interference I steadily and consistently opposed" (House to Lansing, Dec. 1, 1917, Edward M. House Papers, collection in Division of Manuscripts, Yale University Library).

[90] *Literary Digest*, LV (Sept. 15, 1917), 12; *ibid.*, LV (Oct. 13, 1917), 25; Gregory Mason, "Shall We Send an Army to Russia," *Outlook*, XVII (Oct. 24, 1917), 292-297.

[91] Office of Naval Intelligence, Oct. 31, 1917. Notes on Russian Situation as It Affects the Allied Cause (Naval Records Collection in the Office of Naval Records and Library, WA-6, Russian Situation, 1917-1919, in the National Archives), hereinafter referred to as Naval Records Collection.

[92] Reading to Lansing, Nov. 1, 1917, United States, *Foreign Relations, 1918, Russia*, II, 1.

[93] Francis to Lansing, Nov. 6, 1917, United States, *Foreign Relations, 1918, Russia*, I, 221.

[94] Frederick Palmer, *Bliss, Peacemaker: The Life and Letters of General Tasker Howard Bliss* (New York, 1934), p. 169; Peyton C. March, *The Nation at War* (New York, 1932), p. 113.

CHAPTER II

Wilson Says No

DURING the first six months of 1918 Wilson was besieged with appeals for military intervention in Siberia. They came not only from his Allies and the Supreme War Council,[1] but also from his own diplomatic staff abroad. Although the cry for intervention became practically unanimous among American foreign representatives in Russia and the Far East, Wilson found strong resistance to these proposals among his military advisers. Wilson, indeed, was faced with one of the most difficult problems of his career; he informed House that he was "sweating blood" over it. As the Russo-German peace negotiations at Brest-Litovsk neared their conclusion in March, 1918, and the Germans proceeded to withdraw an increasing number of divisions from their Russian front, Britain and France increased their pressure for intervention. The Allies faced what appeared to be a desperate military situation. In the early part of the year they were ready to clutch at every straw. General Tasker H. Bliss, American military representative on the Supreme War Council, later pointed out that the Siberian expedition was a "sideshow born of desperation." Thus the original idea of intervention was not primarily to initiate a war against Bolshevism, but to bring about a renewal of the Russian thrust against Eastern Germany.[2]

[1] The Supreme War Council consisted of the Prime Minister and a permanent military representative from each government fighting on the Western Front. Colonel House represented President Wilson. The military representatives were General Maxime Weygand, France; General Sir Henry Wilson, Great Britain; General Luigi Cadorna, Italy; and General Tasker H. Bliss, United States (Seymour, *Intimate Papers*, III, 246-264).

[2] General Tasker H. Bliss, Final Report on the Supreme War Council, p. 115, file 763.72SU/99, D.S.N.A. As Lloyd George pointed out, "We were not concerned with the internal political trouble of Russia as such. What we had to consider as a war problem was how best to prevent Germany from revictualling herself afresh from the cornfields and the oilfields which would be laid open to her if she succeeded in pene-

Agitation for intervention in Siberia began in earnest toward the close of December, 1917. The chaotic conditions which existed in Vladivostok gave rise to constant rumors of Japanese intervention.[3] On December 13, 1917, Caldwell, the American consul at Vladivostok, advised the landing of an Allied force to preserve order in the city. The suggestion was opposed by the State Department, which advised him to refrain from "considering in any way the advisability of the presence of a foreign force in Vladivostok."[4] The Russian ambassador to Japan suspected that the persistent rumors of a Japanese landing were semiofficial feelers and urged that the United States oppose such action on Japan's part. He was convinced that it would only create resentment in Russia without in any way serving the cause of the Allies.[5] The department concurred in this attitude. It believed that the landing of troops in Vladivostok would undoubtedly result in the unification of the Russians under Bolshevik control in opposition to foreign intervention. This opinion was conveyed to the Japanese government, which professed completed agreement with it.[6]

At the close of December, 1917, the French government reported

---

trating the Don and the rich provinces of the Caucasus. It was for this reason, and not from any anti-communist motives, that we decided to give support to the loyalist Russians . . ." (Lloyd George, *Memoirs*, V, 110). John E. Weeks, later Secretary of War, arrived at a similar conclusion, "Probably the principal underlying idea which was held by those powers, other than the United States and Japan, responsible for the sending of troops to Siberia was that a new Eastern Front might be constituted. . . . In case such a new front could be constituted the Germans would be forced to use troops thereon and would thus be weakened on the Western Front" (Weeks to Hughes, Oct. 7, 1929, A Study of American Participation in the Siberian Expedition, 1918-1920, p. 2, file 861.00/9040, D.S.N.A.). In contrast, General Graves said that "it is evident England, France, and Japan went to Siberia with the distinct idea of fighting bolshevism but, for some reason, they tried to cover up this design by advocating the formation of an Eastern front, which they also hoped could be accomplished" (Graves, *America's Siberian Adventure*, pp. 334-335). The fact that Great Britain was attempting to negotiate with the Bolsheviks, even after the treaty of Brest-Litovsk, to get a renewal of the war against Germany tends to cast doubt on Graves's statement.

[3] Lansing to Caldwell, Dec. 12, 1917, United States, *Foreign Relations, 1918, Russia,* II, 7; Flag, Brooklyn to Office of Naval Operations, Dec. 14, 1917, WA-6, Siberia, Conditions in Vladivostok, Naval Records Collection.

[4] United States, *Foreign Relations, 1918, Russia,* II, 7.

[5] Morris to Lansing, Dec. 16, 1917, United States, *Foreign Relations, 1918, Russia,* II, 9. Throughout early 1918 the Russian ambassadors abroad (representatives of the defunct Provisional government) almost unanimously opposed intervention, particularly by the Japanese. All were united in their suspicions of Japanese intentions (Miles to Lansing, Jan. 4, 1918, file 861.00/938½, D.S.N.A.; Memorandum of the Third Assistant Secretary of State, Jan. 10, 1918, Morris to Lansing, Jan. 13, 1918, Sharp to Lansing, Feb. 3, 1918, United States, *Foreign Relations, 1918, Russia,* II, 23, 27, and 37, respectively).

[6] Memorandum of the Secretary of State of an Interview with the Japanese Minister, Dec. 27, 1917, United States, *Foreign Relations, 1918, Russia,* II, 13.

that inflamed conditions in Irkutsk, Siberia, had resulted in the death of three French citizens. Accounts from that vicinity described the city in flames, "while the Bolsheviki were intent on an orgy of murdering and plundering the inhabitants and ravishing the women, while the corpses of murdered children covered the streets."[7] The French government was considering seriously the possibility of sending a large expeditionary force to aid those "Russian elements in Siberia that have remained true to the cause of the Entente." The expedition would protect Siberia from Bolshevik contagion, secure the use of the Trans-Siberian and South Russian Railways to the advantage of the Allies, and, by isolating Vladivostok, protect the huge quantities of Allied supplies stored there. Such an expedition would be in a position to prevent German influence from extending to Siberia, in case of a separate peace.[8] The United States was unable to give its assent to this proposal.[9]

As early as December 14, 1917, the British ambassador to Japan had discussed informally with the Japanese government the problem of protecting the Amur and Trans-Siberian Railways and the stores and munitions at Vladivostok. The American government was not informed of these discussions.[10] The British Foreign Office was rather concerned about the Japanese attitude:

The Japanese will not tell us what they intend to do, and are very angry if anyone else proposes to do anything. If they were not too unreasonable, the proper plan would undoubtedly be to land a force at Vladivostok to protect our stores there, the force being in substance Japanese, with a few French, Americans and British added for the sake of appearances.[11]

The Anglo-Japanese discussions resulted in the dispatch of warships to Vladivostok. By January 17, 1918, the Japanese had sent a total of four ships, and the British, one.[12] Josephus Daniels, the American Secretary of the Navy, felt this was cause for concern. He suggested that Japan be informed that the United States thought "it a mistake

[7] Caldwell to Lansing, Dec. 30, 1917, file 861.00/888, D.S.N.A.

[8] Jean J. Jusserand (French ambassador to the United States) to Lansing, Jan. 8, 1918, United States, *Foreign Relations, 1918, Russia,* II, 20-21.

[9] Lansing to Jusserand, Jan. 16, 1918, United States, *Foreign Relations, 1918, Russia,* II, 28.

[10] Morris to Lansing, March 22, 1918, United States, *Foreign Relations, 1918, Russia,* II, 84-88.

[11] Lord Robert Cecil to Arthur Balfour, Jan. 8, 1918, Blanche E. Dugdale, *Arthur James Balfour, First Earl of Balfour* (2 vols.; New York, 1937), II, 186-187.

[12] Morris to Lansing, Jan. 17, 1918, United States, *Foreign Relations, 1918, Russia,* II, 30-31.

to create the impression they intended to land." He also advised the dispatch of the *Brooklyn,* an American cruiser, to Vladivostok.[13]

The Japanese government raised no objection to the sending of the *Brooklyn,* but it requested "if conditions should hereafter require the occupation of Vladivostok and the lines of the Chinese Eastern and Amur Railways . . . that this task be left to her alone."[14] Japan had asked the British government to agree to this as evidence of the confidence of the Allies in her good faith.[15] This request, in conjunction with the large naval force at Vladivostok, gave Wilson an "uncomfortable feeling." Since the suggestion seemed to him to be "very significant of possible coming events," he insisted that Japan be told very clearly that the United States would strongly disapprove of military action in that area. Accordingly, Japan was informed that the

common interests of all the powers at war with Germany demand from them an attitude of sympathy with the Russian people in their present unhappy struggle and that any movement looking towards the occupation of Russian territory would at once be construed as one hostile to Russia and would be likely to unite all factions in Russia against us thus aiding the German propaganda in Russia.[16]

The British government was also informed of the American position. Although Balfour professed agreement with the State Department, he believed that events might at any time create a new situation which would necessitate intervention.[17]

That new situation arose very shortly. The counterrevolutionary movement in south and southeast Russia was growing with the aid and encouragement of the British and French governments. Convinced that the Allies should do "anything and everything" to checkmate Germany's exploitation of Russia, Balfour believed that it was obviously to the advantage of the Allies to support the counterrevolu-

[13] Frank L. Polk, Confidential Diary, Jan. 18, 1918 (Division of Manuscripts, Yale University Library).

[14] As early as Jan. 10 a distinguished Frenchman told Colonel Repington that "the Japs were ready to land at Vladivostok and save Siberia from becoming Bolshevist and a granary for Germany, but they wanted to go there alone, and the Americans did not approve of the plan" (Repington, *First World War,* II, 179).

[15] Morris to Lansing, Jan. 17, 1918, United States, *Foreign Relations, 1918, Russia,* II, 29-30. The British government made no reply to this request, while the French government acceded to it (Morris to Lansing, March 22, 1918, United States, *Foreign Relations, 1918, Russia,* II, 85; Morris to Lansing, Feb. 8, 1918, United States, *Foreign Relations, 1918, Russia,* II, 44).

[16] Wilson to Lansing, Jan. 20, 1918, *Lansing Papers,* II, 351; Polk to Morris, Jan. 20, 1918, United States, *Foreign Relations, 1918, Russia,* II, 31.

[17] Page to Lansing, Jan. 24, 1918, United States, *Foreign Relations, 1918, Russia,* II, 33.

tionary movements.[18] He thought this could best be done by inviting Japan to occupy the Trans-Siberian Railway as the mandatory of the Allies. This would keep open a line of communication with the Russian forces in the south and southeast who desired to continue the war against Germany. His Majesty's government believed that the

> Russians would welcome some form of foreign intervention in their affairs, and that it would be more welcome in the shape of the Japanese, engaged as mandatories of the Allies with no thought of annexation or future control than in the shape of the Germans who would make Russia orderly only by making it German. . . .[19]

The President was strongly opposed to the suggested Japanese expedition. He believed that the Japanese themselves had originated the plan for invading Siberia, and that they wished the expedition to be exclusively Japanese in order to secure control of the Maritime Provinces. Wilson intended to prevent such a development.[20] Evidently realizing Wilson's fears, Balfour attempted to overcome them through a personal appeal:

> It may be said that the aggrandizement of Japan whether territorial (as it might be impossible to get her out of, say the maritime provinces when once established there) or morally as consequence of her successful intervention as saviour of the situation, would present grave danger from the spectators point of view. There is force in this but on the other side I would suggest, the Japanese occupation of the maritime provinces is a question which must probably be faced in any case as the state of Russia will probably soon render occupation inevitable. Japan in such circumstances will doubtless take action on her own initiative, whatever the wishes of the Allies will be. As regards danger of Japanese aggrandizement the very fact that the Japanese will be forced into the open against the Germans, and their respective interests brought into open conflict, should do much to lessen Japanese pressure in other directions.[21]

Balfour's appeal yielded no results. House could think of no military advantage that would offset the harm of sending Japanese troops

[18] Dugdale, *Balfour*, II, 187.

[19] British Embassy to Department of State, Jan. 28, 1918, United States, *Foreign Relations, 1918, Russia*, II, 35-36.

[20] Seymour, *Intimate Papers*, III, 391; Statement of the Honorable Breckinridge Long, Third Assistant Secretary of State, before the House Committee on Foreign Affairs, Aug., 1919, file 861.00, vol. 39, D.S.N.A.

[21] Balfour to House, Jan. 30, 1918, marked secret and urgent, Wiseman Papers. Balfour often appealed to Wilson directly through Colonel House, Sir William Wiseman, special British agent in America, or both. See also Seymour, *Intimate Papers*, III, 390-391.

into Siberia.[22] Wilson himself could see nothing "wise or practicable" in the scheme. Said Wilson, "It seems . . . unwise to make a request which would in itself give the Japanese a certain moral advantage with respect to any ultimate desires or purposes she may have with regard to the eastern provinces of Siberia."[23] On February 8 the State Department formally rejected the British proposals. Furthermore, it indicated that any future occupation of the whole or part of the Trans-Siberian Railway should be done through international co-operation and not by any one power acting as the mandatory of the others.[24]

Before the British government received this reply, it sent another note reiterating its position.[25] This was followed by a personal cable from Balfour, who informed House that the Japanese were sending agents to Siberia to investigate conditions, and that if the danger seemed imminent, Japan would take independent steps to meet it.[26]

The State Department was impervious to both appeals. It questioned the advisability of antagonizing the people who controlled Russia, and declared that the necessity for intervention had not yet arisen. Moreover, should the necessity arise, joint military action was to be preferred. In any event, that portion of the Trans-Siberian Railway crossing Chinese territory should be guarded by Chinese rather than Japanese troops.[27] This was the beginning of a diplomatic duel between the Japanese and American governments over the control of the Chinese Eastern Railway.[28]

On February 15, 1918, Lord Reading, the new British ambassador in Washington, had a conference with President Wilson. He came away with the feeling "that the American Government was against any intervention by the Japanese in Siberia with the Allies or for the Allies, and would prefer if Japan should intervene at Vladivostok, that she should do it on her own initiative, thus leaving it open for America and the Allies to make any representation they may hereafter think fit to Japan."[29]

Both the French and British governments were dissatisfied with

[22] House to Wilson, Feb. 2, 1918, Seymour, *Intimate Papers*, III, 391.

[23] Wilson to Lansing, Feb. 4, 1918, file 861.00/1097, D.S.N.A.

[24] Department of State to British Embassy, Feb. 8, 1918, United States, *Foreign Relations, 1918, Russia*, II, 42.

[25] British Embassy to Department of State, Feb. 6, 1918, United States, *Foreign Relations, 1918, Russia*, II, 38.

[26] Feb. 8, 1918, Wiseman Papers.

[27] Lansing to Page, Feb. 13, 1918, United States, *Foreign Relations, 1918, Russia*, II, 45.

[28] LaFargue, *China and the World War*, p. 166.

[29] Lord Reading to British Foreign Office, Feb. 15, 1918, Wiseman Papers.

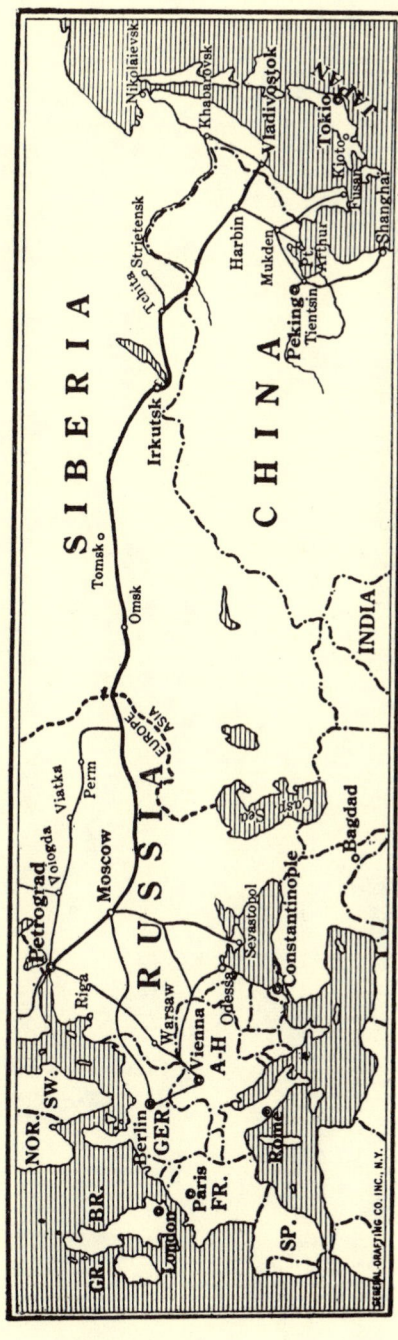

Reprinted from the *Literary Digest*, LVI (March 16, 1918), 15

JAPAN'S RELATION TO THE EUROPEAN CONFLICT

Wilson's stand on intervention. The British, however, assured the State Department that their notes on the subject were nothing more than "preliminary inquiries."[30] The French, too, expressed an appreciation of the American position. Nevertheless, they believed that if events in Russia vitally threatened Japanese interests, Japan would undertake an independent expedition to Siberia without the consent of the Allies. In that event the French Foreign Minister feared a possible German-Japanese alliance providing for the division of Russia.[31] Despite this fear, the French newspapers continued to advocate Japanese intervention in Siberia.[32]

While British and French diplomats in Washington were attempting to persuade Wilson to agree to intervention, similar pressure was being applied to General Bliss. Sir William Wiseman had informed the British Foreign Office that he believed Wilson might agree to intervention if Bliss could be persuaded that the military end was practicable.[33] The British Foreign Office took the hint. It sponsored a scheme for Japanese intervention which was presented to the Supreme War Council by Sir Henry Wilson, British military representative on the Supreme War Council. The plan recommended that the Allies ask Japan to occupy the Trans-Siberian Railway from Vladivostok to Harbin, after first obtaining suitable guarantees from her. An Allied "politics-military mission" was to accompany the expedition. The question of the further occupation of the railway was to be "determined by the Allied Governments concerned according as the circumstances develop."[34]

Although Bliss was not enthusiastic about the project, he agreed to sign the note. It became Joint Military Note No. 16.[35] Bliss reasoned that seizure of the military stores at Vladivostok and Harbin would be

[30] Page to Lansing, Feb. 18, 1918, United States, *Foreign Relations, 1918, Russia*, II, 48-49.

[31] Sharp to Lansing, Feb. 20 and 28, 1918, *United States, Foreign Relations, 1918, Russia*, II, 52, 58-59.

[32] On Feb. 28 the British ambassador to France wrote in his diary, "The French newspapers are booming a Japanese intervention at Vladivostok and in Manchuria. If Japan go thither it will be to stay in a more or less disguised form. It would be foolish of America to object" (Lady Algernon Gordon Lennox, *Diary of Lord Bertie of Thame, 1914-1918*, 2 vols.; London, 1924, II, 271; see also Great Britain, *House of Commons Debates*, 5th series, CVII, 482-483).

[33] Wiseman to Drummond and Balfour, Feb. 4, 1918, Wiseman Papers.

[34] Bliss, Final Report on the Supreme War Council, pp. 119-120, file 763.72SU/99, D.S.N.A.; Bliss to March (chief of staff), Feb. 20, 1918, Tasker H. Bliss Papers (collection in Division of Manuscripts, Library of Congress); March, *Nation at War*, pp. 305-306; Baker, *Woodrow Wilson*, VII, 556.

[35] March, *Nation at War*, pp. 113-115.

of distinct advantage to the Allies, and could be accomplished by a relatively small Japanese force.[36] The Joint Note advanced the argument that Japanese intervention would bring Japan effectively and directly into opposition with Germany and thus eliminate the danger of a German-Japanese alliance.[37]

The Japanese were quite willing to consider intervention in Siberia, but they did not wish to contend with the "humiliation" and "pinpricks" of Allied "show the flag" detachments, in obtaining the willing consent of their people. Bliss believed that Allied insistence upon obtaining suitable guarantees from Japan before inviting her to occupy the Siberian Railway would be regarded by the Japanese as a "pinprick" and something more. Furthermore, Japan might regard the inter-Allied politics-military mission as a "show the flag" detachment. As far as Bliss was concerned, the whole problem was fraught with difficulties. He wrote General March that "the intervention of a large Japanese army over a large portion of Siberia raises the question of how and when they can be made to get out. This Japanese intervention suggests a possible way in which another war may be brought about."[38]

By the end of February Japan appeared ready to act alone, despite the disapproval of the United States and the failure of the British government to consent to independent Japanese action.[39] The Japanese government proposed to the Chinese government a joint military occupation of Siberia and of the Trans-Siberian Railway to restore order in Siberia. The President of China approved in principle, and the Chinese government asked the United States for advice. Lansing repeated his earlier position, namely, that the Chinese Eastern Railway be guarded by Chinese troops.[40]

Reports from Siberia indicated a growing unanimity among American representatives in the Far East concerning intervention in Siberia. General Judson, recently returned from Russia, declared that Russia, if encouraged, would make a stand against the Germans. He urged

[36] Bliss, Final Report on the Supreme War Council, p. 115, file 763.72SU/99, D.S.N.A.

[37] Diplomatic Liaison Officer, Supreme War Council (Frazier) to the Secretary of State, Feb. 19, 1918, United States, Foreign Relations, 1918, Russia, II, 49-50.

[38] Bliss to March, Feb. 20, 1918, Bliss Papers. When March received this letter, he took the opportunity to "urge upon the Secretary of War that we keep out of Siberia" (March, Nation at War, p. 115).

[39] Reinsch to Lansing, Feb. 21, 1918, March to Lansing, Feb. 24 and 27, 1918, United States, Foreign Relations, 1918, Russia, II, 53, 56, 57, respectively.

[40] Reinsch to Lansing, Feb. 23, 1918, Lansing to Page, Feb. 27, 1918, United States, Foreign Relations, 1918, Russia, II, 55, 57-58; Memorandum of Long, Feb. 26, 1918, file 861.00/1249, D.S.N.A.

that American and Japanese troops be sent to assist her.[41] Consular reports from Moscow urged similar action, while Ambassador Francis advocated immediate occupation of Vladivostok, Murmansk, and Archangel.[42] Minister Reinsch reported that a majority of Russians would welcome Allied intervention to prevent German control, but would be most "unfriendly" to the entry of Japanese troops unless accompanied by Allied forces.[43] Even John F. Stevens, who had been solidly opposed to any kind of intervention in Russia, advised that German influence in Siberia was growing and would have to be met by force in the near future. Now that German prisoners were being released and armed, he believed that Japanese action was necessary if Siberia was to be saved from German control.[44]

On February 26 Ferdinand Foch, Generalissimo of the Allied Armies, advocated active intervention in Siberia by Japan and the United States.[45] From Versailles General Bliss reported a feeling of "desperation" in regard to the war. He urged Washington to bear this in mind as a probable explanation for such proposals as Japanese intervention.[46]

On February 27 Lord Reading presented President Wilson with two secret messages from Balfour. The first message urged that the United States, Great Britain, France, and Italy invite Japan to occupy the Siberian Railway, in order to protect the Allied military stores lying at Vladivostok and to prevent the enemy from obtaining access to the vast stores of agricultural resources available to the west of Lake Baikal. Great Britain admitted reluctantly that, although Japan desired a mandatory, she would not tolerate co-operation. Since the Bolsheviks had completely surrendered to the Germans, the British government believed that intervention had become an urgent necessity. France was eager for the decision. Italy approved of the project. The

[41] Polk, Confidential Diary, Feb. 21, 1918.

[42] Summers to Lansing, Feb. 23, 1918, United States, *Foreign Relations, 1918, Russia*, II, 53-54; Summers to Lansing, Feb. 24, 1918, file 861.00/1145, D.S.N.A.; Francis to Lansing, Feb. 24, 1918, United States, *Foreign Relations, 1918, Russia*, I, 387.

[43] Reinsch to Lansing, Feb. 24, 1918, United States, *Foreign Relations, 1918, Russia*, II, 55.

[44] Morris to Lansing, Feb. 24, 1918, file 861.00/1148, D.S.N.A.; Scidmore (consul general at Yokahama) to Lansing, Feb. 26, 1918, file 861.00/1158, D.S.N.A.

[45] New York *Times*, Feb. 26, 1918; Stewart, *White Armies of Russia*, p. 127.

[46] Bliss also reported that the British admitted that Japanese intervention alone was undesirable, as Japan was "probably out for her own best interests." Further, they agreed that "it was not inconceivable for her to make a deal with Germany" (Bliss to Baker, Frank L. Polk Papers, collection in Division of Manuscripts, Yale University Library).

final decision rested with the United States. Furthermore, common action would be impossible if a different view were taken by the United States. In that event, Great Britain feared that Japan would act alone, and would not then be subjected to the safeguards applied by the Allies.[47] The second message dealt with the actions of German prisoners in Siberia.[48]

Balfour's appeal was a powerful one. It was followed by a telegram from the French Embassy, which reported that Viscount Ichiro Motono, Japanese Minister of Foreign Affairs, was willing to announce publicly Japan's disinterestedness and to pledge to carry on military activities as far as the Ural Mountains, that is, to the confines of Asia. Japan agreed to comply with all Allied demands. Believing that the French telegram cast a new light on the problem, Lansing urged a reconsideration of intervention.[49]

Wilson found it very difficult to resist these appeals. Too often he had found himself opposing Allied schemes. There had been friction between the United States and the Allies over America's insistence on being termed an associate rather than an ally.[50] Wilson's insistence on the separateness of the armies of the United States at the front had been a more serious point of friction with England and France. Furthermore, the United States had at first refused to send a military representative to participate in the activities of the Supreme War Council.[51] In addition, there was disagreement over the terms of the peace settlement. Wilson was strongly opposed to the Allied eagerness for territory, and the secret agreements to acquire it were particularly difficult for him to accept.[52] Now, he found himself again in the position of refusing to agree to a plan which had the support of all of the Allies.

Wilson decided to agree. His decision was the result of Anglo-French pressure. He drafted a new declaration of policy stating that, although "the United States has not thought it wise to join the governments of the Entente in asking the Japanese government to act in Siberia," it would not object to such a request being made by the other Allies. The United States realized that in putting an armed force into Siberia, the Japanese government was "doing so as an ally of Russia,

[47] Balfour to Reading, Feb. 26, 1918, Wilson Papers, series II.
[48] Baker, Woodrow Wilson, VII, 568, 569 n.
[49] Lansing to Wilson, Feb. 27, 1918, Lansing Papers, II, 354-355.
[50] Baker, Woodrow Wilson, VII, 221.
[51] Seymour, Intimate Papers, III, 306-307; Baker, Woodrow Wilson, VII, 304 414-415.
[52] Baker, Woodrow Wilson, VII, 474-475.

with no purpose but to save Siberia from the invasion of the armies and intrigues of Germany and with entire willingness to leave the determination of all questions that may affect the permanent fortunes of Siberia to the Council of Peace."[53] On March 1 Wilson sent this statement to the State Department for the information of the Allied ambassadors.[54] On that same day Frank L. Polk, counselor for the Department of State, showed it to the French ambassador and the British chargé. The following day it was shown to the Italian ambassador. The statement was not given to the Japanese chargé when he called at the State Department on March 2.[55]

As soon as the Russian Embassy in Washington learned of the proposed note, it moved quickly in an attempt to prevent American acquiescence to independent Japanese action. Boris A. Bakhmetev, the Russian ambassador, appealed to Colonel House, while John Sookine, onetime secretary of the Russian Embassy, presented his arguments against the plan to the State Department. Both men averred that the Russians preferred the Germans to the Japanese, and that a Japanese expeditionary force would throw the Russians into the arms of the Germans. Sookine advocated the formation of a military-political expedition composed of military units from the United States, Great Britain, France, and Japan under the political leadership of an Allied committee or an American diplomatic representative.[56] House informed Wilson of the Russian ambassador's views, and wrote in opposition to Japanese action:

We are treading upon exceedingly delicate and dangerous ground, and are likely to lose that fine moral position you have given the Entente cause. The whole structure which you have built up so carefully may be destroyed over night, and our position will be no better than that of the Germans.

I cannot understand the . . . determination of the British and French to urge the Japanese to take such a step. Leaving out the loss of moral advantage, it is doubtful whether there will be any material gain. . . .[57]

House's letter was followed by one from William C. Bullitt sent by Gordon Auchincloss (assistant counselor to the Department of State)

[53] *Lansing Papers*, II, 393.

[54] Baker, *Woodrow Wilson*, VIII, 1-2.

[55] Polk to Lansing, March 15, 1918, United States, *Foreign Relations, 1918, Russia*, II, 68.

[56] Memorandum of Long, March 2, 1918, United States, *Foreign Relations, 1918, Russia*, II, 61-63; Seymour, *Intimate Papers*, III, 392.

[57] At the top of this letter there was a note in House's handwriting "after the President received this he recalled from the State Department the note that was to have been sent to Japan" (House to Wilson, March 3, 1918, House Papers; text of letter in Seymour, *Intimate Papers*, III, 393).

to the President. Bullitt stressed the point that America's position would be irretrievably compromised unless the United States protested publicly against Japan's invasion of Siberia. He pointed out that Japan wanted to annex Eastern Siberia, and that the Allies and the United States realized it. Moreover, they appeared willing to assist Japan because they feared she might take it with the assistance of Germany. Bullitt continued with a moving plea:

We shall have to throw Japan out of Siberia some day unless we are willing to compromise on all the principles for which we are asking our soldiers to die. . . . If we stand aside while Japan invades Siberia with the assent of the Government of England and France, the President's moral position as leader of the common people of the world will be fatally compromised. . . . The President must oppose invasion of Siberia by Japan in the name of democracy and liberalism. He must act, or his position as moral leader of the liberals of the worlds will be lost. We cannot wash our hands of this matter. Unless we oppose, we assent.[58]

On March 4 Colonel House cabled a similar plea to the British Foreign Secretary. He stressed the moral position of the United States and argued that independent Japanese action would push Russia into the arms of Germany.[59] On March 6 Balfour replied that Britain had already agreed to give Japan a free hand in Siberia. He justified this action on the grounds that since the Bolsheviks had surrendered unconditionally at Brest-Litovsk it was of the utmost importance to prevent the rich supplies in Siberia from falling into German hands. Furthermore, the Japanese government was preparing to take action in Eastern Siberia; and considerable resentment would be aroused in Japan if the Allies refused to give her a mandate.[60]

Influenced by the views of House and Bullitt, Wilson reverted to his earlier stand on intervention.[61] On March 5 he telephoned a new note to Counselor Polk and instructed him to communicate it formally to the Allied ambassadors in Washington and to the Japanese government.[62] The new note was influenced by Wilson's concern over the moral issues involved in intervention. It rested the case against

---

[58] Bullitt to Polk, March 2, 1918, file 861.00/1290½, D.S.N.A. On March 4 Congress discussed the matter, and Mr. Meyer London proposed a joint resolution in the House of Representatives protesting against the suggested invasion of Russian territory (*Congressional Record*, vol. 56, pt. 3, p. 3028).

[59] House to Balfour, March 4, 1918, Seymour, *Intimate Papers*, III, 394.

[60] Balfour to House, March 6, 1918, Wiseman Papers; Seymour, *Intimate Papers*, III, 397.

[61] Gordon Auchincloss, Diary, March 3, 1918 (Division of Manuscripts, Yale University Library).

[62] Seymour, *Intimate Papers*, III, 396.

intervention upon two assumptions: first, that such a policy would strengthen the extreme revolutionary elements in Russia and would alienate Russian opinion from faith in the Allies and America; second, that the course proposed was contrary to America's democratic war aims and that it would fatally compromise the American moral position. For these reasons the United States was opposed to Japanese intervention in Siberia, even if Japan gave every assurance that she would not impair the political or territorial integrity of Siberia.[63]

House was pleased with the new note and sent his congratulations to Wilson. Auchincloss considered it infinitely better than the first one.[64] The Russian ambassador also approved. He thought it would be a great mistake for anyone to go into Siberia, and particularly the Japanese.[65] Polk, however, had "argued the question . . . a little" with the President. He felt somewhat embarrassed about transmitting the new note to the Allies as he had already given the contents of the earlier note to all of them except Japan.[66] Moreover, as a result of the first note, the British government had agreed that Japan should take independent action in Siberia as the mandatory of the Allies.[67]

On March 6 Polk read the new note to the Japanese chargé, who wanted to know whether American opposition was based on insufficient facts. Polk told him no, and stressed the point that the United States objected to the Japanese intervention in Siberia only because of the bad effect it would have on Russia.[68]

When Ambassador Morris read the American note to the Japanese Foreign Minister on March 7, the latter "expressed his deep appreciation of the frankness and friendly spirit of the communication."[69]

[63] Polk to Morris, March 5, 1918, United States, *Foreign Relations, 1918, Russia,* II, 67. For a sympathetic appraisal of the note, see Lincoln Colcord, "Japan in Siberia," *Nation,* CX (Jan. 10, 1920), 36-38. John Spargo, *Russia as an American Problem,* p. 239, hailed the note as "one of the few bright spots in our Far Eastern diplomacy. . . . That refusal was one of the few decisive diplomatic acts of the war of which Americans can be wholeheartedly proud."

[64] Auchincloss, Diary, March 5, 1918.

[65] Polk, Confidential Diary, March 6, 1918.

[66] Seymour, *Intimate Papers,* III, 396; Polk to Lansing, March 15, 1918, United States, *Foreign Relations, 1918, Russia,* II, 68.

[67] Seymour, *Intimate Papers,* III, 397. At the same time Balfour had instructed Lockhart in Russia to suggest to the Bolsheviks that they invite Japan to intervene in Siberia to aid them in resisting German aggression (British Foreign Office to British representative in Petrograd, March 4, 1918, United States, *Foreign Relations, 1918, Russia,* I, 391-393). The mere mention of Japanese intervention "never failed to rouse the fire in Trotsky's eyes" (Lockhart, *British Agent,* p. 241).

[68] Polk, Confidential Diary, March 6, 1918.

[69] Morris to Lansing, March 12, 1918, United States, *Foreign Relations, 1918, Russia,* II, 78.

Since Great Britain had already consented to Japanese intervention in Siberia as the mandatory of the Allies, the Japanese government was now in possession of counsel which advised both "yes" and "no."[70] Actually, Japan chose to follow the United States. Japan's formal reply to the American declaration was very conciliatory. The note stated that Japan would refrain from taking "any action on which due understanding has not been reached between the United States and the other great powers of the Entente." The reply added, however, that if developments in Siberia should "jeopardize the national security or vital interests of Japan she may be compelled to resort to prompt and efficient measures of self-protection." In any event, whatever action the Japanese government might take in Russian territory would be "wholly uninfluenced by any aggressive motives or tendencies."[71]

Whatever may have been the true temper of the official Japanese mind, the American declaration of March 5 did not meet with the approval of the European Allies.[72] The British and French continued to press for Japanese intervention in Siberia.[73] Sir William Wiseman

[70] Japanese opinion was divided on the subject. Tatsuji Takeuchi, *War and Diplomacy in the Japanese Empire* (New York, 1935), p. 204, states: "By March, 1918, keen interest was manifested on all sides, but the consensus of opinion was opposed to any undertaking." Morris, however, reported that military preparations were being completed rapidly, and that troops were concentrating in the west coast ports (Morris to Lansing, March 7, 1918, United States, *Foreign Relations, 1918, Russia*, II, 71-72; see also A. Morgan Young, *Japan Under Taisho Tenno*, London, 1928, pp. 126-127).

[71] Morris to Lansing, March 19, 1918, United States, *Foreign Relations, 1918, Russia*, II, 81-82. On March 26 Viscount Motono admitted to both houses of the Japanese legislature that negotiations regarding Siberia were in progress (Takeuchi, *War and Diplomacy*, pp. 204-205). Motono may have been referring to the Sino-Japanese negotiations then in progress for action in Siberia.

[72] Page reported from London that there was a great misunderstanding among newspapers and the public concerning America's attitude toward Japanese occupation of Siberia. He suggested that at the earliest moment the President make clear to the world "that whatever we do or not do is in no way predicated on suspicion of Japanese motives" (Page to Lansing, March 7, 1918, file 861.00/1250, D.S.N.A.). As a result, the State Department sent a note to Japan, begging "most" earnestly that the Japanese government understand that the attitude taken was in no way based on suspicion of Japanese motives (Lansing to Morris, March 20, 1918, United States, *Foreign Relations, 1918, Russia*, II, 82. Lord Bertie wrote in his diary on April 5, 1918: ". . . it was more than foolish of President Wilson not encouraging Japanese intervention. What section of the Russian people will he conciliate by his attitude to the so-called 'Russian people'? There is no such thing: it is nothing but an agglomeration of different races which has tumbled to pieces" (Lennox, *Diary of Bertie*, II, 294).

[73] The following entry appears in Sir Henry Wilson's diary: "Much talk at [War] Cabinet about the Japanese joining us and going into Siberia. I have written a paper saying they must come in" (Major-General Sir C. E. Callwell, *Field Marshall Sir Henry Wilson*, 2 vols.; New York, 1927, II, 68). On March 9 Colonel Repington recorded: "All attention is just now directed to the question of Japan and Siberia" (Repington,

thought it still possible to secure the assent of President Wilson to the scheme, although he thought Wilson would never be enthusiastic about it. He urged the Foreign Office, in its appeals, to stress the importance of preventing Siberia from becoming a granary for Germany.[74]

Wilson's March 5 declaration marked the beginning of renewed Allied pressure upon the United States for intervention in Siberia. On March 12 the French Embassy in Washington again presented a note recommending immediate Japanese action in Siberia to establish order. The note played on the fear of a German-Japanese alliance, if Japan intervened independently.[75] If she intervened as the mandatory of the Allies, they could secure pledges of disinterestedness from her. After outlining a plan for seizing the Trans-Siberian Railway and establishing an anti-Bolshevik government to resist German encroachments, the note closed with a warning of Japanese sensitivity and the need for quick action.[76] The State Department replied on March 16 that it was "unable . . . to alter its opinion and attitude toward this question."[77] The appeals, however, were beginning to move Wilson, for Wiseman reported on March 14 that Wilson was trying to find a way to reconcile the American people to the need for intervention, and to allay Russia's fears of it. He was studying the feasibility of a joint Japanese-American enterprise whereby the United States would collaborate with the Russians in the reorganization of Russian elements with Japanese military assistance.[78]

The First World War, II, 241). Lord Bertie recorded on March 7, "There has been too much hesitation and delay in letting loose Japan in Siberia" (Lennox, *Diary of Bertie,* II, 278).

[74] Notes for a cable from the British ambassador to the British Foreign Office, March 9, 1918, Wiseman Papers.

[75] Marshal Joffre in Paris expressed the same fear. See memorandum of conversation between Warrington Dawson of the American Embassy and Marshal Joffre, March 16, 1918, Warrington Dawson, ed., *War Memoirs of William G. Sharp* (London, 1931), pp. 283-284. Ambassador Francis also feared a possible Japanese-German understanding (Francis to Lansing, March 9, 1918, United States, *Foreign Relations, 1918, Russia,* II, 73-74).

[76] Jusserand to Lansing, March 12, 1918, United States, *Foreign Relations, 1918, Russia,* II, 75-77.

[77] Lansing to Jusserand, March 16, 1918, United States, *Foreign Relations, 1918, Russia,* II, 80.

[78] Wiseman to Drummond, March 14, 1918, Wiseman Papers. The American press generally approved of intervention, and those who vetoed the suggestions did so on the grounds of immorality and inexpediency rather than fear of Japan. Only the Hearst press whipped up the Japanese bogey (*Literary Digest,* LVI, March 16, 1918, 136). On March 14 Balfour had been called upon in the House of Commons to defend Japanese motives regarding Siberia (Great Britain, *House of Commons Debates,* 5th series, CIV, 553-554; for further parliamentary reaction to Japanese intervention, see *ibid.,* pp. 530-556.

In the meantime, Allied reports from Russia were optimistic concerning the possibility of Bolshevik continuance in the war. At the height of the negotiations at Brest-Litovsk, Trotsky had sent a French officer to ask Ambassador Francis what moral and material assistance the Allies could render if peace were not ratified at Moscow. Francis had assured him that he would recommend moral and material cooperation provided organized resistance was sincerely established.[79] Trotsky also sent a note via Raymond Robins which specifically asked the kind of support Russia could expect from the Allies in general and the United States in particular, if they continued in the war.[80]

President Wilson's message to the Russian people which had been sent on March 11 was considered an adequate response to Trotsky's appeal.[81] The message had been written at the request of Colonel House, who was not so much concerned about Russia as he was eager to seize the opportunity of clearing up the Far Eastern situation without mentioning Japan specifically: "What you would say about Russia and against Germany could be made to apply to Japan or any other power seeking to do what we know Germany is attempting."[82]

The presidential message expressed sympathy with the Russian people and added that although the United States was not then "in a position to render the direct and effective aid" it desired, nevertheless it would utilize "every opportunity to secure for Russia once more complete sovereignty and independence in her own affairs and full restoration to her great role in the life of Europe and the modern world."[83]

In view of the critical peace negotiations at Brest-Litovsk, Ambassador Francis opposed any action to intervene in Russia.[84] Maddin Summers, consul general at Moscow, opposed particularly the Japanese moving into Siberia alone.[85] Lockhart, the British agent in Russia, who had intimate contact with Trotsky, reported that Trotsky

[79] Francis to Lansing, March 5, 1918, United States, *Foreign Relations, 1918, Russia,* I, 392.

[80] Francis to Lansing, March 12, 1918, United States, *Foreign Relations, 1918, Russia,* I, 397-398; Graves, *America's Siberian Adventure,* pp. 122-123; John A. White, *The Siberian Intervention* (Princeton, 1950), pp. 90-91.

[81] Lansing to Francis, March 19, 1918, United States, *Foreign Relations, 1918, Russia,* I, 402.

[82] House to Wilson, March 10, 1918, Seymour, *Intimate Papers,* III, 399; Polk to Summers, March 11, 1918, United States, *Foreign Relations, 1918, Russia,* I, 395-396.

[83] Pauline Tompkins, *American-Russian Relations in the Far East* (New York, 1949), p. 61; W. A. Williams, *American-Russian Relations, 1781-1947* (New York, 1952), pp. 140-141; Seymour, *Intimate Papers,* III, 420.

[84] Francis to Lansing, March 10, 1918, United States, *Foreign Relations, 1918, Russia,* I, 394-395.

[85] Summers to Lansing, March 18, 1918, file 861.00/1398, D.S.N.A.

really wanted a working agreement with the Allies, and that a Japanese expedition would throw all of Russia into the hands of Germany.[86] Similar views were reported by Sadoul, the French special agent in Russia, and Raymond Robins.[87]

Despite these reassuring reports from Russia, the Supreme War Council, in mid-March, adopted a resolution admitting the "principle of Japanese intervention in Siberia."[88] The French and Italian representatives were anxious to send a joint note to President Wilson, appealing for his consent to Japanese intervention as the mandatory of the Allies. Balfour and Lloyd George, however, advocated delay in view of the recent reports from Russia.[89] During the course of the meeting Clemenceau could not help expressing himself on the attitude of President Wilson:

> President Wilson was pursuing an extraordinary policy. He was willing to fight side by side with us, but does not wish to be our political ally, he wishes to reserve his action in Europe and Asia; so far as Europe is concerned I understand the President's attitude because there are shades of policy unintelligible across the Atlantic; I am nevertheless not uneasy as I have great confidence in the President. . . .[90]

Balfour finally agreed to join in a joint note to President Wilson on March 16. The arguments for intervention were again repeated, and the note concluded that without

> the active support of the United States . . . it would be useless to approach the Japanese Government, and even if the Japanese Government consented to act on the representations of France, Italy and Great Britain, such action, without the approval of the United States Government, would lose half its moral authority.[91]

Wilson, sustained by House, replied to Lord Reading: "I have not changed my mind."[92]

Wilson was fortified in his decision by Admiral Austin M. Knight,

[86] Lockhart to British Foreign Office, March 5, 1918, C. K. Cumming and Walter W. Pettit, *Russian-American Relations* (New York, 1920), pp. 82-83.

[87] Jacques Sadoul, *Notes sur la révolution bolshévique, octobre, 1917-janvier, 1919* (Paris, 1926), pp. 284-285; Robins to Francis, March 27, 1918, Cumming and Pettit, *Russian-American Relations*, p. 116. See also John W. Wheeler-Bennett, *Brest-Litovsk, the Forgotten Peace, March, 1918* (London, 1938), pp. 288-303.

[88] General Jean Jules Henry Mordacq, *Le Ministère Clemenceau, journal d'un témoin* (4 vols.; Paris, 1931), I, 219; Palmer, *Bliss*, p. 290; Seymour, *Intimate Papers*, III, 400.

[89] Seymour, *Intimate Papers*, III, 400; Lloyd George, *Memoirs*, VI, 167; Baker, *Woodrow Wilson*, VIII, 29.

[90] Frazier to Lansing, March 16, 1918, House Papers.

[91] Text of Balfour's dispatch in Lloyd George, *Memoirs*, VI, 165-166.

[92] Baker, *Woodrow Wilson*, VIII, 33; Seymour, *Intimate Papers*, III, 401.

commander-in-chief of the Asiatic fleet, who cabled that there was absolutely no danger that munitions at Vladivostok would reach the hands of the Germans. Furthermore, he could see no signs of German influences at work in support of the Bolsheviks:

It is safe to say that no real necessity exists for armed intervention in Siberia unless such intervention is desirable for the establishment of order. If, however, intervention should be decided upon, it is of the first importance that Japan should not be permitted to act alone. This is the one point upon which everybody who knows conditions and sentiment in Russia is absolutely agreed. It is universally believed by Russians that Japan desires to take over a large part of Siberia and no arguments can shake their belief.[93]

Although rebuffed by Wilson's opposition to the Allied joint appeal, the British soon devised a new plan of action. They proposed that an inter-Allied expedition of American, British, and Japanese troops be substituted for lone Japanese intervention. By this scheme they hoped to overcome not only Bolshevik objections to military action in Siberia, but also President Wilson's opposition.[94] On March 26 Wiseman discussed the new proposal with House, who appeared sympathetic. House believed that many objections to intervention would disappear if it could be put upon an inter-Allied basis and that it was of the utmost importance to secure an invitation from Trotsky.[95]

Meanwhile, by the beginning of April it appeared that the American policy of nonintervention in Siberia had triumphed. President Wilson had successfully resisted all Allied appeals. The Japanese government had agreed to follow American rather than British advice, and the Allies themselves had admitted that Japanese intervention without the approval of the United States "would lose half its moral authority." When Wilson was handed a stack of memoranda on the Siberian question, he wrote Lansing, "I must say that none of these memoranda has anything in it that is at all persuasive with me. I hope that you feel the same way."[96]

[93] Knight to Daniels, March 18, 1918, Polk Papers. When Admiral W. S. Benson received this report he was very much opposed to sending it to Bliss, as Benson was so much in favor of intervention (Auchincloss, Diary, March 20, 1918).

[94] Lloyd George, *Memoirs,* VI, 167; Seymour, *Intimate Papers,* III, 402.

[95] Reading to Balfour, March 7, 1918, Wiseman Papers; Seymour, *Intimate Papers,* III, 402.

[96] Wilson to Lansing, April 4, 1918, file 861.00/1439½, D.S.N.A.

CHAPTER III

The Pressure Increases

O N APRIL 5, 1918, a Japanese armed force landed at Vladivostok and began to patrol the city. The announced reason was the murder of three Japanese nationals in the business district of the city the day previous. The Japanese admiral acted immediately without waiting for an investigation by the local Russian authorities. He notified Russian officials that this action was taken to protect the lives of Japanese residents.[1] The British also landed fifty armed sailors on the afternoon of April 5, ostensibly to protect the British Consulate, but in reality "to ensure that any move made would be an Allied one, not an independent Japanese venture."[2] On the next day the Japanese landed two hundred and fifty additional sailors. Although the French consul asked the Japanese to guard the French Consulate, the American consul did not feel it necessary to ask for protection.[3] The British government urged the United States to land troops and thus to insure unity of action; but the American government was unmoved by the appeal. The language used by the British Foreign Office was significant: "It is unnecessary for me to point out the essential importance of our acting together in this question."[4]

[1] Lansing to Francis, April 5, 1918, United States, *Foreign Relations, 1918, Russia,* II, 100-101. The Japanese admiral furnished a copy of his statement to the commanders of both the British and American vessels (Noulens, *Mon ambassade en Russie,* II, 65). According to Noulens the news of the Japanese landing was greeted with joy by the Allied missions in Russia.

[2] Lloyd George, *Memoirs,* VI, 167; Caldwell to Lansing, April 6, 1918, file 861.00/1439, D.S.N.A.; London *Times,* April 12, 1918; C. H. Smith to H. H. Fisher, Feb. 14, 1931, Railway Service Corps Papers.

[3] Caldwell to Lansing, April 6, 1918, United States, *Foreign Relations, 1918, Russia,* II, 105.

[4] British Foreign Office to British Ambassador in Washington, April 7, 1918, United States, *Foreign Relations, 1918, Russia,* II, 108. Ambassador Francis at Vologda also urged Allied unity of action (Francis to Lansing, April 7, 1918, United States, *Foreign Relations, 1918, Russia,* II, 107).

In Bolshevik circles the Japanese-British landing was regarded as the beginning of intervention against the Bolsheviks. Protests arose immediately from both the Vladivostok Soviet, and the Soviet authorities in Moscow. They denounced the landing bitterly, stating that the murder of the Japanese subjects was a part of a carefully laid plan to seize Russia's Far Eastern outlet. The Council of Peoples' Commissars called upon the "toiling masses" to resist the "imperialist blow from the east."[5] George Chicherin, the Acting Commissar for Foreign Affairs, addressed a note to the French consul general in Moscow, to Bruce Lockhart, and to Raymond Robins, protesting against the Japanese-British descent on Vladivostok, and demanding immediate withdrawal. Although the Bolsheviks indicated by their manner that they regarded the landing as a hostile act against the Soviet government, they appeared willing to negotiate on intervention in Siberia, provided it was an Allied rather than an exclusively Japanese affair.[6]

The Soviet protest was not without effect among the Allies. The British government instructed Lockhart to assure Trotsky that the landing was made "solely with the object of affording security for the life and property of foreign residents in Vladivostok," and had no relation to the larger question of Allied intervention in the Far East. The captain of the *Suffolk*, British cruiser at Vladivostok, had been directed to settle the difficulties with the local authorities and end the incident peaceably. The Japanese government professed agreement with this position.[7] The official silence maintained by the United States was regarded by the British as an indication of disapproval.[8]

Throughout the month of April the Allies continued their diplomatic appeals to President Wilson. The French government resumed the offensive in a note to Lansing, April 8, 1918. The usual arguments for Japanese intervention with Allied consent were repeated. Attention was called to the increased activity of the prisoners of war and to the importance of organizing resistance against German domination in

[5] Noulens, *Mon ambassade en Russie*, II, 66-67; Bunyan, *Intervention*, pp. 68-95; Cumming and Pettit, *Russian-American Relations*, pp. 194-195.

[6] DeWitt C. Poole (consul at Moscow) to Lansing, April 6, 1918, United States, *Foreign Relations, 1918, Russia*, II, 104-105. For selected documents on the Bolshevik reaction to the Anglo-Japanese landing, see Jane Degras, ed., *Soviet Documents on Foreign Policy* (2 vols.; London, 1951), I, 67-69.

[7] Lockhart, *British Agent*, pp. 268-269; British Foreign Office to Lockhart, April 7, 1918, Morris to Lansing, April 13, 1918, United States, *Foreign Relations, 1918, Russia*, II, 109, 121.

[8] Great Britain, *House of Commons Debates*, 5th series, CIV, 1611-1612; London *Times*, April 12, 1918.

Russia and Siberia. The French pointed to the possibility that the Bolsheviks in Moscow might be induced to accept Japanese intervention.[9] The French ambassador also indicated that independent Japanese action in Vladivostok "without any guarantee to the Allies or Russia . . . would seem to be a departure that may draw it away from us and nearer to the Germans."[10]

Jusserand addressed a second note to Secretary Lansing on April 21, in which he reported that the French ambassador in Tokyo had been assured of the willingness of the Japanese government to guarantee noninterference in the domestic affairs of Russia.[11] Two days later the French government informed Lansing of the views of Joseph Noulens, the French ambassador to Russia, who urged Japanese military action to prevent German control of Russia. He believed that "in order to offer the required guarantees to the Entente powers as well as to Russian opinion, the Japanese intervention should bear an inter-allied character which of course implies the consent of the United States."[12] The State Department found nothing in the French notes that necessitated a change in policy in the Far East.[13]

While the French government was pressing notes upon the State Department, the British did not remain quiescent. They were attempting through Bruce Lockhart to persuade the Soviet authorities to participate in the war against Germany with Allied military assistance. They desired an invitation from the Bolsheviks for military assistance through the ports of Murmansk in North Russia and Vladivostok.[14] The British Foreign Office had requested earlier that Colonel Robins co-operate with Lockhart in obtaining from the Soviet authorities a request for Allied intervention. Lord Reading wrote Secretary Lansing that Japan might intervene alone in Siberia in "self-defense," if

[9] On Feb. 19, 1918, William Phillips, Assistant Secretary of State, reported that the French had intimated to the Bolsheviks that they were ready to give assistance if the Bolsheviks would resist the German menace and defend Russia. The French government asked if the United States would give similar instructions to its ambassador in Petrograd. Below the note appears the following in pencil: "It is out of the question. Submitted to president who says the same thing" (Phillips to Lansing, Feb. 19, 1918, file 861.00/1125, D.S.N.A.).

[10] Jusserand to Lansing, April 8, 1918, United States, *Foreign Relations, 1918, Russia*, II, 109-112.

[11] United States, *Foreign Relations, 1918, Russia*, II, 128-129.

[12] Jusserand to Lansing, April 23, 1918, United States, *Foreign Relations, 1918, Russia*, II, 132-133.

[13] Lansing to Jusserand, May 7, 1918, United States, *Foreign Relations, 1918, Russia*, II, 154.

[14] Reading to Lansing, April 16, 1918, United States, *Foreign Relations, 1918, Russia*, I, 500.

the Bolsheviks did not invite intervention. This was a possibility which the British government desired to forestall.[15]

On April 25 Lansing received a cable from Balfour containing a new proposal for intervention.[16] Emphasizing the importance of treating Europe and Asia as a single front, Balfour urged the re-establishment of an Allied front in Russia. This could best be done by sending Allied assistance from Murmansk in the north, Transcaucasia in the south, and Siberia in the east. The eastern approach was regarded as the most important, and in that theater "Japan would clearly have to furnish the greater part of any considerable military force which might be used." Although the British desired that all the Allies participate, they wanted the force sent to Siberia to be composed predominantly of Japanese and American troops. The War Cabinet inquired whether President Wilson would agree to:

1. Great Britain and the United States to make a simultaneous proposal to the Bolshevist government for intervention by the Allies on the lines indicated, an undertaking to be given for the withdrawal of all Allied forces at the conclusion of hostilities.
2. An American force, composed as described above, to be sent to the Far East.[17]

Balfour suggested that Japan be given the military command of the proposed expedition, and that the expedition be accompanied by "a mission from each Allied country, including a strong propaganda detachment." Balfour pointed out that if the President did not concur with the British proposals, the British government would proceed no further with them.[18]

Two days later, on April 27, Lansing received another telegram from the British Foreign Secretary, which indicated that Trotsky, Soviet Commissar for War, appeared willing to accept military assistance through Vladivostok under Japanese command, provided that Russian

[15] Reading to Lansing, April 16, 1918, United States, *Foreign Relations, 1918, Russia,* I, 499-501; Baker, *Woodrow Wilson,* VIII, 97-98.

[16] Colonel House wrote Wilson earlier that Balfour had sent an entirely new proposal regarding Russia—"one that I think you will approve." Reading asked for an appointment in order to discuss it with the President, and called at the White House on April 25 (House to Wilson, April 24, 1918, House Papers; Baker, *Woodrow Wilson,* VIII, 105).

[17] Balfour to Reading, April 25, 1918, United States, *Foreign Relations, 1918, Russia,* II, 136.

[18] Balfour to Reading, April 25, 1918, United States, *Foreign Relations, 1918, Russia,* II, 135-137; Bunyan, *Intervention,* pp. 73-74; Seymour, *Intimate Papers,* III, 403-407.

territorial integrity was guaranteed.[19] On May 1 Lord Reading informed Secretary Lansing of three courses open to the Allies in regard to Trotsky, namely: "to defy him, to work with him, or to do nothing." Balfour considered the first alternative dangerous, and the last, fatal. Thus, only the second remained, "whatever misgivings this may cause us."[20]

To this point certainly, one of the main reasons for the American refusal to intervene in Siberia was that no invitation was forthcoming from the Russians. The British, therefore, were exerting every effort to secure an invitation which would be acceptable to the President. Lord Reading believed that since the Soviets were the *de facto* government, they should be approached and induced to extend the invitation. Count Vincenzo Macchi di Cellere, the Italian ambassador in Washington, feared that British negotiations might constitute a recognition of the Soviet regime. Lord Reading admitted that the possibility existed. However, he believed that such a course was justified if it secured President Wilson's approval of inter-Allied action in Siberia. As the Assistant Secretary of State pointed out, "The British are trying to create a situation in Siberia to suit the President, even though in so doing, they may be obliged to come to some form of agreement with the Soviets."[21]

American resistance to French and British pressure was fortified by reports from the Far East during April. Viscount Ishii, newly appointed Japanese ambassador to the United States, was reported to advocate "a policy of no action in Siberia without the fullest understanding" with the United States.[22] From China, Minister Reinsch approved his government's position on intervention, and added that "only reactionaries want intervention at all costs even in the last resort by Japan alone." Reinsch advocated economic aid rather than military action to save Siberia and Russia from German domination.[23] Professor Thomas G. Masaryk, President of the Czechoslovak National Council, also proposed economic action and emphasized the necessity

[19] Balfour to Reading, April 26, 1918, United States, *Foreign Relations, 1918, Russia*, II, 140; Lockhart, *British Agent*, pp. 267-269.

[20] Balfour to Reading, April 29, 1918, United States, *Foreign Relations, 1918, Russia*, II, 148-149; Seymour, *Intimate Papers*, III, 420-422.

[21] Memorandum of a Conversation between the Italian Ambassador and the Assistant Secretary of State, May 7, 1918, file 861.00/1827, D.S.N.A. At the end of April, the British Foreign Office instructed its consul in Vladivostok that intervention must have Bolshevik consent, as they represented the *de facto* government (Dugdale, *Balfour*, II, 260).

[22] April 5, 1918, United States, *Foreign Relations, 1918, Russia*, II, 101.

[23] Reinsch to Lansing, April 10, 1918, United States, *Foreign Relations, 1918, Russia*, II, 117-118.

of a unified Allied policy toward Russia. He recommended *de facto* recognition of the Bolshevik government as well as "extensive propaganda under American supervision throughout eastern Siberia."[24]

The State Department took no immediate action on these economic proposals. However, it did not give up consideration of military intervention. This was indicated by a significant event. The Italian and Belgian governments requested the United States War Department to aid them in transporting some of their troops from the Far East to Europe. The State Department advised the withdrawal of these requests. The Department deemed it advisable that "as many as possible of the governments at war with Germany should be temporarily represented by military forces in the Far East." If Allied troops were withdrawn "it might be embarrassing to send back there other such troops." Lansing hastened to inform the American ambassador in Paris that this note did not commit the United States to intervention. He added that America was guided by political expediency and the possibility of intervention.[25]

On April 28 Lansing had an interview with Viscount Ishii concerning intervention. Ishii said that he would personally welcome American or Allied participation in a military expedition to Siberia. He believed his government held the same view. The ambassador added "that it was evident that the presence at least of troops of the United States, Japan, and China would go far to remove the suspicion of the Russians as to the purpose of territorial conquest which might be inferred if Japan acted alone." He informed Lansing that Japan could send 250,000 men into Siberia immediately, and could add an additional 150,000 men later. Although the British government desired to push the Japanese forces as far as the Ural Mountains, Ishii believed that it would be impractical to go further than Irkutsk, which was only half the distance to the Urals.[26] When Minister Reinsch learned that the Japanese government was willing to "advance only as far as Irkutsk," he reported: "So far as disclosed the Japanese plans exhibit little advantage to the Allies and offer prospect of Japan's creating for herself an exclusive position in Eastern Asia."[27] Throughout the inter-

[24] Morris to Lansing, April 13, 1918, United States, *Foreign Relations, 1918, Russia*, II, 122; Masaryk to Charles R. Crane, April 10, 1918, Wilson Papers, series II; Masaryk, *The Making of a State*, pp. 192-194.

[25] Lansing to Sharp, April 23, 1918, United States, *Foreign Relations, 1918, Russia*, II, 134-135.

[26] Lansing to Wilson, April 29, 1918, United States, *Foreign Relations, 1918, Russia*, II, 144-145.

[27] Reinsch to Lansing, April 27, 1918, United States, *Foreign Relations, 1918, Russia*, II, 141.

view with Lansing, Ishii expressed his government's willingness to co-operate with the United States in the war and to be guided by American policy with respect to military action in the Russian Far East.

The State Department found it difficult to accept these views at face value, because of the opposing views which existed on the subject within official Japanese circles. It was well-known that Viscount Motono, Minister for Foreign Affairs, the entire Japanese War Office, and most of the leading officers of the army favored immediate intervention, but were held back by Count Masakata Terauchi, Premier, and Baron Shimpei Goto, Minister for Home Affairs. In an authorized interview, Terauchi pointed out that unless the German menace grew considerably stronger, Japan would not intervene except with the warm approval of her allies and the assurance of economic support. She preferred to have no foreign troops co-operating, except possibly small contingents of Chinese. However, she would consent to Allied co-operation, if the Allies insisted. If she did intervene, she had no intention of going beyond a limited objective, probably Irkutsk. Her intervention would be taken primarily to stop the spread of anarchy and German intrigue in the Far East; it would be purely a measure of national self-defense for Japan. Thus, it would probably have little effect toward relieving the pressure of German arms on the Western Front.[28]

Throughout 1918 the threatened activities of Austro-German war prisoners were a vital factor in the Allied pleas for intervention. Camps for war prisoners existed in the vicinity of Irkutsk, Chita, Habarovsk, and Nikolsk. As early as December 15, 1917, Major Walter S. Drysdale, American military attaché at Peking, had reported that there were about thirty thousand Austrian and German prisoners in the Baikal region and in Eastern Siberia. However, he believed they constituted no serious menace to Allied interests.[29] A week later Caldwell reported that many of these prisoners were escaping. He believed that in case of a separate peace between Russia and Germany, the acts of these prisoners of war would necessitate Allied control of Vladivostok and the Priamur District.[30] Throughout February and early March, 1918, Stevens, Colonel Emerson, Ernest L. Harris (consul

[28] Gregory Mason, "Japan, Germany, Russia and the Allies; An Authorized Interview with Count Masakata Terauchi, Premier of Japan," *Outlook*, CXIX (May 1, 1918), 18-22. For the reaction of the American press to Japanese intervention, see *Current Opinion*, LXIV (April, 1918), 234-235.

[29] Drysdale to Reinsch, Feb. 5, 1918, file 861.00/1280, D.S.N.A.

[30] Caldwell to Lansing, Dec. 22, 1917, United States, *Foreign Relations, 1918, Russia*, II, 10.

general at Irkutsk), and Willing Spencer (chargé at Peking) reported an increased activity among German war prisoners.[31]   Spencer, however, admitted that most of the news emanating from Irkutsk came from the French consul general, whose views were "slightly colored by his desire for immediate intervention on the part of Japan."[32]   After the signing of the Treaty of Brest-Litovsk, rumors increased to the effect that the prisoners of war were being armed and were a dangerous menace to the Allies.   Some observers disagreed with these reports. Admiral Knight wrote Secretary Daniels that "there was no danger of German influences at work in Siberia and that there was no real need for intervention."[33]

When Major Drysdale was sent on a special mission to investigate the rumors, he reported that the prisoners of war were armed only in certain localities.[34]   Both Trotsky and Raymond Robins denied the rumors.   A special mission of investigation was sent from Moscow under the leadership of Captain William B. Webster of the American Red Cross Mission, and Captain W. L. Hicks, a member of the British Mission in Moscow.[35]   They reported that the activities of the war prisoners did not endanger Allied interests.   Yet it is to be noted that the views of the Webster-Hicks Mission differed materially from those of the Allied consuls and other sources of information in Siberia.   Webster believed the differences were due to three major factors.   First the Allied consuls at Irkutsk were anti-Bolshevik in sympathy and had not examined Soviet sources concerning the danger. Second, their information came largely from anti-Bolshevik sources. Third, the consuls had little time to make proper investigations because of their limited staffs.[36]

[31] Morris to Lansing, Feb. 13, 1918, Spencer to Lansing, March 6, 1918, United States, *Foreign Relations, 1918, Russia*, II, 45, 69-70; Morris to Lansing, Feb. 17, 1918, March 1, 1918, United States *Foreign Relations, 1918, Russia*, III, 220-221, 223-224; Spencer to Lansing, March 16, 1918, file 861.00/1306, D.S.N.A.

[32] Spencer. to Lansing, March 6, 1918, United States, *Foreign Relations, 1918, Russia*, II, 69-70.

[33] March 18, 1918, Polk Papers.

[34] United States, *Foreign Relations, 1918, Russia*, II, 80, 91, 94-95.   On March 15 the Japanese Minister of War reported that there were 94,000 German prisoners in Siberia east of Lake Baikal and 60,000 to the west of the Lake (London *Times*, March 19, 1918).

[35] Francis to Lansing, March 21, 1918, United States, *Foreign Relations, 1918, Russia*, II, 83-84.

[36] Cumming and Pettit, *Russian-American Relations*, p. 180.   See also Lockhart, *British Agent*, pp. 248-249, and United States, *Foreign Relations, 1918, Russia*, II, 84, 96-97, 122.   General Graves says that "subsequent events have shown that the information furnished the United States government by these investigators was absolutely correct.   Siberia was a great field for propaganda and even Consular Agents of the

Other observers supported the views of Webster and Hicks. Minister Reinsch advised that "there is no evidence of a concerted plan on the part of the Germans to control Siberia through the prisoners nor could such an attempt succeed. Earlier reports were exaggerated; most of these reports came from one source in Irkutsk. . . ."[37] Masaryk, who traveled through Siberia in early April en route to the United States, was convinced that "there is no organized German influence in eastern Siberia. [I] saw no evidence anywhere of organization of German or Austrian prisoners. . . ."[38] If there were large bodies of armed Austro-German war prisoners in Siberia, they were evidently playing a game of hide-and-seek.

The persistent reports of armed and organized prisoners in Siberia caused Lansing considerable worry. If the reports were true, he believed a change in policy was necessary. Perhaps it might even be wise to sanction Japan's entry into Siberia as the mandatory of the Allies.[39]

Throughout the early spring of 1918 Ambasador Francis at Vologda, Russia, vacillated between intervention and nonintervention. Although he continued to hope that the Bolsheviks would request Allied intervention, he believed the Allies should intervene immediately, if evidence proved that the Bolsheviks were controlled by Germany.[40] However, he was willing to ignore the "mistakes and outrages" practiced by the Soviet government in order to induce them to ask for Allied assistance.[41] By the middle of April Francis had begun to doubt both the ability of the Bolsheviks to remain in power and the possibility of obtaining an invitation to intervene from them. He reported, "I think time is fast approaching for Allied intervention and Allies should be prepared to act promptly."[42] Francis, however, registered his opposition to lone Japanese intervention. Although he did

various Governments had great trouble to know what credence to give reports they received. In this vast country, with a limited means of obtaining information, it was a difficult problem to check the accuracy of information" (Graves, *America's Siberian Adventure*, p. 26).

[37] Reinsch to Lansing, April 10, 1918, United States, *Foreign Relations, 1918, Russia*, II, 117.

[38] Masaryk to Charles R. Crane, April 10, 1918, Wilson Papers, series II; Masaryk, *Making of a State*, pp. 192-194.

[39] Lansing to Wilson, March 24, 1918, *Lansing Papers*, II, 357-358.

[40] Francis to Lansing, April 1, 1918, United States, *Foreign Relations, 1918, Russia*, I, 491.

[41] Francis to Lansing, April 5, 1918, United States, *Foreign Relations, 1918, Russia*, III, 228.

[42] Francis to Lansing, April 13, 1918, United States, *Foreign Relations, 1918, Russia*, II, 123-124.

not believe Japan would intervene against American wishes, he could not close his eyes "to [a] situation which gives a grasping nation a magnificent opportunity."[43]

After Count Wilhelm von Mirbach, German ambassador to the Soviet government, arrived in Moscow on April 26, Francis decided that the Allies ought to intervene without an invitation in order to prevent the extension of German domination over Russia. Francis now believed that Japanese demands for compensation to intervene in Siberia should be met, if they were reasonable. Doubting whether the Allies could "longer afford to overlook principles which Lenin is aggressively championing," he recommended intervention as an anti-Bolshevik measure.[44] Despite this advice, Francis continued to hope that the Bolsheviks would invite intervention.[45] On May 29 Francis repeated his recommendation for intervention without Bolshevik consent. Bruce Lockhart, British unofficial representative, had also begun to urge "prompt intervention regardless of Bolshevik consent."[46] The French and Italian ambassadors at Vologda had been advocating such action for over two months.[47]

Appeals for Allied action in Siberia increased throughout the month of May. Even those American representatives who had opposed intervention earlier now began to urge it. Both Major David P. Barrows, military attaché in Russia and Major Drysdale, military attaché at Peking, began to advocate Allied action. This may have been due to Semenov's victories in Siberia.[48] Minister Reinsch felt that the Siberian situation was distinct from that in Russia, and he recommended that the Allies co-operate in organizing a representative government "for strengthening common defense against German dominion."[49] On May 16 he reiterated his views: "Situation in Siberia seems more favorable than ever for effective joint action of Allies and American initia-

[43] Francis to Lansing, April 18, 1918, United States, *Foreign Relations, 1918, Russia,* II, 126; Noulens, *Mon ambassade en Russie,* II, 50-51.

[44] Francis to Lansing, May 5, 1918, United States, *Foreign Relations, 1918, Russia,* I, 519-520; Francis, *Russia from the American Embassy,* p. 302.

[45] Francis to Lansing, May 20, 1918, United States, *Foreign Relations, 1918, Russia,* I, 526-527.

[46] Francis to Lansing, May 29, 1918, United States, *Foreign Relations, 1918, Russia,* II, 179-180; Lockhart, *British Agent,* pp. 279-281; Noulens, *Mon ambassade en Russie,* II, 117.

[47] Sharp to Lansing, May 26, 1918, United States, *Foreign Relations, 1918, Russia,* II, 173.

[48] Reinsch to Lansing, April 24, 1918, file 861.00/1870, D.S.N.A.; Reinsch to Lansing, May 10, 1918, file 861.00/1776, D.S.N.A.

[49] Reinsch to Lansing, May 10, 1918, United States, *Foreign Relations, 1918, Russia,* II, 158, 160.

tive. A commission authorized to command moderate financial support would be able to reconstruct at least Siberia as an Allied factor. Should America remain inactive longer friendly feeling is likely to fail."[50] By the end of May Reinsch began to suspect that Japan was ready to act independently in the Far East. Japan had concluded successfully a military agreement with China, and was wholeheartedly supporting Semenov. Reinsch, therefore, began to demand Allied action, fearing that delay was dangerous.[51] John F. Stevens also felt that the need for Allied action against the "Bolsheviks in Siberia was imperative." He cabled an urgent appeal: "German propaganda, influence, occupation, increasing daily. Quick effective Allied action Siberia against treacherous combination necessary . . . if Allies expect to save Siberia they should move."[52]

During the first two weeks in May the question of intervention was revived in Tokyo largely as a result of Ishii's talk with Lansing on intervention, Semenov's success in Trans-Baikal, and the activity of the French Major Jean Pichon, who was then in Japan urging immediate action. The British ambassador to Japan was also advocating immediate intervention while the Japanese General Staff was urging Allied intervention under Japanese command.[53] Ambassador Morris noted that there was apparent satisfaction among the members of the Japanese General Staff with the Sino-Japanese military negotiations for cooperation against the Bolsheviks in Siberia.

The news that China and Japan had concluded a military agreement on May 16, 1918, was not welcome in Washington. As early as February 23, 1918, the State Department had been aware that negotiations for such an agreement had been in progress. Reinsch had then informed Lansing that Japan had proposed to China that the two nations co-operate "in restoring order in Siberia." Without knowledge of any of the details, the Chinese President had approved of the measure in principle. China had then turned to the United States for advice on the matter.[54] Lansing found it difficult to protest against the measure since it was ostensibly aimed at a common foe. He did,

---

[50] United States, *Foreign Relations, 1918, Russia*, II, 162.

[51] May 30, 1918, United States, *Foreign Relations, 1918, Russia*, II, 181.

[52] Stevens to Lansing, May 30, 1918, United States, *Foreign Relations, 1918, Russia*, II, 182.

[53] Morris to Lansing, May 16, 1918, United States, *Foreign Relations, 1918, Russia*, II, 162-165.

[54] Reinsch to Lansing, Feb. 23, 1918, United States, *Foreign Relations, 1918, Russia*, II, 55. Reinsch frankly believed that "the revolution in Russia and the rise of Bolshevism" were used as a pretext for the agreement by Japan (Paul S. Reinsch, *An American Diplomat in China*, New York, 1922, p. 351).

however, advise the Chinese government that if Japan deemed military occupation a necessity that China should guard the Chinese Eastern Railway alone.[55] The Sino-Japanese conversations then proceeded, and on March 25, 1918, China and Japan agreed to co-operate against those "hostile influences" in Russian territory which might threaten the peace and security of the Far East. The agreement was to be implemented by further provisions which were to be determined by the military and naval authorities of both countries.[56] Morris, who had managed to secure secretly a copy of the March agreement from his British colleague, pointed out that, although simple in its terms, it could easily lend itself to broad interpretation. He added that China was too weak to resist Japanese encroachments, while military authorities in the north of China were inclined to follow Japan's lead. Nevertheless, Japan met with great difficulties in completing the subsidiary agreement as to plans for military co-operation because China felt that the occasion for such joint action had not yet arisen. For obvious reasons, Chinese officials were reluctant to commit themselves to the full extent desired by Japan, but they did finally consent.[57]

The military agreements of May 16 and 19, 1918, signed in Peking by the military authorities of Japan and China, in accordance with the preliminary agreement of March 25, provided for Sino-Japanese military and naval co-operation in the event that their territories or "the general peace and tranquillity in the extreme Orient" should be menaced by the enemy. Specifically, the agreements provided for joint defense of the Chinese border against "the enemy" for the duration of the war, joint dispatch of troops outside Chinese territory, and use of the Chinese Eastern Railway. Japanese troops were to respect the sovereignty of China. The compacts were to remain secret.[58]

The Chinese government succeeded in introducing certain limiting clauses to the effect that the treaty would not be enforced unless the "general situation" required Chinese-Japanese co-operation in Siberia and Manchuria. Furthermore, Japan agreed that the treaties

[55] Lansing to Page, Feb. 27, 1918, United States, *Foreign Relations, 1918, Russia,* II, 57-58.

[56] Spencer to Lansing, March 29, 1918, file 861.00/1381, D.S.N.A.

[57] Morris to Lansing, April 19, 1918, file 793.94/683, D.S.N.A.

[58] For text of treaties, see United States, *Foreign Relations, 1918,* pp. 222-226; MacMurray, *Treaties,* II, 1407-1412; *Japan Year Book, 1919-1920,* pp. 473-475. These two treaties were supplemented by two additional treaties signed Sept. 6, 1918, and Feb. 5, 1919. They provided for Japanese control of Chinese troops operating in Siberia and fixed the duration of the treaties (United States, *Foreign Relations, 1918,* pp. 475-476; MacMurray, *Treaties,* II, 1413-1414). These treaties bound China even more closely to Japan. See LaFargue, *China and the World War,* p. 177.

would terminate upon the completion of the war, and that co-operation would be confined to military action.[59] Reinsch immediately informed the State Department of the agreement.[60] Since the Sino-Japanese agreements were in terms aimed primarily at combating German intrigue, they seemed to favor the anti-Bolsheviks. Kolchak, however, was well-acquainted with Japanese methods, and expressed the belief that Japan had obtained the "approval of China to bring Japanese forces into north Manchuria and ultimately secure complete control" of the region.[61]

While the Sino-Japanese negotiations were in progress, the Allies continued to press for action in Siberia. Sir Henry Wilson epitomized the attitude of most of the Allied leaders when he wrote in his diary on May 11: "From a military point of view the Japanese Army could not intervene too soon nor go too far, and . . . I was always impressing this on my Government, and hoped that the Japanese General Staff would do the same to their Government."[62] Balfour continued to flood the State Department with telegrams pleading for intervention.

This continued pressure of the Allies, the alleged menace of the Austro-German prisoners in Siberia, and the fear of independent Japanese action as evidenced by the Sino-Japanese Military Agreement were beginning now to wear down American resistance. On May 11 Lansing informed Balfour that the problem of intervention had in reality become two problems. Lansing was quite willing to consider favorably the intervention of Allied troops in North Russia because he could understand the military advantage in that area. However, he could see no military advantage in sending troops into Siberia. This attitude is explained in part by the fact that General March, as well as most of the leaders in the War Department, believed it impossible to send a sufficient military force into Siberia to do anything effective. Wilson, however, agreed with Lansing's view that the Siberian and

[59] Reinsch to Lansing, May 18, 1918, file 793.94/689, D.S.N.A.

[60] The British government, however, had not received the text of the agreement by May 30 (Great Britain, *House of Commons Debates*, 5th series, CVI, 943).

[61] Moser to Lansing, May 23, 1918, United States, *Foreign Relations, 1918, Russia*, II, 170. According to a Chinese scholar, the Sino-Japanese agreement meant nothing but permission to let Japan "occupy North Manchuria" (Shuhsi Hsu, *The Manchurian Question*, Peking, 1929, p. 39). A Japanese scholar frankly admitted that by the agreement, Japan simply "obtained the right to station guards along the northern end of the Chinese Eastern Railway" (Takeuchi, *War and Diplomacy*, p. 209). For a similar view, see also George E. Sokolsky, *The Story of the Chinese Eastern Railway* (Shanghai, 1929), pp. 33-34.

[62] Callwell, *Sir Henry Wilson*, II, 99.

North Russian questions should not be confused or discussed together.[63]

The British government immediately took advantage of Lansing's admission and appealed for American intervention of North Russia, as distinct from action in Siberia. Both Wilson and Secretary of War Baker soon evinced their willingness to send troops to the North Russian ports, where they believed a distinct military advantage could be obtained. Balfour believed that the objections which the President felt to Allied intervention at Vladivostok did not apply to the northern ports because in that area "there is no question of Japanese participation. . . ."[64] By June 1 the President consented to divert American troops from France to North Russia upon the approval of General Foch, provided such operations had the "sure sympathy of the Russian people."[65]

Throughout May the French authorities in Paris attempted to persuade the American ambassador of the need for intervention in Siberia, in the hope that he would influence his government accordingly. On May 12 General Niessel gave his eyewitness account of the situation in Russia. His strongest argument was based on the fear of German control in Russia. Ambassador Sharp found that most prominent French leaders were united in the belief that German control of Russia could only be prevented by immediate Japanese action. At the same time they feared that, unless the Allies supported and approved of that action, Japan would act independently and "in all probability" come to an understanding with Germany.[66]

The French appeals fell on barren soil. Wilson was adamant in his opposition to the Siberian scheme. On May 30, 1918, he sent for Sir William Wiseman to discuss the Russian problem. Wiseman reported that, although Wilson appreciated the arguments presented by the French and British governments, "no military man with whom he had talked had been able to convince him that there was any practical

[63] Lansing to Wilson, May 11, 1918, United States, *Foreign Relations, 1918, Russia,* II, 160; Baker, *Woodrow Wilson,* VIII, 361; Wilson to Lansing, May 20, 1918, *Lansing Papers,* II, 361.

[64] Balfour to Reading, June 11, 1918, Wiseman Papers; Memorandum of the Secretary of State, June 3, 1918, United States, *Foreign Relations, 1918, Russia,* II, 484-485; Noulens, *Mon ambassade en Russie,* II, 114-115.

[65] Reading to Lansing, May 29, 1918, United States, *Foreign Relations, 1918, Russia,* II, 476; Baker, *Woodrow Wilson,* VIII, 175. For the events leading to intervention in North Russia, see Leonid I. Strakhovsky, *The Origins of American Intervention in North Russia, 1918* (Princeton, 1937).

[66] United States, *Foreign Relations, 1918, Russia,* I, 528-529; Sharp to Lansing, May 15, 1918, file 861.00/6237, D.S.N.A.; Dawson, *War Memoirs of Sharp,* pp. 255-256.

scheme which would re-create a Russian front. He remarked that he would go as far as intervening against the wishes of the Russian people —knowing that it was eventually for their good—providing he thought the scheme had any practical chance of success." The President pointed out that the Japanese refused to go any further than Omsk, and he doubted "if they could get as far as that." It was the President's view that the Japanese were eager to have an invitation from the Allies "so that they might occupy the maritime provinces, but had no intention of engaging in a vast military enterprise sufficient to reach even the Ural mountains."[67]

When General Bliss learned that the Supreme War Council, scheduled to assemble at Versailles for its sixth session on June 1, was planning to discuss the subject of Japanese intervention in Siberia and Allied policy toward Russia, he cabled for instructions. He outlined the arguments to be used and ventured the thought that "perhaps French interest in the Russian debt partly accounts for their unanimity in favoring Japanese intervention." Bliss reported that the European Allies generally conceded that the United States must finance Japanese military operations. Bliss admitted that he distrusted everything he heard on the subject, and that France and Britain were rabid in their denunciation of the Bolsheviks. He believed that the United States should "consent only to a recommendation that the Allied governments ascertain beyond [a] shadow of a doubt what the real attitude of the Russian people will be toward this intervention."[68]

When General March replied to Bliss's cable, he stated the President's views in forceful language: "The President's attitude is that Russia's misfortune imposes upon us at this time the obligation of unswerving fidelity to the principle of Russian territorial integrity and political independence. Intervention via Vladivostok is deemed impracticable" while "the idea of compensating Japan by territory in Asiatic Russia is inadmissible."[69]

Throughout the sixth session of the Supreme War Council, much energy was expended "trying to get the Siberian expedition launched."[70] This time the Allies tried a new approach; they determined to ask

[67] Wiseman to Sir Eric Drummond, May 30, 1918, Wiseman Papers.

[68] Bliss to Baker, May 27, 1918, Wilson Papers, series II.

[69] March to Bliss, May 28, 1918, Wilson Papers, series II; Frederick Palmer, *Newton D. Baker, America at War* (2 vols.; New York, 1931), II, 314-315; Baker, *Woodrow Wilson*, VIII, 175. These instructions were probably responsible for the following entry in Sir Henry Wilson's Diary on June 1: "The President, U.S.A., has now ordered Bliss not to back Japanese intervention" (Callwell, *Sir Henry Wilson*, II, 104). Sir Henry Wilson was now Chief of the Imperial General Staff.

[70] Palmer, *Bliss*, p. 271.

Japan for certain guarantees in advance of intervention, in order to remove President Wilson's objections to the proposed expedition. The three conditions proposed to Japan were: "(1) that Japan should promise to respect the territorial integrity of Russia; (2) that she would take no side in the internal politics of the country; (3) that she would advance as far west as possible for the purpose of encountering the Germans."[71]

The appeals of the Supreme War Council were supported by insistent pleas for intervention from American representatives throughout Asia and Europe, as well as from Allied statesmen. Non-Bolshevik Russians added their entreaties to the swelling cries for action. Wilson found it increasingly difficult to maintain his position of opposition. And, as the month of June advanced, a new situation arose in Siberia, which threatened to draw Wilson into action, despite his better judgment.

In March, 1918, a force of some seventy thousand Czechoslovaks, former prisoners of war and deserters from the Austrian Army, had started across Siberia to Vladivostok with the consent of the Bolshevik government. From Vladivostok they expected to be transported to France to fight on the Western Front.[72] The French and British governments disagreed as to the best means of utilizing the Czech forces. On April 1 the British War Office suggested that Czech troops either occupy Siberia in the vicinity of Omsk, or else join Semenov's force in Trans-Baikal.[73] Both the French government, under whose leadership the Czech forces were operating, and the Czechs themselves were opposed to this. While the French and British governments argued, the Czechs continued their eastward journey via the Trans-Siberian Railway with no advance preparations made for their arrival at Vladivostok.[74] Anticipating the French request for vessels to transport the Czechs to France, the State Department had instructed its ambassador in Paris that it could not "provide tonnage for transportation across Pacific."[75]

[71] Frazier to Lansing, June 10, 1918, United States, *Foreign Relations, 1918, Russia,* II, 202-203; Bliss to Baker, June 3, 1918, Bliss Papers.

[72] For a detailed account of the Czech trek across Siberia, see Bunyan, *Intervention,* pp. 75-101; Margarete Klante, *Von der Wolga zum Amur. Die tschechische Legion und der russische Bürgerkrieg* (Berlin, 1931); Henry P. S. Baerlein, *March of the Seventy Thousand* (London, 1926).

[73] Eduard Beneš, *My War Memoirs* (Boston, 1928), p. 357.

[74] Caldwell to Lansing, April 19, 1918, United States, *Foreign Relations, 1918, Russia,* II, 126-127.

[75] Lansing to Sharp, April 22, 1918, United States, *Foreign Relations, 1918, Russia,* II, 130.

Meanwhile, contingents of the Czechoslovak Army were arriving at Vladivostok. By May 27 their number had reached ten thousand but no preparations had been made to transport them to Europe. Admiral Knight informed Secretary Daniels on May 27 that the Czechs "have been approached as to willingness to conduct military operations in Siberia and Russia and they are positively opposed to this believing it would bring them at least virtually into conflict [with the] Russian faction. . . ."[76]

The Czech problem was discussed at a Franco-British conference in London on May 28. Again, the French insisted on the immediate transfer of the Czechs to France, while the British wanted them to remain in Siberia to aid in the establishment of an Eastern Front. The British finally compromised reluctantly and agreed to find some means of transportation for five thousand Czechs from Vladivostok.[77]

At the Supreme War Council meeting in early June the Allies finally agreed to bring to Europe as many Czechs as possible and a resolution was adopted to that effect.[78] The British were requested to ask Japan to furnish tonnage for the transport of Czech troops. The British were not very sympathetic to this suggestion, as they feared it would interfere with the plans for a Japanese expedition to Siberia. The French, however, were so insistent that the British government finally made the request. Although the British Foreign Office expressed to Japan the belief that all Japanese tonnage must be used for the expedition to Siberia to the "exclusion of all less important objects," nevertheless, it hoped that Japan would help in the transport of Czech troops until the expedition should take place.[79]

When the Allied decision regarding the Czechs was sent to the State Department, William Phillips, Assistant Secretary of State, drafted a memorandum in which he suggested the advisability of "retaining these forces in the far east for the present, pending the development of the situation on the eastern front where they may be needed to reinforce possible Russian opposition to further encroachments by Germany."[80] His note was sent for approval to Basil Miles, acting chief

[76] United States, *Foreign Relations, 1918, Russia,* II, 174.

[77] Dugdale, *Balfour,* II, 260; Beneš, *War Memoirs,* p. 378; Masaryk, *The Making of a State,* p. 183.

[78] Palmer, *Bliss,* pp. 277-278; Beneš, *War Memoirs,* p. 392; Dugdale, *Balfour,* II, 190; Masaryk, *The Making of a State,* p. 191.

[79] Memorandum from the British Foreign Office to the Department of State, June 10, 1918, file 763.72/10309, D.S.N.A.; World War Records of the Supreme War Council, 6th Session, June 1-2, 1918, Old Records Section, Department of War, National Archives.

[80] Memorandum drafted June 20, 1918, file 763.72/10309, D.S.N.A.

of the Russian Division, and Joseph E. Grew, acting chief of the Western European Division. The latter replied:

> Mr. Miles and I agree that it would be highly desirable to have these Czecho-Slovak troops remain in Siberia, but to go on record as recommending it to the British government might prove embarrassing in connection with our attitude toward Japanese intervention. Would it not be better to concur with the British in their plan for transporting them if and when it is found practicable to spare sufficient tonnage from allied needs? Mr. Miles informs me that there are now about 16,000 Czecho-Slovak troops in Vladivostok, about 30,000 between Irkutsk and the sea, and another 30,000 to 50,000 in other parts of Russia. It seems very improbable that sufficient tonnage will be available to transport all or even a great part of this number in the near future. . . .[81]

Although never sent, the American memorandum, and the correspondence concerning it, indicated that the State Department was beginning to think along the same lines as the British Foreign Office.

On June 3, 1918, the military representatives of the Supreme War Council discussed the utilization of Czech troops at the Russian Arctic ports. They believed that such an occupation was an indispensable corollary of Allied intervention in Siberia. Utilization of the available Serbian and Czech units would render the land defense of the maritime bases possible without the transport of any considerable expeditionary force. The military representatives finally agreed on securing the approval of the National Czechoslovak Council to retain some Czech units, with the understanding that the remainder would be sent to France as previously agreed.[82]

While the Allied military representatives discussed the best disposition of Czech troops, relations between the Czechs and the Bolsheviks had been strained to the breaking point. On March 26, 1918, the Czechs and the Soviets had signed an agreement which provided for the transportation of the Czechs to Vladivostok via the Trans-Siberian Railway, not as military detachments but as free citizens. They were to surrender most of their arms at Penza.[83] The agreement was signed by Stalin.[84] Neither side lived up to the letter of the agreement. Czech detachments frequently concealed arms in excess of the permitted

[81] Grew to Phillips, June 25, 1918, file 763.72/10308, D.S.N.A.

[82] Joint Note No. 31, Supreme War Council, Military Representatives, June 3, 1918, file 861.00/6731, D.S.N.A.

[83] Klante, *Von der Wolga zum Amur*, pp. 137, 138; Baerlein, *March of the Seventy Thousand*, pp. 109-110; B. O. Johnson to H. H. Fisher, April 29, 1931, Railway Service Corps Papers.

[84] White, *The Siberian Intervention*, p. 245.

quota, while the Soviet authorities often delayed the passage of the Czechs and insisted on the surrender of more arms than prescribed by the Penza agreement. Suspicion and mistrust grew rapidly between the Czechs and the Soviets, and was intensified by the disorderly condition of the country and the delays in transportation.[85] By the end of May fighting had broken out between the two groups in Central and Western Siberia. As a result the Czechs in Vladivostok feared for the safe exit of their brothers from the interior.[86] On June 20, 1918, the Czechs in Vladivostok decided to act. They placed guards over the military stores in Vladivostok to prevent their shipment to the west, and determined to return to rescue the Czechs in Central and Western Siberia from the armed war prisoners and Bolsheviks.[87] At the same time members of the Czech National Council in Vladivostok appealed to the Allied consuls for a supporting force of "from 50 to 100,000 Allied troops to establish [a] permanent front against Germany."[88]

On June 29 the Czecks overthrew the Vladivostok Soviet and assumed control of the city.[89] Immediately the Allied powers, having war ships in port, went into action. The British and Japanese landed large armed parties in the morning; the Chinese landed marines in the afternoon; and a small detachment of American marines was landed to guard the American consulate in the evening. Shortly thereafter the action taken by the naval commanders on the scene was sanctioned by the powers.[90]

Evidence indicates that the struggle which broke out between the Czechs and the Bolsheviks may have been influenced by a third party. Chicherin, Soviet Foreign Minister, advised Lockhart on May 28 that

[85] Chamberlin, *Russian Revolution*, II, 4; Carl W. Ackerman, *Trailing the Bolsheviki; Twelve Thousand Miles with the Allies in Siberia* (New York, 1919), p. 123; B. O. Johnson to H. H. Fisher, April 29, 1931, Railway Service Corps Papers.

[86] Caldwell to Lansing, June 1, 1918, file 861.00/1926, D.S.N.A.

[87] Caldwell to Lansing, June 20, 1918, United States, *Foreign Relations, 1918, Russia*, II, 219.

[88] Caldwell to Lansing, June 25, 1918, United States, *Foreign Relations, 1918, Russia*, II, 226. Caldwell reported that all of the Allied consuls agreed to recommend favorable action to their respective governments.

[89] Caldwell to Lansing, June 28, 1918, United States, *Foreign Relations, 1918, Russia*, II, 226. The Vladivostok Soviet had governed Vladivostok since April 30. Allied representatives had consistently reported that it was a transitory affair, maintained in power by the support of armed prisoners of war (Caldwell to Lansing, April 30, 1918; Knight to Daniels, May 27, 1918, June 26, 1918, United States, *Foreign Relations, 1918, Russia*, II, 148, 174, 230, respectively).

[90] Knight to Daniels, June 3, 1918, WA-66, Siberia, Conditions in Vladivostok, Naval Records Collection; Caldwell to Lansing, June 29, 1918, United States, *Foreign Relations, 1918, Russia*, II, 235; Bunyan, *Intervention*, p. 316.

telegrams had been seized "showing the connection between this movement and the counter-revolutionary plots. Now military commissaries are informing us that connections have been disclosed between the Czechs and British representatives." Chicherin urged Lockhart to use his "moral influence" to induce the Czechs to cease the struggle, deliver their weapons, and leave the country.[91]

Many Russian Whites and Siberians believed that "the return of the Czechoslovak units from Eastern Siberia to the Volga and the Ural front, the overthrow by them of the Soviet rule at Vladivostok, and the strengthening of their control along the Trans-Siberian, which were officially explained as protective measures, were undoubtedly the execution of a part of the Allied or at least the French plans for intervention." Professor Georgii K. Guins, a member of the Kolchak regime, wrote:

> The secret of the Czechs' return westward was in a decision made in Paris. War with Germany was not yet concluded. To provide sufficient ships to carry 40,000 Czechs to France appeared difficult. It seemed more purposeful to return all the Czechs to the Volga and thus create for Germany the threat of re-establishing an eastern front. President Masaryk, then only president of the Czechoslovak National Committee in Paris, sent the Czechoslovak Army his greetings and blessed it to continued the fight. Political considerations dictated a return to the Volga . . . and the re-establishment of a Russia loyal to the Allies.[92]

Colonel George Emerson, who was on a tour of inspection along

[91] *Correspondance se rapportant à la déscente à Vladivostok* (Paris, 1919), p. 7. The Bolsheviks pointed out that the direct reason for the taking of decisive and severe measures for the disarming of the Czecks was their own action, which constituted "counter-revolutionary armed rebellion," against the Soviets" (Cumming and Pettit, *Russian-American Relations*, pp. 224-226; Bunyan, *Intervention*, pp. 102-103).

[92] Varneck and Fisher, *Testimony of Kolchak*, pp. 241-242. Professor H. K. Norton, *Far Eastern Republic of Siberia* (New York, 1927), p. 68, who spent considerable time in Siberia investigating the history of this period, endorses the view of Guins, to the effect that the "Czecks were prevailed upon by the Allies under the urgence of France, to attack the Russians from the rear in return for recognition and assistance." He believes this hypothesis receives additional support from the fact that France recognized the Czechoslovak Republic on June 30, 1918, and Great Britain on August 13. The United States and Japan followed this lead on September 2, and September 9, respectively. For similar views, see also E. A. Ross, *The Russian Soviet Republic*, p. 135; William P. and Selda K. Coates, *Armed Intervention in Russia, 1918-1922* (London, 1935), pp. 110-111. Bruce Lockhart wrote, "But for the folly of the French I am convinced that the Czecks would have been evacuated without incident. . . . How I wish today that President Mazaryk had remained in Russia during this trying period. I am convinced that he would never have sanctioned the Siberian revolt" (*British Agent*, pp. 269-270). See also Frederick L. Schuman, *American Policy toward Russia since 1917* (New York, 1928), pp. 93-94.

the Trans-Siberian Railway, became an eyewitness to the events which led to the Czech revolt, and offered his services as a mediator. He reported that it "was impossible to come to any understanding between Captain Kadlets [Czech Army] and the Soviet Government, as the Captain advised us at that time that action of the Czechish troops was a concerted movement, that all officers had instructions to act at a certain time to take the towns in the vicinity that they were located."[93] When the Soviet President of Marinsk learned of Czech military success along the Trans-Siberian Railway, he exclaimed with an apparently ingenuous ejaculation, "France has, through concerted action with the Czech Troops, *en route,* taken Siberia in 24 hours."[94]

In the spring of 1919 the American Military Intelligence prepared a report on the activities of the Czechs in Siberia from the materials which were then available to them. Although recognizing the inadequacy of the materials examined, the report concluded that the Czech claims of a treacherous attack by Bolsheviks, German agents, and war prisoners were unfounded in fact; that the Czechs could have safely accomplished their original purpose to withdraw; and that the Czechs did not fully abide by their promise to surrender their arms and keep out of Russian internal affairs. The report also indicated that the Czech diversion from their original purpose to withdraw was probably due to the interference of one of the Allied powers. The one big fact in the complete change of the Czechoslovak mission was the subsequent, and almost immediate, erection of anti-Bolshevik authorities at all those points seized by the Czechoslovak echelons.[95]

[93] Report of Colonel George H. Emerson of the Russian Railway Service Corps, covering his movements from April 26, 1918, to Sept. 9, 1918, signed also by Major H. H. Slaughter, assistant military attaché to American Embassy, file 861.77/541, D.S.N.A., pp. 43-44; B. O. Johnson to H. H. Fisher, April 29, 1931, George H. Emerson to H. H. Fisher, May 13, 1932, Railway Service Corps Papers.

[94] Emerson Report, file 861.77/541, D.S.N.A., p. 12. The report showed further that the Czecks never were in danger from the aggressive acts of the Soviets, as long as they maintained their original purpose of traveling to Vladivostok via the Trans-Siberian Railway. General Graves believed that the Czechs were the aggressors, and that the Soviets wanted to get the Czechs out of Siberia, and were willing to meet them half-way in effecting their announced purpose (Graves, *America's Siberian Adventure,* pp. 51-52). It must be remembered that on June 3 the military representatives of the Supreme War Council had already decided to retain some of the Czech troops in Siberia. Baerlein, *March of the Seventy Thousand,* p. 125, writes, "One can but wonder whether the Allies really planned to remove the Czechs from Siberia. Trotsky has been blamed for impeding the movement of the Czechs toward the east; but his apprehension that the Entente proposed to make use of them against Soviet Russia was by no means the view of a mere alarmist."

[95] Laurance Packard, Captain, U.S.A., The Czecho-Slovaks in Russia, Aug., 1914 to Feb., 1919. Prepared in the Office of the Chief of Staff, Confidential, file 861.00/6052,

Whether the Czech revolt was due to international intrigue or to some insignificant and chance incident, the fact remains that the "rescue of the Czechs" gave President Wilson a moral reason for sending American troops to Siberia, and initiated the final phase in the campaign which resulted in his acquiescence to intervention in Siberia. By early June Minister Reinsch was urging joint action and the utilization of the Czechs. In regard to the Czechs he wrote:

It is the general opinion of Allied representatives here in which I concur that it would be a serious mistake to remove the Czecho-Slovak troops from Siberia. With only slight countenance and support they could control all of Siberia against the Germans. They are sympathetic to the Russian population, eager to be accessories to the Allied cause, the most serious means [menace] to extension of German influence in Russia. Their removal would greatly benefit Germany and further discourage Russia. If they were not in Siberia it would be worth while to bring them there from a distance.[96]

Wilson was profoundly influenced by the suggestion from Reinsch, and wrote Lansing, "There seems to me to emerge from this suggestion the shadow of a plan that might be worked with Japanese and other assistance. These people [the Czecho-Slovaks] are the cousins of the Russians."[97]

By the end of May both Breckinridge Long and Basil Miles were convinced of the need for intervention. All the Americans in Russia, Siberia, and China, with one or two exceptions, were now united in supporting the call of the British, French, and Japanese for immediate action. Reports also indicated that this was the desire of a large part of the Russian people. Ambassador Francis had satisfied himself that the Bolsheviks were accepting German domination and no longer deserved American assistance. Both Long and Miles felt that the men in the field knew the situation better than those in Washington.[98]

D.S.N.A., pp. 1-5. When Secretary Baker read this report, he wrote Wilson as follows, "The paper is much too long for your reading, but I have talked with Mr. Lansing about it, and indicated to him that, in my judgment, the report shows with fair conclusiveness that the Czecho-Slovak forces could have gotten out of Russia, but that influence was brought to bear (perhaps by the French who were interested in having them remain in Russia), and that at least a part of their difficulties with the Russians grew out of this changed desire on their part" (Baker to Wilson, July 31, 1919, Wilson Papers, series VI).

[96] Reinsch to Lansing, June 13, 1918, United States, *Foreign Relations, 1918, Russia*, II, 206-207. The need for action was also urged by consuls at Vladivostok and Harbin. See United States, *Foreign Relations, 1918, Russia*, II, 191, 208-209, 226.

[97] June 17, 1918, file 861.00/2145½, D.S.N.A.; *Lansing Papers*, II, 226.

[98] Long to Miles, May 31, 1918, file 861.00/1900, D.S.N.A. Leading editorials also

Throughout June Ambassador Francis continued to urge action in Siberia. He believed such action was necessary to aid not only the Czechs, but also the Russian people who were "confidently" awaiting deliverance. France was evidently convinced that the Bolshevik government would soon collapse, and that if Allied intervention were not forthcoming the people would turn to Germany as a last resort. Russia trusted the United States, said Francis, and expected her to take the lead in intervention. If she did not, Francis believed the war would be prolonged by two years.[99]

The recommendations of Francis were supplemented by pressure from the Russian representatives of the defunct Provisional government who had earlier been opposed to intervention. Ambassador Bakhmetev urged intervention of an Allied character in preference to lone Japanese action, and advised the use of the Czechs in Siberia.[100] Alexander Konovalov and John Sookine, both attached to the Russian Embassy at Washington, favored the participation of Czech troops, as well as Japanese soldiers. Although opposed to Japanese command of such an expedition, they agreed to accept such a possibility if the whole Allied expedition were put under a civil high commissioner of either American or French nationality. They also advocated, in addition to a military expedition, a political department to publicize the Allied aims and an economic department to establish trade relations and bring relief to the population of Siberia and Russia.[101]

By the end of May the State Department began considering concrete proposals for action in Siberia. Fearing the dangers of Allied military intervention in Russia, it considered the possibility of using the Russian Railway Service Corps as the chief factor in a policy of Allied

---

preached the need for intervention urging that Bolshevism was a greater threat than the menace of Japan. They insisted that the only means of helping Russia was by overthrowing Bolshevism. See "Intervention in Russia," *New Republic*, XX (June 1, 1918), 130-133; Gregory Mason, "Japan and Bolshevism," *Outlook*, CXIX (June 12, 1918), 259-261; London *Times*, June 15, 19, 1918, July 4, 1918; New York *Times*, June 3, 4, 1918. By June of 1918 even members of Congress had begun to urge that the United States adopt the policy of Siberian intervention (*Congressional Record*, vol. 56, pt. 8, pp. 7557, 7997-8001, 8065-8067, 8580).

[99] United States, *Foreign Relations, 1918, Russia*, I, 561; II, 214, 220-223. For reports from Consul Poole in Moscow and Consul General Harris at Irkutsk, supporting these views, see United States, *Foreign Relations, 1918, Russia*, II, 205-206, 210-211, 215-216, 239-241.

[100] Memorandum of Long, June 7, 1918, United States, *Foreign Relations, 1918, Russia*, II, 192-193. The Central Committee of the Constitutional Democratic Party passed a resolution favoring Allied intervention (United States, *Foreign Relations, 1918, Russia*, II, 198-199).

[101] Konovalov to Lansing, June 26, 1918, Phillips to Lansing, June 27, 1918, United States, *Foreign Relations, 1918, Russia*, II, 227-229, 232-233.

economic assistance to Russia. The activities of the corps would be protected by an Allied military force. Although it would be difficult to attain numerically equal participation by the Allies in such a military policy, the State Department felt that Japanese participation could be equalized by means of American and Chinese forces, and also by the immediate utilization of the "valuable Bohemian troops now gathering at Vladivostok." Lansing also informed Francis that,

while an invitation by the 'de facto' authorities for such Allied action might reduce opposition thereto, compliance therewith might give a color of recognition and thereby prove undesirable. If, however, as a result of your conference and cooperation with Emerson it might be arranged that any reasonable and proper suggestions or requests by the Soviet authorities be favorably considered by the Embassy and the Railway Corps with the distinct proviso and 'quid pro quo' that railway assistance in European Russia should be accompanied by permission for the Corps to extend its activities in Siberia, this program might immediately be commenced with the advantage of the tacit acquiescence of such authorities.[102]

This suggestion was followed by another from Colonel House, who advised the formation of a committee on Russian affairs to act in conjunction with the President and the Department of State.[103] By June 11 the President had begun to consider the possibility of a "Russian Relief Commission." The idea evidently originated with Colonel House and his son-in-law, Gordon Auchincloss. Both House and Lansing urged the President to create such a commission as concrete proof of American desires to stand by Russia.[104] Sir William Wiseman also approved of the idea. Conferring with the President, Wiseman found him still opposed to intervention by the Japanese alone. Moreover, the President was also opposed to Allied intervention on the ground that this would amount to the same thing as independent Japanese action, as Japan would supply the greater part of the military force. Furthermore, the President still desired an invitation to enter Russia from either the Bolsheviks or some body really representing Russian opinion. Nevertheless, things were not completely hopeless, according to Wiseman, as the President had been thinking rather seriously of a civil commission. Wiseman hoped that the commission might be used as an entering wedge for military intervention. He advised the British Foreign Office to encourage the scheme.[105]

[102] Lansing to Francis, May 29, 1918, file 861.00/2079½, D.S.N.A.

[103] Baker, *Woodrow Wilson*, VIII, 190.

[104] Seymour, *Intimate Papers*, III, 409; Auchincloss, Diary, June 12 and 13, 1918; Baker, *Woodrow Wilson*, VIII, 210; *Lansing Papers*, II, 362-363.

[105] Wiseman to Drummond, June 14, 1918, Wiseman Papers.

Meanwhile, British authorities were becoming impatient at the delay. The military leaders insisted that a Japanese expedition to Siberia was an immediate necessity. On June 20 a message was dispatched to Washington stating that armed action in Siberia was essential if the Allies desired victory in 1919. Immediate action was necessary before winter set in.[106] Colonel House urged the President that "something must be done immediately" or Russia would become the prey of Germany. He advised Wilson to make an address to Congress, stating his plan for sending a relief commission to Russia for the purpose of speeding up her food production and coordinating the activities of the various relief agencies in that country. Since the commission and its assistants would need a "safe and orderly" field in which to work, the President might ask for the cooperation and assistance of England, France, Italy, and Japan. These nations would then promise not to "interfere with Russia's political affairs or encroach in any way upon her territorial integrity." House believed that the Russian people would approve of this type of intervention.[107] Lord Reading was enthusiastic over the plan. Wilson, who also thought well of the scheme, discussed it with his Cabinet the next day.[108]

Throughout the month of June the President deliberated over the Russian question. Auchincloss reported that it was "the matter of most interest at the present time," and that "no one seems to know what the President is going to do."[109] The French government brought increasing pressure to bear on the President by the dispatch of two special emissaries, Marcel Delanney, French ambassador to Japan en route to Tokyo, and Henri Bergson, the noted French philosopher. Both of these men also called on Colonel House.[110]

Despite the increasing pressure for intervention in Siberia, American military authorities remained firm in their opposition. They were opposed to any diversion of American forces from France. Secretary Baker told Wilson that, if he had his own way about Russia, he

---

[106] Callwell, *Sir Henry Wilson*, II, 109; Seymour, *Intimate Papers*, III, 412.

[107] Baker, *Woodrow Wilson*, VIII, 225; Seymour, *Intimate Papers*, III, 412-414; Memorandum of J. Butler Wright (former counselor of American Embassy in Petrograd), June 3, 1918, file 861.00/2166½, D.S.N.A.

[108] Baker, *Woodrow Wilson*, VIII, 231, 235.

[109] Auchincloss, Diary, June 21, 1918.

[110] Noulens, *Mon ambassade en Russie*, II, 114; Seymour, *Intimate Papers*, III, 407-408; Baker, *Woodrow Wilson*, VIII, 215, 233. President Wilson told M. Delanney that he was considering "anew the entire situation, and would express his conclusions within the next ten days" (Morris to Lansing, June 22, 1918, United States, *Foreign Relations, 1918, Russia*, II, 219).

"would like to take everybody out of Russia, except the Russians, including diplomatic representatives, military representatives, political agents, propagandists and casual visitors, and let the Russians settle down and settle their own affairs." Baker continued to adhere to this point of view.[111] Later, Baker said that the North Russian and Siberian expeditions were practically the only decisions of a military nature which President Wilson had determined personally throughout America's participation in the war. Wilson attempted to explain his position to the Secretary of War: "Baker, I wholly agree with all you say from a military point of view, but we are fighting this war with Allies and I have felt obliged to fall in with their wishes here."[112]

General March also registered his opposition, not only because he was a pronounced "western fronter," but also because he was convinced that Japanese intervention would "draw Russia together and throw her into the arms of Germany." There was no doubt in his mind but that "as between Germany and Japan *as their master* they would infinitely prefer Germany."[113] Generals Pershing and Bliss were also opposed to any diversion of American troops."[114] Their views were not shared by General Foch, Generalissimo of the Allied armies, who sent an appeal directly to the President urging intervention:

In my opinion the sending by you of American troops to Russia is justified, for no appreciable diminution of the number of troops to be sent to France will result therefrom. I conceive the expedition to Siberia as having to be mainly formed with Japanese elements. The Allies' contingents would be reduced to modest numbers; some 12,000 men or thereabouts. America could supply at once two regiments, and the Allies the rest. Under those conditions the American troops sent to France would only be reduced in an insignificant way.

More than ever, in the interest of military success in Europe, I consider the expedition to Siberia as a very important factor for victory, provided action be immediate, on account of the season being already advanced. I take the liberty of insisting on this last point.[115]

Although Great Britain and France continued to maneuver for

[111] Baker to Wilson, June 19, 1918, Newton D. Baker Papers (collection in custody of Baker, Hostetler, and Patterson, Cleveland, Ohio); Baker, *Woodrow Wilson*, VIII, 219.

[112] Baker to Mrs. John B. Casserly, Nov. 15, 1924, Wilson Papers, Ac. 6190. See also Baker, Foreword in Graves, *America's Siberian Adventure*, p. viii.

[113] March, *A Nation at War*, p. 118.

[114] John J. Pershing, *My Experiences in the World War* (2 vols.; New York, 1931), II, 49; Baker to Mrs. John B. Casserly, Nov. 15, 1924, Wilson Papers, Ac. 6190.

[115] Foch to Wilson, June 27, 1918, Baker Papers; partially reproduced in Baker, *Woodrow Wilson*, VIII, 235.

American approval of their Siberian plans, they were not yet certain of the Japanese attitude toward the three conditions set forth by the Supreme War Council on June 3. Japan finally replied on June 24 that she did not "feel at liberty" to express a decision on the matter before a satisfactory understanding had been reached among the three European powers and the United States. President Wilson "read this communication with genuine pleasure."[116]

Despite this apparently friendly attitude on the part of Japan toward the United States, American consuls in Siberia reported a strong anti-American campaign by the Japanese, who appeared to be endeavoring by every means in their power to persuade the Russians to place all intervention in Japanese hands. Some attacks even suggested that America meant to share with Germany in despoiling Russia.[117]

The British War Cabinet feared that the Japanese reply of June 24 might encourage President Wilson to declare publicly his opposition to military intervention in the Far East. This was to be avoided at all costs. Lloyd George, therefore, immediately sent a message to the President asking him to refrain from making any decision on the matter until after the next meeting of the Supreme War Council.[118]

Although President Wilson was still "sweating blood" over the question of intervention, many of the policy-making members of the State Department were now enthusiastic about the scheme. When news reached Washington that the Czechs were favorable to the idea of remaining in Siberia, and that they had become the dominating factor in the Russian situation, both Basil Miles and J. Butler Wright, former counselor of the Russian Embassy, were overjoyed. Said Wright to Miles, "This is a god-send. It's just the news we want. Masaryk is in town! Let's concentrate on this with all our power at once!"[119] E. T. Williams, chief of the Division of Far Eastern Affairs, told Long that "Professor Masaryk is decidedly opposed to the retention of the Czech-Slovak forces in Russia and Siberia." When Joseph Grew was informed of this discussion, he penciled a notation on the memorandum, "Prof. Masaryk has changed his mind." Thus between June 20 and June 24 Masaryk had evidently agreed to the retention of Czech troops in Siberia. It is quite likely that this decision was in part due to the influence of certain members of the State

[116] *Lansing Papers*, II, 365.

[117] Moser to Lansing, June 10, 1918, file 861.00/1996, D.S.N.A.; Moser to Lansing, June 14, 1918, United States, *Foreign Relations, 1918, Russia*, II, 208-209.

[118] Baker, *Woodrow Wilson*, VIII, 237.

[119] Knight to Daniels, June 21, 1918, Wright to Miles, June 22, 1918, file 861.00/2165½, D.S.N.A.

Department.[120] Even Lansing believed that the Czech situation had created a new condition which should receive careful consideration. He asked President Wilson if it was not possible that "in this body of capable and loyal troops may be found a nucleus for military occupation of the Siberian railway?"[121] Moreover, Admiral Knight had reported that if the Allies contemplated the establishment of an Eastern Front, they would find their plans enormously facilitated by "the present condition with the notable advantage that Czech influence would greatly overcome that of Japanese removing chief antagonism of Russians to movement against German power and influence."[122]

As the month of June ended, events seemed to be forcing President Wilson's hand. All of his Allies as well as the vast majority of his diplomatic advisers at home and abroad were urging action. In addition, the threat of independent Japanese action loomed on the horizon. The machinery for such action had already been provided by the Sino-Japanese Military Agreement of May 16, 1918. Moreover, although Semenov had been defeated and had retired to the safety of the Chinese Eastern Railway, Japanese advisers were encouraging him to resist disarmament by the Chinese authorities, despite the fact that he had crossed the Chinese boundary. The Chinese government was aware that failure to disarm the Cossack troops entering its territory would indicate sympathy with Semenov, and might result in war with the Bolsheviks. Apparently, Japan was attempting to create a situation which would necessitate independent Japanese action in North Manchuria, according to the terms of the recent Sino-Japanese Military Agreement.[123] At the same time the Czechs had taken over control of Vladivostok and strategic terminals along the Trans-Siberian Railway. They appeared ready and willing to remain in Siberia, if the Allies desired it. The decision apparently rested with the President.

[120] Williams to Long, June 20, 1918, Memorandum of Grew, June 24, 1918, file 861.00/10309, D.S.N.A.

[121] Lansing to Wilson, June 23, 1918, Lansing Papers, II, 364.

[122] Knight to Daniels, June 21, 1918, file 861.00/2165½, D.S.N.A.

[123] Reinsch to Lansing, June 26, 1918, United States, Foreign Relations, 1918, Russia, II, 231-232. The Soviet government had already directed a note to China asking her either to refrain from harboring Semenov, or to permit Soviet troops to pursue him into Chinese territory (Francis to Lansing, May 26, 1918, United States, Foreign Relations, 1918, Russia, II, 172).

CHAPTER IV

Wilson Says Yes

A T THE beginning of July, 1918, the Allies faced a dilemma in regard to Siberia. Japan refused to undertake a military expedition into Siberia as the mandate of the Allies without the approval and support of the United States. The Allies, therefore, had to obtain President Wilson's consent or abandon entirely the idea of action in Siberia. Refusing to consider the second alternative, the Supreme War Council decided upon an urgent appeal to President Wilson. On July 2 Lloyd George presented the draft of such a message to the Supreme War Council. It was approved with very few corrections. At the request of M. Stephen Pichon, French Minister of Foreign Affairs, the word *considerable* was replaced by *adequate* in describing the forces for intervention in the belief that the term *considerable* might cause Wilson to vote against intervention.[1]

The appeal of July 2 summarized in a masterly way all of the reasons for immediate intervention. First, since the Czechs were in control of Western Siberia and were in danger of being cut off by the organization of German and Austrian prisoners at Irkutsk, the Allies were obligated to take immediate action before these "gallant allies" were overwhelmed. Furthermore, intervention to save the Czechs provided an excellent opportunity for gaining control of Siberia. Second, Allied intervention was necessary to save the Russian people from domination by German autocracy. Germany must be prevented from gaining control of Western Siberia and its resources, for if she seized this granary, she could compel the Russian people to her will by the threat of starvation. Finally, Allied intervention was necessary to win the war. The re-creation of an Eastern Front would prevent Germany from withdrawing her eastern divisions to fight on

[1] Frazier to Lansing, July 2, 1918, file 763.72SU/61, D.S.N.A.; Bliss to March, July 2, 1918, Wilson Papers, series II.

the Western Front, and would thus result in a decisive shortening of the war. Japan had agreed to the intervention, if the United States approved. Moreover, Japan had also agreed to respect Russia's territorial integrity and to maintain neutrality in Russia's internal politics. The Czech forces were already in control of Western Siberia. If action were taken immediately, Allied control of the entire Trans-Siberian Railway could be achieved in a few weeks. The appeal closed by urging the President to approve the policy recommended before it was too late.[2]

Lord Reading presented the appeal to the President on July 3. He found that the President's mind was "crystallizing" in the direction of an economic commission accompanied by an armed protective force. Reading believed that "the addition of the Czecho-Slovak incidents in Vladivostok and elsewhere and the resolution of the Supreme War Council endorsed by General Foch" would "cause him to decide in favour of a military force accompanying the Commission and of a more important character than he had originally intended." However, Reading thought that the President would never agree to a new Eastern Front.[3]

On July 4 the views of the State Department were incorporated in a memorandum, which emphasized the changed situation created by the capture of Vladivostok by the Czechoslovaks and the success of their fellow countrymen in Western Siberia. Lansing believed that it was the responsibility of the United States to aid the Czechs; the responsibility was increased and made almost imperative since they were being attacked by released German and Austrian prisoners of war. Lansing advised that the United States adopt a policy of aiding the loyal Czech troops at Vladivostok with arms, artillery, ammunition, and supplies. Moreover, he suggested the dispatch of additional troops to aid the Czechs in policing the railroad as they advanced and to co-operate in disarming and dispersing the Germans and Austrians who opposed them. He believed that both the United States and the Allies should participate with Japan in supplying the necessary troops. In addition, the Secretary advised that the proposed assistance to the

[2] Frazier to Lansing, July 2 and 3, 1918, United States, *Foreign Relations, 1918, Russia*, II, 241-248; Palmer, *Bliss*, pp. 298-299; Lloyd George, *Memoirs*, VI, 178; Bliss to March, July 2, 1918, Wilson Papers, series II.

[3] Reading to Foreign Office, July 3, 1918, Wiseman Papers. When Wiseman informed Auchincloss of Reading's talk with the President, Auchincloss advised "the best way for Reading to act for the next few days." He suggested that Reading get the President's permission to discuss the matter with Baker in order to ascertain "whether there was not some way of reconciling the British and American military opinion on the feasibility of intervention in Russia" (Auchincloss, Diary, July 3, 1918).

Czechs be preceded by a declaration pledging noninterference in the internal affairs of Russia and the withdrawal of military forces as soon as the danger from German and Austrian aggression was over. Lansing's final suggestion was that a peaceful commission of representatives of moral, industrial, financial, commercial, and agricultural interests with a High Commissioner at its head should proceed at once to Vladivostok to assist the Russian people to restore normal conditions of trade, industry, and social order. Lansing was convinced that "furnishing protection and assistance to the Czechoslovaks, who are so loyal to our cause, is a very different thing from sending an army into Siberia to restore order or to save the Russians from themselves. There is a moral obligation to save these men from our common enemies, if we are able to do so."[4]

Basil Miles shared Secretary Lansing's viewpoint. On July 5 he wrote Lansing, "I do not believe the Allies can excuse themselves if they leave these gallant men unsupported. If the U.S. and the Allies are ever going to do anything in Siberia, the time is now." A final and somewhat ambiguous sentence was added in pencil, "Otherwise they should get these men out of Russia."[5] Lansing's reply to this communication was to send a preliminary telegram to the American consul at Vladivostok, advising him to inform the Czech leaders verbally that the American government regarded the "Czech forces in Russia as an inspiring element of the military forces now engaged against the Central Powers." Furthermore, the conduct of the leaders at Vladivostok and in Western Siberia was beyond criticism and "deserving of the support and approval of all Governments engaged in war against Germany and Austria."[6]

On July 6 the President had a conference on the Russian situation with Secretaries Lansing, Baker, and Daniels, General March, and Admiral Benson. The President informed them of his decision to embark upon an expedition to Siberia in co-operation with Japan. Instead of wholly accepting the plan recommended by the Supreme War Council, the President was attempting to devise a new scheme for intervention, based to a large extent upon Lansing's memorandum of July 4. The conferees agreed that the establishment of an Eastern Front was militarily unfeasible. Therefore, they refused to consider any advance westward beyond Irkutsk. However, they agreed

[4] Memorandum of the Secretary of State, July 4, 1918, file 861.00/2292½, D.S.N.A.

[5] Basil Miles to Lansing, July 5, 1918, file 861.00/2908, D.S.N.A.

[6] Lansing to Caldwell, July 5, 1918, file 861.00/2181, D.S.N.A.

to aid the Czechoslovaks if the Japanese government would co-operate in the following program:

(a) The furnishing of small arms, machine guns, and ammunition to the Czecho-Slovaks at Vladivostok by the Japanese Government; this Government to share the expense and to supplement the supplies as rapidly as possible;

(b) The assembling of a military force at Vladivostok composed of approximately 7000 Americans and 7000 Japanese to guard the line of communication of the Czecho-Slovaks proceeding toward Irkutsk; the Japanese to send troops at once;

(c) The landing of available forces from the American and Allied naval vessels to hold possession of Vladivostok and co-operate with the Czecho-Slovaks;

(d) The public announcement by this and Japanese Governments that the purpose of landing troops is to aid Czecho-Slovaks against German and Austrian prisoners, that there is no purpose to interfere with internal affairs of Russia, and that they guarantee not to impair the political or territorial sovereignty of Russia; and

(e) To await further developments before taking further steps.[7]

When President Wilson read the program to the conferees, General March indicated his opposition by shaking his head. The President then said, "You are opposed to this because you do not think Japan will limit herself to 7,000 men, and that this decision will further her schemes for territorial aggrandizement." When General March replied in the affirmative, the President said, "Well, we will have to take that chance."[8]

Thus it was that on July 6 the United States government decided to act in Siberia, ostensibly to save the Czechoslovaks who had started for Vladivostok on their way to France. Immediately after the White House conference, Admiral Knight was instructed to keep Vladivostok "available as a base for the safety of Czechs and as a means of egress for them should the necessity arise."[9] On the same day the Allied powers issued a proclamation taking Vladivostok and its vicinity under their temporary protection.[10]

[7] Memorandum of the Secretary of State of a Conference at the White House in Reference to the Siberian Situation, July 6, 1918, United States, *Foreign Relations, 1918, Russia,* II, 262-263; Baker, *Woodrow Wilson,* VIII, 256.

[8] March, *A Nation at War,* p. 126; Baker, *Woodrow Wilson,* VIII, 256.

[9] Lansing to Morris, July 6, 1918, United States, *Foreign Relations, 1918, Russia,* II, 263.

[10] Bunyan, *Intervention,* pp. 317-318. The Czechs, assisted by British and Japanese forces, had been policing the city since June 29. American marines had been guarding the American Consulate (Caldwell to Lansing, July 5, 1918, United States, *Foreign Relations 1918, Russia.* II, 261).

The State Department now faced the task of getting Japanese approval of the American policy as determined by the President at the White House conference. On July 8 Secretary Lansing informed Viscount Ishii of the American program. Ishii approved the plan and agreed to convey it to his government immediately. He "spoke as if he was sure the suggestion of a small force of 14,000 men equally divided between the United States and Japan would be acceptable to his Government."[11] House also had a discussion with Ishii, whom he described as being "very receptive."[12]

Meanwhile Lansing was concerned about the secrecy of the negotiations with Japan. He feared that Japan might consult the British government about the American proposal. If this should happen, Lansing wrote Wilson, "we may be embarrassed in our relations with those Governments who will consider us not frank. I am very sure that a secretive attitude will deeply offend Reading and Jusserand, and, to a lesser degree, Cellere and Koo. My own disposition is to be candid with them, now that the Japanese government has had time to consider our proposed program."[13]

Lansing's concern was not without foundation. The Italian ambassador reported that the news of independent Japanese-American negotiations "came as a shock" to the three Allied ambassadors, "especially after the diplomatic exchanges of the last few weeks looking towards an Allied movement."[14] When the British ambassador, together with the French and Italian ambassadors, called upon Secretary Lansing on the afternoon of July 9, it was Lord Reading who did the talking, despite the fact that Jusserand was the *doyen* of the corps and therefore the natural spokesman. Reading bluntly asked whether it was the intention of the American government to ask the Allies to participate in the "initial landing of troops at Vladivostok or whether it was our purpose to confine the enterprise to Japanese and American troops." Lansing replied that he thought it useless to con-

[11] Memorandum of the Secretary of State of a Conference with the Japanese Ambassador concerning a Siberian Program July 8, 1918, United States, *Foreign Relations, 1918, Russia,* II, 267-268.

[12] In writing Wilson of this conversation, House said, "It has been my opinion for a long time that unless Japan was treated with more consideration regarding the right of her citizens to expand in nearby Asiatic undeveloped countries she would have to be reckoned with—and rightly so" (July 6, 1918, Wilson Papers, series II).

[13] Lansing to Wilson, July 8, 1918, file 861.00/2292½, D.S.N.A. For popular knowledge of American negotiations regarding Siberia, see New York *Times,* July 9, 1918.

[14] Phillips to Acting Secretary of State, July 12, 1918, United States, *Foreign Relations, 1918, Russia,* II, 276.

sider the question until the Japanese government had agreed to the principle of "joint equal military action." However, Lansing indicated that it had always been his purpose to confer with the Allies, once the Japanese had accepted the American program. When Lord Reading said that he "feared his government would not understand action which did not include all parties," Lansing expressed his regret but replied that the President "had no intention of submitting the questions to the Allied Governments until Japan had declared that she was favorable to the general plan." Lansing went even further when he repeated that "expediency should control and that if expediency was opposed to British participation, that . . . ended it." Although the British ambassador appeared "manifestly disturbed," Lansing had the feeling that the French and Italian ambassadors approved of the American program.[15]

On July 10 Lansing assured Reading that the only reason for conducting independent negotiations with Japan was to save time and avoid preliminary discussions with the five governments. The President also sent a message to Reading which emphasized the idea that opportunity for consultation would be given the Allied governments as soon as Japan replied. These assurances and explanations were the result of Reading's statement that he feared the "Allied Governments would be surprised at the course taken by the U. S. Government." Lord Reading had informed Lansing "that it was a pity a course had been pursued which was capable of being misunderstood. . . ."

Despite his disapproval of American methods of negotiation, Reading regarded the new move as real progress, attributing it largely to the Supreme War Council's appeal of July 2 and General Foch's personal message to the President. His conversation with Lansing led Reading to believe that the expedition would eventually become the means of creating a Russian front. Reading informed the Prime Minister that the President was still unwilling to agree to the creation of an Eastern Front, because of the disapproval of his military advisers. However, a first step had been made, and Reading regarded this as a

[15] Lansing to Wilson, July 9, 1918, United States, *Foreign Relations, 1918, Russia,* II, 269-270. Auchincloss also noted Reading's concern about the American plan. Reading feared that it involved the elimination of the English, French, and Italians from participation in the expedition. Auchincloss confided to his Diary on July 9 that "Lord Reading is really very nervous about the situation and particularly because he feels that the President and Secretary Lansing are under the impression that the British are not very particular about consulting us before they act, and consequently, why should we be very particular about consulting them. The truth is the whole thing is not very scientifically handled and there is cause for complaint on both sides."

great triumph, suggesting "much for the future."[16] Wiseman was also pleased that the President was "now committed to intervention," even though on a small scale. He believed that "we must now work to [the] end that he commit himself finally and irrevocably, when I think we will find the whole matter will go through in entire accordance with our wishes."[17] Although Lord Balfour welcomed Wilson's decision to intervene, he felt that fourteen thousand troops were entirely inadequate for the purpose.[18]

It was quite evident that the British government was disturbed by American independence in the Siberian matter. On July 10 the British battalion at Hong Kong was ordered to proceed immediately to Vladivostok "to replace the Czechs there," who had started back to Irkutsk.[19] Balfour carefully informed the American government that the British action had not been "adopted with any intention to start intervention but for the sole purposes of ensuring order in Vladivostok, securing the communications of the Czech forces, and safeguarding the Allied stores in the city."[20]

The British continued along their independent course. On July 11 the British government decided to use for other purposes the tonnage which had been originally intended for transporting the Czechs from Vladivostok. At the same time they withdrew their request for Japanese shipping for the transportation of the Czechs. This decision was made because the Czech commander believed that every available Czech soldier would be needed to assist the other Czech forces at Irkutsk.[21]

[16] Reading to Lloyd George and Balfour, July 10, 1918, Wiseman Papers.

[17] Wiseman to Arthur Murray (British Military Intelligence), July 10, 1918, Wiseman Papers.

[18] Balfour to Reading, July 10, 1918, Wiseman Papers; New York *Times,* July 10, 1918.

[19] Reading to Lansing, July 11, 1918, United States, *Foreign Relations, 1918, Russia,* II, 274.

[20] Reading to Lansing, United States, *Foreign Relations, 1918, Russia,* II, 275. Lord Reading was disturbed over the sending of British troops from Hong Kong without consulting the United States. He assured Frank L. Polk that it had nothing to do with America's proposed plan, and was not an attempt to forestall American action. Reading did indicate to Polk, that "of course it looked a little bit on the surface as though we intended to leave out the British, and French . . ." (Polk, Confidential Diary, July 12, 1918). The Japanese ambassador also called when he heard that the British had sent troops to Vladivostok. He was anxious to know whether this would make any difference in the American proposal for joint action. Polk assured him that it would not affect in any way any arrangement between Japan and the United States (Polk, Confidential Diary, July 13, 1918).

[21] Reading to Lansing, July 12, 1918, United States, *Foreign Relations, 1918, Russia,* II, 275; General Maurice Janin, *Ma mission en Sibérie, 1918-1920* (Paris, 1933), p. 8; Beneš, *War Memoirs,* p. 369.

On July 16 the British asked Japan to furnish the necessary destroyers for strengthening the naval patrol at Vladivostok. Lord Reading expressed the hope that the State Department would support the request made by the British government.[22] On the same day the British War Cabinet, despite President Wilson's disapproval, decided to send General Alfred W. F. Knox, former military attaché in Petrograd, to Vladivostok as head of a British military mission.[23]

In the meantime the British, French, and Japanese ambassadors had requested permission from the Russian railway authorities at Harbin to transport Czech troops by the Chinese Eastern Railway. When a favorable reply was received to this request, they proposed "simply to inform the Chinese Government that these forces are to pass through Manchuria."[24] Wilson was profoundly disturbed by the independent action of his Allies:

I do not understand or like the way in which the governments mentioned are acting independently of us in this matter, but I think that perhaps it would be all right to advise Reinsch not to object, while not cooperating where his cooperation is apparently not asked. It is my clear judgment, however, that the Chinese Government should be much more than "informed" about this business. Their acquiescence and approval should be sought. Do you not think so?[25]

British actions throughout July indicated a desire to assume leadership of the expedition to Siberia. Colonel John Ward, who commanded the British battalion at Hong Kong, later wrote that once the British had agreed that a "diversion through Russia was the surest way of relieving pressure on the French front, the English apparently decided to be the first in."[26] The French and Italians were also unwilling to be left out of the expedition. On July 12 the Italian ambassador informed the State Department that a contingent of Italian troops at Tientsin was ready to proceed at once to Siberia as a part of an inter-Allied expedition.[27] Jusserand, too, informed Polk that his govern-

[22] Reading to Lansing, July 16, 1918, United States, *Foreign Relations, 1918, Russia*, II, 284.

[23] Murray to Wiseman, July 17, 1918, Wiseman Papers; Callwell, *Sir Henry Wilson*, II, 116; Lloyd George, *Memoirs*, VI, 176-177. General Knox reached Vladivostok on Sept. 5, 1918 (London *Times*, Sept. 9, 1918).

[24] MacMurray to Lansing, July 9, 1918, United States, *Foreign Relations, 1918, Russia*, II, 271-272.

[25] Wilson to Polk, July 15, 1918, file 861.00/2241, D.S.N.A. Wilson's suggestion was carried out (Polk to MacMurray, July 15, 1918, United States, *Foreign Relations, 1918, Russia*, II, 283).

[26] John Ward, *With the Die-Hards in Siberia* (London, 1920), p. 20.

[27] Phillips to Polk, July 12, 1918, United States, *Foreign Relations, 1918, Russia*, II, 276.

ment approved of the American plan of action and desired to co-operate in sending troops to Siberia.[28]

While Great Britain prepared for action in Siberia, the State Department patiently awaited the Japanese reply to its note suggesting a joint Japanese-American expedition. Despite Lansing's plea for haste, Japanese officialdom was deliberate; and while their deliberations continued, events were moving very rapidly in Siberia and Manchuria. On July 7 General Horvat left Harbin for Vladivostok, where he planned to proclaim himself the head of a new Siberian government. He frankly admitted the guarantee of Japanese assistance.[29] Upon Horvat's departure, China indicated her desire to regain control over the Chinese Eastern Railway and the zone through which it ran. The Chinese governor told the American consul at Harbin that "Horvat's departure constituted Russia's abandonment" and that Horvat could not come back in any administrative capacity, but only as the railway manager. Charles K. Moser, the American consul at Harbin, suspected that Japan was behind China's attitude. John MacMurray, the chargé in China, was advised to tell the Chinese Minister for Foreign Affairs that the American government would regret "any attempt by China to take advantage of Russia's present distress to regain control of the Chinese Eastern Railway."[30]

On July 10, 1918, Ambassador Ishii introduced a new note into Japanese-American negotiations concerning a program of action in Siberia. He told Lansing that a decision on the matter might be expedited if some arrangement could be made regarding the high command of the joint expedition. Although Lansing made light of the question, he regarded it as a very serious matter, particularly as he knew the Japanese expected to have the high command.[31] The question of command had been discussed considerably at Washington. General March had made the "rather rash statement that no American Officer would serve under the Japanese." This statement had been repeated and criticized. Wiseman's solution to the problem of com-

---

[28] Baker, *Woodrow Wilson*, VIII, 280.

[29] MacMurray to Lansing, July 9, 1918, file 861.00/2262, D.S.N.A. Horvat issued his proclamation on July 9. When the United States indicated its disapproval of Japanese assistance to the new government, the Japanese Foreign Minister assured Lansing that Japan would not interfere in the internal politics of Siberia (MacMurray to Lansing, July 9, 1918, United States, *Foreign Relations, 1918, Russia*, II, 273).

[30] Lansing to MacMurray, July 9, 1918, July 18, 1918, United States, *Foreign Relations, 1918, Russia*, II, 273-292; LaFargue, *China and the World War*, pp. 170-171.

[31] Lansing to Wilson, July 10, 1918, *Lansing Papers*, II, 373; Baker, *Woodrow Wilson*, VIII, 272.

mand was to appoint an American as High Commissioner in charge of the whole expedition and to place a Japanese officer in command of the military part of the expedition.[32]

On July 15 Counselor Polk informed the President of his views concerning the Japanese delay in replying to the American proposals: "I think if we were disposed to tell him [Viscount Ishii] that we had no objection to a Japanese officer being the senior military officer, and therefore in command of the troops, we would hear very shortly that the Japanese Government were willing to cooperate."[33] Wilson evidently approved of this suggestion, for on July 16, he informed Polk that "the Japanese were to have the supreme command when they landed in Vladivostok." Polk was authorized to convey this information to the Japanese ambassador. That evening, when Polk informed Ambassador Ishii of the President's decision, he "suggested that no formal statement be given out, but that they send an officer of sufficient rank with their forces, and it would be understood that our forces would be under his command."[34] On the next day the American ambassador to Japan was informed that the Japanese would have the high command of the expedition.[35]

Evidently the War Department was not informed of this decision, for on August 8 Secretary Baker was quoted as saying, "I should suppose the ranking officer would be the Japanese General. I understand they are going to send a Lieutenant General and we are sending a Major General. . . . Whether there will be any more definite Commander-in-chief I do not know."[36] This confusion between the State and War Departments concerning the high command in Siberia was to place both General Graves and the Japanese commander in Siberia in an awkward position at the very outset of the expedition.

As the month of July progressed and Japan continued to delay in replying to the American proposals, President Wilson determined to draft an *aide memoire* to the Allied ambassadors, carefully defining the objectives of America's proposed expedition to Siberia.[37] Circulated on July 17, the *aide memoire* informed the Allied powers that since the United States government was bending every effort towards

[32] Wiseman to House, July 4, 1918, Wiseman Papers.

[33] Polk to Wilson, July 15, 1918, Baker, *Woodrow Wilson*, VIII, 280.

[34] Polk, Confidential Diary, July 16, 1918.

[35] Polk to Morris, July 17, 1918, United States, *Foreign Relations, 1918, Russia*, II, 292.

[36] New York *Times*, Aug. 9, 1918. For General Graves's views on the supreme command, see Graves, *America's Siberian Adventure*, pp. 57-59.

[37] Baker, *Woodrow Wilson*, VIII, 285.

winning the war on the Western Front, it could not separate or divert any part of its forces for military operations on a large scale in other parts of the world such as Russia. Furthermore, it was opposed to military intervention in Russia, even in principle:

It is the clear and fixed judgment of the Government of the United States, arrived at after repeated and very searching reconsiderations of the whole situation in Russia, that military intervention there would add to the present sad confusion in Russia rather than cure it, injure her rather than help her, and that it would be of no advantage in the prosecution of our main design, to win the war against Germany. It can not, therefore, take part in such intervention or sanction it in principle. Military intervention would, in its judgment, even supposing it to be efficacious in its immediate avowed object of delivering an attack upon Germany from the east, be merely a method of making use of Russia, not a method of serving her. Her people could not profit by it, if they profited by it at all, in time to save them from their present distresses, and their substance would be used to maintain foreign armies, not to reconstitute their own. Military action is admissible in Russia as the Government of the United States sees the circumstances only to help the Czecho-Slovaks consolidate their forces and get into successful cooperation with their Slavic kinsmen and to steady any efforts at self-government or self-defense in which the Russians themselves may be willing to accept assistance.[38]

The communication added further that American troops would be used only for the purposes stated, and that they would be withdrawn "if the plans in whose execution it is now intended that they should cooperate should develop into others inconsistent with the policy" of the United States. At the same time the United States pointed out that in restricting its own activities, it did not mean, "even by implication, to set limits to the action or to define the policies of its associates." The United States hoped to carry out its plans in close cooperation with a small military force like its own from Japan, and from the other Allies if necessary. It proposed to ask all nations associated in the American program to unite

in assuring the people of Russia in the most public and solemn manner that none of the governments uniting in action either in Siberia or in northern Russia contemplates any interference of any kind with the political sovereignty of Russia, any intervention in her internal affairs, or any impairment of her territorial integrity either now or hereafter, but that each of the associated powers has the single object of affording such aid as shall

---

[38] The Secretary of State to the Allied Ambassadors, July 17, 1918, United States, *Foreign Relations, 1918, Russia*, II, 288. For complete text of *aide memoire*, see Appendix, p. 235.

be acceptable, and only such aid as shall be acceptable, to the Russian people in their endeavor to regain control of their own affairs, their own territory, and their own destiny.

The communication stated finally that the United States proposed to send to Siberia a commission of merchants, agricultural experts, labor advisers, Red Cross representatives, and agents of the Young Men's Christian Association to render educational and economic aid, at the earliest opportunity.[39]

President Wilson's *aide memoire* brought forth varying reactions from Japan and Great Britain. Baron Shimpeii Goto, Japanese Minister for Foreign Affairs, expressed his entire sympathy with the attitude of the United States toward Russia. However, he hoped that Washington "could see its way clear to co-operate for the assistance of the Czecho-Slovaks in the slightly modified manner" suggested by Japan.[40] The formal British reply to Wilson's *aide memoire*, delivered to the State Department on July 30, revealed a clear difference of views between Washington and London. Although approving of aid to the Czechs, the War Cabinet feared that the proposed force would prove inadequate.[41] The British reply took issue with two points, one military, the other political, which seemed to misconceive seriously the attitude of the Entente Powers. In the first place, Washington failed to appreciate the importance of establishing an Eastern Front against Germany. Such a front would force Germany to withdraw important bodies of troops from the Western Front and would thereby relieve pressure in France. Great Britain, therefore, believed that Japan should be willing to employ her unused military strength for this purpose. The second misconception which pervaded the *aide memoire* was the idea that the Allies in advocating intervention in Russia were not thinking of Russia, "but solely of themselves." The British government professed the belief that by helping the Russian people to free themselves from German domination it was performing a

[39] The Secretary of State to the Allied Ambassadors, July 17, 1918, United States, *Foreign Relations, 1918, Russia*, II, 287-290. See also Pauline Tompkins, *American-Russian Relations in the Far East*, pp. 79-80.

[40] Morris to Lansing, July 23, 1918, United States, *Foreign Relations, 1918, Russia*, II, 300-301.

[41] Conveying his real opinion of the *aide memoire* to Lord Reading, Balfour wrote: "On the other hand, we cannot pretend for ourselves, nor ought we to convey to them, that we regard [the] size of American-Japanese force as in any way adequate to the necessities of the case. To us it seems almost certain that either [the] Allied expedition will fail or that it will have to be largely reinforced; we hope the latter. But these are hopes which you can hardly convey to [the] President" (Balfour to Reading, Wiseman Papers).

signal service. The British note ended by denying the American suggestion that intervention had a political as well as a military object. The British government thought it necessary to deal briefly with these various points in order to "remove any possible misconceptions as to the attitude of His Majesty's Government."[42] The State Department was thus aware at the very outset of the expedition of the divergence in views between the two governments.

The French government accepted the American proposal without question, and avoided the issue of participation by ordering troops from Tientsin.[43] The Italian ambassador had already informed Polk that Italy was prepared to participate in the expedition with a force of two thousand men.[44] Secretary Lansing was particularly concerned about the insistence of Great Britain and France in taking part in the movement. Believing that it gave the affair the character of joint intervention, he felt that no declaration would change this impression because of the secret support given by Great Britain and France to factions in various parts of Russia. He wrote of his fears to Polk:

The participation of those two Governments will give the enterprise the character of interference with the domestic affairs of Russia and create the impression that the underlying purpose is to set up a new pro-Ally Government in Siberia, if not in Russia. It is unfortunate that London and Paris do not see this and let the United States and Japan handle the situation without seeking to interfere. It seems to me that the wisdom of this dual action is so evident that I cannot understand why the others do not keep their hands off.[45]

America's European Allies were not the only powers who desired to participate in the American-Japanese expedition to Siberia. As soon as the Chinese government learned of the American proposals to Japan, it announced a desire to participate in the venture. China offered to co-operate to the extent of seven thousand troops and suggested that an invitation from the United States to that effect would be welcome. Later, on the same day, the Acting Minister for Foreign Affairs informed the American chargé in China that the Cabinet had decided to dispatch one thousand troops to Vladivostok immediately via the Chinese Eastern Railway, and to send another thousand in the near future. Although the Japanese minister had insisted that such

[42] British Embassy to Department of State, July 30, 1918, United States, *Foreign Relations, 1918, Russia*, II, 315-317.

[43] Polk to Lansing, file 861.00/3055½, D.S.N.A.; New York *Times*, Aug. 1, 1918.

[44] Polk to Wilson, July 16, 1918, file 861.00/2837, D.S.N.A.

[45] Lansing to Polk, Aug. 3, 1918, Lansing Papers. See also Lloyd George, *Memoirs*, VI, 171.

participation was unnecessary, the Chinese minister at Washington was instructed specially to urge upon the American government the advisability of Chinese co-operation and to "bespeak . . . assistance in such difficulties as may be raised by Japan."[46]

On July 23 the State Department informed V. K. Wellington Koo, the Chinese minister at Washington, that since the Chinese request involved a military matter, it would have to be referred to the Inter-Allied Military Conference in France.[47] Undeterred by this reply, Koo continued to plead for Chinese participation on the grounds that "military participation and control of the Chinese Eastern Railway were integral parts of an aggressive activity which China would like to contribute to the Allied cause." Furthermore, he believed it would have a good effect on China's internal politics, and give her a better standing among the nations of the world.[48]

The State Department was sympathetic to Koo's pleas, and particularly so when rumors reached Washington from Peking that "by the recent military convention with Japan, China might have committed herself to delegate control of that part of the Chinese Eastern Railroad which lies within Chinese territory to some other government." Long informed Koo that, if there should be a military operation of an Allied character in Siberia, "the Chinese Government should control that part of the Chinese Eastern Railway, which lies within Chinese territory, *and should control it alone*."[49] President Wilson approved emphatically of this idea.[50]

The State Department's views concerning Chinese participation were conveyed to Baron Goto on July 31. He was inclined to accede to the American suggestion, not because he believed the Chinese troops would be effective in aiding the Czechs, but because Japan "desired to act in full accord" with the views of the American government.[51]

[46] MacMurray to Lansing, July 20, 1918, United States, *Foreign Relations, 1918, Russia*, II, 298-299.

[47] Memorandum of a Conversation between Long and the Chinese Minister, July 23, 1918, United States, *Foreign Relations, 1918, Russia*, II, 299-300.

[48] Memorandum of a Conversation between Long and Koo, July 26, 1918, United States, *Foreign Relations, 1918, Russia*, II, 305.

[49] Italics inserted. Memorandum of a Conversation between Long and Koo, July 26, 1918, United States, *Foreign Relations, 1918, Russia*, II, 304. This information was conveyed to Japan, along with a statement approving China's request to participate in the international force at Vladivostok with a small contingent (Polk to Morris, July 29, 1918, United States, *Foreign Relations, 1918, Russia*, II, 314).

[50] Wilson to Long, July 26, 1918, Breckinridge Long Papers (collection in Division of Manuscripts, Library of Congress).

[51] Morris to Lansing, Aug. 1, 1918, United States, *Foreign Relations, 1918, Russia*, II, 321-322; Polk to Lansing, July 29, 1918, file 861.00/2403½, D.S.N.A.

While the European allies of China and America hastened to participate in the proposed expedition, Japan continued to deliberate over the American proposal. Japanese imperialists regarded the invitation as an excellent opportunity to improve Japan's prestige and position in Asia. The Terauchi Ministry, then in power, reflected this point of view. Ambassador Morris later pointed out that the Terauchi Ministry "clearly planned to use the joint expedition to Vladivostok . . . as an excuse to take possession of the Chinese Eastern Railway and thus dominate northern Manchuria and eastern Siberia."[52]

On July 12 the Japanese Cabinet, under the leadership of Premier Terauchi and Baron Goto, decided not only to accept the American proposal but also to send an "independent expedition" to Siberia.[53] On July 13 Ambassador Morris reported that the Japanese General Staff was urging the Cabinet to occupy Manchuria immediately. This could be done without offense to China because of the recent military agreement. The plan included taking over control of the Chinese Eastern Railway.[54]

Takashi Hara, president of the Seiyukai party, and Baron Shinken Makino, both influential members of the Advisory Council on Foreign Relations,[55] opposed the independent expedition. Since it was necessary to have the approval of the Advisory Council before making a final decision, Premier Terauchi attempted to overcome their opposition through personal pressure. His efforts failed.[56] Forced to alter his original plans, Terauchi submitted a revised draft to the council on July 16 which accepted the American proposal for a joint expedition to Vladivostok, but added that the Japanese government would dispatch additional troops to Siberia for self-protection and for police purposes. Both Hara and Makino insisted that no necessity existed for an

[52] Morris to Lansing, July 30, 1919, United States, *Foreign Relations, 1919, Russia*, II, 293.

[53] Takeuchi, *War and Diplomacy*, p. 205.

[54] United States, *Foreign Relations, 1918, Russia*, II, 281. The American government protested against these reports (Polk to Morris, July 19, 1918, United States, *Foreign Relations, 1918, Russia*, II, 297-298; LaFargue, *China and the World War*, p. 169).

[55] The Advisory Council on Foreign Relations was established on June 5, 1917, to deliberate upon important diplomatic affairs. The object was to place questions of foreign policy and national defense above partisan politics. The members of the council consisted of the Prime Minister and several other members selected from among cabinet ministers or former cabinet ministers. With the establishment of this council the Foreign Office was reduced to a secondary position in the actual formulation and execution of foreign policies. The council continued to function until Sept. 18, 1922 (Takeuchi, *War and Diplomacy*, chap. v).

[56] Takeuchi, *War and Diplomacy*, p. 206; London *Times*, July 23, 1918.

independent expedition. A compromise was finally made by which Japan reserved the right to send additional troops to Siberia "in case of necessity to protect the Czechoslovak soldiers."[57] The draft reply to the American proposal was finally approved on July 18, and dispatched to Ambassador Morris on July 19.[58]

Ambassador Ishii delivered the Japanese reply orally to Acting Secretary Polk on July 24. The ambassador stated that Japan could not accept the limitation of seven thousand men "for political reasons," because the Japanese people, and particularly the opposition, would say "that the limitation was being imposed because of lack of confidence in Japan and its motives." Since the Japanese government believed that the number of troops suggested by the American government was too small to protect the Czechoslovaks adequately, it proposed to send a division, which would approximate twelve thousand men, with the understanding that the number of troops to be sent would depend on the amount of resistance given by the Bolsheviks and Austro-German prisoners. Unsuccessful in persuading Ishii to limit the number of troops to seven thousand, Polk referred the Japanese reply to the White House for action.[59]

The President was "very much put out" by the Japanese reply. He instructed Polk to tell Ishii that while he did not wish to cause Japan "any embarrassment," nevertheless, their plan was so different from ours that he thought it best not to act at all.[60] On July 25 Polk conferred again with Ishii, informing him that "his answer was a new proposal." Washington took issue with the reference in the Japanese declaration to the "special position of Japan." This phrase was considered unnecessary in view of the Lansing-Ishii Agreement and the fact that Japan would have the supreme command and a larger number of troops than all of the other powers combined. Moreover, such an assertion might "create a misunderstanding in the minds of the Russian people and would be seized on by the Germans as having much greater significance than was intended." Polk again attempted to limit the size of the Japanese expedition, arguing that such a limitation was necessary in order to create the proper impression on the

[57] Takeuchi, *War and Diplomacy*, pp. 206-207; "What Japan Thinks," *New Republic*, XVI (Aug. 31, 1918), 124-125.

[58] Takeuchi, *War and Diplomacy*, p. 207. Communications were also approved to the governments of England, France and Italy, London *Times*, July 23, 1918.

[59] Polk to Wilson, July 24, 1918, United States, *Foreign Relations, 1918, Russia*, II, 301-302. Auchincloss was confident "that the President would be considerably put out" by the Japanese reply (Auchincloss, Diary, July 24, 1918).

[60] Auchincloss, Diary, July 25, 1918.

Russian people. He informed Ishii that although the United States would not object to a Japanese force of ten or twelve thousand soldiers, he felt that the question of sending additional troops should be deferred until after the original expedition had landed. If Japan and the other powers then felt that additional troops were necessary, the United States "could then decide whether it wished to go on or withdraw." Assuring the Japanese ambassador that Washington had the "utmost confidence in Japanese motives," Polk added that if Tokyo and the other Allies considered that a large expedition was a military necessity that the United States "would be compelled to withdraw as that was not our plan."[61]

While Washington awaited Tokyo's reaction to the Polk-Ishii interview, further disquieting news was received from Japan. Ambassador Morris reported that the Japanese Foreign Minister had called upon him and

expressed his clear conviction that a patrol of troops along the line of the Chinese Eastern Railway and Trans-Siberian Railway as far as Karymskaya was a military necessity. He confirmed my advices that the Twelfth Division is prepared to embark for Vladivostok and the Eighth Division is prepared to embark for Harbin to protect the railway. The present plan is to send the Vladivostok expedition first and to follow with the Harbin expedition between two and four weeks later.[62]

Several days later the Japanese Embassy reported that the Japanese government had sent some torpedo boats to Nikolaevsk, at the mouth of the Amur River, to protect Japanese interests there.[63] These developments only served to increase anxiety in Washington. When Admiral Knight questioned Secretary Daniels as to when Allied troops would be sent to Vladivostok, President Wilson wrote, "I wish I could give Knight the information he desires . . . but unhappily the Japanese Government is trying to alter the whole plan in a way to which we cannot consent, and for the time being at any rate the whole matter is in suspense."[64] On the same day the President requested Acting Secretary Polk to cable Ambassador Morris urging the Japanese

[61] Polk to Morris, July 27, 1918, United States, *Foreign Relations, 1918, Russia*, II, 306-307; Baker, *Woodrow Wilson*, VIII, 297-298.

[62] Morris to Lansing, July 23, 1918, United States, *Foreign Relations, 1918, Russia*, II, 300.

[63] Polk to Morris, July 30, 1918, United States, *Foreign Relations, 1918, Russia*, II, 318; Varneck and Fisher, *Testimony of Kolchak*, pp. 334-335.

[64] Baker, *Woodrow Wilson*, VIII, 310-311.

government to hasten its decision, or else the proposed plan of aiding the Czechs would "prove abortive."[65]

The Japanese government deliberated for several days upon Viscount Ishii's report of his July 25 interview with Polk. On July 31, following an informal conference with Baron Goto, Ambassador Morris cabled his belief that the Japanese government would make certain changes in its declaration in accordance with Polk's suggestions.[66] However, no formal statement of Japanese modifications followed Morris's preliminary note. Therefore, Washington was quite surprised to learn that Premier Terauchi had made public the Japanese declaration of intervention on the evening of August 3 without previously informing the American State Department. Baron Goto later explained that "this unexpected action was taken to allow public opinion to accede to all the suggestions" of the American government.[67]

The Japanese declaration did attempt to meet some of Washington's earlier objections. No reference was made either to Japan's "special position," or to the dispatch of additional Japanese troops at a later date. Significantly, the declaration failed to mention the number of troops participating in the venture. The statement declared that the "Japanese Government . . . have decided to proceed at once to dispatch suitable forces for the proposed mission. A certain number of these troops will be sent forthwith to Vladivostok." The purpose of the expedition was to assist the Czechoslovaks in accordance with the proposals made by the United States. It was the avowed policy of the Japanese government to respect the territorial integrity of Russia and to abstain from all interference in her internal politics. In conclusion, the Japanese declaration stated that upon realization of the above object, Japanese troops would be withdrawn immediately from Russian territory, leaving unimpaired the political and military sovereignty of Russia.[68] Significantly, the Japanese declaration made no mention either of the British plan to reconstitute the Eastern Front or of the American proposal to send economic aid to Siberia.

[65] Polk, Confidential Diary, Aug. 2, 1918, United States, *Foreign Relations, 1918, Russia*, II, 322-323. On the same day General Graves received his first orders concerning the Siberian expedition (Graves, *America's Siberian Adventure*, pp. 2-3).

[66] Takeuchi, *War and Diplomacy*, p. 208; Morris to Lansing, Aug. 1, 1918, United States, *Foreign Relations, 1918, Russia*, II, 322. Morris pointed out that the Japanese government was taking unusual precautions to prevent the nature of the negotiations from reaching the public. Evidently the government feared popular resentment.

[67] Morris to Lansing, Aug. 5, 1918, United States, *Foreign Relations, 1918, Russia*, II, 330.

[68] United States, *Foreign Relations, 1918, Russia*, II, 324-325; Takeuchi, *War and Diplomacy*, p. 208; *Japan Year Book, 1919-1920*, pp. 790-791.

On August 3 Ambassador Ishii assured Polk that his government had no intention of sending more men than necessary to assist the Czechs. However, his government still felt that a larger force was necessary than that proposed by the American government. Despite this difference of opinion, Ishii had been authorized to say that Japan accepted the American proposals, "reserving the question as to the sending of additional troops to Vladivostok or elsewhere until circumstances should arise which might make it necessary." In explanation of his last statement, Ishii pointed out that it might be necessary to move out of Vladivostok, or to send reinforcements "to prevent the slaughter of the Czechs." In such an event his government intended to consult the American government as well as the other Allies. However, if an emergency arose, the Japanese government "wished to say frankly that they would be compelled for reasons already stated to move without consultation." When Polk repeatedly inquired as to whether the Japanese forces would be limited to ten or twelve thousand men, Ishii replied that since such a number had been mentioned in a previous conversation, and since his government had stated that "they accepted our proposal, he felt there was no question on that point." Again, when Polk questioned him as to whether his government intended to send troops elsewhere, Ishii said "no, not as far as he knew, and he thought that he had been fully informed on this point."[69]

On August 5 Baron Goto assured Morris that the number of troops would not exceed twelve thousand, as mentioned by the American government. Goto, however, expressed some doubts as to whether this force would be sufficient to meet the increasingly serious conditions developing in Northern Manchuria and Eastern Siberia.[70]

Once Japan had made public its declaration on intervention, the United States quickly announced its position to the world. President Wilson had begun working on a public announcement shortly after the circulation of his *aide memoire,* and the announcement actually

[69] Polk to Wilson, Aug. 3, 1918, United States, *Foreign Relations, 1918, Russia,* II, 325-326; Polk, Confidential Diary, Aug. 3, 1918. On Aug. 6, 1918, MacMurray, chargé in China, reported that the Chinese Acting Minister for Foreign Affairs had informed him that although no representations had been made through diplomatic channels, the Japanese military attaché, who was also attached to the Chinese General Staff, had repeatedly urged that China should undertake an expedition into Siberia in co-operation with Japan under the terms of the recent military convention. The Chinese government had assented in principle to such co-operation although no definite proposal had yet been made by the Japanese as to when this expedition was to be undertaken (MacMurray to Lansing, United States, *Foreign Relations, 1918, Russia,* II, 331).

[70] Morris to Lansing, Aug. 5, 1918, United States, *Foreign Relations, 1918, Russia,* II, 330.

paraphrased it to a large degree.[71] Released to the press on the afternoon of August 3, the American declaration announced that the objectives of the expedition were to aid the Czechs, to guard military stores which might be needed subsequently by Russian forces, and "to steady any efforts at self-government or self-defense in which the Russians may be willing to accept assistance." The declaration carefully pointed out that since the United States and Japan were the only powers in a position to act in Siberia with a sufficient force to accomplish the stated objectives, the United States had proposed to Japan that "each of the two governments send a force of a few thousand men to Vladivostok, with the purpose of co-operating as a single force in the occupation of Vladivostok, and in safeguarding so far as it may, the country to the rear of the westward-moving Czecho-Slovaks." The British, French, and Italian governments had agreed to the American plans and purposes "in principle." The announcement also declared that American actions on the matter were not intended to restrict or interfere with the independent judgment of the other Allies. The American government again announced its neutral position in Russian affairs in strong and decisive language.[72]

The British issued a similar declaration on August 8, after British troops had already landed in Vladivostok. The British statement did not mention the Czech need of assistance. It stated that the Allies were coming as friends to stop German penetration of Russia, and to bring economic relief. The announcement concluded with a stirring plea: "Peoples of Russia! Unite with us in defense of your liberties. Our one desire is to see Russia strong and free and then to retire and watch the Russian people work out its destinies in accordance with the freely expressed wishes of the people."[73]

[71] Baker, *Woodrow Wilson,* VIII, 286.

[72] Polk to Morris, Aug. 3, 1918, United States, *Foreign Relations, 1918, Russia,* II, 328-329. The British Foreign Minister had expressed a similar attitude in a somewhat more realistic manner several weeks earlier. He had written, "It is of course perfectly true that, however strong and genuine be our desire to keep out of Russian politics, it will probably be in practice almost impossible to prevent intervention having some (perhaps a great) effect on Russian parties. . . . We can do no more than attempt to the best of our ability to keep aloof from these internal divisions, and to give full opportunity to the Russian people to determine the future of their country" (Balfour to Lloyd George, July 16, 1918, Lloyd George, *Memoirs,* VI, 177-178). On Aug. 5, 1918, Mr. Balfour declared in the House of Commons, "The aim of his Majesty's Government is to secure the political and economic restoration of Russia without internal interference of any kind, and to bring about the expulsion of enemy forces from Russian soil" (Great Britain, *House of Commons Debates,* 5th series, CIX, 904-906).

[73] Barclay to Lansing, Aug. 8, 1918, United States, *Foreign Relations, 1918, Russia,* II, 334.

The public announcements brought forth varied reactions throughout the interested countries. Ambassador Morris reported from Tokyo that as far as one could observe the final decision of the Japanese government "to fall in with the American proposals" met with general approval, although there seemed to be no enthusiasm for the enterprise.[74] In the United States the policy of intervention was generally supported by the American press.[75] George Kennan, the man whom Lansing regarded as the highest American authority on Russia, congratulated Lansing on the decision to intervene. Kennan assumed that the expedition proposed to overthrow the Bolshevik government, which he evidently regarded as the puppet of Germany. He predicted early success for the venture with a resulting "regeneration of Russia as a true democracy."[76]

From Vladivostok the American consul cabled that the Japanese declaration was "evoking favorable comment."[77] The London *Times* of August 13 reported that the British declaration had been "heartily welcomed," and had "increased the popularity of the Allied troops." In contrast to these statements came a report from Harbin on the American declaration, which was compared unfavorably with the Japanese. The *Vestnik Manchurii,* the principal organ of the Horvat government, declared that the American program was too narrow in scope and too materialistic in its aims.[78]

The public declarations of Japan, Great Britain, and the United States clearly revealed the differences of opinion among the three nations concerning the scope, character, and purposes of the expedition to Siberia. As time went on, these differences tended to increase rather than decrease, and the next months were to reveal a three-way diplomatic struggle for leadership in Siberia.

Wilson's decision to intervene in Siberia was based on several reasons. He had placed the winning of the war first. This implied no quarrel with the Allies. When the Allies insisted on going into Siberia, Wilson had resisted, but had finally yielded on the theory that if he participated in the venture, he would later be able to say,

[74] Morris to Lansing, Aug. 5, 1918, United States, *Foreign Relations, 1918, Russia,* II, 330. Yamato Ichihashi, *The Washington Conference and After* (Stanford, 1928), p. 320, later wrote that "the people of Japan had never looked with favor upon Japan's venture in Siberia."

[75] New York *Times,* Aug. 4, 1918; *Literary Digest,* LVIII (Aug. 17, 1918), 10.

[76] George Kennan to Lansing, Aug. 9, 1918, Lansing Papers. For a similar view, see *Outlook,* CXIX (July 24, 1918), 478.

[77] Caldwell to Lansing, Aug. 6, 1918, United States, *Foreign Relations, 1918, Russia,* II, 332.

[78] Moser to Lansing, United States, *Foreign Relations, 1918, Russia,* II, 338-339.

"Now let us come out," instead of, "Now you come out."[79] He made his decision after it became evident that intervention would take place despite his opposition and probably with Japan in charge of the expedition. He joined it, not because he believed in it, but because he thought he could "impose greater restraint on Japan within rather than outside it."[80]

It is quite true that the much publicized plight of the Czechs in Siberia gave Wilson the necessary "moral" reason for intervention, but the number of troops proposed for rescuing seventy thousand Czechs was ludicrously small. And by the time the United States took action for their safety they had already been in possession of important points on the Trans-Siberian Railway for some two months. Moreover, the Supreme War Council had already decided on June 3 to retain certain of the Czech units in Russia to co-operate in holding Murmansk and Archangel.[81]

Despite the publicized reasons for intervention, the documents reveal that once Japan had indicated her intentions to undertake an independent expedition to Siberia and Northern Manchuria under the terms of the Sino-Japanese Military Agreements of May, 1918, the hand of the United States was forced. The "open door" in China was at stake. If Japan went into Siberia, the United States must also go.[82]

[79] Lincoln Steffens to Laura Suggett, reporting a conversation with Colonel House, Oct. 16, 1918; Steffens to James H. McGill, Oct. 31, 1918; Lincoln Steffens, *Letters* (2 vols.; New York, 1938), I, 433, 438. See also Baker, *Woodrow Wilson*, VIII, 284.

[80] Griswold, *Far Eastern Policy*, p. 234; Newton D. Baker, Foreword in Graves, *America's Siberian Adventure*, pp. viii-ix; Schuman, *American Policy toward Russia since 1917*, p. 103.

[81] Dugdale, *Arthur Balfour*, II, 190; Stewart, *White Armies of Russia*, p. 114. General Graves points out that both DeWitt C. Poole and Consul General Harris in Irkutsk knew that the Czechs were not in need of help at least one month before his arrival (Graves, *America's Siberian Adventure*, pp. 343-346).

[82] Statement of the Honorable Breckinridge Long before the House Committee on Foreign Affairs, Aug., 1919, file 861.00, vol. 39, D.S.N.A.; Palmer, *Newton D. Baker*, II, 321. See also Tompkins, *American-Russian Relations in the Far East*, p. 86.

CHAPTER V

The Allies Enter Siberia

ALLIED troops began to land at Vladivostok on August 3, 1918. The British and French landed first, followed by the Japanese and Americans.[1] Although the French and American troops were cheered by the crowds, the British and Japanese were received in silence. It was evident that the Russians felt considerable hostility toward the Japanese.[2]

Major General William S. Graves commanded the American troops. Both Secretary Baker and General March regarded him as a loyal, self-reliant, levelheaded, and highly trained soldier.[3] His only orders were those contained in the President's *aide memoire* which had been handed to him by Secretary Baker in early August. He received no further information on the social, economic, political, or military situation in Russia until a few days before his departure from San Francisco. He was then informed that Japan's probable policy would be to "keep Russian forces apart and oppose any strong Russian central authority, but to support a number of weak Russian forces which could not form more than a screen for Japanese action."[4]

When General Graves arrived in Vladivostok on September 3, he immediately called upon General Kikuzo Otani of the Japanese Army, who was the senior in rank of the Allied commanders. General Otani informed Graves that he had been notified by the American State Department that he, Otani, would be in command of American troops. Graves replied that although he desired to co-operate with the Japanese,

[1] Caldwell to Lansing, Aug. 3, 1918, Aug. 20, 1918, United States, *Foreign Relations, 1918, Russia*, II, 327, 352; Ward, *Die-Hards in Siberia*, p. 3; Graves, *America's Siberian Adventure*, p. 55.

[2] United States, *Foreign Relations, 1918, Russia*, II, 352.

[3] Baker, Foreword in Graves, *America's Siberian Adventure*, p. ix; March, *A Nation at War*, p. 130.

[4] Graves, *America's Siberian Adventure*, p. 55. This proved to be an excellent prognosis of Japan's policy in Siberia.

he had no orders to place American troops under Japanese command.[5]

General Graves soon found that American soldiers were confused as to their purpose in Siberia. Upon their arrival they had been given no information concerning their duties. Some American soldiers believed that their purpose was to aid the Czechoslovaks, who were supposedly fighting their way out of Siberia. Others believed that American troops were to be used to recapture the German and Austrian prisoners who were running loose in Siberia and were reported to be gathering arms and moving back toward Germany. Still others thought that the American army was to lend its assistance in the establishment of an Eastern Front against Germany. Lastly, many believed that the American Army had been sent to Siberia to crusade against Bolshevism.[6] General Graves found that this last idea had been generally accepted among American officers and men. When he learned that a young American officer had arrested a Russian, simply because he was a Bolshevik, Graves delivered the following statement:

Whoever gave you those orders must have made them up himself. The United States is not at war with the Bolsheviki or any other faction of Russia. You have no orders to arrest Bolsheviks or anybody else unless they disturb the peace of the community, attack the people or the Allied soldiers. The United States army is not here to fight Russia or any group or faction in Russia. Because a man is a Bolshevik is no reason for his arrest. You are to arrest only those who attack you. The United States is only fighting the Bolsheviki when the American troops are attacked by an armed force.

Carl Ackerman, correspondent for the New York *Times,* was present during the incident, and later remarked that General Graves's

[5] United States Army War College, *Order of Battle of the United States Land Forces in the World War, American Expeditionary Forces in the World War* (Washington, 1937), p. 387; Graves, *America's Siberian Adventure,* p. 58. Evidently the War Department had not been informed of Wilson's decision to give Japan the supreme command. See above, pp. 75-76. See also Sylvian G. Kindall, *American Soldiers in Siberia* (New York, 1945), pp. 17-18. The British government recognized that the Japanese would have the supreme command in Siberia and announced that General Knox would be the head of the British military mission attached to the staff of the Japanese commander-in-chief (*Lansing Papers,* II, 373). When the French military representative on the Supreme War Council questioned General Bliss on the subject of the Japanese supreme command, Bliss wrote that there had been no formal acceptance of a commanding general of the Allied forces in Siberia. "The Japanese General is the senior officer on the ground and the Japanese have requested that we send a liaison officer to the Japanese headquarters and ask authority to send one to ours" (Bliss to Permanent French Military Representative, Supreme War Council, Aug. 16, 1918, Bliss Papers).

[6] Kindall, *American Soldiers in Siberia,* p. 17.

statement was his "first intimation that the United States did not consider the Bolsheviki everywhere as enemies of the Allies." As Ackerman traveled into the interior of Siberia, he found that not all American representatives had the same ideas as General Graves.[7]

The same divergence of views concerning the purpose of intervention which existed in Siberia existed also among Allied and American councils at home. While Great Britain and France attempted to extend the scope of military and political action in Siberia, and Japan proceeded with her plans to occupy the Russian Far East, the United States spent its efforts attempting to limit and restrain the independent operations of its Allies.

In early August the State Department made quite clear its opposition to any expansion of the Siberian expedition.[8] When the British Foreign Office requested that more troops be sent to Siberia, the State Deparment replied that it would not consider any change of plans until American troops en route to Vladivostok had arrived and the military authorities there had time to consider the situation thoroughly and make their own recommendations. The British government was not discouraged by this opposition, for on August 12 it presented a carefully worded memorandum which emphasized the alleged critical position of the Czech forces in Siberia, and advocated the need for immediate reinforcements by the Japanese. The British government hoped that American authorities would "feel it possible formally to request the Japanese Government to despatch at the earliest possible moment such military assistance as the military experts of the Czech and Japanese forces may consider desirable and necessary."[9] The French government made a similar request, suggesting that approximately eighty thousand men would suffice.[10]

The British proposal aroused no enthusiasm in Washington. Lansing quickly announced American opposition to the scheme:

I am bound in candor to say that this Government would be gravely embarrassed if the British Government should take the action suggested. The plan of action recently proposed by the Government of the United

[7] Ackerman, *Trailing the Bolsheviki,* pp. 188-189; Graves, *America's Siberian Adventure,* pp. 91-92.

[8] Reading to British Foreign Office, Aug. 9, 1918, Wiseman Papers.

[9] United States, *Foreign Relations, 1918, Russia,* II, 341-342. The London *Times* of August 15 reported that the Czechs "were wholly destitute of supplies of all kinds," and were "being opposed by large bodies of prisoners armed by the Bolshevists."

[10] Jusserand to Lansing, Aug. 17, 1918, *Lansing Papers,* II, 376-377. The American consul at Vladivostok also recommended immediate reinforcements to aid the Czechs (Caldwell to Lansing, Aug. 15, 1918, United States, *Foreign Relations, 1918, Russia,* II, 346-348).

States, accepted by Japan and acquiesced in principle by the Government of Great Britain is now in course of execution. Only a small part of the troops have reached Vladivostok. When all are assembled there they will number, approximately, 25,000. It should, in the judgment of the Government of the United States, be left to a later time and other circumstances, not yet developed, to consider radical alterations of the whole scale and character of action in Siberia. The President advises me that on several occasions he has stated to Lord Reading the unalterable facts which must of necessity limit military action and the supplying of armies in Siberia, and the President hopes that Lord Reading will be kind enough to set those facts before his Government in London more fully than is possible in a cable message.[11]

Rebuffed by the State Department, the British Foreign Office attempted to appeal to the President through Colonel House. Balfour cabled a lengthy appeal to Wiseman urging that the facts be laid before House, who might offer suggestions which would be acceptable to the President.[12] Although not fully informed about the latest developments in Siberia, House suggested that since the Japanese had the military direction of the expedition, they were the "right people to press U.S.G. to increase the expedition to whatever size they consider necessary in order to enable the Czecho-Slovaks to retire in safety."[13]

On August 23 Wiseman informed Lord Reading of the State Department's real attitude toward Britain's request to enlarge the size of the expedition in Siberia. The Department believed that the United States and the Allies were at cross-purposes regarding the objects of the expedition to Siberia. Although the United States government had consented to lend its aid to help the Czechs escape from their "dangerous situation" and leave the country, it was beginning to think that the Allies wanted to use the expedition not only to assist the Czechs, but also to help them maintain and increase their position in Russia. The State Department was concerned because the Czechs were making no attempt to retire. Disturbed by the Department's attitude, Wiseman offered his advice to Lord Reading:

I have always thought that time and circumstances would modify the President's original policy regarding Russia, and I see indications even now that this is so. The danger now is—to be quite frank—that he is beginning to feel that the Allies are trying to rush, even trick, him into a policy which he has refused to accept. He is well aware that he is committed to

[11] Lansing to Barclay, Aug. 14, 1918, United States, *Foreign Relations, 1918, Russia,* II, 344-345.
[12] Reading to Wiseman, Aug. 20, 1918, House Papers.
[13] Wiseman to Reading, Aug. 22, 1918, Wiseman Papers.

the task of rescuing the Czechs, but thinks the Allies are already trying to change the character of the expedition into a full-fledged military intervention with the object of reconstituting the Eastern front.

If I may offer a suggestion it is that the Japanese Commander should report that he cannot be responsible for the safety of Czech forces unless further troops are despatched at once, and that message should be conveyed to the President together with the statement that the Japanese are only awaiting his agreement to rush more troops to the rescue.[14]

Balfour evidently approved of Wiseman's suggestion, for on August 28 he informed the British Embassy in Washington, that he was "asking the Japanese to take the necessary action." At the same time, he was directing Dr. Beneš to inform Masaryk of the seriousness of the Czech position.[15]

The British government desired not only increased military strength in Siberia, but also a more coherent direction of political affairs in that area. At first the British simply suggested that the Allies establish and preserve order in Vladivostok, since the Russians were "too divided amongst themselves to do so effectively and impartially." The Czech force could be used for policing purposes. The French government supported this view, while the American consul at Vladivostok considered that some measure of martial law was necessary.[16]

Washington rejected these suggestions. Caldwell was informed that the United States government did not believe it wise to interfere in Russian local governmental affairs.[17] When the United States continued to oppose Anglo-French desires to establish a unified political control of affairs in Siberia, London and Paris decided to disregard Washington's opposition. After all, Wilson himself had carefully stated in his *aide memoire* of July 17 that, while restricting American activities, he did not wish, "even by implication, to set limits to the

[14] Aug. 23, 1918, Wiseman Papers. Wiseman indicated that Masaryk did not make the task of the British government any easier, for he seemed quite satisfied with the whole situation.

Sir William Wiseman recently pointed out that certain of the excerpts quoted from his papers might, as he put it, "give the impression that we tried to trick Wilson into adopting a policy in which he did not believe. This of course is not true. He was always against a big military enterprise in that theatre, and I so reported to my Government. The thing we did persuade him to do, and which he thought was quite proper, was to lend his support in the task of rescuing the Czechs" (Wiseman to Dr. Charles Seymour, March 8, 1954, copy sent to present writer, March 22, 1954).

[15] Balfour to Barclay, Aug. 28, 1918, Wiseman Papers.

[16] Barclay to Lansing, Aug. 16, 1918, British Embassy to Department of State, Aug. 23, 1918, Caldwell to Lansing, Aug. 24, 1918, United States, *Foreign Relations, 1918, Russia,* II, 349-350, 354, 355.

[17] Lansing to Caldwell, Aug. 30, 1918, United States, *Foreign Relations, 1918, Russia,* II, 361.

actions or to define the policies" of his associates. Therefore, on August 11 the State Department was informed that Sir Charles Eliot had been appointed British High Commissioner in Siberia. He was to represent Great Britain in all political matters which confronted the Allies. An important part of his duties was to "promote the closest possible cooperation amongst the Allied forces and their leaders." The British government hoped that the United States would follow its example, so as to facilitate co-operative action by the Allies.[18]

On the next day the French government suggested that an inter-Allied civilian board be set up for the purpose of settling any political, economic, or technical questions which might arise in Siberia. A few Russians could be admitted to the board in an advisory capacity. The French government offered the chairmanship of the board to the United States.[19]

State Department officials were not agreed on their response to the Anglo-French request. Phillips, the Assistant Secretary of State, felt that the French request should be answered in the affirmative.[20] Long was also in apparent agreement with the idea. He advised Lansing that it seemed "really necessary that some one person be designated to supervise, control and coordinate the different efforts, civil, political, and humanitarian, which are being exerted for the Czechs and Siberians through the State, War and Navy Departments, and the Red Cross." He pointed out that only confusion and lack of accomplishment could result under the present arrangement where no one had authority.[21] Similar arguments were presented by Ambassador Morris and Consul Caldwell. The latter suggested that he be authorized to act with the Allied commissioners then in Vladivostok, pending the arrival of an American commissioner. He was informed that Washington did not intend to send a High Commissioner to Siberia.[22]

Secretary Lansing believed it would be unwise to follow the Anglo-French request, which he considered as "another move to impress our action in Siberia with the character of intervention rather than relief of the Czechs." Furthermore, the suggestion that an American High

---

[18] Barclay to Acting Secretary of State, United States, *Foreign Relations, 1918, Russia*, II, 339-340.

[19] Jusserand to Lansing, Aug. 12, 1918, United States, *Foreign Relations, 1918, Russia*, II, 340-341. On Aug. 22 the French government appointed Eugene L. O. Regnault as representative on the board and French High Commissioner at Vladivostok.

[20] Phillips to Lansing, Aug. 22, 1918, file 861.00/2659, D.S.N.A.

[21] Long to Lansing, Aug. 17, 1918, file 861.00/2601½, D.S.N.A.

[22] Morris to Lansing, Aug. 23, 1918, Caldwell to Lansing, Aug. 29, 1918, Lansing to Caldwell, Sept. 3, 1918, United States, *Foreign Relations, 1918, Russia*, III, 139-140; II, 360, 364.

Commissioner be the head of the civilian board, seemed to Lansing to
"be a bait to draw us into a policy which has been so insistently urged
by Great Britain for the past six months."[23]

Wilson was in complete agreement with his Secretary of State.
He revealed his anxiety in a letter to Lansing:

> I hope you will do just what you here suggest. The other govern-
> ments are going much further than we—and much faster—are, indeed,
> acting upon a plan which is altogether foreign from ours and inconsistent
> with it.
>
> Please make it plain to the French Ambassador that we do not think
> co-operation in *political* action necessary or desirable in eastern Siberia
> because we contemplate no political action of any kind there, but only the
> action of friends who stand at hand and wait to see how they can help.
> The more plain and emphatic that is made, the less danger will there be or
> [of?] subsequent misunderstandings and irritations.[24]

While Washington resisted Anglo-French efforts to broaden the
scope of the Siberian expedition, Tokyo was proceeding along its own
independent course. On August 5 the Japanese Foreign Minister informed Ambassador Morris of his concern over the "increasingly serious condition developing in northern Manchuria and eastern Siberia."
He stated that Semenov's defeat and "the invasion of Chinese territory
by Bolsheviks and organized German war prisoners was giving them
more concern than the Czech situation."[25] The Chinese government,
however, denied repeatedly and emphatically that its borders had been
violated by Bolsheviks or German prisoners of war.[26] Despite this
denial, on August 5 the Japanese Cabinet decided to station guards in
the Manchouli region.[27] On August 13, Tokyo informed the American government that it would send an independent Japanese force to
Manchouli Station to protect the Manchurian border from invasion by
the Bolsheviks. The action would be taken under the terms of the
Sino-Japanese Military Agreement of May 16, 1918. Tokyo stated that
the Chinese government had consented to the operation and that troops
would be withdrawn as soon as the temporary emergency was over.

[23] Lansing to Wilson, Aug. 22, 1918, *Lansing Papers*, II, 378.

[24] Wilson to Lansing, Aug. 23, 1918, *Lansing Papers*, II, 378-379. Lansing carried out Wilson's request (Lansing to Jusserand, Aug. 31, 1918, United States, *Foreign Relations, 1918, Russia*, II, 362).

[25] Morris to Lansing, Aug. 5, 1918, United States, *Foreign Relations, 1918, Russia*,
II, 330.

[26] Memorandum of a Conversation between Long and Koo, Aug. 6, 1918, MacMurray to Lansing, Aug. 8, 1918, Aug. 15, 1918, United States, *Foreign Relations, 1918,
Russia*, II, 330-331, 334-335, 348-349.

[27] Takeuchi, *War and Diplomacy*, p. 209.

The Japanese government added that its expedition into the Chinese Eastern Railway zone was "entirely different in nature from the present joint intervention in Vladivostok, or from military action within Russian territory, and the only nations that have interests involved are Japan and China."[28]

The Chinese version of the affair differed from the Japanese. Koo reported to Lansing that on August 8 the Japanese minister at Peking had asked for China's consent to the execution of measures for joint defense against the enemy according to the terms of the Sino-Japanese Military Agreement. The Chinese Premier replied that when the necessity arose China would give her consent in accordance with the agreement. The Japanese then proceeded to move troops into Northern Manchuria. Koo pointed out that apparently the Japanese government had interpreted the casual reply of the Premier as China's consent to immediate co-operation. China held, however, that Article 11 of the agreement provided that defensive measures must be decided upon and initiated by the highest military commands of the two countries. Therefore, an answer to a mere inquiry from the Japanese minister at Peking should not be construed to be consent by the Chinese government to the execution of the agreement.[29]

By August 21 the Japanese had stationed twelve thousand troops along the line of the Chinese Eastern Railway.[30] A few days later Tokyo announced its intention to send ten thousand additional troops to the Maritime Province. Its justification for such action was the critical situation of the Czechs, the increased activity of armed German war prisoners, and pressure by the European Allies as well as the Czechs.[31]

[28] Morris to Lansing, Aug. 13, 1918, United States, *Foreign Relations, 1918, Russia,* II, 343-344. See also New York *Times*, Aug. 18, 1918.

[29] Koo to Lansing, Sept. 13, 1918, United States, *Foreign Relations, 1918, Russia,* II, 378.

[30] Memorandum of a Conversation between Long and Koo, United States, *Foreign Relations, 1918, Russia,* II, 353.

[31] Morris to Lansing, Aug. 26, 1918, Ishii to Lansing, Aug. 27, 1918, United States, *Foreign Relations, 1918, Russia,* II, 356-358. America had originally announced its intention of sending 7,000 men to Siberia, but the actual count was 9,000, of which 7,368 were combatant troops and 251 officers. When the Japanese ambassador was informed of this, he replied that "he feared his Government would feel that they would have to give way to the pressure which other Governments were exerting upon them to send an increased military force into Siberia since the American Government had sent a force in excess of the 7,000 which it had announced would be sent" (Memorandum of a Conversation between Long and Ishii, Aug. 15, 1918, file 861.00/2751, D.S.N.A.). Ambassador Morris had warned the State Department earlier concerning "the wisdom of limiting our present contingent to 7,000 as originally suggested to the

The State Department was perplexed by Japan's independent course of action. Long was convinced that the Siberian affair was "getting out of control." He advocated a change in policy and wrote a long memorandum on the subject to Lansing.[32] The latter introduced many of Long's views in a letter to Wilson, in which he pointed out that it might be wiser to assent to the Japanese increase of troops under existing conditions, since Japan was going to send such troops "whether we liked it or not."[33]

Actually, the State Department made no comment to Japan on the recent developments in Siberia. When Ambassador Morris requested an expression of attitude on the subject, Lansing replied that the "American Government does not intend to approve or disapprove the sending by Japan of forces to Manchouli."[34] Lansing later learned that the Minister for Foreign Affairs was "greatly embarrassed by his inability to report definitely on the American attitude toward recent developments in Siberia."[35] Ambassador Morris soon revealed further information concerning Japan's sudden decision to send additional troops to Siberia. He learned that Ambassador Ishii was "greatly shocked" by the Japanese action. Ishii felt that it was contrary to the recent Japanese-American understanding on the subject.[36] Morris himself believed that the recent developments in Siberia seemed to support the idea that "the General Staff has a definite policy in Siberia and that it proposes to pursue this policy leaving to the Foreign Office and Viscount Ishii the task of explaining after the event."[37]

Further developments seemed to justify rather than deny Ambassador Morris's viewpoint. Japan continued to pour troops into Siberia. By the time the Armistice was signed on November 11, 1918, she had sent three divisions, or some seventy thousand men, all of them under the direct control of the General Staff in Tokyo.[38] Japanese troops continued to arrive in Siberia even after reports indicated

Japanese Government." He pointed out that if American forces were increased beyond the original number, "it would make a most unfortunate impression" (Morris to Lansing, Aug. 7, 1918, United States, *Foreign Relations, 1918, Russia*, II, 333).

[32] Long to Lansing, Aug. 17, 1918, file 861.00/2601½, D.S.N.A.

[33] Lansing to Wilson, Aug. 18, 1918, *Lansing Papers*, II, 374-375.

[34] Lansing to Morris, Aug. 30, 1918, United States, *Foreign Relations, 1918, Russia*, III, 240.

[35] Morris to Lansing, Sept. 8, 1918, United States, *Foreign Relations, 1918, Russia*, II, 371.

[36] Morris to Lansing, August 27, 1918, file 861.00/2601, D.S.N.A.

[37] Morris to Lansing, Sept. 8, 1918, United States, *Foreign Relations, 1918, Russia* III, 245-246.

[38] David P. Barrows, "Japan as an Ally in Siberia," *Asia*, XIX (1919), 930.

that the Czech forces were out of danger and had been joined by a Russian military force of equal strength.[39] It appeared to Wilson that the object of the Japanese was "to do the fighting on their own plans and let the Czechs tag along, instead of acting themselves as a supporting force."[40]   Actually, the Czechs had very easily overcome Bolshevik opposition. By the first week in September railway connections between Eastern and Western Siberia were re-established. The Czechs were thus in a position to withdraw to Vladivostok and from there return to France. However, they showed no indication of retiring. Instead, they seemed bent on active participation in the threatened civil war.[41]

By the middle of September President Wilson had become vitally concerned about the disposition of Japanese and Czech troops in Siberia. He considered the possibility of asking Japan what she proposed to do with the large army she had sent to Siberia, in view of the fact that the Trans-Siberian Railway was open and controlled by friends from Vladivostok to Samara. Wilson feared that there was "some influence at work to pull absolutely away from the plan which we proposed and to which the other governments assented, and proceed to do what we have said we would not do, namely form a new Eastern front." Wilson believed that the United States government should "insist" that the Czechoslovaks be brought out eastward to Vladivostok and conveyed to the Western Front in Europe. He advised Lansing to inform the Allies of the American viewpoint on this subject and to emphasize the point that the United States would "not be a party to any attempt to form an Eastern front."[42]

Although Lansing concurred with the President's views, he called Wilson's attention to the *aide memoire* of July 17, which carefully pointed out that the United States government would not seek, even by implication, to set limits to the action or define the policies of its associates. In these circumstances, Lansing could scarcely "insist" that the Czechs be brought out to Vladivostok and conveyed to Europe.

[39] Lansing to Wilson, Sept. 4, 1918, Wilson Papers, series II.

[40] Wilson to Lansing, Sept. 2, 1918, *Lansing Papers*, II, 380.

[41] Morris to Lansing, Sept. 5, 1918, United States, *Foreign Relations, 1918, Russia*, II, 368; Varneck and Fisher, *Testimony of Kolchak*, pp. 371-372; Baerlein, *March of the Seventy Thousand*, p. 186. For Masaryk's criticism of this action, see Masaryk, *The Making of a State*, p. 281.

[42] Wilson to Lansing, Sept. 17 and 18, 1918, file 861.00/3009, 861.00/3010, D.S.N.A. Wilson considered the formation of an Eastern Front "absolutely impracticable from a military point of view and unwise as a matter of political action. . . ." Masaryk concurred with this view (Baker, *Woodrow Wilson*, VIII, 419).

He could merely restate American policy on the matter and emphasize the impracticality of the restoration of an Eastern Front.[43]

It was becoming extremely difficult for the State Department to formulate a Siberian policy on the basis of the conflicting reports being sent from the Far East. In an attempt to get firsthand information on affairs in Siberia, the State Department decided to order Ambassador Morris to go to Vladivostok in an unofficial capacity. His purpose was to investigate economic, social, financial, political, and military conditions in Siberia and send the Department his views on the best method of aiding the Russian people under existing conditions.[44]

Morris soon discovered that the Czechs were actively engaged in the civil war in Western Siberia and were making no real effort to proceed to Vladivostok. Reports from the Volga region showed that the Czech forces were in serious danger from various directions. Their leaders were pleading for immediate assistance. Without such assistance the Czechs would be forced to retire east of the Ural Mountains. They were opposed to such a retreat because it would leave defenseless those Russians who had supported them against the Bolsheviks. Morris recommended that American troops be sent to the vicinity of Omsk to co-operate with British and French troops in aiding the Czechs and their Russian friends to maintain their position in European Russia. He believed that the Russian people would welcome such action. Moreover, General Graves's presence in Western Siberia would be a strong influence in counteracting impracticable plans for establishing an Eastern Front. Both General Graves and Admiral Knight supported these views.[45]

Lansing was thoroughly perplexed and distressed by Morris's report. He sympathized with "the spirit of the Czecho-Slovaks when they say that they cannot abandon their helpless friends to certain massacre and pillage." Moreover, he feared that the United States government would be generally criticized if it told the Czechs that it was their duty, regardless of their Russian allies, to join their compatriots in Siberia. Revealing his perplexity to the President, Lansing

---

[43] Lansing to Wilson, Sept. 21, 1918, file 861.00/3010, D.S.N.A. Wilson agreed to Lansing's modifications (Wilson to Lansing, Sept. 23, 1918, file 861.00/3013, D.S.N.A.). Basil Miles considered the President's query concerning Japanese forces in Siberia, and suggested that the President's views be presented to Viscount Ishii in an oral conversation. This suggestion was followed (Miles to Lansing, Sept. 23, 1918, file 861.00/2763½, D.S.N.A.).

[44] Lansing to Morris, Sept. 4, 1918, United States, *Foreign Relations, 1918, Russia,* II, 366.

[45] Morris to Lansing, Sept. 23, 1918, United States, *Foreign Relations, 1918, Russia,* II, 387-390.

wrote, "We cannot abandon the Czecho-Slovaks on the ground that they will not abandon their Russian friends. Of course that would never do. And yet, what is the alternative, or is there any?"[46] Lansing indicated that he would appreciate Wilson's advice or suggestions on the matter.

In conjunction with Wilson's suggestions and the advice of his counselors, Lansing directed a forceful reply to Morris's proposals of September 23. His note pointed out, in accordance with Wilson's earlier views, that if the Czechs desired American co-operation, they should retire to the eastern side of the Urals. Although the United States intended to send all available supplies to the Czechoslovaks as rapidly as possible, it would not undertake to send them west of the Urals. The suggestion that General Graves establish himself at Omsk was disapproved. However, General Graves was to be given authority to establish himself at Harbin or a similar place agreeable to the Chinese government, so that he could be in touch with an open port during the winter. This would enable him to make the best use of his force to carry out the plans for safeguarding the rear of the Czechoslovaks. Lansing concluded on a confidential note:

The ideas and purposes of the Allies with respect to military operations in Siberia and on the "Volga front" are ideas and purposes with which we have no sympathy. We do not believe them to be practical or based upon sound reason or good military judgment. Consequently, while we have said that we do not desire to set the limits of the actions or to define the policies of our associates, we are not prepared and do not intend to follow their lead and do not desire our representatives to be influenced by their persistent representations as to facts and as to plans for action which, to us, seem chimerical and wholly impossible. You will please impress upon the military, naval, and civil authorities of the United States Government at Vladivostok that, notwithstanding any pressure to the contrary, they are expected to be governed wholly and absolutely by the policy of this Government as expressed herein.[47]

The policy defined in the note to Morris was sent to all the Allied governments.[48] The British government replied that the decision to hold American troops in Eastern Siberia would not affect Britain's determination to aid the Czechs in holding their position west of the Urals. Great Britain felt obligated to assist those Russians who had

---

[46] Lansing to Wilson, Sept. 24, 1918, *Lansing Papers*, II, 386-387.

[47] Lansing to Morris, Sept. 26, 1918, United States, *Foreign Relations, 1918, Russia,* II, 392-394.

[48] United States, *Foreign Relations, 1918, Russia,* II, 394.

been loyal to the Allies throughout the war. If the Czechs withdrew to the east of the Urals, the "loyal" Russians would be left to the mercy of their enemies. In these circumstances Great Britain intended to continue her efforts in their behalf and to request the French and Japanese governments to follow British policy in standing by the "loyal" Russians against the Bolsheviks. Britain added that if the United States was "unable to assist us beyond the point indicated, we hope they will not discourage our other Allies from helping us."[49] In the face of such determination, the State Department anxiously awaited Japan's reply to the British request. Therefore, Lansing was gratified to hear of Japan's refusal to send troops to Western Siberia.[50]

Having clearly defined its policy in regard to an Eastern Front, the Department now turned its attention to the progresssive Japanese occupation of Eastern Siberia and North Manchuria. Attempting to curb Japanese actions along the Chinese Eastern Railway zone, the United States formally requested permission from China to station American troops at Harbin for the winter. The Chinese government immediately granted the necessary permission, adding informally that it "heartily welcomed the presence of American troops in the railway zone although it feared that any expression of that sort might be resented by Japan."[51]

Despite Chinese permission, American soldiers found it almost impossible to establish themselves in Harbin. Japanese troops occupied all available barracks. Thus, only one American company was able to remain there. General Graves reported that it was evidently the Japanese desire to keep American troops from being stationed alone at any Siberian town. Therefore, they had occupied all important points along the railway. As a result, Graves had been "practically sewed up to the railway line between Vladivostok and Habarovsk."[52]

The Japanese occupation of Eastern Siberia was quite thorough. By the beginning of November they were in full military control. Furthermore, they were also subsidizing General Horvat as well as

[49] Barclay to Lansing, Oct. 3, 1918, United States, *Foreign Relations, 1918, Russia*, II, 403-404.

[50] Morris to Lansing, Oct. 27, 1918, United States, *Foreign Relations, 1918, Russia*, II, 418.

[51] Lansing to MacMurray, Sept. 26, 1918, file 861.00/2791a, D.S.N.A.; MacMurray to Lansing, Sept. 28, 1918, United States, *Foreign Relations, 1918, Russia*, II, 396.

[52] Graves to Adjutant General, Oct. 25, 1918, Records of Adjutant General, file 370.22, Russian Expedition, War Records Collection.

several Cossack leaders, whose actions served as a convenient screen for Japanese military and commercial ventures.[53]

Graves did not see the necessity for the large numbers of Japanese troops in Siberia. He reported that the Japanese commanders constantly exaggerated disorderly conditions in order to justify the large numbers of troops in the various towns. Graves was absolutely convinced that fifty soldiers would be perfectly safe in any of the towns, and that he would not hesitate to station six men in the great majority of them.[54]

Conditions in Siberia grew worse daily. Graves described the situation graphically in his reports to the War Department. He was particularly disturbed by General Horvat's appointment as the representative of the Omsk government in Eastern Siberia. He regarded Horvat as a typical reactionary, supported by the Russian army officer class, who, if he did not favor monarchy, was certainly in favor of some form of autocratic government. Graves reported that Horvat's views were opposed by the great majority of Russians:

The opinion just now is that this crowd could not remain in power 24 hours in eastern Siberia after allied troops are removed. As I see the situation they know the poorer class will not attack them as long as allied troops are here and they are utilizing this to the fullest extent . . . to entrench themselves, to get together a military force which they hope will be strong enough to hold them in power when allied troops are removed. I think some blood will be shed when troops move out but the longer we stay the greater will be the bloodshed when allied troops do go, as in effect each day we remain here, now that war with Germany is over, we are by our mere presence helping establish a form of autocratic government which the people of Siberia will not stand for and our stay is creating some feeling against the allied governments because of the effect it has. The classes seem to be growing wider apart and the feeling between them more bitter daily.[55]

General Graves's reports finally aroused Secretary Baker to action. Confessing his anxiety to President Wilson, Baker wrote of his inability to understand the necessity for keeping American troops in Siberia,

[53] Graves to Adjutant General, Oct. 1, 1918, Wilson Papers, series II; United States, *Foreign Relations, 1918, Russia,* II, 427, 428, 432.

[54] Graves to Adjutant General, Oct. 31, 1918, file 370.22, Russian Expedition, War Records Collection. Graves's reports sorely disturbed Secretary Baker, who told Wilson that he heartily wished "it were possible . . . to arrange affairs in such a way as to withdraw entirely from that expedition" (Baker to Wilson, Nov. 6, 1918, Wilson Papers, series II).

[55] Graves to Adjutant General, Nov. 21, 1918, Wilson Papers, series II. Copy sent to President Wilson.

now that the war was over. He felt that the Americans were being "used by the Japanese as a cloak for their own presence and operations there." Pleading for a complete and immediate withdrawal of American troops from Siberia, Baker wrote:

Two reasons are assigned for our remaining in Siberia. One is that having entered we cannot withdraw and leave the Japanese. If there be any answer to this it lies in the fact that the longer we stay, the more Japanese there are and the more difficult it will be to induce Japan to withdraw her forces if we set the example. The second reason given is that we must have a military force to act as guardians and police for any civil relief effort we are able to direct toward Siberia. I frankly do not believe this, nor do I believe we have a right to use military force to compel the reception of our relief agencies. . . .

I do not know that I rightly understand Bolshevikism. So much of it as I do understand I don't like, but I have a feeling that if the Russians do like it, they are entitled to have it. . . .

I have always believed that if we compelled the withdrawal of the Germans and Austrians we ought then to let the Russians work out their own problem. Neither the method nor the result may be to our liking, but I am not very sure that the Russians may not be able to work it out better if left to themselves and more speedily, than if their primitive deliberations are confused by the imposition of ideas from the outside, and I am especially fearful that the Japanese intervention in Siberia is growing so rapidly and is so obviously beyond any interest Japan could have of a humanitarian or philanthropic character that the difficulty of securing Japanese withdrawal is growing every hour and I dread to think how we should all feel if we are rudely awakened some day to a realization that Japan has gone in under our wing and so completely mastered the country that she cannot be either induced out or forced out by any action either of the Russians or of the Allies.[56]

American officialdom was concerned over Japan's commercial as well as military occupation of Siberia. Admiral Knight reported that there was much speculation among all classes of the population in Siberia as to the intentions of Japan. It was generally believed that if Japan ever secured a foothold in Siberia she would never withdraw. This belief was strengthened by the large Japanese forces in occupation. Significantly, this large military force had been accompanied and followed by large numbers of civilians. The military and civil contingents were apparently working in perfect harmony toward the accomplishment of thinly disguised commercial aims. Japanese goods were smuggled into Russia free of customs duties. Japanese merchants were given every advantage, while obstacles prevented the free movement of foreign goods. The whole operation was aptly described as "a commercial invasion under military convoy."[57]

Although the signing of the Armistice ended hostilities on the Western Front, it had no effect on the factional strife among the Russians. However, it did change the status of Allied troops in Siberia. Their presence could no longer be justified on the grounds of danger from war prisoners, the need for forming an Eastern Front against Germany, protecting military stores, or aiding the Czechs, who long since could have been safely evacuated. American troops did not know why they were being retained in Siberia, any more than they knew why they had been sent. While England, France, and Japan had already committed themselves to an anti-Bolshevik policy, General Graves clung to a strict interpretation of his *aide memoire* and withdrew American troops to the vicinity of Vladivostok, where they remained until the spring of 1919.[58] Secretary Baker had his own solution to the problem:

My own judgment is that we ought simply to order our forces home by the first boat and notify the Japanese that in our judgment our mission is fully accomplished and that nothing more can be done there which will be acceptable to or beneficial to the Russian people by force of arms, and that we propose to limit our assistance to Russia hereafter to an economic aid in view of the fact that our armies by the armistice have been required to withdraw their armed forces from Russian territory.[59]

The State Department did not share Baker's views. On November 16, 1918, Secretary Lansing made the first of numerous representations to Tokyo concerning Japanese actions in Siberia and North Manchuria. The United States protested against the number of Japanese troops in Eastern Asia and the monopoly of control which they exercised there. The note stressed the need for placing Stevens and the Russian Railway Service Corps in charge of operating the Siberian railways in be-

[57] Knight to Daniels, Nov. 4, 1918, WA-6, Russian Situation, Naval Records Collection; H. E. Ingersoll to F. Leonard, Nov. 17, 1921, file 861A.00/131, D.S.N.A.; Memorandum on the Japanese Role in the Intervention of Siberia, Oct. 15, 1918, Wiseman Papers; Kindall, *American Troops in Siberia*, p. 153; Raymond L. Buell, *The Washington Conference* (New York, 1922), p. 27. For a strongly anti-Japanese account of Japan's economic plans and policies in Siberia, see Spargo, *Russia as an American Problem*, pp. 217-220.

[58] Stewart, *The White Armies of Russia*, p. 329; Kindall, *American Troops in Siberia*, pp. 21, 74-75.

[59] Baker to Wilson, Nov. 27, 1918, Baker Papers; Palmer, *Baker*, II, 395.

half of Russia. The State Department also questioned Morris as to "the effect of withdrawing from Siberia all American forces, including Stevens and the Russian Railway Service Corps, as evidence of our unwillingness to be associated with a policy so contrary to our declared purpose regarding Russia."[60]

The Japanese Minister for Foreign Affairs admitted that the total number of Japanese troops sent to Siberia was 72,400. This number had been reduced to 58,000, who were protecting 3,400 miles of railway. He did not believe this was an excessive guard. Tokyo was not the "least disturbed" by Washington's threatened withdrawal. Morris feared that such action would be welcomed by Japanese military authorities and interpreted as an end of American efforts to assist in the reconstruction of Siberia. Morris advised against withdrawal.[61]

The United States received little support from either Great Britain or France in its representations to Japan. This was not surprising since both Great Britain and France had requested Japan to send troops into Western Siberia only one month earlier. Pleading ignorance of the Japanese activities to which the United States referred, the French Foreign Minister added that "France would not tolerate any step toward imperialism by Japan."[62] Great Britain did not express sympathy with American representations to Japan although she agreed with the American position that one nation should not exercise a monopoly of control in either China or Russia. Balfour stated unequivocally that "His Majesty's Government have always been anxious for the active participation of American and Japanese troops in Siberia and they see no reason therefore for criticizing from their own point of view the mere presence of considerable bodies of Japanese troops in Russian territory."[63]

[60] Lansing to Morris, Nov. 16, 1918, United States, *Foreign Relations, 1918, Russia*, II, 433-435. Copies of the telegram were also sent to London, Paris, and Rome (United States, *Foreign Relations, 1918, Russia*, II, 433).

[61] Morris to Lansing, Nov. 20, 1918, United States, *Foreign Relations, 1918, Russia*, II, 436-437.

[62] Sharp to Lansing, Nov. 22, 1918, United States, *Foreign Relations, 1918, Russia*, II, 440-441. Italy wholeheartedly supported the American cause (Page to Lansing, Nov. 28, 1918, United States, *Foreign Relations, 1918, Russia*, II, 449).

[63] Laughlin (chargé in Great Britain) to Lansing, Dec. 9, 1918, United States, *Foreign Relations, 1918, Russia*, II, 456-457. Great Britain's apparent approval of the Japanese position in Siberia gave weight to certain remarks made by Arthur Bullard some weeks earlier. From Japan he wrote that American diplomacy was faced quite as much by an Anglo-American as by a Japanese-American problem. The growing prestige of the American ambassador had made the British representatives in the Far East bitter and had probably colored all their reports home. Bullard was convinced that most British representatives in Japan had the "fairly conscious desire to make discord." In an effort to show concrete gains resulting from the Anglo-Japanese Alli-

Great Britain's attitude did not provoke a modification of America's position. When Japan failed to make a formal reply to American representations, the State Department dispatched a second protest. This time the Department indicated its disapproval of Japanese support of local Russian factions and protested against Japan's commercial policy in Siberia and Manchuria, which jeopardized the open door.[64]

Japan made no formal reply to American protests until the end of December. However, about the middle of November, Premier Hara, who had assumed office in September, asked Ambassador Morris to discuss the Siberian situation informally with his confidential agent, Viscount Kaneko, with a view to better understanding. Morris was informed that the dispatch of additional forces into Manchuria and Siberia was a serious mistake made by the last ministry, without the knowledge of the diplomatic advisory council. Hara himself was trying to free the Japanese government from the domination of the General Staff, but was having considerable difficulty. Realizing the necessity of co-operating with the United States in China and Siberia, Hara was withdrawing troops quietly in order not to arouse public feeling.[65] On December 23 Viscount Ishii announced the withdrawal of thirty thousand troops from Manchuria.[66] A few days later Japan announced its readiness to "reexamine the Siberian situation in the light of changed circumstances." Japan's reply ended a month of discussion and controversy in government circles. Morris considered the results quite encouraging. Hara had won an initial victory over the reactionary forces of the General Staff.[67]

ance, they tended to encourage extreme Japanese annexationists, promising British diplomatic support if the United States made trouble (Bullard to House, Oct. 21, 1918, House Papers).

[64] Polk to Morris, Dec. 16, 1918, United States, *Foreign Relations, 1918, Russia*, II, 462-463.

[65] Morris to Reinsch, Dec. 2, 1918, file 861.00/3326, D.S.N.A.; Norton, *Far Eastern Republic*, pp. 82-83.

[66] Polk, Confidential Diary, Dec. 23, 1918.

[67] Morris to Lansing, Dec. 29, 1918, United States, *Foreign Relations, 1918, Russia*, II, 465-466.

CHAPTER VI

Rivalries over a Railroad

THROUGHOUT the course of the Siberian intervention, the United States was engaged in a struggle to prevent Japan from gaining control of the Chinese Eastern Railway. When the work of John F. Stevens and the Russian Railway Service Corps was interrupted by the Bolshevik revolution, Stevens returned to Japan. There he remained until the major disturbances along the Chinese Eastern Railway subsided. In February, 1918, he returned to Harbin to confer with General Horvat on the best means of utilizing the services of the Russian Railway Service Corps.[1]

The Japanese government watched these conversations closely. Stevens reported that the Japanese were unsympathetic to American endeavors, as they desired railway control themselves. Moser, consul at Harbin, had written earlier that unless America took over direction of the railroads Japan would do so.[2] As a result of the negotiations between Stevens and Horvat, part of the Russian Railway Service Corps came to Harbin in March, 1918, and began the task of improving the railway. This move was approved by Bakhmetev, who proposed to pay their salaries from Russian funds.[3] Stevens was further assured that if the Russian funds gave out, the State Department would guarantee the salaries of the railroad men as long as their services lasted.[4]

After a month of exasperating delays Stevens succeeded in distrib-

[1] Stevens to Lansing, Feb. 1, 1918, United States, *Foreign Relations, 1918, Russia*, III, 218-219.

[2] Moser to Lansing, Feb. 3, 1918, Stevens to Lansing, Feb. 10, 1918, United States, *Foreign Relations, 1918, Russia*, III, 219-222.

[3] Lansing to Wilson, Feb. 19, 1918, file 861.77/309, D.S.N.A.; Morris to Lansing, Feb. 21, 1918, Stevens to Lansing, March 28, 1918, United States, *Foreign Relations, 1918, Russia*, III, 222, 226; Sokolsky, *Chinese Eastern Railway*, p. 34.

[4] Lansing to Scidmore, Feb. 19, 1918, United States, *Foreign Relations, 1918 Russia*, III, 221.

uting units of the corps along the entire line of the Chinese Eastern Railway. He reported that Japan was opposing him constantly, "undoubtedly with the view of controlling the entire transportation system of Manchuria."[5] Despite this opposition and the disruption of service caused by the anti-Bolshevik armed detachments in the railway zone, the corps made many improvements in the operation and management of the railway in the months preceding armed intervention.

This matter of efficient management and operation of the Trans-Siberian Railway became vital, of course, after Allied troops reached Siberia. As Japanese troops began to pour into Siberia and North Manchuria, Stevens registered his anxiety with the State Department. He reported that Japan was making every effort to control the operation of the railways and would succeed unless the United States took a firm stand. He recommended that the railways be taken under military control at once and that he and the Russian Railway Service Corps be authorized to operate them.[6]

The State Department immediately presented Stevens's proposal to Japan and China. Lansing informed the Chinese government that the suggested policy seemed to be the "only solution of a problem which is very complicated and which may otherwise become most embarrassing."[7]

Although favorable to the American plan, China hesitated to give her formal consent in the fear of antagonizing Japan. On the other hand, the Japanese formally rejected the plan as "constituting intervention in Russia's domestic administration which it has always been the avowed policy of Associated Governments to denounce."[8] In a confidential interview with Ambassador Morris, Baron Goto stated that the Japanese government had three major objections to the American proposal. First, the Allied representatives at Vladivostok and the Japanese General Staff disapproved of any proposition that would mean the elimination of General Horvat. Second, the representatives of France and Great Britain were "very much transcended" [sic] over

[5] Stevens to Lansing, April 10, 1918, Stevens to Lansing, April 29, 1918, United States, *Foreign Relations, 1918, Russia*, III, 229, 231.

[6] Caldwell to Lansing, Aug. 26, 1918, United States, *Foreign Relations, 1918, Russia*, III, 239. As soon as the Czechs had taken over control of Vladivostok, Stevens had been instructed to bring over the remainder of his men from Nagasaki, for use in the administration of the railway (Lansing to Morris, July 10, 1918, United States, *Foreign Relations, 1918, Russia*, III, 237).

[7] Lansing to Morris, Aug. 30, 1918, Aug. 31, 1918, United States, *Foreign Relations, 1918, Russia*, III, 239-240, 241.

[8] United States, *Foreign Relations, 1918, Russia*, III, 243-244, 248, 255-256, 257-258.

what they called American control of the railways, and were earnestly backing the Japanese group in their opposition. Third, the Chinese government had expressed opposition to the operation of the Chinese Eastern Railway by the Stevens mission. Goto realized the railways ought to be taken out of political controversy and operated on a businesslike plan, but the "attitude of the Allies and the possible suspicion that some of them might hold, as to America's object, would make it difficult to accomplish, what in fact was a very excellent purpose."[9]

The American government was unimpressed by Japan's objections, and with good reason. On September 3 Stevens had cabled that General Otani had issued an order placing all of the Siberian railroads under military control. Stevens expected that a Japanese would probably be placed in charge of the operation of the railways. He urged quick action or "American railroad men are out of business completely."[10] From Irkutsk Harris urged that "all measures permissible be taken to block any ulterior motives which Japan may have on the railway as being inimical to Allied interests in Siberia."[11] President Wilson was "very much disturbed" by these reports and sent an emphatic protest to the Japanese government.[12] At the same time the State Department tried to gain support for its railway plan from Great Britain, France, and Italy. Stressing the fact that Stevens and the Russian Railway Service Corps were "agents of the Russian people," the State Department denied the suggestion that it was trying to obtain control of the Russian railways. It was merely doing what it thought best for the Russian people in a spirit of unselfishness and disinterestedness.[13]

The French and Italian governments promised to support the American proposal.[14] However, Great Britain appeared unwilling to follow their example. Refraining from taking sides on the question, the Foreign Office finally replied that it "would prefer that the United States and Japanese Governments should arrange the question of actual control, since they are primarily interested," and that Great Britain

[9] Morris to Lansing, Sept. 11, 1918, file 861.00/2663, D.S.N.A.
[10] Lansing to Morris, Sept. 6, 1918, United States, *Foreign Relations, 1918, Russia*, III, 242.
[11] MacMurray to Lansing, Sept. 7, 1918, United States, *Foreign Relations, 1918, Russia*, III, 245.
[12] Lansing to Morris, Sept. 6, 1918, United States, *Foreign Relations, 1918, Russia*, III, 243.
[13] Lansing to Page, Sept. 13, 1918, United States, *Foreign Relations, 1918, Russia*, III, 249-252.
[14] Sharp to Lansing, Sept. 18, 1918, Macchi di Cellere to Lansing, Sept. 20, 1918, United States, *Foreign Relations, 1918, Russia*, III, 259, 261.

would "fall in with any agreement which may ultimately be reached by those two Governments."[15] England thus refused to influence the Japanese authorities.

While the State Department tried to secure Japan's agreement to its railway proposals through regular diplomatic channels, Ambassador Morris went to Vladivostok in an effort to negotiate an agreement with the Allied and Russian representatives on the spot. After a month of patient and persistent effort he finally succeeded in devising an agreement satisfactory to Allied, Russian, and Japanese representatives at Vladivostok. The informal agreement of October 13, 1918, provided that the Siberian railways, including the Chinese Eastern, be placed under the protection of the Allied military forces in Siberia, and that the technical, administrative, and financial management of the railways be entrusted to Stevens and the Russian Railway Service Corps. Stevens was to share the supervision of the railways with an inter-Allied committee composed of one representative from each of the powers having military forces in Siberia, including Russia.[16]

Despite the approval of the Japanese representative at Vladivostok, the Japanese government was reluctant to approve the scheme. Fearing the establishment of American influence on the Chinese Eastern Railway, Tokyo presented certain alternatives to the agreement of October 13, which in effect would be a new agreement. She desired sole Japanese operation of the Chinese Eastern Railway, a joint management of the Siberian railways under Stevens and Kinoshita, a Japanese railway expert then in Siberia, and the appointment of an Allied committee to advise the Russian management.[17]

Stevens was adamantly opposed to sharing the management of the railways with a Japanese expert. He felt it would only lead to further complications. The State Department supported this view. Moreover, the United States government was absolutely against sole Japanese operation of the Chinese Eastern Railway. This, in effect, was what it was seeking to prevent.[18]

As the informal conversations over the operation of the Siberian railways continued between Morris and Viscount Uchida, the Japanese Foreign Minister, reports from Harbin indicated that to all outward

[15] Barclay to Lansing, Oct. 3, 1918, United States, *Foreign Relations, 1918, Russia,* III, 272.

[16] Morris to Lansing, Oct. 13, 1918, United States, *Foreign Relations, 1918, Russia,* III, 277.

[17] Morris to Lansing, Nov. 10, 1918, United States, *Foreign Relations, 1918, Russia,* III, 282-283.

[18] Morris to Lansing, Nov. 8, 1918, United States, *Foreign Relations, 1918, Russia,* III, 281-282.

appearances the Japanese military authorities had taken over the management of the Chinese Eastern Railway. Calculations by the Russian Railway Service Corps revealed that forty thousand Japanese troops had passed through North Manchuria during a six weeks' period. General Horvat had frankly admitted to Stevens that the control and operation of the Chinese Eastern Railway had passed entirely out of his hands. Although Colonel Emerson and his railway men were continuing their efforts to retain their positions as instructors to the Russian personnel of the Chinese Eastern, Japanese interference was daily narrowing their field.[19]

Miles informed Lansing that what the State Department feared had actually happened. The Japanese General Staff had practically absorbed the Chinese Eastern Railway, leaving to the Japanese Foreign Office the task of explaining the accomplished fact.[20] Vance C. McCormick, chairman of the War Trade Board, informed Lansing that Japanese activities were preventing American economic and railway aid to Siberia. He urged the State Department to take immediate action to thwart Japan's imperialistic plans in Siberia.[21]

The Japanese Minister for Foreign Affairs confidentially informed Morris that the Japanese General Staff refused to consent to Stevens's operation of the Siberian railways. Having contributed so much to the opening of the railways, the Japanese military authorities felt they should not be forced to surrender entire control to Stevens and his corps. Uchida emphasized the existence of widespread suspicions concerning the motives of the United States in regard to the Chinese Eastern Railway.[22] Morris considered it questionable whether the Japanese Ministry was strong enough to overcome the opposition of the General Staff.[23]

On December 3, 1918, after a bitter struggle between the Ministry and the General Staff, Tokyo submitted certain informal counterproposals for the operation of the railways. The Japanese govern-

[19] Morris to Lansing, Oct. 25, 1918, United States, *Foreign Relations, 1918, Russia,* III, 278-280.

[20] Oct. 28, 1918, Wilson Papers, series II.

[21] Nov. 8, 1918, file 861.00/3214½, D.S.N.A.

[22] The American Naval Intelligence also reported that such suspicions persisted in Japan among considerable sections of public opinion (Polk to Lansing, Dec. 7, 1918, file 861.00/3317, D.S.N.A.). Polk advised Morris to discuss the rumors quite frankly with members of the Japanese government, and attempt to assure them that the United States had "no deep policy or hidden purpose in any of the measures it is endeavoring to take in order to assist Russia" (Polk to Morris, Dec. 11, 1918, file 861.77/585a, D.S.N.A.).

[23] Morris to Lansing, Nov. 8, 1918, file 861.77/544, D.S.N.A. Morris feared that the British attitude had strengthened the position of the Japanese General Staff.

ment advocated the creation of a technical board composed of one representative from each of the Allied powers having military forces in Siberia. The technical board, with Stevens as its president, would act in an advisory capacity to the Russian railway administration.[24]

Although Ambassador Morris and the State Department were willing to consent to the Japanese counterproposals, Stevens refused. He felt that he could accomplish nothing in an advisory capacity, as he would have no way of enforcing his decisions.[25] Thus, the State Department was thrown into a quandary. Since Secretary Lansing and President Wilson had already departed for the Paris Peace Conference, Polk and Long attempted to thrash out the problem in Washington.

Morris had reported earlier that the "unsympathetic indifference" of the British ambassador in Tokyo was strengthening the opposition of the General Staff to American railway proposals. Morris asked whether it would be expedient to indicate to the British government "the broader reasons affecting the entire situation in the Far East and particularly China which call for closest cooperation of our two Governments in establishing a policy which shall limit spheres of exclusive commercial or political control." In raising this question, Morris was evidently thinking of the Twenty-One Demands, Japan's loan policy to China, the Sino-Japanese Military Agreements of May, 1918, and the general tendency of Japanese policy to combine commercial and political activities in such a way as to exclude all foreign interests.

Polk, also, had been concerned about the problem. He believed that if no action were taken, "the doctrine of equal opportunity for all will tend to disappear as the Japanese political and commercial program extends and that herein lies an actual danger of future complications between the powers concerned in the Far East." Both Polk and Morris believed that the problem would be solved more easily if Great Britain would co-ordinate her policy with that of the United States and bring pressure to bear on Japan in Chinese and Siberian matters.[26]

Counselor Long was opposed to pleading for Britain's support. He felt it would be "a confession of weakness on our part and of our inability to come to an understanding with Japan." He thought that

[24] Morris to Lansing, Dec. 3, 1918, United States, *Foreign Relations, 1918, Russia,* III, 288-291.

[25] Polk to Morris, Dec. 7, 1918, Morris to Lansing, Dec. 6 and 7, 1918, United States, *Foreign Relations, 1918, Russia,* III, 291-292, 292-293, 295.

[26] Draft of a cable from Polk to Lansing, Dec. 21, 1918, Long Papers. Consul General Harris advocated a strong collective note from England, France, Italy, and America in regard to Japan's actions in Siberia and Manchuria (Polk to Lansing, Dec. 27, 1918, file 861.00/3614a, D.S.N.A,).

England would immediately inform Japan of the proposal and thus "our single influence with Japan will be decreased." He advised a continuation of the present policy in an attempt to come to an agreement with Japan. If no understanding could be reached, the matter could be brought to the Peace Conference, where it could be treated publicly to Japan's disadvantage.[27]

While Polk and Long discussed the possibilities of seeking British support, Morris succeeded in persuading the Japanese government to modify its proposals to meet Stevens's objections. The modified plan was accepted by Stevens and Morris on January 9, 1919.[28]

On January 15, 1919, Viscount Ishii formally submitted to the State Department the plan for operating the Trans-Siberian and Chinese Eastern Railways. From this time forth it was termed the Japanese Plan.[29] On paper the plan appeared rather simple. The general supervision of the railways was placed in the hands of an Inter-Allied Committee, composed of one representative from each of the Allied powers having military forces in Russia, including Russia. The chairman was to be a Russian. Two additional boards were created and placed under the control of the Inter-Allied Committee. The Technical Board, composed of Allied railway experts, was to administer the technical and economic management of the railways in the Allied zone, while the Military Transportation Board was to co-ordinate military transportation. The railways were placed under the protection of the Allied military forces.

The Technical Board was authorized to elect a president, who would be entrusted with the technical operation of the railways. He, in turn, was to select his staff from among the nationals of Allied powers in Siberia. However, a Russian manager was to remain at the head of each railway. In matters of technical operation the president might issue instructions to the Russian managers. *The whole arrangement was to cease upon the withdrawal of Allied military forces from Siberia, at which time all foreign railway experts appointed under the arrangement would be recalled.*[30] According to a previous under-

<hr>

[27] Long to Polk, Dec. 21, 1918, Long Papers.

[28] Morris to Department of State, Dec. 27, 1918, United States, *Foreign Relations, 1918, Russia*, III, 301-302; Morris to Polk, January 9, 1919, United States, *Foreign Relations, 1919, Russia*, pp. 236-237; LaFargue, *China and the World War*, pp. 171-172.

[29] Ishii to Polk, Jan. 15, 1919, United States, *Foreign Relations, 1919, Russia*, p. 239.

[30] United States, *Foreign Relations, 1919, Russia*, pp. 239-240; Ken Shen Weigh, *Russo-Chinese Diplomacy* (Shanghai, 1928), pp. 229-231; italics inserted.

standing between Japan and the United States, Stevens was to be made president of the Technical Board.[31]

The State Department had finally succeeded in securing a railway plan acceptable to both Japan and the United States. By this time, however, American public opinion was becoming "extremely restive" on the whole subject of Russia. At the same time General March was preparing to withdraw American forces from Siberia.[32] Since the railway plan provided that American troops remain in Siberia to support Stevens and guard the railway, the situation was made somewhat awkward by Secretary Baker's insistence on adhering rigidly to the policy laid down for the use of American troops in Siberia by President Wilson in his *aide memoire* of July 17. Baker told the State Department that the "War Department does not believe that the small force which we now have there is large enough to give Mr. Stevens support with reference to the policing of the Chinese Eastern and Trans-Siberian Railroads, and cannot approve of sending any more troops to Siberia for such purpose."[33]

The execution of the railway plan was endangered by lack of funds as well as the opposition of the War Department. Since the Russian ambassador had already exhausted the money set aside for maintaining the Railway Service Corps, additional funds would have to be appropriated either by Congress, which was unlikely, or from the President's private fund.[34] In view of this problem, Acting Secretary Polk sought presidential guidance before formally accepting the Japanese railway plan.

After carefully considering the whole Siberian picture, Lansing, with the approval of President Wilson, cabled full instructions to Polk. He was told to request a secret hearing before the appropriate committee or committees in Congress and to tell them fully and frankly about the entire Siberian situation:

You will then develop the strategic importance both from the point of view of Russia and of the United States of the Trans-Siberian Railway as being a principal means of access to and from the Russian people and as affording an opportunity for economic aid to Siberia where the people are relatively friendly and resistant to Bolshevik influence and where there

[31] Morris to Polk, Jan. 9, 1919, United States, *Foreign Relations, 1919, Russia*, pp. 236-237.

[32] Polk to Commission to Negotiate Peace, Jan. 7, 1919, United States, *Foreign Relations, 1919, Russia*, p. 461.

[33] Baker to Department of State, Jan. 14, 1918, file 861.00/3651, D.S.N.A.

[34] Polk to Commission to Negotiate Peace, Jan. 24, 1919, United States, *Foreign Relations, 1919, Russia*, p. 245.

are large bodies of Czecho-Slovaks who rely upon our support as well as large numbers of enemy prisoners of war whose activities must be watched and in all cases [*if necessary*] controlled. The potential value of this railroad as a means for developing American commerce particularly from the west coast of the United States to Russia might be mentioned.[35]

Polk was then instructed to describe in detail the activities of Japan in Siberia and Manchuria, stressing particularly the large number of troops sent and Japan's actions in practically seizing the Chinese Eastern Railway. Polk was then to indicate how the United States, after considerable effort, had finally succeeded in getting Japan to withdraw a substantial number of troops from Siberia and to accept a railway plan which "may be of inestimable value to the people of Russia and to the United States, as well as the world in general . . . thereby giving practical effect to the principle of the open door." The purpose of the hearing was to secure Congressional approval of the necessary appropriations for executing the railway plan. Lansing's instructions to Polk closed on an interesting note: "We feel that it may be a wise practice to take Congress more into confidence on such matters and we at least desire to make the experiment in this case."[36]

Polk discussed Lansing's suggestions with other men in the State Department and brought the "question up at Cabinet." He found that "everyone" advised against his going to Congress with any plan having anything to do with Russia or with the acquisition of money for expenditure abroad. Polk reported that it was the unanimous opinion of all who had been consulted that "to get Congress to commit itself to any proposal for financing the railroad—in its present mood when it is badly frightened over the amount of money we are spending and when it is so completely at sea as to what should be done in Russia—would be hopeless."[37]

When the President received Polk's report of the prevailing attitudes in Congress, he withdrew his original proposal. However, he did authorize Polk to accept formally the Japanese railway plan on behalf of the United States, reserving the question of financial responsibility for future discussions. Secretary Baker was to inform General Graves of his duties under the railway plan. Ambassador Morris was then instructed to proceed with the inauguration of the plan.

[35] Commission to Negotiate Peace to Polk, Jan. 31, 1919, United States, *Foreign Relations, 1919, Russia*, p. 246.

[36] United States, *Foreign Relations, 1919, Russia*, pp. 246-248.

[37] Polk to Lansing, Feb. 4, 1919, United States, *Foreign Relations, 1919, Russia*, pp. 248-249.

Although in deference to Polk's views the President withdrew his suggestion of placing the Siberian situation frankly before Congress, he requested that Polk take advantage of the appropriate opportunity to advise Congress of American policy in reference to the Trans-Siberian and Chinese Eastern Railways. He concluded on a significant note:

It is felt that this matter can be treated entirely apart from the general Russian problem, as, irrespective of what our policy may be toward Russia, and irrespective of further [future] Russian developments, it is essential that we maintain the policy of the open door with reference to the Siberian and particularly the Chinese Eastern Railway.[38]

The United States formally accepted the Japanese railway plan on February 10, 1919.[39] France, Great Britain, and Italy soon followed her example.[40] The Chinese government held back. Early in February the Chinese government had suggested that it be permitted to operate the Chinese Eastern Railway as a unit. The United States had assured China that her interests would be fully protected under the Inter-Allied Railway Agreement. Nevertheless, the Chinese government was the last to appoint a representative to the Technical Board. The British, French, and Italian civil and military representatives showed a fine spirit of co-operation. The Japanese military officials sought every excuse for delay and endeavored to make mere questions of detail matters for further diplomatic discussion.[41] Despite these various delays, on March 5, 1919, the machinery for the international administration and operation of the Trans-Siberian and Chinese Eastern Railways was formally inaugurated in Vladivostok.[42]

[38] Lansing to Polk, Jan. 21, 1919, Feb. 9, 1919, United States, *Foreign Relations, 1919, Russia*, pp. 244, 250-251. America's formal acceptance was probably hastened by the persistent reports that Japan was making desperate efforts to maintain control of the Chinese Eastern Railway. Even the Omsk government had asked that the managing control of the Siberian railways be taken over by Stevens and the railway mission (Reinsch to Lansing, Dec. 30, 1918, file 861.77/595, D.S.N.A.; Polk to Lansing, Dec. 27, 1918, United States, *Foreign Relations, 1919, Paris Peace Conference*, II, 480; Polk to Page, Jan. 3, 1919, file 861.77/588, D.S.N.A.; Polk to Morris, Jan. 11, 1919, United States, *Foreign Relations, 1919, Russia*, pp. 237-238).

[39] Polk to Ishii, United States, *Foreign Relations, 1919, Russia*, pp. 251-252.

[40] United States, *Foreign Relations, 1919, Russia*, pp. 254, 255.

[41] Polk to Reinsch, Feb. 4, 1919, Morris to Polk, Feb. 24, 1919, files 861.77/660, 861.77/690, D.S.N.A.; Weigh, *Russo-Chinese Diplomacy*, p. 231.

[42] Morris to Polk, March 5, 1919, United States, *Foreign Relations, 1919, Russia*, p. 256. At the first meeting the question was raised as to whether committee decisions should be by majority vote. The Japanese and Chinese representatives insisted on unanimity. On the grounds that nothing could be accomplished under such an arrangement, Great Britain brought pressure to bear on both governments to submit to a ma-

The Inter-Allied Railway Agreement completely changed the character of intervention in Siberia. The primary concern of American military forces now became the restoration and protection of the railways instead of the rescue of the Czechs. The latter were now participating in the execution of the railway plan. In effect, the improvement of the transportation situation served to aid the anti-Bolshevik cause. Thus, despite its denials, the United States became an active participant in the Russian civil war. President Wilson justified this course on the grounds of maintaining the open door in Siberia and North Manchuria and preserving Russia's territorial integrity.[43] In this respect, the conclusion of the railway agreement represented a victory for the United States and the liberal civilian elements in the Japanese government.[44] It was one of the few victories achieved by the United States in the whole Siberian affair.

jority vote (Reading to Polk, March 15, 1919, file 861.77/747, D.S.N.A.). Reading was evidently anxious to inform Polk of British co-operation on this matter, since Polk had told him earlier "rather bluntly if his government had shown more patriotism and had not been neutral Japan would have come to terms long ago" (Polk, Confidential Diary, Jan. 7, 1919).

[43] Polk to Lansing, May 9, 1919, United States, *Foreign Relations, 1919, Russia,* p. 494; Memorandum of John F. Stevens, Railway Service Corps Papers.

[44] Benjamin Bock, "The Origins of the Inter-Allied Intervention in Eastern Asia, 1918-1920" (unpublished doctoral dissertation, Stanford University, 1940), p. 297.

CHAPTER VII

New Sources of Trouble: The Cossacks

THE JAPANESE military were not slow in revealing their real attitude toward co-operation with the United States in Siberia. Despite the railway agreement and continuous efforts to avoid factional strife, American forces were constantly embroiled in difficulty either with Japan or with the Siberian factions which she supported. At times scrapes with both almost led to actual hostilities.

By the end of 1918 political affairs in Siberia revolved about two distinct geographic units. The Kolchak or Omsk government, established in November, 1918, was supreme in Western Siberia. Supported by the Czechs, the Kolchak government maintained an army which was engaged in conducting a campaign against the Bolsheviks. Kolchak was supported strongly by the British and French representatives in Siberia, who were eager to have the Allied governments recognize his rule.[1]

American diplomatic and military representatives in Siberia recognized Admiral Kolchak as an honest and courageous man of limited experience in public affairs. He had served with distinction in both the Russo-Japanese and the World Wars. Consul General Harris believed that Kolchak had the best interests of all Russia at heart, while Consul Moser, who knew Kolchak well, considered him a capable and honest patriot. Both feared that Kolchak would be helpless without aid from the Allies. On the other hand, Kolchak was denounced by many Siberians because of his methods in gaining control of the Omsk government and because he called himself "Dictator." Although he evinced a desire to call a constituent assembly, his officers always spoke of this as a matter for the far distant future. Among the ex-

[1] Rudolph Medek, *The Czechoslovak Anabasis across Russia and Siberia* (London, 1929), pp. 2-3.

treme Russian reactionaries, Kolchak was denounced as a liberal, while the middle class considered him too reactionary.[2]

Governmental affairs were more complex in Eastern Siberia. There, four different men claimed some degree of authority at various places throughout the region. General Horvat called himself the "supreme representative of the Kolchak government in the Far East," while Major General Pavel Pavlovich Ivanov-Rinov represented Admiral Kolchak as commander of all the Russian troops in Eastern Siberia. Although Horvat was a man of education and refinement, he had absolutely no control over Ivanov-Rinov, who terrorized and pillaged villages throughout Eastern Siberia. Eichelberger described Ivanov-Rinov as "absolutely unscrupulous."[3] In addition to Horvat and Ivanov-Rinov, there were two independent Cossack leaders, Semenov and Kalmikov, who used the chaotic conditions in Siberia solely as a means of increasing their own wealth and power. Semenov was a complete scoundrel. About twenty-nine years of age, he was fond of carrying his hand thrust in his coat in the manner characteristic of Napoleon Bonaparte. He always carried Napoleon's *Maxims* in his pocket. Dominated to a large extent by his mistress, he spent hundreds of thousands of rubles upon her. He ruled as a dictator at Chita, robbing the banks and custom houses in the area. He shipped in military supplies to Chita on trains without paying freight or duty and sold the goods to the civilian population in "Semenoff stores." His officers went even further. When in need of funds, they simply robbed the Chinese merchants. Kalmikov was no better. He had acquired his position as Ataman of the Ussuri Cossacks by killing the legitimate candidate. General Graves described Kalmikov as the worst scoundrel he had ever met. He seriously doubted if one could think of a crime which Kalmikov had not committed. The chief difference between Kalmikov and Semenov was that Kalmikov murdered with his own hands, whereas Semenov ordered others to kill.[4]

The confusion in Siberia was increased by the friction which existed

[2] Robert L. Eichelberger, Lieutenant Colonel, to Director of Military Intelligence, March 31, 1919, file 861.00/4967, D.S.N.A.; Harris to Lansing, Nov. 25, 1918, Moser to Lansing, Nov. 27, 1918, United States, *Foreign Relations, 1918, Russia,* II, 443-444, 448.

[3] Eichelberger to Director of Military Intelligence, March 31, 1919, file 861.00/4967, D.S.N.A.; Varneck and Fisher, *Testimony of Kolchak,* pp. 231, 233.

[4] Eichelberger to Director of Military Intelligence, March 31, 1919, file 861.00/4967, D.S.N.A.; Graves to Adjutant General, Dec. 1, 1918, Office of the Adjutant General, file 370.22, Russian Expedition, Siberia, War Records Collection; Graves, *America's Siberian Adventure,* pp. 90-91; Emil Lengyel, *Siberia* (New York, 1943), pp. 222-228.

between Kolchak and Semenov. Refusing to recognize Admiral Kolchak, Semenov conducted independent activities in the Trans-Baikal region. He destroyed railway transportation, interrupted telegraphic communications, and terrorized the eastern regions with his irresponsible activities. Kolchak wrote to the Russian ambassador in America:

By reason of such activities of Semenoff, I have dismissed him from his offices and have ordered that he be brought to subordination by force so as to check his arbitrary actions and the ensuing anarchy. I have, however, met opposition in this matter on behalf of Japan, which is openly sympathizing with Semenoff and am prevented from rendering the necessary aid to the population. The Japanese General declared that no troops could be despatched for the suppressing of the bands of Semenoff.[5]

Kolchak indicated that such acts represented a direct interference in the internal affairs of Russia. Many American observers believed that Semenov's activities were directly encouraged and supported by Japan.[6]

Since the dispute between Kolchak and Semenov had resulted in the suspension of communications on the Trans-Siberian Railway, Great Britain requested Japan to urge Semenov to cease his activities.[7] Although Japan promised her support, conditions grew worse rather than better.

Once the campaigns of the Japanese and Czechs had driven the Bolshevik elements into hiding, the way was opened for Cossack military leaders and groups of former officials to begin a campaign of their own against the more liberal parties and organizations in Siberia. Although the Kolchak government did not actually support this campaign, it was too weak to prevent it. The campaign consisted of attacks on peasant villages, the beating of women, the killing of workmen and peasants alleged to have Bolshevik tendencies, and the arbitrary arrest of officials whose chief fault consisted of trying to establish a form of representative government. General Graves was constantly receiving appeals from Zemstvo representatives, individuals of liberal views, and groups of peasants, asking either for protection or for assurances from the Allied commanders that if they resisted these outrages Allied troops would not interfere on the ground of suppressing Bolshevism. Ambassador Morris believed that these unfortunate conditions could be traced almost completely to the Japanese military

[5] Kolchak to Bakhmetev, Dec. 8, 1918, file 861.00/3462, D.S.N.A.

[6] Reinsch to Polk, Dec. 9, 1918, Polk to Lansing, Jan. 2, 1919, Morris to Lansing, Jan. 10, 1919, files 861.00/3368, 861.00/3617b, 861.00/3622, D.S.N.A.; Reinsch to Polk, Jan. 3, 1919, United States, *Foreign Relations, 1919, Russia*, p. 460.

[7] Barclay to Polk, Jan. 16, 1919, United States, *Foreign Relations, 1919, Russia*, pp 462-463.

authorities who were disappointed over the results of the railway negotiations, which they feared would seriously interfere with their own plans in Eastern Siberia.[8] There was no doubt in General Graves's mind that as long as Japan continued the policy of "equipping and financing unscrupulous Cossack leaders there can be no such thing as security of life and property in Eastern Siberia."[9]

Morris shared Graves's viewpoint. While investigating conditions in Siberia, he discussed the problem with General Graves, Admiral William L. Rodgers, then in command of the Asiatic fleet, and Consul Caldwell. The question which troubled the conferees was whether the United States could "remain in Siberia and permit reactionary groups in Siberia to inauguarate a campaign the purpose of which was suppression of all local representative institutions." After considerable discussion the group agreed that since the United States had initiated the expedition and had acquiesced in the action of both the Czechs and Japanese in restoring order along the railways, American troops would have to remain in Siberia for the present. Furthermore, they believed that the population in the cities and towns along the railway, where Allied troops were quartered, should be protected from the arbitrary actions of any faction. However, they feared that such a proposal would be unacceptable to the Japanese.[10]

When Morris advised the State Department of the results of this consultation, a note was immediately sent to Harris at Irkutsk, instructing him to discuss informally with the Omsk government the actions of the Cossack leaders. Thereupon, Harris informed the Omsk authorities that the activities of the Cossacks were creating an unfortunate effect on public opinion in America, which might result in "embarrassing" the support which the United States was then lending to the authorities in Siberia.[11]

The Omsk government replied promptly with a confidential note. It frankly admitted its failure to secure control over Eastern Siberia. It was too involved in military operations against the Bolsheviks to control Semenov and Kalmikov. Moreover, a serious obstacle prevented the establishment of Omsk authority in Eastern Siberia. The obstacle was Japan. She was supporting Semenov, who in turn was preventing Kolchak from extending his influence into the Far East. Thus the

[8] Morris to Polk, March 7, 1919, file 861.77/727, D.S.N.A.

[9] Graves to Adjutant General, Feb. 25, 1919, United States, *Foreign Relations, 1919, Russia,* pp. 468-472.

[10] Morris to Polk, March 8, 1919, file 861.77/736, D.S.N.A.

[11] Lansing to Polk, March 23, 1919, file 861.00/4128, D.S.N.A.

Kolchak government could not take complete responsibility for the actions of these reactionary officials.[12]

While negotiations proceeded between Omsk and Washington, the Cossack leaders continued their efforts to make trouble. They sought to make everyone believe that most of their difficulties were due to the presence of American troops in Siberia. At the same time the Japanese and Cossacks endeavored to get the Bolshevik elements to attack American troops. The United States would then be forced to join the Cossacks and Japanese against the Bolsheviks. In these circumstances General Graves felt he had more to fear from the Cossacks than from the Bolsheviks. He reported that the situation in Siberia was just what the Japanese had been trying to achieve for the past few months.[13] The views of General Graves were corroborated by Admiral Rodgers and American consuls at various places in Siberia. Lansing himself admitted that "reports received from American consuls at various places in Siberia seem, however, to confirm on the whole General Graves's opinion of Japanese activities as intended to aid the reactionary party and as conducted with a view to the eventual domination of Eastern Siberia by Japan."[14]

In view of the tense uncertainties in Siberia, Admiral Rodgers believed that it would be wise to have a battleship fleet in the Pacific. He thought it might have a beneficial effect on diplomacy. Secretary Lansing opposed this suggestion:

I understand from Admiral Benson that in less than two months in the natural order of events as prescribed in naval orders a substantial fleet will be in the Pacific or ready to proceed there. To specifically order a fleet to the Pacific at this time, when the friction is just developing, would seem to tend to aggravate and intensify the situation for all concerned rather than help matters.[15]

Although there was no change in the attitude of the Cossack and Japanese leaders in Siberia during the next few months, there was considerable change in the attitude of the Omsk authorities, who began

[12] Harris to Polk, March 25, 1919, United States, *Foreign Relations, 1919, Russia*, pp. 484-485.

[13] Graves to Adjutant General, March 21, 1919, file 861.00/4967, D.S.N.A. General Graves later pointed out that his refusal to permit American troops to be used against the Bolsheviks accounted for nine-tenths of the criticism directed against him in Siberia. He was told by General Leonard Wood upon his return from the Far East in 1920 that if he had not had copies of his papers, he would have been "torn limb from limb, in the United States," because he had not taken part "in fighting Bolshevism" (Graves, *America's Siberian Adventure*, p. 93).

[14] Lansing to Wilson, March 22, 1919, Wilson Papers, series VIII-A.

[15] Lansing to Wilson, March 22, 1919, Wilson Papers, series II.

to protest against the "unneutral policy" of American troops. The Omsk government was particularly angered because General Graves persisted in treating the Bolsheviks as a political party of ordinary character. It flatly stated that American troops were accomplishing no useful purpose in Siberia, but were doing actual harm in tending to prolong disturbed conditions. The British and French governments sustained the objections of the Omsk government.[16]

In view of Omsk representations, both Consul Caldwell and General Graves believed that the time had come either to withdraw all American troops or to support actively the Omsk government. The British government was already aiding Kolchak.[17] On April 14 Commodore Edwards of the British cruiser *Kent* had notified the American consul in writing of his authorization by the British admiralty to give active support to the forces of the Kolchak government when necessary. The necessity arose immediately.[18] Moreover, the British government was quite displeased with the attitude and actions of American troops in Siberia. It informed the State Department of nine specific instances when General Graves had taken a stand against the Omsk government. The State Department was urged to insist upon co-operation among all the representatives and troops in Siberia.[19] General Knox, commander of the British forces in Siberia, was also annoyed with the attitude of General Graves, particularly the cables which he was sending to Washington. He criticized Graves as being ignorant of the real situation outside of the Vladivostok district, unsympathetic with the efforts of the Kolchak and British governments, and "hypnotized" by the cases involving mistreatment of peasants.[20] On the other hand, General Graves considered Knox to be a natural autocrat who "could not, if he had desired to do so, give sympathetic consideration to the aspirations of the peasant class in Russia, whom he characterized as swine."[21] However, Knox was

[16] Omsk Government to Bakhmetev, April 24, 1919, United States, *Foreign Relations, 1919, Russia*, pp. 494-496.

[17] Caldwell to Polk, May 5, 1919, file 861.00/4435, D.S.N.A.

[18] Miles to Polk, May 6, 1919, file 861.00/4976, D.S.N.A.

[19] George T. Clerk to Lansing, May 19, 1919, United States, *Foreign Relations, 1919, Russia*, pp. 499-500.

[20] Caldwell to Polk, March 3, 1919, United States, *Foreign Relations, 1919, Russia*, pp. 473-474. Carl Ackerman had reported earlier that Knox was hostile to the United States. The British general had told him at one time that "all America meant by her program of economic relief was to sell more harvester machines, shows and films to the Russians." Polk declared that Knox's attitude was injuring the Allies and making it more difficult for them to work together in Russia (Polk to John W. Davis, ambassador to Great Britain, Feb. 11, 1919, file 861.00/4058c, D.S.N.A.).

[21] Graves, *America's Siberian Adventure*, pp. 18-19.

speaking with conviction when he pointed out that the divergence in views between the British and American military authorities in Siberia was giving the Japanese a clear field.[22]

Knox was not alone in his criticism of Graves. The Russian Division of the State Department, as well as other important policy-making officials, were also opposed to his views. It was quite evident that they desired Graves to help Kolchak actively against the Bolsheviks. Graves, however, refused to comply. His orders, which had come directly from the President, instructed him not to interfere in Russian domestic affairs. To Graves this meant no participation in man hunts against the Bolsheviks and strict neutrality in all factional strife.[23] Because he refused to allow his command to become implicated in the depredations against the Bolsheviks, Graves earned the reputation of being a Bolshevik himself.[24]

General Graves, however, found it almost impossible to obey his *aide memoire* implicitly. By refusing to support Kolchak he was aiding the Bolsheviks; yet, by helping to guard the railway, he was working to the advantage of Kolchak.[25] The War Department expected Graves to follow his instructions strictly, while the Russian Division of the State Department desired him to follow a looser interpretation. The entire situation baffled even Secretary Baker, who later wrote:

I cannot even guess at the explanation of the apparent conflict between the War Department and the State Department of the United States with regard to the Siberian venture, nor can I understand why the State Department undertook to convey its ideas on Siberian policy, as it seems occasionally to have done, directly to General Graves. Perhaps the State Department was more impressed than I was with some of the Allied views as to the desirability of cooperation beyond the scope of *Aide Memoire*. Possibly some of these comments were mere reflections of Allied criticism, forwarded for what they were worth, but without being first presented to the Secretary of State or considered by him as affecting the maturely formulated policy of the United States in the adventure.[26]

[22] Caldwell to Polk, March 3, 1919, United States, *Foreign Relations, 1919, Russia,* p. 474.

[23] Lengyel, *Siberia,* pp. 235-236; Graves, *America's Siberian Adventure,* pp. 191-192.

[24] Stewart, *The White Armies of Russia,* p. 279. Graves himself pointed out that military representatives of England, France, and Japan "not only did not deny, but boasted about their efforts to destroy, what they called Bolshevism" (Graves, *America's Siberian Adventure,* pp. 81-82).

[25] Stewart, *The White Armies of Russia,* p. 286.

[26] Baker, Foreword in Graves, *America's Siberian Adventure,* p. xiv.

Throughout his stay in Siberia the attitudes, actions, and reports of General Graves were constantly criticized by the State Department. Typical was the comment written by Basil Miles on one of General Graves's reports: "I consider this report of little real value . . . it is entirely out of perspective and written with little real knowledge of Russia and Russian ways of doing things."[27] Assistant Secretary Phillips shared Miles's viewpoint. He believed that many of the difficulties described by Graves were not insurmountable and might be solved by an officer with exceptionally large experience and delicacy. He implied that these were characteristics which Graves did not have. Polk, too, considered Graves incapable of exercising discretion and lacking in tact. He conveyed these sentiments to Lansing, adding, "I understand one of the results is that the British regard him as apparently sympathizing with the Bolsheviks rather than with the Omsk authorities."[28]

On the other hand, Secretary Baker was quite "exercised" over the reports from Graves. They fully justified all of his predictions concerning the results of military intervention in Siberia.[29] Both General March and Secretary Baker appreciated Graves's difficulties and supported him. When the going was particularly rough, General March wrote: "Keep a stiff upper lip, I am going to stand by you until——freezes over."[30]

Graves's attitude even became a subject for discussion at the Peace Conference. When Lloyd George remarked that British authorities believed that much of the trouble in Siberia was due to the attitude of General Graves, President Wilson replied that "General Graves was a man of most unprovocative character, and wherever the fault might lie he felt sure it was not with him."[31]

Criticisms of Graves continued as did also the troublesome activities of the Cossacks. Although American protests to the Omsk government finally resulted in the recall of General Ivanov-Rinov from Vladivostok, Semenov continued to stop trains, examine baggage, and collect dues on any part of the Siberian railway he controlled. His actions now had the substance of legality since he had recently agreed to recognize Kolchak and submit unconditionally to his command. The agreement, however, did not stop him from continued interference

[27] March 31, 1919, file 861.00/4967, D.S.N.A.

[28] Polk, Confidential Diary, May 10, 1919; Polk to Lansing, May 9, 1919, United States, *Foreign Relations, 1919, Russia*, pp. 493-494.

[29] Phillips to Lansing, March 28, 1919, file 861.00/4174a, D.S.N.A.

[30] Graves, *America's Siberian Adventure*, p. 160.

[31] United States, *Foreign Relations, 1919, Russia*, pp. 496-497.

with the Siberian railways. In an effort to restrain Semenov, Assistant Secretary Phillips asked the British government to urge him to discontinue his activities. When Great Britain refused to take the initiative in the matter,[32] the Inter-Allied Railway Committee took action. It sent a vigorous protest to the Omsk government denouncing the activities of Semenov.[33] The protest brought no remedy. On the contrary, a few weeks later Kolchak promoted Semenov to a full general. In reality Kolchak had little choice in the matter. Since his support was rapidly diminishing throughout Siberia, he was compelled to rely on the Cossacks for the maintenance of his authority.[34]

With the nominal support of Kolchak the Cossacks continued their irresponsible activities. On September 5 Kalmikov arrested two American soldiers, a captain and a corporal, because they had no Russian passports. He released the captain but had the corporal whipped. Graves naturally considered the action an outrage and informed Kalmikov that a repetition of the incident would result in his arrest. Semenov immediately denounced Graves and declared his willingness to assist Kalmikov in case of trouble with the Americans.[35] As a result of this anti-American activity, General Graves refused to deliver one hundred thousand rifles ordered by Kolchak from the United States. He feared that they might fall into the hands of Kalmikov or Semenov. If this should happen, Graves wrote: "We will be helping to arm the worst criminals in Siberia; we will be neglectful of the interests of the people . . . and will be helping Japan to delay the settlement of conditions in Siberia."[36] Ambassador Morris approved of this action. Badly in need of the rifles, the Omsk government insisted that it did not have the power to suppress the disorderly elements. Finally, upon urgent representations from the State and War Departments, Graves agreed to deliver the rifles directly to Kolchak.[37]

Incidents of this nature continued to pile up. Conditions at Vladivostok were made considerably worse when Kolchak appointed General Sergei N. Rozanov as his representative in the Far East to suc-

[32] Phillips to Davis, June 28, 1919, Polk to Caldwell, July 17, 1919, files 861.00/4752, 861.00/4838, D.S.N.A.

[33] July 19, 1919, United States, Foreign Relations, 1919, Russia, pp. 511-512.

[34] Morris to Lansing, Aug. 13, 1919, United States, Foreign Relations, 1919, Russia, p. 514.

[35] Tenney to Polk, Sept. 22, 1919, United States, Foreign Relations, 1919, Russia, p. 516; Polk to Lansing, Oct. 5, 1919, file 861.00/5514, D.S.N.A.

[36] Graves to Adjutant General, Oct. 29, 1919, United States, Foreign Relations, 1919, Russia, pp. 540-541.

[37] Graves to Adjutant General, Sept. 26, 1919, Sept. 28, 1919, United States. Foreign Relations, 1919, Russia, pp. 519, 522.

ceed Horvat. Since Rozanov was a reactionary hostile to America, the State Department protested informally against his appointment. The protest was wasted. Rozanov brought four thousand soldiers into Vladivostok and assumed nominal control of the city. His rule brought serious disorder. Kalmikov and his Cossacks were permitted to come into Vladivostok. Shortly thereafter two men in Cossack uniforms murdered a Cossack colonel in broad daylight. This was followed by the murder of one American and one Czech soldier by Russian officers. The Allied military representatives immediately demanded that Rozanov remove Russian troops from Vladivostok. They indicated that a failure to comply by noon of September 29 would result in the use of force.[38]

The Omsk government protested the removal of Russian troops on the grounds that Allied troops did not exercise any extra-territorial rights in Vladivostok. Thereupon the Allied commanders withdrew their demand. The Omsk government later reported that an investigation of the incident indicated that one of the chief promoters of the affair was General Graves, "whose conduct recently has become entirely incomprehensible" to Omsk. The Omsk authorities added that "his remaining at Vladivostok will lead to perpetual misunderstanding and to the growing of public discontent with Americans."[39] Although shifting the blame to General Graves, the Omsk government recalled Rozanov from Vladivostok to explain himself. Consul General Harris believed that this meant the definite elimination of Rozanov from the Far Eastern situation.[40]

While the United States attempted to solve its difficulties with the Omsk government, it faced another problem involving the Czechs. As early as January, 1919, the Czechs had expressed their displeasure at having to remain in Siberia after the Armistice. They were tired of fighting; their morale was low. They had become dissatisfied with the character of the Kolchak regime, and now refused to fight for the purpose of securing his rule in Siberia.[41] Many Czechs believed that by aiding Kolchak they were perpetuating a government whose ideas

[38] Caldwell to Lansing, Sept. 30, 1919, United States, *Foreign Relations, 1919, Russia*, pp. 522-523. The Japanese government refused to sanction the use of force.
[39] De Bach (Russian chargé) to DeWitt C. Poole (Chief of Russian Division), Oct. 3, 1919, United States, *Foreign Relations, 1919, Russia*, pp. 530-531.
[40] Tenney (secretary to American Legation in China) to Lansing, Oct. 28, 1919, United States, *Foreign Relations, 1919, Russia*, p. 539.
[41] Harris to Department of State, Jan. 25, 1919, United States, *Foreign Relations, 1919, Russia*, pp. 274-275; Harris to Department of State, Feb. 3, 1919, file 861.00/3805, D.S.N.A. Harris reported that their attitude was becoming more annoying daily.

were directly opposed to the democratic ideas of the Czechs.[42] Moreover, they saw no reason for continuing the fight against the Bolsheviks while the Allies were doing no fighting themselves.[43] By the end of March friction was so intense that combat between the Czechs and Kolchak Russians seemed imminent. Major Slaughter believed the Czechs could not be asked to guard the railroad because they would obstruct traffic passively and permit local disorder. The only hope of preventing disaster was to send them home or promise to send them home. However, if this were done without replacing them within a few months, the Kolchak government would probably collapse. Therefore, if the Czechs left, it would have to be slowly so that men could be recruited to take their places.[44]

By June, the problem had not yet been solved. The Czechs had been absent from home for five years. They had been out of communication with their homes and families throughout their entire stay in Siberia. With the attainment of Czechoslovakian independence, the soldiers felt that they were needed at home to protect the new state. When, however, the Peace Conference proposed that the Czechs fight their way out to Archangel without asking the consent of the Bolsheviks, the suggestion was refused by the Czechs and General Janin.[45]

Stevens, in the meantime, desired to know whether the Czechs were to go or stay. Unless the Czechs were replaced by Allied troops, Stevens would have to withdraw American inspectors from west of Lake Baikal, since they could not remain at their posts without military protection. Even Kolchak realized that in their present stage of demoralization the Czechs were of no use. He advised their evacuation by sea from Vladivostok and their replacement by Allied troops. After Ambassador Morris had carefully studied the Czech problem he was led to conclude that Allied operation of the railways would not be possible beyond Irkutsk, unless the Allies were prepared to supply addi-

[42] Baker to Department of State, Feb. 11, 1919, United States, *Foreign Relations, 1919, Russia,* pp. 277-278. Masaryk wrote later, "I cannot and do not wish to defend all that was done politically and strategically in our army after my departure. I perceived that there was some lack of cohesion, political wavering, outbreaks of an adventurous spirit and, often, fits of bewilderment in various units; and I deplore that our command in Siberia should not have recognized forthwith the incapacity of Kolchak . . ." (Masaryk, *The Making of a State,* p. 281).

[43] Sharp to Department of State, Feb. 12, 1919, file 861.00/3837, D.S.N.A.

[44] Phillips to Lansing, March 29, 1919, United States, *Foreign Relations, 1919, Russia,* pp. 279-280.

[45] Harris to Department of State, July 6, 1919, file 861.00/4802, D.S.N.A.; Bliss Diary, June 11 1919.

tional troops to replace the Czechs. Morris was convinced that no arrangement with Japan would prove satisfactory which did not provide that the United States contribute at least one half of the necessary replacements. He informed the State Department that there was a fundamental difference in purpose governing the Siberian policy of Japan and the United States. The Japanese military authorities still desired to use the expedition to Siberia as an excuse to take the Chinese Eastern Railway and dominate North Manchuria and Eastern Siberia. Despite the failure to accomplish their object directly, the purpose still remained. Although the civil party under the leadership of Hara was opposed to this purpose, it was hampered by the powerful military clique. Morris was convinced that Japan was pursuing in Siberia the same methods which had produced "such tragic results in China. . . ." He indicated the necessary remedy:

The Seminoff controversy is, as I see it, simply a sordid conspiracy to practice extortion upon the people of Siberia through control of the customs service at Manchuria Station and of distribution at Chita. We cannot meet this conspiracy and enforce the "Open Door," necessary for the economic salvation of Russia, merely by frank discussions and formal protests in Tokyo. We must speak our determined purpose in the only language the Japanese military clique can understand. This will not lead to friction; on the contrary it will bring about a better understanding. We shall not only help the liberals in Russia; we shall render an even greater service to the liberal and progressive movement in Japan.

The presence of a substantial number of American troops will serve to impress upon the Cossack leaders and other reactionaries . . . the character and extent of the protection we are prepared to give to American agencies.[46]

Despite Morris's reasoned plea and Clemenceau's appeal on the same subject, President Wilson replied "with the utmost regret" that he found it impracticable to furnish additional American troops for the purpose of replacing the Czechs.[47] Thus the Czech problem continued unsolved.

The problem of maintaining harmonious relations with Japan in Siberia also remained unsolved. The State Department knew that Japan was behind many of the outrages committed by the Cossacks. Yet, whenever representations were made concerning them, Japan al-

[46] Morris to Lansing, July 30, 1919, United States, *Foreign Relations, 1919, Russia*, pp. 292-294. Polk had already informed President Wilson that all reports indicated that Allied troops would probably be required to replace the Czechs when they were withdrawn (Polk to Wilson, July 16, 1919, Wilson Papers, series II).

[47] Lansing to the Commission to Negotiate Peace, Aug. 8, 1919, United States, *Foreign Relations, 1919, Russia*, p. 295.

ways politely and courteously disclaimed all connections with them. The Japanese War Office found it more difficult to explain its actions in Siberia to the Japanese Diet.[48] On March 31, after a heated debate in the Diet, General Giichi Tanaka, the Minister of War, called upon Morris to discuss the apparent conflict of policy between American and Japanese forces in Siberia. He explained that since Japan was changing its troops, substituting new divisions for old ones, the time had come to redefine a joint policy in Siberia. He expressed his personal conviction that military activities should be confined thereafter to the guarding of the railroad. Morris interpreted Tanaka's friendliness as an indication that the dominant influences in the General Staff had abandoned their plans for independent action in Siberia and were prepared to co-operate with General Graves and to modify their previous policy of supporting local Cossack leaders.[49]

Wilson was deliberating over the Siberian problem while Morris and Tanaka conferred in Tokyo. His solution was similar to that of Tanaka. In order to insure uninterrupted operation of the Trans-Siberian and Chinese Eastern Railroads, the President proposed that a zone of three miles be established on either side of the railroad and that the Allies exercise definite police power within that region and prevent any disturbance that might interfere with the operation of the railways.[50]

Although General March declared that the proposition was "ridiculous,"[51] Secretary Baker thought it might be workable if modified. He pointed out that if the Allies assumed responsibility for a six-mile zone along the Trans-Siberian Railway, they would need a military force of perhaps five hundred thousand men, which would necessitate large additions to the American or Japanese forces. In any case, it would place a large section of the railway under Japanese control. Moreover, the establishment of such a long zone would tend to increase the frequency of conflicts between the Allied forces and the various elements of the native population. Such conflicts would appear to justify assumption of civil control, and perhaps military repression, which in effect would mean occupation and administration of Siberia by Japan. Therefore, Baker suggested that the objectives of Allied military forces be limited to the preservation of order in the immedi-

[48] Takeuchi, *War and Diplomacy*, pp. 210-211.

[49] Morris to Polk, March 31, 1919, United States, *Foreign Relations, 1919, Russia*, pp. 551-552.

[50] Commission to Negotiate Peace to the Acting Secretary of State, April 1, 1919, United States, *Foreign Relations, 1919, Russia*, pp. 552-553.

[51] Polk, Confidential Diary, April 4, 1919.

ate vicinity of the railroad and its stations as those in charge of the railroad might request. Baker suggested that the State Department clearly indicate its disinclination to send additional troops to Siberia, or to see additions made by other nations. Baker believed that this plan would limit military activity to the railroad and to existing forces, and give no implied sanction to the extension of military or political activities by any other nation.[52]

President Wilson approved Baker's policy. So also did Ambassador Morris, who thought it might be agreeable to Japan since Baron Tanaka himself had presented a somewhat similar scheme. Morris's assumption was correct. Tanaka was quite agreeable and made a real effort to be cordial. Referring of his own accord to the recent newspaper campaign in the United States and Japan which tended to disturb friendly relations, Tanaka announced his intention to issue a statement as War Minister emphasizing the frank and cordial relations now existing between the two nations. He also planned to have an entertainment in Morris's honor and significantly asked the ambassador to submit to him the names of any American writers or newspapermen to whom he might extend invitations.[53]

On May 2 the Japanese government transmitted to Morris a suggested military policy in Siberia. It provided for the establishment of a zone for the protection of railways, rivers, and waterways in Siberia. Associated troops were to maintain order within the limits of the zone. The Russians were to be responsible for the maintenance of order outside the zone. However, the Omsk government was to be aided morally and materially in its efforts to re-establish order, peace, and security in Siberia. Furthermore, if the Russian troops found their strength inadequate to maintain order in the regions outside the specified zone and sought Allied assistance, the Associated powers upon consultation might extend to them the necessary assistance.[54]

Although interested in protecting the railways in Manchuria and Siberia, the United States was opposed to the establishment of a definite zone of military action along the rivers or waterways. The State De-

[52] Baker to Wilson, April 3, 1919, file 861.77/780, D.S.N.A.

[53] Morris to Polk, April 25, 1919, United States, *Foreign Relations, 1919, Russia,* pp. 556-557. The statement given to the newspapers appears quite humorous in retrospect: "There have recently been some rumors of unpleasant relations between Japanese and American troops in Siberia. This is, however, mournful guesswork of those who do not know the true conditions . . . there exists [*sic*] no reasons or facilities liable to harm the friendly relations between the troops of the two nations in Siberia" (Morris to Polk, April 29, 1919, United States, *Foreign Relations, 1919, Russia,* p. 558).

[54] Morris to Polk, May 2, 1919, United States, *Foreign Relations, 1919, Russia,* p. 559.

partment felt that it would be wiser to define Allied policy in the following terms:

The Governments interested in the protection of Chinese Eastern and Trans-Siberian Railways and having military forces in Siberia agree that the use of these military forces shall be limited to the preservation of order in the immediate vicinity of the railway, its stations and trains, when those in charge so request and in the suppression of local violence by conflicting Russian forces only when such conflicts affect the dispatch of troops or operation of the railways and even then only to the extent necessary to protect the railway and those engaged in its operation.[55]

Before the State Department presented its statement to Japan, it had secured London's agreement to the idea that the Inter-Allied Committee "take preeminence in all matters affecting policy so that both the Technical Board and the military boards may act along lines consistent with attitude assumed by Inter-Allied Committee."[56]

The Japanese government did not approve of the American modification of its military plan. The American note, in effect, gave to the Inter-Allied Committee the authority to determine when troops should be used for the preservation of order along the railways. The Minister for Foreign Affairs felt that the protection of the railways was clearly a matter for the Allied military forces and fell outside the function of the Inter-Allied Committee. The Japanese note of June 2 stated the attitude of the General Staff quite bluntly: "The military forces should be authorized to act on their own initiative within the scope of the object above defined. It appears neither wise nor practicable to call upon them to withhold their actions until a request for it is made by those in charge of the railways." Japan also retained her idea of military protection not only for rivers and waterways, but also for mines and other establishments which had a direct bearing upon the supply of materials needed for the railway.

Morris was quite disappointed in the. Japanese attitude. It revealed to him the inherent difficulty of any real co-operation with the Japanese military forces in Siberia through civilian control. As Morris pointed out, "the General Staff insist upon retaining the initiative. They can not understand and will not tolerate any arrangement which would deprive them of independent action and it is this attitude, adopted not only by the General Staff but by every subordinate mili-

[55] Morris to Polk, May 23, 1919, United States, *Foreign Relations, 1919, Russia*, pp. 562, 563.
[56] Polk to Davis, April 26, 1919, Davis to Polk, May 3, 1919, United States, *Foreign Relations, 1919, Russia*, pp. 537, 560.

tary official, which is so exasperating to our representatives in Siberia."[57]
It appeared that the United States and Japan had reached an impasse
over the formulation of a policy in Siberia.

An equally exasperating state of affairs existed along the Trans-
Siberian and Chinese Eastern Railways. The Japanese military authorities refused to protect the representatives of the Technical Board in
the performance of their duties and the enforcement of their orders.
The Russian military authorities were constantly interfering with the
dispatching of trains and other technical details of operation, while
the Russian railway managers refused to obey the directions of the
Technical Board, insisting that such directions were in conflict with
Russian laws and regulations which had never been repealed.[58] At
the same time, while Semenov's hostile acts against American inspectors grew worse, Japanese soldiers gave Stevens "absolutely no
protection." Japanese military authorities refused to restrain Semenov
on the grounds that such actions would be interference in Russian
internal affairs.[59] To Ambassador Morris the Japanese plan was perfectly clear:

Baffled by the railway agreement in their organized attempt to take possession of the Chinese Eastern and Trans-Siberian Railways as far as Chita
and thus dominate eastern Siberia and northern Manchuria the Japanese
Government is countenancing a less obvious, but a more insidious scheme
of operating through the Cossack organization which is the only substantial support Kolchak has east of Chita. It will not be difficult for
Japan to dispose of the eastern Cossacks when they have served the purpose.[60]

Whereas the Japanese military authorities refused to restrain Semenov, the Omsk government was powerless to control him or prevent
his interference with the railroad in the territory which he dominated.
Semenov, emboldened by the passive attitude of Japan, defied the
authority of the Inter-Allied representatives and terrorized the railway
employees. Thus, American engineers found themselves alone at
widely separated stations along the railway, surrounded by hostile
Cossacks, and unable to rely on the protection of the Japanese soldiers.

[57] Morris to Polk, June 7, 1919, United States, *Foreign Relations, 1919, Russia*, pp.
563-565.
[58] Morris to Polk, July 27, 1919, United States, *Foreign Relations, 1919, Russia*, pp.
567-568.
[59] Stevens to Polk, Aug. 15, 1919, Lansing to Caldwell, Aug. 21, 1919, United
States, *Foreign Relations, 1919, Russia*, pp. 570, 572-573.
[60] Morris to Polk, July 17, 1919, United States, *Foreign Relations, 1919, Russia*,
p. 567.

In these circumstances Stevens and Emerson did not feel justified in risking the lives of American engineers and were preparing to withdraw them from the Semenov area.[61] Relations between Japan and the United States were critical. If the two nations could come to no agreement, the United States was faced with two alternatives: either to send more troops to protect Stevens in the execution of the railway agreement or to withdraw American troops entirely.

[61] Morris to Lansing, Aug. 15, 1919, file 861.00/1025, D.S.N.A.

CHAPTER VIII

Wanted: A Russian Policy

PRESIDENT Wilson's Russian policy received little criticism in Congress or in the press as long as the war in Europe was in progress. The enormousness of the task of crushing Germany prevented such criticism as long as the Russian policy might be interpreted as a means of stopping Germany. However, after the signing of the Armistice, attitudes changed. Congress began to show a keen interest in what seemed to many to be a little war with Russia. Criticism of Wilson's Russian policy grew louder and more intense as the year 1919 wore on. Political partisans, isolationists, and constituents who desired the return of their husbands and sons demanded the withdrawal of troops from Russia. Many people found it difficult to reconcile Wilson's idealistic phrases concerning Russia with his policy of military intervention.[1] Many were opposed to the extent of the intervention. Others condemned the vacillation in policy rather than the policy itself. Time and again newspapers and periodicals urged either a complete withdrawal of troops or a reinforcement sufficient to crush Bolshevism. Interestingly enough, the general run of articles assumed that American policy was aimed at crushing Bolshevism. Thus the writers could not understand how a small contingent of American troops could be of any value.[2] Few guessed that Wilson's Russian policy might be more concerned with keeping the open door in Siberia.

Throughout December, 1918, and January, 1919, a group of Republican senators assailed vigorously the policy of intervention, demanding information concerning Russia and Siberia. What was most irritating to the opposition was their lack of knowledge concerning the admin-

[1] *Congressional Record,* vol. 57, part 1, p. 346.
[2] For representative articles expressing these points of view, see the following: "Withdraw from Russia," *Dial,* LXV (Dec. 14, 1918), 525-528; "Justice to Russia," *Nation,* CVIII (Jan. 4, 1919), 6-7; "American Policy in Russia," *New Republic,* XVIII (Feb. 8, 1919), 37-39; *Literary Digest,* LXIII (Oct. 4, 1919), 17-18.

istration policy in Russia. On December 12, 1918, Hiram Johnson, Republican senator from California, introduced a resolution asking for all data, documents, and information showing or bearing upon American relations with Russia as to peace or war. Said Johnson: "I have made diligent private inquiry without success and because I do not know and we do not know, the situation in Russia today, what we are fighting for there and what ultimately we seek to obtain, I publicly now repeat the inquiries unsuccessfully made privately."[3]

Wilson's supporters in Congress were able to give only a weak defense for the administration as they knew no more about the policy than did the opposition. Those Congressmen who favored the policy advocated sending more troops to save all the Czechs from the "hell of Bolshevism," salvage every dollar of Allied equipment, and help the people of Russia to get a government of their own choosing. Their speeches generally ended with tirades against Bolshevism.[4]

Although the Congressional debates resulted in no definite action, they were not completely without effect. The debates disturbed Acting Secretary Polk, who believed that American troops in North Russia should be withdrawn. General March had been urging such action upon him. And on February 17, 1919, Secretary Baker announced that American troops would be withdrawn from North Russia at the earliest possible moment.[5] Polk, however, did not favor withdrawing American troops from Siberia. There, the United States had finally come to an arrangement with the Japanese on the operation of the railways. If troops were withdrawn, it would be impossible to keep Stevens and his men there. Thus Siberia presented a more complicated problem than North Russia.[6]

On January 31, 1919, President Wilson decided that perhaps the best method of dealing with Congress was to be completely frank. He instructed Polk to request a hearing before certain Congressional committees and explain the Siberian situation in complete and strict

[3] *Congressional Record*, vol. 57, part 1, pp. 342-346. The Senate Committee on Foreign Affairs also registered its intention to ask the State Department to explain its policy in an executive session. Although Acting Secretary Polk thought it best to agree to appear, he doubted the desirability of discussing at length the difficulties with Japan (Polk to Commission to Negotiate Peace, Dec. 31, 1918, United States, *Foreign Relations, Paris Peace Conference*, II, 483).

[4] *Congressional Record*, vol. 57, part 2, pp. 1391-1393.

[5] Polk to Commission to Negotiate Peace, Dec. 31, 1918, United States, *Foreign Relations, Paris Peace Conference*, II, 483; Polk, Confidential Diary, Dec. 14, 1918; New York *Times*, Feb. 18, 1919.

[6] Polk to Commission to Negotiate Peace, Dec. 31, 1918, United States, *Foreign Relations, Paris Peace Conference*, II, 483.

confidence. When Polk advised against the scheme, the plan was dropped. However, Polk was told to take the first opportunity to inform Congress of the policy adopted in regard to the Siberian railways, and to stress the importance of maintaining the policy of the open door with reference to the Siberian and particularly the Chinese Eastern Railway.[7]

Throughout 1919 public sentiment against the Bolsheviks grew in intensity throughout the United States. Senators, congressmen, respected government officials, and the newspapers described the brutalities of the Bolsheviks in lurid language. Porter J. McCumber, Republican Senator from North Dakota, favored "maintaining war against Lenin and Trotsky, and . . . fighting the battles of the poor, innocent Russian people, who are in the grasp of these damnable beasts." After reciting a long list of Bolshevik atrocities, McCumber declared that "the civilization of the world demands the extermination of such beasts."[8] Speeches such as these gained powerful supporters for the intervention policy. In view of such propaganda and despite strong isolationist sentiment in the Senate, Senator Johnson was unable to secure the passage of a resolution demanding the withdrawal of soldiers from Russia.[9] On the other hand, a resolution providing for the *de facto* recognition of the Omsk government and assistance to it in overthrowing the "Bolshevist tyranny and anarchy" was buried in the Committee on Foreign Relations.[10]

The publication of the so-called "Sisson Documents" contributed to the American feeling against Bolshevism. Edgar Sisson, the associate chairman of the Committee on Public Information, had obtained these documents under dramatic circumstances in Petrograd.[11] He accepted them as proving that the Bolshevik government was not a Russian government at all but a German government "acting solely in the interests of Germany and betraying the Russian people as it betrays Russia's Allies, for the benefit of the Imperial German Gov-

[7] Polk to Commission to Negotiate Peace, Feb. 4, 1919, United States, *Foreign Relations, 1919, Russia,* pp. 248-249.

[8] *Congressional Record,* vol. 57, part 4, p. 37455, part 5, pp. 4883-4887. Congress conducted a full-scale investigation of such stories and emerged with some 1,200 pages of evidence which depicted Russia as a completely barbaric state. See U. S. Congress, Senate, Committee on the Judiciary, *Brewing and Liquor Interests and German and Bolshevik Propaganda* (66th Congress, 1st Session, Senate Document No. 61).

[9] *Congressional Record,* vol. 57, part 2, p. 1313; *Literary Digest,* LX (March 1, 1919), 18.

[10] *Congressional Record,* vol. 58, part 1, p. 157.

[11] Sisson, *One Hundred Red Days,* pp. 358-369.

ernment alone."[12] Sisson's report was placed in President Wilson's hands on May 9, 1918, and was released to the press on September 15, 1918, apparently with the President's approval. The report was generally accepted at face value.[13]

By the middle of May the weight of Congressional opinion had begun to turn against the retention of troops in Siberia. Even the increasing hatred of Bolshevism could not stem the tide of isolationism

[12] *The German-Bolshevik Conspiracy* (War Information Series, No. 20: Washington, Oct., 1918), p. 3.

[13] James R. Mock and Cedric Larson, *Words That Won the War: The Story of the Committee on Public Information 1917-1919* (Princeton, 1939), pp. 314-317; Sisson, *One Hundred Red Days*, p. 366. Prior to publication, charges of forgery were made, and George Creel, chairman of the Committee on Public Information, submitted the documents to a committee of the National Board of Historical Service (Dr. J. Franklin Jameson and Professor Samuel N. Harper), who upheld their authenticity in "every essential particular" (*The German-Bolshevik Conspiracy*, p. 3; Baker, *Woodrow Wilson*, VIII, 402). Professor Harper later wrote: "Professor Jameson and I had access to the original documents where Sisson had such. . . . With respect to those documents which we had in the original, we expressed the view that, as students of history, we would accept them. We refused to express an opinion on those documents for which only translations had been obtained. . . . We flatly refused to comment on Sisson's conclusions as to what the documents proved, namely, that Lenin not only had had contacts with the German general staff when he journeyed across Germany but had been and still was a German agent. . . . But the general view current at the time was that he had declared all the documents genuine beyond any question" (Samuel N. Harper, *The Russia I Believe In: The Memoirs of Samuel N. Harper, 1902-1941,* Chicago, 1945, pp. 111-112). Many attacks have since been made on the documents, some with evidence, others without evidence. See Ross, *Soviet Republic,* p. 140; Schuman, *American Policy towards Russia since 1917,* pp. 152-153; Mock and Larson, *Words That Won the War,* pp. 316-320; E. H. Wilcox, *Russia's Ruin* (New York, 1919), pp. 248-249; W. A. Williams, *American-Russian Relations,* pp. 136, 154-155. President Masaryk is quoted as saying in his *Memoirs:* "I do not know what the Americans, the English and the French paid for these documents, but to anyone accustomed to dealing with matters of this kind, their contents alone are sufficient to reveal that our friends had purchased forgeries" (Boris Souvarine, *Stalin, a Critical Survey of Bolshevism,* New York, 1939, p. 165). The Soviet authorities pronounced the documents to be forgeries soon after their appearance (Van Santwood Merle-Smith, Third Assistant Secretary of State, to Evan D. Young, American Commissioner to the Baltic Provinces, Oct. 21, 1921, file 861.00/7603a, D.S.N.A.). Captain George A. Hill of the British Secret Service later wrote: "I can say at once and definitely that the more important of these are forgeries, for afterwards with Sidney Reilly's help, I succeeded in running to earth the man who forged them" (Hill, *Go Spy the Land,* London, 1932, p. 201). Early in October of 1918, Balfour sent the President a confidential message "that English experts and authorities had gone over the Sisson papers carefully and had come to the conclusion that they were forgeries" (Baker, *Woodrow Wilson,* VIII, 402). A check of the Sisson documents and the correspondence relating to them in the State Department revealed that information concerning the authenticity of the documents was still being sought by the department as late as 1921 (Secretary of State to Evan D. Young, Oct. 21, 1921, file 861.00/7603a, D.S.N.A.; Ellis Loring Dresel to Secretary of State, Jan. 3, 1921, file 861.00/8014; Alvey A. Adee to Rudolph Forster, Executive Secretary of the White House, May 24, 1921, file 861.00/8663a, D.S.N.A.).

which was sweeping the country. On May 20, 1919, Senator Johnson presented a resolution directing the Secretary of State to inform the Senate immediately of the reasons for sending American troops to Siberia.[14] On June 27 the Senate by unanimous consent finally approved Senator Johnson's resolution with amendments and addressed the inquiry to the President.[15]

In the meantime the President's Russian policy was attacked in the House. On May 22 Representative Mason of Illinois introduced a resolution providing for the withdrawal of all American troops from Russia.[16] Representative Wood of Indiana charged that American troops were being kept in Siberia to protect the investments of private American citizens in the Trans-Siberian Railway.[17] The discussion resulted in no official action.

On July 22 President Wilson replied to Senator Johnson's resolution for information. Referring to the declaration of August 3, 1918, Wilson pointed out that American troops were sent to Siberia in order to save the Czechoslovaks from destruction at the hands of "hostile armies apparently organized by, and often largely composed of, enemy prisoners of war," and to steady the efforts of the Russians at self-defense and the establishment of law and order. Allied efforts had succeeded in reuniting the separated Czechoslovak armies. The President then indicated why American troops remained in Siberia. The United States had accepted the Japanese railway plan, which provided for an efficient operation of the Trans-Siberian and Chinese Eastern Railways, essential arteries of transportation for extending economic aid to the vast population of Siberia. Since the line was constantly menaced by Cossacks and Bolsheviks, military protection was necessary for the engineers as well as the railways. Wilson stated that such protection was a vital necessity, since the population of Western Siberia and Admiral Kolchak were entirely dependent upon the railways.[18] The President's explanation was generally accepted as adequate.[19]

Although President Wilson made no public reference to the difficulties with Japan or the necessity for maintaining the policy of the

---

[14] *Congressional Record*, vol. 58, part 1, pp. 63, 64.

[15] *Congressional Record*, vol. 58, part 2, p. 1864.

[16] *Congressional Record*, vol. 58, part 3, pp. 1783-1784.

[17] *Congressional Record*, vol. 58, part 2, p. 1530.

[18] *Senate Document* 60 (66th Congess, 1st Session), pp. 2-4; *Congressional Record*, vol. 58, part 5, p. 4816.

[19] For bitter attacks on the President's explanation, see "The Crime against Russia," *Nation*, CIX (Aug. 2, 1919), 136; "President Masaryk on Intervention," *New Republic*, XIX (July 23, 1919), 377.

open door in Siberia and Manchuria, these were certainly basic reasons for retaining American troops in Siberia. In August, 1919, Breckinridge Long, Third Assistant Secretary of State, went before the House Committee on Foreign Affairs and in careful detail described all of the events which led to the sending of American troops to Siberia and to their retention there.[20] He answered the questions of the committee fully and frankly. His testimony clearly revealed that the guiding motive of American policy in Siberia and Northern Manchuria had been the maintenance of the open door free from Japanese imperialistic designs.[21]

While Congress discussed the problem of Russia, so also did Allied statesmen at the Paris Peace Conference. Many of the reasons which had originally been given to justify intervention could no longer be used. Thus, the Allies were faced with the task of adopting a common policy toward Russia.

From the very outset there was little unity in the views of the Allies in regard to Russia. When the Russian problem was discussed on January 12, 1919, Marshal Foch immediately urged a quick peace with Germany in order to permit the Allies to begin an anti-Bolshevik crusade. He wished to crush Bolshevism by force, using American troops primarily.[22] Wilson objected. Although Communism was indeed a "social and political danger," he doubted whether it could be checked by force of arms.[23] He believed that food would be the best weapon to stop Bolshevism. With this end in mind, he proposed to negotiate with the Russians.[24] Clemenceau disagreed. He believed that if the Allies continued to furnish the various governments fighting against the Bolsheviks with money, arms, and such military support as was practicable, the Soviet government would ultimately collapse.[25]

The lack of unity among the Associated powers in regard to Russia was also noticeable among the various statesmen from the individual

[20] This was in accordance with the President's instructions (Commission to Negotiate Peace to Polk, Feb. 9, 1919, United States, *Foreign Relations, 1919, Russia,* p. 251).

[21] Statement of the Honorable Breckinridge Long before the House Committee on Foreign Affairs, Aug., 1919, file 861.00, Vol. XXXIX, D.S.N.A.

[22] Supreme War Council, 9th Session, Jan. 12, 1919, World War I Records of the Supreme War Council, Old Records Section, Department of War, National Archives.

[23] Ray Stannard Baker, *Woodrow Wilson and World Settlement* (3 vols.; New York, 1922), I, 166.

[24] Wilson to Lansing, Jan. 10, 1919, Wilson Papers, series VIII-A.

[25] Barclay to Polk, Jan. 13, 1919, United States, *Foreign Relations, 1919, Russia,* p. 7.

nations, particularly the United States and Great Britain. Although Britain had made the greatest contribution to the interventionist cause, her Prime Minister, Lloyd George, more than once voiced his opposition to the policy of intervention, and at times even advocated coming to terms with the Bolsheviks.[26]   On the other hand, War Minister Churchill, a strong and steady advocate of maximum intervention, was quite often directly opposed to the views of Lloyd George.[27]   He was supported by General Henry Wilson, who advocated arming Russian prisoners of war in Germany to fight against the Bolsheviks. General Wilson could not understand why Lloyd George was "such a fool" about Bolshevism.[28]   The interventionist policies of both Churchill and General Wilson were approved by British military representatives in Russia. A somewhat similar situation existed in American councils. Ambassador Francis was implacably opposed to the Soviet regime. Considering Bolshevism a disgrace to civilization, he advocated its complete extermination.[29]   He was convinced that nothing but military intervention would cure the situation in Russia. General Bliss found both Francis and Riggs, the American military attaché in Russia, thoroughly obsessed with this idea, and in a state of mind to condemn as Bolsheviks all those who had different views.[30]   Consul General Poole in Moscow was also completely opposed to any dealings with the Bolsheviks, and agreed with Francis's views on intervention. In this respect he was supported by most of the men who were close to the scene in Russia. However, these views were not held by either Wilson or House, who were completely opposed to any further thought of intervention. They believed it had only served to strengthen the cause of the Bolsheviks.

The French statesmen appeared the most violent in their hatred of the Soviet regime. They firmly refused to have any dealings with the Bolsheviks. Both France and Great Britain bitterly resented the Soviet repudiation of the Russian prewar debts and the confiscation of

[26] Winston Churchill, *The World Crisis* (4 vols.; New York, 1923-1929), IV (*The Aftermath*), 266-268.

[27] Lloyd George wrote that "the most formidable and irrepressible protagonist for an anti-Bolshevik war was Mr. Winston Churchill" (Lloyd George, *Memoirs of the Peace Conference*, 2 vols.; New Haven, 1939, I, 214).

[28] Callwell, *Sir Henry Wilson*, II, 163, 165.

[29] Francis, *Russia from the American Embassy*, pp. 313-318. Apparently he believed that from the outset American policy had been aimed at exterminating Bolshevism. At one point, he wrote, "It may be that our policy toward Russia is influenced by threats of Japanese aggression or maybe Japanese invasion, but if so you have never advised me thereof" (Francis to Lansing, Jan. 11, 1919, Lansing Papers).

[30] Bliss, Paris Peace Conference Diary, Feb. 3, 1919, Bliss Papers.

foreign property. In addition, some statesmen still regarded as shameful Russia's desertion of the Allies during the war. Although the Allies were all agreed in their opposition to Bolshevism, none would pledge to send additional troops to fight against it.[31]

As early as January 3, 1919, the British government had dispatched notes to Paris, Rome, Washington, and Tokyo, suggesting that the Allies propose a truce to Admiral Kolchak, General A. I. Deniken, commander-in-chief of the armed forces of South Russia, Nicholas Tchaikovsky, President of the North Russian government, and the Soviet authorities for the duration of the Peace Conference, and invite them to send delegates to Paris.[32]

The French Foreign Minister was outraged at the idea of negotiating with the Soviets. He would make "no contract with crime." Attempting to explain the British proposal at a meeting of the Big Five, Lloyd George pointed out that the scheme did not contemplate recognition of the Soviet regime. It merely suggested a truce among the various factions in Russia.[33] Once such a truce had been made, representatives of the various Russian governments could be invited to come to Paris to explain their positions and receive suggestions from the Allies for the alleviation of their differences. To Lloyd George this seemed to be the only solution to the problem. The idea of suppressing Bolshevism by force was not only "pure madness" but also militarily unfeasible, while the suggested project of a *cordon sanitaire* was too inhumane for consideration since it would mean the starvation of millions. In these circumstances the British proposal seemed the only reasonable alternative.[34]

President Wilson favored the proposal. He was confirmed in his position by a report which he had just received from W. H. Buckler, attaché of the American Embassy at London. Just back from a conference with Maxim Litvinov in Russia, Buckler reported that the Soviet government was eager for permanent peace and was willing to compromise on all points.[35] Wilson presented Litvinov's peace pro-

[31] Lansing to Polk, Jan. 27, 1919, United States, *Foreign Relations, 1919, Russia,* p. 35.

[32] Barclay to Polk, Jan. 3, 1919, United States, *Foreign Relations, 1919, Russia,* pp. 2-3.

[33] Lord Bertie, British ambassador to France, pointed out that Lloyd George "would not have had such a triumphant majority at the General Election if the public had known his intentions at the Paris Peace Conference in regard to the Bolsheviks" (Lennox, *Diary of Lord Bertie,* II, 314).

[34] United States, *Foreign Relations, 1919, Russia,* pp. 10-14.

[35] Buckler to Lansing, Jan. 18, 1919, United States, *Foreign Relations, 1919, Russia,* p. 15; Lloyd George, *Memoirs of the Peace Conference,* I, 225.

posals to his colleagues and urged the French to swallow their pride and repulsion and see the representatives of all organized Russian groups. Later in the day, in deference to Clemenceau, Wilson suggested that the British proposal be modified to permit the Russian representatives to meet at some other place besides Paris.[36] On January 22 Wilson suggested as a site for the meeting Prinkipo or Prince's Island in the Sea of Marmora. The invitation, drafted by Wilson, proposed a free and frank exchange of views so that the desires of all groups of the Russian people might be made known and so that an agreement might be reached by means of which Russia could define its own intentions and establish a basis of co-operation with other nations. The invitation proposed a general armistice between the contending forces in Russia and set February 15 as the date for the conference. The French and Italians yielded very reluctantly to Wilson's insistence.[37] Neither Balfour nor Churchill approved of the scheme, while General Wilson considered it absolutely "disgraceful."[38] Lord Bertie recorded in his diary his belief that "Clemenceau found it advisable to make a concession to the inexperience of President Wilson and to the obstinacy of Lloyd George in the expectation that, even if the Soviet Government accept the invitation and terms, they will not observe the conditions of the invitation. This may prove a very dangerous and costly way of demonstrating to Messrs. Wilson and Lloyd George that they have been, to say the least, very foolish."[39]

The opposition of Churchill, Balfour, and General Wilson was supported by certain members of the State Department, who condemned any policy which meant dealing with the Bolsheviks.[40] From England Ambassador Francis presented a lengthy protest against the proposal,[41] while Chargé DeWitt C. Poole in Moscow offered his resignation on the grounds that he could not serve under a Russian policy which contained no word of condemnation for the "utter wickedness and evilness" of the Bolsheviks.[42]

When Acting Secretary Polk learned of the call for the Prinkipo

[36] United States, *Foreign Relations, 1919, Russia*, pp. 18-25.

[37] United States, *Foreign Relations, 1919, Russia*, p. 31.

[38] Callwell, *Sir Henry Wilson*, II, 167.

[39] Lennox, *Diary of Lord Bertie*, II, 314-315.

[40] New York *Times*, Jan. 24 and 25, 1919; United States, *Foreign Relations, 1919, Russia*, pp. 32, 37-38, 44-46, 54-55.

[41] United States, *Foreign Relations, 1919, Russia*, pp. 27-30.

[42] Poole to Polk, Feb. 4, 1919, United States, *Foreign Relations, 1919, Russia*, p. 42. Poole was urged not to resign because of the effect on the morale of American troops in the Archangel district (Polk to Commission to Negotiate Peace, Feb. 7, 1919, United States, *Foreign Relations, 1919, Russia*, p. 46).

Conference, he pointed out that it would probably destroy the morale of all parties opposing the Bolsheviks. He suggested that Lansing consider the possibility of recognizing the Omsk government. "This would undoubtedly strengthen it so it could withstand the crisis created by the recent action of the Peace Conference." Polk thought that if recognition were not deemed wise, at least some statement should be made to the Omsk government so as "not to entirely discourage" it.[43]

From Siberia, Archangel, and Southern Russia the Prinkipo proposal was indignantly rejected. "Under no circumstances whatever, would there be any question of an exchange of ideas on this matter with the participation of the Bolshevists, in whom the conscience of the Russian people sees only traitors."[44]

The Soviet reply to the Prinkipo proposal was quite conciliatory. The Bolsheviks expressed a desire to end hostilities and begin negotiations at once. They offered to make territorial and economic concessions in return for peace. Moreover, they evinced a readiness to make certain concessions in regard to Russia's financial obligations. Although they agreed to refrain from interference in the internal affairs of the Allied powers, they refused to "limit the freedom of the revolutionary press."[45] Since the White Russian governments refused to consider a conference with the Bolsheviks, and since the Bolsheviks, although willing to confer, would make no specific pledges to stop the advance of their armies, the Prinkipo proposal came to a lingering end.

February 15, the deadline set for the final acceptance or rejection of the Prinkipo plan, was also the date of President Wilson's first return to the United States. The day before Wilson left Paris, Churchill came over from England specifically for the purpose of getting the President's views on the Russian problem. The conference sat long that day, and it was past seven by the time the Russian

[43] Polk to Lansing, Feb. 1, 1919, United States, *Foreign Relations, 1919, Russia*, pp. 38-39.

[44] Russian Embassy in France to Secretariat-General of the Paris Peace Conference, Feb. 12, 1919, United States, *Foreign Relations, 1919, Russia*, pp. 53-54; New York *Times*, Feb. 20, 1919. For replies of other Russian groups, see Cumming and Pettit, *Russian-American Relations*, pp. 298-306.

[45] Soviet Commissar for Foreign Affairs (Chicherin) to the Principal Allied and Associated Governments, Feb. 4, 1919, United States, *Foreign Relations, 1919, Russia*, pp. 39-42. Nabokov, Russian chargé d'affaires in London, felt that White Russian prestige had suffered by this refusal to accept the Prinkipo proposal when the Soviets had appeared so eager to accept the invitation (Nabokov, *The Ordeal of a Diplomat*, pp. 286-287).

item was reached. The President was actually ready to leave when Churchill asked for some decision on Russia. What was to be the policy, peace or war? Surely the President would not leave Paris without answering so important a question.[46]

The President was quite affable. He had a very clear opinion on two points. First, he believed that Allied intervention was doing no good in Russia. Therefore he advocated the withdrawal of Allied and Associated troops from all parts of Russian territory. The second point related to Prinkipo. The President was not opposed to an informal meeting between American representatives and the representatives of the Bolsheviks for the purpose of securing information.[47] Wilson pointed out that since official and unofficial reports were conflicting, it was impossible to obtain a coherent picture of Russian affairs. Some light might be cast on the subject by a meeting with the Russian representatives.

Churchill agreed that the withdrawal of troops from Russia was a logical and clear-cut policy. However, it would leave some five hundred thousand non-Bolshevik troops at the mercy of the Bolsheviks. Thus there would be no further armed resistance to the Bolsheviks in Russia. All that remained then for Russia was "an interminable vista of violence and misery."

President Wilson replied that since the existing Allied troops in Russia could not stop the Bolsheviks, and since none of the Allies could reinforce its armies there, withdrawal seemed the best solution. Moreover, even when the Allies supplied the non-Bolsheviks with arms, they "made very little use of them." Undeterred by Wilson's evident lack of confidence in the anti-Bolsheviks, Churchill again raised the question of arming them if the Prinkipo Conference proved a failure.

President Wilson replied that "he hesitated to express any definite opinion on this question. He had explained to the Council how he would act if alone. He would, however, cast in his lot with the rest."[48] Churchill recorded the President's concluding statement as follows: "Nevertheless, if Prinkipo came to nothing, he would do his share with the other Allies in any military measures which they considered neces-

---

[46] Churchill, *The Aftermath*, pp. 173-174.

[47] General Sir Henry Wilson recorded this conversation to the effect that the President had stated that "(a) he would withdraw all Allied troops from Russia, and (b) he would meet Bolsheviks alone at Prinkipo" (Callwell, *Sir Henry Wilson*, II, 170).

[48] Minutes of the 14th Session of the Supreme War Council held in M. Pichon's Room at the Quai d'Orsay, Paris, Feb. 14, 1919, United States, *Foreign Relations, 1919, Russia*, pp. 57-59.

sary and practicable to help the Russian armies now in the field."[49]

On February 17, 1919, at the next meeting of the Supreme War Council, Churchill submitted a resolution directing the military representatives to report on the possibilities of joint military action by the Associated powers to aid the White Russian armies to maintain themselves against Bolshevik coercion. They were also directed to report on the measures and precautions necessary to safeguard Finland, Esthonia, Livonia, Poland, and Romania. The American representatives opposed the adoption of the resolution.[50]

Greatly surprised by Churchill's action, President Wilson registered his immediate opposition. He pointed out that the views which he had expressed on February 14 were only meant to convey the idea that he would "take no separate action" himself. However, he was not in favor of any course which did not mean the "earliest practicable withdrawal of military forces."[51] Wilson cabled House to make it plain to the Allied statesmen that "we are not at war with Russia and will in no circumstances that we can now foresee, take part in military operations there against the Russians."[52]

General Bliss immediately explained Wilson's views to Churchill, and the project was dropped.[53] In the notes which Bliss prepared for discussing Churchill's proposal, he used a rather significant argument: "There can be no possible doubt that the United States will decline to take part in any hostile action in Russia as long as the present general conditions *elsewhere* exist."[54] Japan was undoubtedly the *elsewhere* referred to.

The next device adopted in dealing with the Russian problem was the sending of a special emissary to the Soviet government. This project was in line with Wilson's views expressed on the last day of his

[49] Churchill, *The Aftermath*, p. 174.

[50] Lansing to Polk, Feb. 17, 1919, United States, *Foreign Relations, 1919, Russia*, pp. 68-69; Lloyd George, *Memoirs of the Peace Conference*, I, 242.

[51] Wilson to Commission to Negotiate Peace, Feb. 19, 1919, United States, *Foreign Relations, 1919, Russia*, pp. 71-72.

[52] Seymour, *Intimate Papers*, IV, 348. Lloyd George also protested against Churchill's project (Lloyd George, *Memoirs of the Peace Conference*, I, 243-244).

[53] Commission to Negotiate Peace to Polk, Feb. 23, 1919, United States, *Foreign Relations, 1919, Russia*, p. 73; Seymour, *Intimate Papers*, IV, 348. Lieut. General Walter Bedell Smith, ambassador to Russia from 1946 to 1949, reported a conversation with Stalin in which he asked why Stalin thought any power or group of powers was a threat to the U.S.S.R. "Churchill," Stalin replied. "He tried to instigate war against Russia, and persuaded the United States to join him in an armed occupation against part of our territory in 1919. Lately he has been at it again" (Smith, *My Three Years in Moscow*, Philadelphia, 1950, p. 52).

[54] Bliss to House, Feb. 17, 1919, Bliss Papers. Not sent.

stay in Paris. The immediate idea evidently originated with Lincoln Steffens, who conveyed it to his friend, Colonel House. The proposal took shape on February 18, 1919, when Lansing ordered William C. Bullitt, a member of the staff of the American delegation at Paris, to go to Moscow. He was to make a report on the general situation in Russia, and find out what peace conditions were acceptable to the Soviet government.[55] The mission was to be a secret from all except the British delegation. Bullitt discussed the matter with Phillip Kerr, Lloyd George's secretary, who informed him of the British point of view. Both Great Britain and the United States agreed on an outline of peace terms for the Soviet government. The terms included cessation of hostilities on all fronts, continued occupation by the *de facto* governments of the territory which they controlled, free right of entry into Soviet Russia for Allied subjects, general amnesty to all political prisoners on both sides, restoration of trade relations and the withdrawal of Allied troops.[56]

Bullitt reached Petrograd on March 8. He was accompanied by Walter W. Pettit, R. E. Lynch, and Lincoln Steffens. After a week in Russia he returned to Paris with a document containing the terms of peace which the Soviet government pledged itself to accept. The terms differed from the British desires only in a few particulars.[57] Believing that they constituted a practicable basis for peace between the Soviet government and the Allied powers, Bullitt wrote a moving plea to Colonel House: "You must do your utmost for it, for if you had seen the things I have seen during the past week and talked with men I have talked with, I know that you would not rest until you had put through this peace."[58]

The American peace commissioners as well as Lloyd George seemed favorably impressed. According to Bullitt's testimony before the Senate Committee, Colonel House, Secretary Lansing, General Bliss, and Henry White thought it desirable to attempt to bring about peace on the basis of the Moscow proposition. Bullitt was instructed

[55] William C. Bullitt, *Bullitt Mission to Russia; Testimony before the Committee on Foreign Relations, United States* (New York, 1919), p. 4. Steffens reported that House first proposed the idea, Lloyd George planned the visit, while Bullitt's instructions came from House and Lloyd George (Steffens, *Autobiography,* New York, 1931, pp. 790-791).

[56] Bullitt, *Testimony,* pp. 35-37. The Commission to Negotiate Peace informed Polk of the mission, describing it as unofficial and for information only (Feb. 24, 1919, United States, *Foreign Relations, 1919, Russia,* p. 74). Instructions for the mission can be found in *Senate Document 106* (66th Congress, 1st Session), p. 1234.

[57] Cumming and Pettit, *Russian-American Relations,* pp. 317, 320.

[58] Bullitt to House, March 18 (?), 1919, United States, *Foreign Relations, 1919, Russia,* p. 84.

by Colonel House to draft a proposal to the Soviet government similar to theirs.[59]   The day after Bullitt's return he breakfasted with Lloyd George, who thought Bullitt's report of the "utmost importance." However, he did not know what to do with it in the face of British public opinion, which was hysterical on the subject of Russia.   He admitted that all reports received from the people they had sent in for information purposes were similar to Bullitt's.   If someone known to the world as an archconservative made a report similar to Bullitt's, Lloyd George believed it might be accepted by the British people. Balfour also favored the proposal.[60]

Although Lloyd George and Balfour were sympathetic to Bullitt's report, President Wilson did not express his viewpoint to Bullitt directly.   Bullitt made every effort to secure official approval to the Soviet proposals but no action was taken on them.   April 10, the deadline set by the Soviet government, passed and Bullitt resigned in disgust, bitterly criticizing both Wilson and the Peace Conference.[61]

The reasons for the death of the Bullitt proposal could be seen in the rise of a Soviet government in Hungary, led by Bela Kun, and Kolchak's successful advance toward the Volga in March and April.[62] The French government and press were overjoyed at Kolchak's victories and joyfully predicted an early destruction of the Bolshevik regime.   At the same time Lloyd George attempted to convince Parliament of the necessity for sending immediate aid to the White Russians.[63]   Thus was inaugurated a new program for solving Russia's ills: aid to, and recognition of the Kolchak regime.

[59] Bullitt, *Testimony*, pp. 65-73.

[60] Bullitt, *Testimony*, p. 67.

[61] Both Phillip Kerr and Lloyd George denounced Bullitt's testimony before the Senate as a "tissue of lies."   New York *Times*, Sept. 16, 1919.

[62] William H. Chamberlin, *The Russian Revolution, 1917-1921* (2 vols.; New York, 1935), II, 60; Bullitt, *Testimony*, pp. 90-91.   The vacillations in Allied policy toward Russia were cleverly described by Churchill: "The fitful and fluid operations of the Russian armies found a counterpart in the policy, or want of policy, of the Allies. Were they at war with Soviet Russia?   Certainly not; but they shot Soviet Russians at sight.   They stood as invaders on Russian soil.   They armed the enemies of the Soviet Government.   They blockaded its ports, and sunk its battleships.   They earnestly desired and schemed its downfall.   But war—shocking!   Interference—shame!   It was, they repeated, a matter of indifference to them how Russians settled their own affairs. They were impartial—Bang!   And then—parley and try to trade" (Churchill, *The Aftermath*, pp. 243-244).

[63] Great Britain, *House of Commons Debates*, fifth series, CXIV, 2936-2943.

CHAPTER IX

Kolchak and the Allies

AS SOON AS Kolchak established his government at Omsk in November, 1918, the State Department was besieged with pleas from American representatives in Asia advocating support and assistance to the new government. Many members of the State Department favored the idea. President Wilson, however, still expressed opposition to any active intervention in the internal affairs of Russia. France and Great Britain had no such scruples to bind them. Early in 1919 Great Britain expressed its "warmest sympathy" with the Kolchak cause, while the French government expressed to Omsk its pleasure at Kolchak's recent union with General Denikin in Southern Russia.[1] These sentiments pointed to the hope of eventual recognition of the Omsk government.

On January 2 Consul General Harris at Irkutsk recommended that the United States government lend "friendly sympathy and assistance" to the Omsk government in its attempts to "restore law and order" in Siberia.[2] Harris believed that assistance to Kolchak was the best means of combating Bolshevism, which he regarded as a "real world danger." He recommended that the Allies deal with Bolshevism not as a Russian problem, but as a world problem. He added that "unless a systematic and definite military campaign is launched against it, there can be no such thing as peace. Half hearted measures will not suffice."[3]

Secretary Lansing questioned the expediency of either recognizing the Kolchak government or committing the United States to an extensive military undertaking in Siberia. However, he saw nothing contradictory in making a declaration which reiterated America's re-

[1] Reinsch to Polk, Jan. 23 (?), 1919, United States, *Foreign Relations, 1919, Russia*, pp. 327-329.
[2] Polk to Commission to Negotiate Peace, Jan. 2, 1919, United States, *Foreign Relations, 1919, Russia*, p. 322.
[3] Harris to Polk, Jan. 16, 1919, file 861.00/3666, D.S.N.A.

fusal to interfere in Russian internal affairs, and at the same time promised assistance to Kolchak in the form of economic and financial aid and military supplies.[4] Although Polk agreed with Lansing's views, he felt that before the Allies took any further steps, the United States should define its attitude toward the Bolsheviks, decide how far it was prepared and able to go in supporting the elements of law and order, and determine what funds for military supplies could be used for granting aid. The most important step was control of the railroads. As soon as the railroad plan went through, the Allies could decide on the next step.[5] In the meantime the State Department would have to move slowly because Congress was becoming quite concerned about the policy in Russia. While the State Department discussed the possibility of lending assistance to Kolchak, the Red Cross, the YMCA, and the War Trade Board were rendering effective aid and assistance to the people of Siberia. The consular service was co-operating with these three institutions.[6]

While Harris pleaded for assistance to Kolchak, Arthur Bullard, director of the Russian Division of the Committee on Public Information, urged Colonel House to oppose the extension of formal recognition to Kolchak, whose personality, he said, was of small significance. Bullard reported that Kolchak was "surrounded and dependent on the support of reactionary elements whose principal idea of government is the reconquest of former grafts. His army is being organized on old lines of Tsarist discipline. Several units have already revolted against brutality of officers." Furthermore, his vengeance against the Bolsheviks was as red as the Bolshevik terror in Moscow.[7] These divergent reports concerning Kolchak increased the difficulty in formulating a Siberian policy.

As the negotiations over the Trans-Siberian and Chinese Eastern Railways neared completion, the movement to recognize Kolchak gained momentum. On February 26 the British Foreign Office explained its attitude. It praised the Allied intervention policy in the Far East for preventing the extension of enemy activities to Siberia. Unfortunately, the Armistice had not affected the Soviet government,

[4] Lansing to Polk, Jan. 8, 1919, United States, *Foreign Relations, 1919, Russia,* p. 323.

[5] Polk to Lansing, Jan. 11, 1919, United States, *Foreign Relations, 1919, Russia,* p. 325.

[6] Reinsch to Polk, Jan. 15 (?), 1919, United States, *Foreign Relations, 1919, Russia,* pp. 325-326.

[7] MacMurray to Polk, Jan. 23, 1919, United States, *Foreign Relations, 1919, Russia,* p. 327.

"which continued their efforts to overwhelm the friendly Russian forces opposed to them and to bring the whole country under their disastrous sway." Admitting that affairs in Siberia were complicated by indecision on the part of the Allies, and by the divergent interests of the various Russian groups in Siberia, His Majesty's government believed that its paramount consideration was loyalty to the Russian forces opposing the Bolsheviks. The anti-Bolsheviks had co-operated with the British as soon as troops had been dispatched to Siberia. Therefore the British could not withdraw support from their forces at a critical stage in their operations simply because the primary Allied objectives had been achieved. Moreover, since Great Britain had consistently supported the government of Admiral Kolchak, she considered it essential that whatever the eventual outcome of the deliberations in Paris regarding the Russian Soviet government, the Allies should co-operate in taking all measures necessary to support the Kolchak government. Both Harris and Poole supported British representations.[8]

In its formal reply to the British note, the State Department expressed its sympathy with the Kolchak government but added that it was not "disposed to afford formal recognition." The note continued rather vaguely:

The American Government has been glad, however, to participate in the measures taken to reorganize and repair the Trans-Siberian Railway which is believed will make possible the transport of needed supplies. Support to this extent is being given and the American Government is disposed to continue such support and desires that peace and order shall be maintained throughout Siberia.[9]

The American reply did not satisfy all the members of the State Department. The acting chief of the Russian Division, who urged immediate recognition of Kolchak, wrote, "My view has not changed since 1917; that we should support any reputable and sound elements of order wherever they may be found. You cannot expect the Russians to work out their own salvation if you refuse to give them a fair start."[10] D. C. Poole, later chief of the Russian Division, added his plea for recognition of Kolchak. He pointed out:

Its main effects would be to give clear definition and therefore strength to Allied policy in Russia and to deal a heavy moral blow to the Bolsheviks. . . . Every blow struck at the Moscow Government is a blow as

[8] Davis to Lansing, March 1, 1919, file 861.00/3976, D.S.N.A.
[9] Commission to Negotiate Peace to Polk, April 1, 1919, file 861.00/4195, D.S.N.A.
[10] Miles to Lansing, April 15, 1919, file 861.77/791½, D.S.N.A.

necessary and as potent for decency, justice and liberty in the world as those which have been struck on the western front.[11]

The agitation for military aid to Kolchak caused Secretary Baker grave concern. He believed that "if Congress and the people want war to be made upon Bolshevism by force of arms," it should be undertaken "by such a force as would enable us to be independent of any Japanese, Chinese or Russian allies." He did not think American troops should be permitted to come under the command of the Japanese commander-in-chief. Of this much Baker was convinced: "Either General Graves should be directed to cooperate with the Kolchak government or he ought to be withdrawn."[12]

Baker's views were not shared by the State Department, which was assisting the Russian forces in its own way. Ever since American troops had entered Vladivostok, the American government had been lending its good offices to the Russian Embassy in shipping Russian rifles and boots, railway material, and other military equipment to Siberia. These materials had been consigned to General Ivanov-Rinov for use on the Volga front and in Siberia. The American Peace Commission was evidently unacquainted with these activities, for Polk was questioned concerning the kind of military equipment being sent to the authorities, and the purpose for which it was being used. The Acting Secretary of State immediately answered that along with the American "efforts to aid the Czecho-Slovak armies it seemed proper to cooperate in measures to strengthen the Russians who were acting with them."[13]

The State Department continued to consider the recognition of Kolchak. Lansing instructed Consul Harris, Admiral Rodgers, General Graves, Consul Caldwell, and Charles H. Smith of the Railway Commission to pool their views on the question. The conferees all agreed that Kolchak appeared to be sincerely committed to the good of Russia. Moreover, his movement was increasing in strength. Although he was surrounded by a number of reactionaries, he probably represented the most acceptable type of man Russia had available. The conferees believed that the Siberian picture would be considerably improved by some form of encouragement to Kolchak outside of actual

[11] Poole to Polk, May 7, 1919, United States, *Foreign Relations, 1919, Russia*, pp. 343-344.

[12] Bliss to Wilson, May 9, 1919, Wilson Papers, series VIII-A.

[13] Commission to Negotiate Peace to Phillips, March 23, 1919, Phillips to Commission to Negotiate Peace, March 27, 1919, United States, *Foreign Relations, 1919, Russia*, p. 331.

recognition.[14] They also urged financial and material support given openly and not as the Japanese were doing through secret gifts of arms to Semenov and Kalmikov. In addition, they advocated an agreement on the part of the Allies to refrain from assisting or supporting any of the Cossack factions embarrassing Kolchak. They felt that every means short of force should be taken to weaken the strength of these reactionary Cossack leaders. The conferees also expressed their views on the attitude of the other powers in Siberia. Not only was there a divergence of views between the Japanese military party and the incumbent Japanese government, but it appeared that both the English and French military representatives in Siberia personally had very reactionary views on Russian politics and were not in harmony with the representatives of their own governments on the Inter-Allied Committee. Consequently the governments of England and France did not get clear-cut views on affairs in Siberia. The American representatives believed that "if the powers will unify the expression of views by their respective representatives, the Inter-Allied Railway Committee will be able to arrive at harmonious decisions promotive of their law, order, good feeling, and prosperity in Siberia."[15] Ambassador Morris was in general agreement with these views. Although he believed that Kolchak should be treated encouragingly, he hesitated to suggest even a *de facto* recognition of the Omsk government, as he had serious doubts concerning its permanency.[16]

Throughout April the State Department considered the advisability of a provisional recognition of Kolchak. It was encouraged in its deliberations by Kolchak's recent successes. On April 29 Acting Secretary Polk asked Ambassador Morris if he were willing to modify his opinion concerning recognition in view of Kolchak's substantial successes.[17] Morris replied:

If Great Britain and France decide to recognize the Kolchak Government I think we should do likewise and urge similar action by Japan. Unity of action in Siberia is more important than the character of the action. Frankly I would prefer to see recognition postponed until the Kolchak Government shows more willingness to define its purposes and policy and less subserviency to reactionary influence. If, however, the

[14] Stevens also urged some measure of recognition to the Siberian government in order to strengthen its hand (Polk to Commission to Negotiate Peace, May 6, 1919, United States, *Foreign Relations, 1919, Russia*, p. 339).

[15] Morris to Department of State, April 19, 1919, file 861.00/4332, D.S.N.A.

[16] Morris to Polk, April 12, 1919, United States, *Foreign Relations, 1919, Russia*, pp. 331-332.

[17] United States, *Foreign Relations, 1919, Russia*, p. 337.

Associated Governments decide that the general situation in Russia as a whole calls for recognition of a Siberian Government, [it is] important that a statement will be first obtained from Kolchak and his colleagues defining their own position on the fundamental issues of the revolution, the land problem, the state of self-government, freedom of speech and uncensored communication and the calling as soon as practicable of a con-stituent assembly.[18]

Morris's views in conjunction with other reports received from Siberia bore out Polk's personal opinion that all governments concerned in the railway plan should recognize Omsk as the *de facto* government in Siberia and in all other parts of Russia that might be brought under its control. He felt that if the Omsk government knew recognition was at hand it would willingly provide for the convening of a Constituent Assembly at the earliest practicable date and provide for other democratic safeguards.[19]

President Wilson apparently did not share Polk's views. Troubled by the entire Siberian situation, he presented his problem to the Council of Four. He pointed out that although the United States did not believe in Kolchak, the British and French military representatives in Siberia were supporting him. Kolchak, who regarded American soldiers as neutrals, was quite irritated by their presence on the railway. Moreover, the Cossacks were antagonistic to American soldiers. Wilson suspected that the Japanese would be glad to see a collision between the two groups. In these circumstances, Wilson believed that the United States must either take sides wth Kolchak and send a much stronger force to Siberia, or withdraw. If the United States aided Kolchak and increased its forces in Siberia, Japan would increase hers still more. If American troops continued merely to guard the railroad and to maintain a neutral position, Wilson was advised that collisions would occur, which might result in actual war. If American troops were withdrawn, Siberia would be left to the Japanese and Kolchak, who was supported by the Allies. The President's dilemma was quite evident. Although he favored a neutral policy toward Russia and Siberia, at the same time he did not wish to withdraw American soldiers from Siberia and leave Japan in control of the situation. This would mean an end to the cherished open-door policy. Personally, Wilson had always believed that the proper policy for the

[18] Polk to Commission to Negotiate Peace, May 6, 1919, United States, *Foreign Relations, 1919, Russia*, pp. 339-340.
[19] Polk to Commission to Negotiate Peace, May 6, 1919, United States, *Foreign Relations, 1919, Russia*, pp. 340-341.

Allied and Associated powers was "to clear out of Russia and leave it to the Russians to fight it out among themselves."[20]

On May 20 the Council of Four again attempted to devise a Russian policy. Wilson pointed out that the only reason America had gone into Siberia was to get the Czechs out and then they refused to go. Lloyd George replied that the British had gone in to reconstitute the Eastern Front and now that they had succeeded in doing this, they could not leave the loyal Russians in the lurch. Wilson believed that if the Allies continued to support Kolchak, they should at least secure democratic pledges from him. The Council of Four finally decided to draft a letter stating the conditions under which the Allies would continue to help certain of the Russian governments.[21]

On May 26 the Council of Four addressed a formal note to Admiral Kolchak explaining Allied policy toward Russia and making a conditional offer of further assistance. Declaring that it had always been a cardinal policy of the Allied governments not to interfere in the internal affairs of Russia, the Council added that their original intervention was for the dual purpose of aiding those Russians who wished to continue the struggle against Germany and to rescue the Czechs who faced destruction at the hands of the Bolsheviks. In direct contradiction to its first statement the note then indicated that since the Armistice Allied forces and supplies had been kept in various parts of Russia at considerable cost. Blaming the Soviet government for the failure of the Peace Conference to bring peace and food relief to Russia, the note stated that the Allied and Associated powers were prepared to continue their assistance to the anti-Bolsheviks under certain conditions. Among the assurances requested were pledges that a freely elected constitutent assembly would be convoked as soon as Kolchak reached Moscow, that no attempt would be made to restore the special class privileges of the Czarist regime, that Russia's debts would be recognized, and that the new democratic government of Russia would join the League of Nations and co-operate with it in the settlement of Russia's relations with the border states and the limitation of armaments.[22]

---

[20] Notes of a Meeting Held at President Wilson's House in the Place des Etats-Unis, Paris, May 9, 1919, United States, *Foreign Relations, 1919, Russia*, pp. 345-347.

[21] Notes of a Meeting Held at President Wilson's House, May 20, 1919, United States, *Foreign Relations, 1919, Russia*, pp. 351-353.

[22] United States, *Foreign Relations, 1919, Russia*, pp. 367-370; New York *Times*, June 13, 1919. The proposal to force Kolchak to make certain democratic pledges in return for recognition aroused considerable protest in certain Western reactionary groups friendly to the Kolchak government (Coates and Coates, *Armed Intervention in Russia*, p. 214).

On June 4 Kolchak sent a carefully worded affirmative reply which generally complied with the Allied conditions. He acknowledged the national debt and disavowed any intention of restoring the old regime. However, he added that the final sanction of all the decisions taken in the name of Russia rested with the Constituent Assembly.[23]   On June 12 his reply was accepted by Wilson, Clemenceau, Lloyd George, and Baron Nobuaki Makino. The promised aid was dispatched without delay.[24]

Since the joint action taken by the Supreme Council in respect to Kolchak still left open the question of formal recognition, President Wilson instructed Ambassador Morris to proceed to Omsk to determine whether Kolchak deserved recognition. The President was also "desirous that Ambassador Morris should so utilize his visit to Omsk as to impress upon the Japanese Government our great interest in the Siberian situation and our intention to adopt a definite policy which will include the 'open door' to Russia, free from Japanese domination."[25]

In accordance with his instructions, Morris arrived at Vladivostok on July 11, and arranged to have General Graves accompany him on his mission.[26]   They arrived at Omsk at a very serious moment. The people and government of Omsk had evidently misunderstood the nature and extent of the assistance which the Allies were willing to grant. They lamented the fact that the Allies had not sent fifty thousand troops to their assistance when the Czechs were in possession of Samara and Kazan in October of 1918. They also criticized the Prinkipo proposal, which had greatly discouraged the anti-Bolsheviks. Moreover, the failure of the Allies to grant recognition had resulted in

[23] United States, *Foreign Relations, 1919, Russia,* pp. 375-378; New York *Times,* June 14, 1919.

[24] Notes of a Meeting Held at President Wilson's House, June 2, 1919, United States, *Foreign Relations, 1919, Russia,* p. 379. For American attempts to live up to tthe agreement to support Kolchak, see United States, *Foreign Relations, 1919, Russia,* pp. 381-453.

[25] Wilson to Polk, June 24, 1919, Wilson Papers, series VIII-A; Phillips to Morris, June 30, 1919, United States, *Foreign Relations, 1919, Russia,* p. 388. On the next day Wilson wrote to Lansing, "I think that we should omit no step by which we can get nearer to the situation in Siberia and know more clearly what we are about" (June 25, 1919, Wilson Papers, series VIII-A). The State Department had been informed by Minister Reinsch in China that "one of the chief motives for Japanese support is their desire to secure extensive concessions in the mineral and other resources of Manchuria. It is stated that it is believed that the gold resources of the Upper Amur river alone are sufficient, if developed properly, to pay off the entire Russian National debt" (Reinsch to Department of State, May 9, 1919, file 861.00/4726, D.S.N.A.).

[26] Morris to Acting Secretary of State, July 10, 1919, United States, *Foreign Relations, 1919, Russia,* p. 389.

a depressing reaction. There was no enthusiasm among the people for recruiting. The morale of the soldiers had deteriorated until they were completely demoralized at the front. An order had been issued to retreat, which would mean the sacrifice of several Siberian towns. Omsk itself was threatened.[27] The situation was made worse by the attitude of the Czechs, who desired to return home immediately. Morris believed that if their wish was not granted, the men might take matters into their own hands and possibly negotiate with the Bolsheviks for a safe conduct through European Russia. At any rate, Morris was convinced that they could not be relied upon for assistance after November of 1919. Without the Czechs or other military guard, the railway could not be operated beyond Irkutsk.[28]

Morris painted a depressing picture of the conditions observed en route to Omsk:

> I had expected to find on approaching Omsk a considerable sentiment in favor of Kolchak, or at least an anti-Bolshevik sentiment. I must report, however, that the Kolchak government has failed to command the confidence of anybody in Siberia except a small discredited group of reactionaries, Monarchists and former military officials. It is the judgment of all with whom I have conferred,—representative Czechs, British and French military officers, our own railway-service men, Allied Consuls, and even thoughtful and moderate Russians such as the Orthodox Bishop at Krasnoyarsk and Kolchak's appointed governor of the Province of Tomsk,—that the withdrawal of the Czechs would be a signal for a formidable anti-Kolchak if not pro-Bolshevik uprising in every town on the railway from Irkutsk to Omsk.[29]

Members of the Omsk government were aware of the conditions described by Ambassador Morris. Sookine, now Acting Minister for Foreign Affairs of the Omsk government, admitted the extreme seriousness of the military situation, but hoped for an improvement in the future. Sookine referred to the "persistent scare" of Japan and to the

---

[27] Reinsch to Acting Secretary of State, July 14 (?), 1919, United States, *Foreign Relations, 1919, Russia*, pp. 390-391.

[28] Morris to Acting Secretary of State, July 22, 1919, United States, *Foreign Relations, 1919, Russia*, p. 395.

[29] Morris to Acting Secretary of State, July 22, 1919, United States, *Foreign Relations, 1919, Russia*, p. 395. As Ambassador Morris left Tomsk, he said to General Graves: "You and I have been much criticized because of our attitude towards the Kolchak regime; it has been repeatedly said we have the Far Eastern orientation and that if we would come West, we would find an entirely different situation after we left Irkutsk; and with all the people questioned by us and, through the interpreters, we have not found a single individual who spoke a good word for the Kolchak regime" (Graves, *America's Siberian Adventure*, pp. 216-217).

efforts of Japanese officials to discredit American activities. Frankly acknowledging that Semenov was under Japanese control, he added that Kolchak had only nominal authority over·him. It was the Japanese representatives who had urged Semenov's promotion to a full generalship, and their "request" had to be granted immediately. Although Sookine pointed out that there was bitter resentment among all classes of Russians against the American policy of neutrality in Siberia, he expressed his personal conviction that Russia's future must be worked out in harmony with the progressive forces represented by Great Britain and the United States.[30]

In conducting his inquiries, Morris was proceeding on three assumptions, which were not refuted by the State Department: first, that the action of the Supreme Council definitely and finally placed the United States and its associates in opposition to Bolshevism; second, that there was still a reasonable hope that the Kolchak movement would survive the present military crisis; third, that in such an event, the United States was prepared to give its help and support if practicable means could be devised.[31]

As Ambassador Morris continued his investigations, he conferred with the British and French military leaders in Siberia, Generals Knox and Janin. Both generals stated with brutal frankness the difficulties met in delivering supplies to the Kolchak army during the last eight months. They reported that "the army staff and supply departments were completely disorganized, inefficient, corrupt and unsettled; that personal ambition, jealousy and intrigue prevailed; and that repeated appeals to the Admiral to correct the abuses had been without result because in their judgment he was powerless to act." They felt it would be useless to continue further shipments of supplies unless the Allied governments were "prepared to exercise supervision and control not only over the distribution but also over the organization of the army itself." Admitting that the criticisms were just, if slightly exaggerated, the Omsk Minister for Foreign Affairs and his colleagues agreed that they would not oppose in principle any plan for the supervision of distribution. All the experts present, including General Graves, agreed that some plan of supervision was essential. They differed, however, as to the nature and extent of the supervision.[32]

[30] Morris to Lansing, July 24, 1919, United States, *Foreign Relations, 1919, Russia,* pp. 396-398.

[31] Morris to Lansing, July 27, 1919, file 861.00/4931, D.S.N.A.; Long to Lansing, Aug. 14, 1919, Long Papers.

[32] Morris to Lansing, July 31, 1919, United States, *Foreign Relations, 1919, Russia,* pp. 401-402.

On August 4 Morris submitted his report on the personnel of the Kolchak government. He believed that Kolchak was an honest, courageous, and narrow-minded patriot of limited experience in public affairs and small administrative ability. Although a dictator in name, he exercised little influence on his Council of Ministers. Despite his good intentions, he had little or no knowledge of the political and economic dangers which threatened his government. In this respect he had little help from his Council of Ministers. Although probably as representative as Sibera could produce, the civilian members were all young and inexperienced, while nothing favorable could be said of the military members and the officers of the General Staff, who, as a body, were intolerant, reactionary, and corrupt. Commenting on the strength of the Kolchak government, Morris reported: "The Government has failed in administration; has failed in the organization of the army; has failed to retain the confidence of the moderate groups." Still it had elements of strength. In the first place, no one doubted the Admiral's patriotism or honesty of purpose. In spite of the intrigue around him he still retained a large measure of sympathy and respect. In the second place, despite its helplessness, the Kolchak government was the only one around which those opposed to Bolshevism could rally. The choice, therefore, which confronted every moderate in Siberia was either Kolchak or Bolshevism.[33] However, Morris believed that the Kolchak government was not sufficiently strong to rescue Russia from the grip of Bolshevism. Furthermore, Morris was convinced that "only drastic changes in its personnel and methods would render it equal to such a task, no matter how much support the Allied governments might give it."[34]

On August 11 Morris telegraphed his final recommendations. Briefly, he believed that with Allied assistance and counsel, the Kolchak government might be so strengthened as ultimately to be able to rescue the Russian people from the Bolshevik tyranny. There were certain steps necessary to insure that success. These included the formal recognition of Kolchak and his associates as the Provisional government of Russia, the extension of some two hundred million dollars in military, commercial, and railway credits, the stabilization of non-Bolshevik currency, the continuation of the Inter-Allied Railway Agreement, and the dispatch of forty thousand additional troops to take the place of

[33] Morris to Lansing, Aug. 4, 1919, United States, *Foreign Relations, 1919, Russia*, pp. 403-405.

[34] Morris to Lansing, Aug. 8, 1919, United States, *Foreign Relations, 1919, Russia*, pp. 407-408.

the Czechs. Moreover, an Allied military supply committee and a committee of commercial experts were necessary to provide an honest and efficient use of credits and distribution of supplies. Finally, Morris recommended that the United States appoint a diplomatic representative and certain other experts to help and advise the Omsk government. In conclusion, Ambassador Morris emphasized that no plan would be successful unless it included at least the formal recognition of Kolchak, a grant of credits, and the dispatch of twenty-five thousand American troops to assist in guarding the railway. He added, "Unless our policy includes all of these measures, we can do little if anything to help Russia by way of Siberia and we will be forced to abandon eastern Siberia to Japanese domination."[35]

On August 16 Morris, fearing that he had perhaps emphasized too strongly the weaknesses of the Kolchak government, informed the State Department that it was the best, perhaps the only available, agency through which the United States could give its promised aid to Russia. Morris elaborated further:

Perhaps I am too close to see the Russian situation clearly in its true proportions, but I am sure that whatever the outcome of this crisis may be the Kolchak government cannot continue without the open support of our government. To come to its aid in the hour of discouragement and defeat is, I admit, to take a great risk: But it is also to take advantage of a great opportunity. If the Kolchak government should collapse we could not be worse off than if we stood and waited for the event. On the other hand, if by our timely and active service Kolchak should survive, we should be in a preeminent position to assist and even to lead in the reconstruction of Russia, to maintain the "open door" now in imminent peril of being closed, and to preserve the integrity of Siberia.[36]

The State Department gave careful consideration to Morris's recommendations. Long pointed out that the only part of the program which could be effected without going to Congress was the recognition of the Kolchak government. As Long saw it, here was an opportunity for the President to condemn Bolshevism and to place squarely before Congress the burden of future aid for Russia.[37] The President, however, had already acted on one part of Morris's program. On August 8, in response to a direct inquiry by Clemenceau, the President had stated that the United States would be unable to "furnish additional

[35] Morris to Lansing, Aug. 11, 1919, United States, *Foreign Relations, 1919, Russia,* pp. 408-410.

[36] Morris to Lansing, Aug. 16, 1919, United States, *Foreign Relations, 1919, Russia,* p. 415.

[37] Memorandum by Long, Aug. 14, 1919, Long Papers.

troops in Siberia to replace Czechs in guarding the railways."[38] The State Department immediately informed Morris. Believing that this decision rendered his entire plan impracticable, Morris questioned the wisdom of recognizing Kolchak. He thought it would be better to await the outcome of the military crisis in Siberia, at which time he would submit further suggestions.[39]

On August 25 the State Department informed Morris of its decision in regard to his other recommendations. It could not recognize Kolchak because of its inability to give him the support which Morris had insisted was necessary to insure success. The United States was unable to assist Kolchak with credits for military supplies unless he was recognized as a cobelligerent against the Central Powers, which he was not, or unless the State Department received specific authorization from Congress, which it had not. Furthermore, commercial credits could not be granted without authorization of Congress. No action by Congress could be urged until the ratification of the peace treaty was out of the way. On the credit side of the ledger, the State Department declared its intention to aid Kolchak through the shipment of rifles and increased contracts for goods with the Siberian co-operatives. British and American banks were planning a fifty-million-dollar loan to Kolchak. Morris was urged to explain to Kolchak that American limitations were due solely to existing legislation, to the state of public opinion, and to the lack of appropriations.[40]

Morris decided to withhold this final statement from Kolchak in view of the crisis at Omsk. He feared that "any formal statement . . . if followed by the fall of Kolchak, might place on our Government responsibility for a result due to entirely different causes."[41] The department approved this action.[42]

Morris departed to Vladivostok, leaving Harris to report the tenor

[38] Lansing to Harris, Aug. 12, 1919, United States, *Foreign Relations, 1919, Russia,* pp. 412-413. The British, French, and Italians had also refused to send additional troops (Bliss, Paris Peace Conference Diary, June 11, 1919, Bliss Papers). On August 12 Sir Charles Eliot, British High Commissioner in Siberia, had informed Morris that he had received instructions which indicated the intention of his government to retire entirely from the Siberian enterprise and concentrate all its attention hereafter on Denikin (Morris to Lansing, Aug. 12, 1919, file 861.00/5020, D.S.N.A.).

[39] Morris to Lansing, Aug. 27, 1919, United States, *Foreign Relations, 1919, Russia,* pp. 422-423.

[40] Lansing to Morris, Aug. 25, 1919, United States, *Foreign Relations, 1919, Russia,* pp. 421-422.

[41] Morris to Lansing, Aug. 30, 1919, United States, *Foreign Relations, 1919, Russia,* p. 423.

[42] Phillips to Jenkins, Sept. 5, 1919, United States, *Foreign Relations, 1919, Russia,* p. 423.

of affairs in Omsk. The air was full of rumors concerning America's threatened withdrawal from Siberia. Harris received reports from Vladivostok quoting Morris to the effect that the Omsk government could last only a few more days, and that a government formed of the revolutionary parties was pending.[43] Despite these rumors, American rifles and ammunition were being shipped to Kolchak's representatives, while clothing was being sent to the co-operatives and railway materials to Stevens.[44] The State Department believed that the failure to assist Kolchak would not be understood in Russia and would not only weaken Kolchak but also affect unfavorably America's position in Siberia to the immediate, and possibly permanent, advantage of Japan. The State Department, therefore, sent an urgent note to President Wilson asking him to authorize the Secretary of War "to sell to the Russian Ambassador or other Russian representatives in America for shipment to Kolchak on a credit basis, shoes, underclothing, cloth surplus, overcoats. . . ."[45]

On the very day on which Wilson approved further aid to Kolchak, August Heid, the representative of the War Trade Board at Vladivostok, reported that he considered his work fiinshed. He was convinced that political, financial, military, and railway transportation conditions were too unsettled to undertake any further economic relief. He saw no chance for improvement. Affairs were worse than at any time since Kolchak had come to power. Heid reported that the Omsk government had conceded military control of the territory from Irkutsk to Vladivostok to the Cossack leaders, who aided and supported morally and materially by Japan, "insult, beat and even kill peasants and civilians, obstruct and delay transportation, requisition and pilfer goods in transit, in fact generally pursue a policy calculated to prohibit relief reaching the masses especially if such relief be attempted by Americans."[46]

While Heid was telegraphing in this vein, Harris, now at Omsk, was urging the *de facto* recognition of Kolchak and the fullest support possible. He urged President-Wilson to send Kolchak a personal

[43] Tenney to Acting Secretary of State, Sept. 14 (?), 1919, United States, *Foreign Relations, 1919, Russia,* p. 424.

[44] Phillips to Harris, Sept. 19, 1919, United States, *Foreign Relations, 1919, Russia,* p. 424.

[45] Phillips to Wilson, Sept. 19, 1919, United States, *Foreign Relations, 1919, Russia,* p. 425. Sookine, Kolchak's Foreign Minister, pointed out that the "United States considers her own quarrels with Japan of more importance than her relations with Russia . . ." (enclosure in Baker to Lansing, Nov. 7, 1919, file 861.00/5608, D.S.N.A.).

[46] Heid to Phillips, Sept. 20, 1919, United States, *Foreign Relations, 1919, Russia.* pp. 426-427.

message expressing confidence in his motives and purposes, and appreciation of the serious difficulties which confronted him. At the same time Harris wrote that the Siberian army was making progress and more than holding its own. He believed that Omsk would not be captured and that the city and the front would be held through the winter.[47]

Harris's military reports were in direct conflict with those of Major Slaughter, who reported that Kolchak's forces were scarcely making any progress and that bad morale and desertions continued. Harris was urged to confer with Slaughter and come to some agreement.[48]

Ambassador Morris was quite discouraged about the entire Siberian picture, and particularly so in view of Kolchak's formal recognition of both Kalmikov and Semenov and the increasingly antagonistic attitude of the Czechs toward the Kolchak government. Morris expressed his views aptly:

> As it is impossible for our agencies to cooperate with these Atamans we now find ourselves in disagreement not only with the Japanese policy but also with the official representatives of the Kolchak government in Eastern Siberia. We thus have the doubly anomalous situation that the Czechs by their presence are responsible for the continued existence of a Government against which they are now intriguing while we are endeavoring to find means of cooperation with a Government many of whose representatives are openly hostile.[49]

Morris was convinced that Kolchak did not have sufficient strength or popular support to control these conditions without Allied assistance of the type he had described in earlier reports. In regard to immediate

[47] Tenney to Phillips, Sept. 22, 1919, United States, *Foreign Relations, 1919, Russia,* pp. 427-430. General Graves wondered whether "President Wilson knew of the unneutral attitude of Consul General Harris in Siberia and approved of his attitude, but the President, as all knew, was fully occupied with the questions arising in the Peace Conference and could not give any of his personal attention to Siberia. It was apparent to me that Consul General Harris had the full support of the Russian Section of the State Department, and I believe he had the support one step higher in the hierarchy of the State Department" (Graves, *America's Siberian Adventure,* pp. 217-218).

[48] United States, *Foreign Relations, 1919, Russia,* p. 218.

[49] Morris to Phillips, Sept. 23, 1919, file 861.00/5264, D.S.N.A. Morris had reported earlier that "much of the discontent with the present Government, the demoralization and panic, is . . . due to the utter insecurity of person and property. All over Siberia there is an orgy of arrest without charges; of execution without even the pretense of a trial; and of confiscation without color of authority. Fear—panic fear—has seized everyone. Men suspect each other and live in constant terror that some spy or enemy will cry 'Bolshevik' and condemn them to instant death" (Morris to Lansing, July 27 [?], 1919, United States, *Foreign Relations, 1919, Russia,* p. 400).

policy Morris advocated an agreement with the Japanese government for guarding the railways and for the treatment of Semenov and Kalmikov. In addition, he advised a continuation of the Railway Service Corps and an Allied credit of seventy-five million dollars for the purchase of required commodities. Finally, he suggested that the port of Vladivostok be placed temporarily under an Allied economic commission, that American military forces be continued at their present strength, and that the Red Cross work be continued.[50]

On October 1 Polk, then at Paris, was confidentially informed that as soon as President Wilson was well enough to attend to business, the Secretary was seriously considering asking him to grant formal recognition to the Kolchak government.[51] At the same time, Phillips, the Acting Secretary of State, sent a note to the American representatives in Siberia urging them to give publicity to an American note which emphasized the fact that the United States intended to continue its support to the government of Admiral Kolchak, and that in return it hoped to receive the co-operation of all elements in Russia which were devoted to the establishment of democratic institutions among the Russian people.[52] August Heid was told to continue his work for carrying out economic aid through the co-operative societies.[53]

When General Bliss heard of the trend of American policy toward the Kolchak government, he reported his reaction to Secretary Baker:

Some people say that there can be no disarmament while Bolshevism exists in Russia. But Bolshevism exists everywhere; and it will exist after we have killed the last Bolshevik. The trouble is that we are trying to kill Bolsheviks and not Bolshevism. The latter can be killed, but not by force of arms. After most thinking men here have come to the conclusion that a way must and can be found to combat Bolshevism otherwise than by armies, I am sorry to see from statements in the American press that our government has decided to lend material aid to the Koltchak Government. The real trouble in Russia will begin after the Koltchak Government wins out.[54]

Consul General Harris continued to urge greater assistance to Kolchak and formal recognition. His entreaties were supported by many

[50] Morris to Phillips, Sept. 23, 1919, United States, *Foreign Relations, 1919, Russia,* pp. 432-434.

[51] Phillips to Commission to Negotiate Peace, Oct. 1, 1919, United States, *Foreign Relations, 1919, Russia,* p. 436.

[52] Phillips to Caldwell, Oct. 2, 1919, United States, *Foreign Relations, 1919, Russia,* p. 437.

[53] Lansing to Caldwell, Oct. 7, 1919, United States, *Foreign Relations, 1919, Russia,* p. 439.

[54] Bliss to Baker, Oct. 5, 1919, Bliss Papers.

Russian officials in Washington and Paris. Even Polk was urging recognition of Kolchak. However, no decision on the matter could be made due to President Wilson's illness.[55] Even after Kolchak had decided upon a general evacuation of Omsk, Harris continued to plead for his recognition:

While there is nothing immediately alarming yet it may shortly become so. I reiterate that if Kolchak falls Bolshevism will extend at least to Lake Baikal. I respectfully suggest that the Department take the initiative [in urging?] Prague government to issue an order for 25,000 Czechs to advance to this front and save the situation. At the same time, I respectfully suggest that the Allies recognize Kolchak. Such a step would strengthen Kolchak in the same degree as it would dishearten the Bolsheviki. The time has now arrived to make the issue clean cut. Any delay simply encourages and spreads Bolshevism and all that it stands for. All other governments in Russia opposed to Bolshevism have recognized Kolchak. Why do the Allies delay longer? I am now satisfied that Kolchak cannot last much longer unaided and the above suggestions appear the only way out. The Siberian Army is fighting well, yet if the Bolsheviki continue to advance as rapidly as at present Omsk will fall in four weeks time. It is believed that at least 50 per cent of the Czech soldiers are willing to fight the Bolsheviki again, and thus secure their return home across European Russia. The situation is extremely serious and urgent.[56]

Harris was at least correct in his belief that the Kolchak government was nearing its end. Despite this fact, as late as November 4, 1919, Lansing seriously considered recognizing Kolchak.[57]

[55] Polk to Lansing, Oct. 24, 1919, Commission to Negotiate Peace to Lansing, Oct. 22, 1919, Tenney to Lansing, Oct. 31, 1919, United States, *Foreign Relations, 1919, Russia*, pp. 444-445.
[56] Tenney to Lansing, Oct. 31, 1919, United States, *Foreign Relations, 1919, Russia*, pp. 445-446.
[57] Lansing to Polk, Nov. 4, 1919, United States, *Foreign Relations, 1919, Russia*, p. 443.

CHAPTER X

The Doughboys Go Home

WHILE the State Department was formulating its policy in regard to Admiral Kolchak, it continued its efforts to co-operate with and restrain Japan in Siberia. The task grew increasingly difficult. By the end of August, 1919, affairs had reached a crisis. The major points of friction involved radical differences of interpretation of the Inter-Allied Railway Agreement. Thus, while the United States felt that protection of the railway engineers was a vital element in the protection of the railways, Japan felt that Japanese troops should limit themselves to safeguarding railway property and keeping the line open. If a disagreement occurred between a Russian under the authority of the Omsk government and a national of any country engaged in the operation or protection of the railways, Japan considered it a matter for 'discussion between the Omsk government and the government of the other persons involved. In practice this understanding had resulted in a definite refusal on the part of Japanese military commanders to protect the lives and property of the Allied inspectors in the territory controlled by General Semenov. By the middle of August the situation was so grave that Stevens advised the withdrawal of American engineers from those sections of the railway guarded by Japanese troops.[1]

This crisis prompted the State Department to draft a note to Japan threatening the withdrawal of American troops unless the outstanding differences between the United States and Japan were settled. The proposed note was not approved by all the members of the State Department. Basil Miles was particularly disturbed over the sudden decision of the government to withdraw, especially in view of the sympathetic telegram which had been sent to Kolchak only a few days

[1] Lansing to Ray Atherton (chargé in Japan), Aug. 30, 1919, United States, *Foreign Relations, 1919, Russia*, pp. 575-578.

earlier. He felt that withdrawal amounted to a "betrayal of our word." He wrote his views to Long:

We are shipping arms and ammunition to Kolchak; we have told Bakhmeteff he could have the rouble notes; we are executing contracts with the Cooperatives of Siberia; we are helping the Embassy in loans for Kolchak, etc. etc.

I would be glad to know how these facts are to be squared with any decision to withdraw from Siberia while the present crisis lasts?

It occurs to me that if we withdraw before the future of Kolchak is determined—moreover at a time when Kolchak and his outfit know that our special representative, Ambassador Morris has favored formal recognition—our position will be fatally vulnerable. Furthermore we shall be unable to answer effectively the Japanese retort that our action in blaming them is merely a cloak for our decision to quit and get out of a bad mess for some more promising venture.

These points seem to me to affect the international position of the Government. They certainly affect my status in the Department. I cannot be associated with policies which I believe pernicious nor in good faith continue to draw pay from the Government if they are adopted.[2]

Miles's views were taken under careful consideration as were those of the Secretary of War. Although Baker did not object to the withdrawal of American troops, he was opposed to the proposed method of doing it. If withdrawal were desired, Baker advised that it be done as an exercise of the discretion reserved by the President in his *aide memoire*. Furthermore, he believed that the real explanation for withdrawal should be made after American troops had all returned home. Since the feeling between Japanese and American troops had at times been hostile, Baker believed that withdrawal might provoke feelings of irritation on the part of Japanese troops, especially if responsibility for withdrawal were placed upon the actions of Japan. Since the force of General Graves was small as compared with the Japanese force, Baker thought it ought to be gotten out of the country safely "to the last man" before anything was said which might be taken by the Japanese government as a pretext for interfering with the American withdrawal. Thus, Baker recommended that the President discontinue American military co-operation in Siberia on the ground that the Czechoslovak forces had been rescued and that the subsequent restoration of order in Siberia was the business of the Siberian people. Once withdrawal had been completed, the question of further explanation to the Japanese

[2] Miles to Long, Aug. 26, 1919, Long Papers.

government and further public statements in America could then be considered.[3]

Breckinridge Long did not agree with all of Baker's recommendations. Believing that there were distinct advantages to America in notifying Japan that publicity might be used, Long added, "It is an instrument of torture under their form of Government and is the only effective modern weapon short of force to combat their antiquated method of diplomacy. I believe it will be productive of good—not the use of it only, but the thought that we might use it." Long also disagreed with Baker's criticism of the proposed reasons for withdrawal. He stated his views as follows:

First—Siberia, and all Anti-Bolshevik Russia, look to us for friendship and help. We have extended both. Further help is made impracticable by the actions of Japan. If we withdraw without making known our reason we may sacrifice the friendship of all those people. The reasons actuating the decision are set forth in the note. If the people of Siberia know the reasons they will appreciate what we have done up to now and will blame Japan as [sic] the discontinuance of our efforts.

Second—The fear, I think is ill-founded, that Japan will harry our soldiers if we tell that Government the truth about the reasons for our withdrawal. It is the only moral thing to do. It may produce further enmity on the part of Japan, but there is little indication we shall be overburdened with the real affection of Japan in the near future—and it may cost us the friendship of the good citizens of all Siberia and Russia which we now enjoy, if we fail to state the true reasons—out of fear of Japan, no matter how well founded.[4]

Long believed that the projected note was advantageous in that it gave Japan an opportunity to change her tactics and prevent withdrawal.

Long's suggestions were accepted by Lansing. However, the Secretary informed Baker that the note would be phrased in such a way as simply to warn Japan that publicity might be used. Baker was further assured that no public statement would be issued until after the matter had been discussed with him as to the possible effect on the soldiers in Siberia.[5]

As finally sent on August 30, 1919, the note carefully reviewed the events which led to intervention and the later developments which contributed to the making of the Inter-Allied Railway Agreement.

[3] Baker to Lansing, Aug. 29, 1919, Baker Papers.

[4] Long to Lansing, Aug. 29, 1919, Long Papers.

[5] Lansing to Baker, Aug. 30, 1919, Baker Papers. President Wilson approved the note in principle (Lansing to Wilson, Aug. 30, 1919, Wilson Papers, series II).

Citing the major differences which existed between the United States and Japan in regard to Siberian policy, the note frankly placed the blame for the failure of the railway plan upon the lack of co-operation of Japanese officials. Lansing then suggested the possibility of withdrawing American troops and making public the reasons. He added:

—the Government of the United States has a clear appreciation of the consequences of such action, especially as it is burdened with a deep sense of obligation towards Russia, whose people contributed such a vital share in the triumph of the Allied and Associated Governments over the Central Powers. Moreover, my Government is firmly convinced that the future welfare of all Governments is to be based upon a community of interest which is about to replace permanently the former balances of power and other bargains of self-interest and aggrandizement on the part of one nation or group of nations at the expense of others. With the deepest regret my Government finds that the attitude of Japan in this matter raises the question as to whether this view of international relations is shared by the Imperial Government.[6]

The Japanese government showed little immediate reaction to the American protest. The Omsk government, however, was very much perturbed. On September 4 the Russian ambassador called on Long to ask if the note meant definite withdrawal on the part of America. Replying in the negative, Long said that if Japan would live up to her agreements, the United States would not necessarily withdraw; that although the United States government wanted to remain in Siberia, it could not be placed in the position of being responsible for a situation for which it was not actually accountable. Therefore, the consideration of further help to Siberia would be suspended until Japan faithfully executed the railroad agreement and her prior agreements made with the United States on entering Siberia. If Japan refused to live up to those agreements, the United States would withdraw all of her troops.[7] The Russian ambassador communicated these views to Sazanov, Minister of Foreign Affairs under Kolchak, who was then in Paris. Sazanov indicated that the withdrawal of the United States "would never in the world be understood by the Russian people; that it would be regarded as deserting the Russians in favor of Japan to the advantage of Japan."[8]

Although the United States received no official word from Japan

[6] Lansing to Atherton, Aug. 30, 1919, United States, *Foreign Relations, 1919, Russia*, pp. 573-578.
[7] Memorandum of Conversation between Long and Bakhmetev, Sept. 4, 1919, Long Papers.
[8] Long to Miles, Sept. 16, 1919, file 861.00/5260, D.S.N.A.

concerning the note, Katsuji Debuchi, the Japanese chargé d'affaires, called on Miles and discussed the protest informally. Informing Miles that the note was quite unexpected, Debuchi was concerned over the abruptness of the language. He felt that the difficulty lay entirely with Semenov. Miles concurred but reminded Debuchi that although Japan had agreed that China should protect the Chinese Eastern Railway from Manchuria to Harbin, Japanese forces had remained all along the line and Japanese flags had been flying for six months over every station. While criticizing the Japanese military, Miles pointed out that "we found by our own experience that our own military authorities some times took the bit in their mouths and ran away with us during the war and that, as far as I could see, the Japanese military were doing the same thing with his Government." Throughout the discussion Debuchi appeared very friendly, and closed the interview by inviting Miles to lunch![9]

Apparently the Japanese Foreign Office did not share the same friendliness. The French ambassador to Japan informed Atherton, the American chargé, that the American protest was received by the Japanese government with considerable resentment. The Japanese Minister for Foreign Affairs apparently saw in the note nothing more than a series of minor disagreements between Semenov, American engineers, and certain Japanese military commanders. Although these disagreements were being investigated, the Minister stated that a long time must elapse before a reply could be given. The American protest did not prevent the Japanese press from reporting a discussion by the Diplomatic Advisory Council concerning the possibility of either increasing Japanese forces in Siberia, or withdrawing to the borders of Manchuria and Mongolia to prevent the spread of Bolshevik influence.[10]

Although Japan sent no formal reply to the American protest, the attitude of the Japanese military in Siberia seemed to be undergoing a change. General Narimoto Oi, who had succeeded Otani as commander of the Japanese forces, expressed to Stevens and Morris his opinion that the future operation of the railway required imperatively that the representatives of the Technical Board and railway employees should be protected and supported by the military from all interference in the performance of their duties. He said that all of his officers

[9] Memorandum of a Conversation between Miles and Debuchi, Sept. 4, 1919, file 861.77/1097, D.S.N.A.

[10] Atherton to Phillips, Sept. 16, 1919, United States, *Foreign Relations, 1919, Russia,* pp. 580-581.

would be so instructed "in principle," with orders to refer to their senior commandant any doubtful or delicate cases which might arise.[11] The necessary orders were issued on September 28. Although Caldwell did not approve of the phrase "in principle," and would have preferred "in practice," Stevens believed that the United States should accept the general's statement in good faith.[12]

When no reply to the August 30 note was received by late September, Ambassador Morris was instructed to inform the Japanese government that the United States was neither "indifferent [n]or disposed to evade the issue presented by its note." However, the State Department hoped that the attitude assumed by General Oi indicated a willingness on the part of Japan to co-operate in Siberia.[13]

Meanwhile in Siberia local newspapers seemed to be taking it for granted that American and Allied assistance would be withdrawn from Russia but that Japan would remain in Siberia. One section of the Russian press was actually speculating on the possible means of compensating Japan for her continued assistance to the Omsk government.[14] Anti-American propaganda was becoming more general and more effective.

The British government was also concerned about America's proposed withdrawal from Siberia. It pointed out that withdrawal would leave the Trans-Siberian Railway inadequately guarded, and in all probability make it impossible to keep open the line. Moreover, Japan would be left as the only country maintaining forces in Siberia. Great Britain, therefore, expressed an "earnest hope" that American troops would be retained in Siberia.[15]

The Japanese press had been giving considerable space to America's desire to withdraw. It attributed that desire to a failure of American policies. The newspaper comment indicated that American withdrawal would be welcomed by Japanese "public opinion" because it would leave Japan free to pursue her own purpose in Siberia. One

[11] Morris to Lansing, Sept. 25, 1919, United States, *Foreign Relations, 1919, Russia,* p. 581. Morris was unable to determine whether Tsuneo Matsudaira, Japanese member of the Inter-Allied Railway Committee, and Oi were acting under instructions from Tokyo or on their own initiative.

[12] Smith to Lansing, Sept. 28, 1919, United States, *Foreign Relations, 1919, Russia,* p. 584.

[13] Phillips to Morris, Sept. 27, 1919, United States, *Foreign Relations, 1919, Russia,* pp. 582-583.

[14] Jenkins to Lansing, Oct. 3, 1919, file 861.00/5324, D.S.N.A.

[15] Davis to Lansing, Oct. 1, 1919, United States, *Foreign Relations, 1919, Russia,* p. 585.

of the most significant statements appeared in the *Yamato,* a newspaper which represented the views of the military group in Japan:

Even if America withdraws Japan cannot do likewise. Not only would the Omsk Government be placed in peril if we did so but the Bolsheviks would create disturbances which would threaten the security of Korea and Manchuria. We should therefore like to make Japan's position clear to the whole world. The population of Japan is increasing at the rate of six or seven hundred thousand a year. The difficulty of living is increasing more and more. We ought to seek areas of extension abroad but America is violating the fundamental principles of freedom and equality and is closing the door to our emigrants. Canada, Australia and Africa are also standing in the way of our progress so that our people have no place to go except sparsely settled Manchuria and Siberia. The same applies to China. We should both assist the Russians to develop their land. Of course Japan has no designs to control the Siberian railways as America has, nor has she any territorial ambition. We cannot withdraw from Siberia because we desire to preserve and make ourselves secure. We therefore want the whole world to understand that we are not in the same position with reference to Siberia as the United States.[16]

Conditions in Siberia did not improve to any considerable degree after the dispatch of the American note of August 30. Reports from General Graves and other sources showed that subordinate Japanese commanders in Siberia were continuing to support the conflicting activities of Cossack leaders. Stevens cabled that Semenov was moving troops and occupying stations along the Chinese Eastern. Further reports indicated that an attempt would be made to establish independent Russian authority under Semenov east of Lake Baikal. Semenov would be supported by Japanese military commanders. Moreover, Army and Navy intelligence reports revealed that troops under Kalmikov, Semenov, and Rozanov were planning to attack American troops. Graves believed that they were instigated by the Japanese for the purpose of getting American troops out of Siberia.[17]

In view of this critical situation, Baker urged Lansing to insist upon an answer from Japan. By this time Baker was firmly convinced that the United States should either send a large force to Siberia or withdraw completely.[18] A note was sent immediately to Japan, requesting a reply to the American note of August 30. Morris was also instructed to bring to the attention of the Japanese government the grave condi-

[16] Morris to Lansing, Oct. 8, 1919, file 861.00/5351, D.S.N.A.

[17] Graves to Adjutant General, Oct. 8, 1919, file 861.00/5472, D.S.N.A.; Macgowan to Lansing, Oct. 8, 1919, file 861.00/5360, D.S.N.A.

[18] Baker to Rear Admiral Grayson, Oct. 9, 1919, Baker Papers.

tions which existed in Siberia due to the activities of Japanese subordinate military officers and the Cossack leaders.[19]

The Japanese answer finally arrived on October 31. Although vague and indirect, the note was conciliatory in spirit. It appeared to be a compromise between the military and civilian groups. While reasserting the independence of the Japanese military, the note promised close co-operation with the Inter-Allied Committee and protection of the lives and property of the committee's representatives. This was a distinct gain. In addition, the Japanese government invited formal discussion of specific instances in which "Japanese troops have refused to protect the lives and property of Allied inspectors." The Japanese government also substantiated General Oi's revised orders. These, however, still had to stand the test of execution. The note concluded with a promise to send to Siberia, as civilian High Commissioner, Ambassador Tsunetado Kato, a man of liberal views reputed to be antimilitaristic. There was, however, one significant omission from the reply. No reference was made to the fear suggested in the American note that the Japanese government did not share the American conviction "that the future welfare of all governments is based upon a community of interests."[20] It was Morris's growing conviction that it is of no value to discuss at this time and in the abstract the views or purposes of the Japanese Government. I see no advantage to better relations between Japan and America in reiterated statements of policy, rather we should put Japan's national purposes, so far as they touch our own purposes, to the test of action. When we are prepared as a Government and people to support constructive action in the Orient then we should seek Japan's cooperation and at the same time be ready to proceed without it. Mere mutiny [sic] and protest simply accentuate differences and may lead to serious complications. In the face of crying needs such as exist in China and Siberia we cannot be placed in the position of seeming to stay the hand of Japan while failing to offer any alternative plan of relief.

Morris added that the Siberian problem was different. Even though conditions demanded much more, the United States was not in a position to do more. In these circumstances Morris felt that "we can only make the best of our limitations and with patience continue our efforts to cooperate with Japan. Such a policy may seem unsatisfactory but it is, I submit, far better than entire withdrawal."[21]

[19] Lansing to Morris, Oct. 10, 1919, United States, *Foreign Relations, 1919, Russia*, pp. 586-587.

[20] Morris to Lansing, Oct. 31, 1919, United States, *Foreign Relations, 1919, Russia*, pp. 588-592.

[21] Morris to Lansing, Nov. 1, 1919, United States, *Foreign Relations, 1919, Russia*, pp. 592-594.

The American government followed Morris's suggestion. Accepting the Japanese note at its face value, Lansing expressed pleasure over the Japanese desire to co-operate in forwarding the railway plan in Siberia.[22]

Following the American-Japanese exchange of notes the Japanese Cabinet discussed the problem of formulating a definite Siberian policy. Viscount Takaakira Kato, leader of the Kenseikai party, had subjected the policy to severe criticism, demanding the withdrawal from Siberia of a substantial portion of the Japanese troops. The military, on the other hand, had been agitating for the dispatch of additional reinforcements, using as an argument the possible withdrawal of American troops. The civilian members of the Cabinet opposed such action. Hara, the Prime Minister, thus found himself between two fires, the military on the one side and Viscount Kato, leader of the opposition, on the other.[23]

On November 24 Viscount Uchida attempted to explain Japan's position to Ambassador Morris. Pointing to Kolchak's retirement from Omsk, Uchida expressed his concern over the continued eastward advance of the Bolsheviks. If the Red Army reached Baikal and came into contact with Japanese troops, the situation would be serious; if on the other hand Japan should withdraw, it would mean the surrender of Eastern Siberia to Bolshevism, and this would at once create a serious menace to Korea, Manchuria, and indirectly to Japan itself.

Morris immediately assured Uchida that he did not expect the withdrawal of American troops from Siberia. He then gave his personal recommendations concerning the problem at hand. He advocated that the Allies avoid all participation in local intrigue, that they continue earnestly to support Kolchak, and that they maintain the present force to protect and continue railway operations. Finally, Morris emphasized his personal conviction that some comprehensive plan of economic relief be undertaken by the two governments. Uchida expressed his full accord with these views and his intention to discuss them with the Cabinet.[24]

A few days later Hara attained a sweeping victory over General Tanaka, Minister of War, both in the Cabinet and in the Diplomatic Advisory Council. Tanaka had urged the dispatch of more troops. Hara, however, following the advice of Viscount Uchida, and having

[22] Lansing to Morris, Nov. 12, 1919, United States, *Foreign Relations, 1919, Russia,* pp. 594-595.

[23] Morris to Lansing, Nov. 24, 1919, file 861.00/5742, D.S.N.A.

[24] Morris to Lansing, Nov. 24, 1919, United States, *Foreign Relations, 1919, Russia,* pp. 599-601.

in mind Kato's recent criticism of the military policy, advocated the maintenance of the status quo pending an understanding with the Allied governments, particularly the United States.[25] Thus it seemed that the differences between Japan and America on the Siberian question were about to be resolved. In the meantime Ambassador Shidehara had begun negotiations with the State Department regarding a joint policy in Siberia.[26]

During the next month the State Department was forced to reconsider its entire policy in Siberia. It received suggestions from various quarters. Lloyd George suggested that Georgia, Azerbaijan, Bessarabia, the Ukraine, the Baltic Provinces, Finland, and possibly even Siberia should be independent, since a unified Russia would be a menace to Europe.[27] The American government opposed this view not only on moral grounds, but also because it believed that a divided Russia would be unable to cope with "existing Japanese territorial ambition."[28] Minister Hapgood, telegraphing from Denmark, said that only four possible courses were open. One was to give Germany a free hand. He considered this politically beyond serious discussion. Another was to send in a big Entente Army prepared to stay two years. Hapgood personally thought this also was politically impossible. The third was to treat the Russian situation honestly as a civil war, favoring no faction and backing none. A fourth view stated that since the collapse of Judenitch and Kolchak was so complete and the prospects of Denikin so poor, no civil war would be left if foreign aid were withdrawn; therefore the Moscow government should actually be recognized.[29]

On December 8 the Japanese Embassy presented an *aide memoire*

[25] Morris to Lansing, Nov. 28, 1919, United States, *Foreign Relations, 1919, Russia*, pp. 601-603. A few days later Tanaka called upon Morris and gave an extended summary of his views on the Siberian situation. He stated that the Cabinet recognized the necessity of reinforcements but had decided first to reach an understanding with America. He had therefore telegraphed General Inouye, the military attaché at Washington, to co-operate with Ambassador Shidehara in arriving at an understanding with the State Department. He added that all the Japanese generals in Siberia agreed "that the only purpose of sending reinforcements was to keep the means of transportation protected in the hope our governments would speedily agree on some joint method of economic assistance" (Morris to Lansing, Dec. 1, 1919, file 861.00/5796, D.S.N.A.).

[26] Poole to Lansing, Dec. 8, 1919, file 861.00/6114, D.S.N.A.

[27] Polk to Lansing, Nov. 29, 1919, United States, *Foreign Relations, 1919, Russia*, p. 126; Davis to Lansing, Dec. 3, 1919, United States, *Foreign Relations, 1920*, III, 484.

[28] Lansing to Davis, Dec. 4, 1919, United States, *Foreign Relations, 1919, Russia*, p. 130; Lansing to Morris, Dec. 5, 1919, file 861.00/5828, D.S.N.A.

[29] Hapgood to Lansing, Nov. 30, 1919, United States, *Foreign Relations, 1919, Russia*, pp. 126-127.

to the American government which expressed concern over the military crisis confronting Kolchak and suggested three possible courses of action:

1. To send a re-inforcement of sufficient strength and, acting on the offensive in cooperation with the anti-Bolshevik forces, to crush the Red Army;

2. To avoid direct contact with the Red Army and to effect entire or partial withdrawal of the Allied troops;

3. To maintain the guarding of the districts now under Allied military protection, and, without assuming the offensive, to check the continued eastward advance of the Red Army.

The Japanese government rejected the first idea because the Japanese public opposed the dispatch of more troops to Siberia. The second alternative was also opposed because it meant that Eastern Siberia would become Bolshevik. Thus, the third suggestion seemed to be the only practicable course to take. Under that plan the Japanese government felt that reinforcements should be sent to those points on the railway which were inadequately guarded, so as to fortify them against Bolshevik invasion. The number of reinforcements suggested was five to six thousand men. The note concluded with the request for information as to "whether the United States proposes to maintain the *status quo,* or to proceed to entire or partial withdrawal of its troops, or whether it is ready to send a reinforcement in case of need."[30]

The Japanese government had thus brought the question of withdrawal or reinforcement to a head. Japanese officials impatiently awaited the State Department's reaction to their note of December 8. The delay apparently embarrassed the Foreign Office in formulating a Siberian policy and in resisting the pressure of the military authorities, who were more eager than ever to send reinforcements.[31] While the Foreign Office waited, the American government struggled toward a decision. On December 23 Lansing presented a memorandum to the President. Written as a projected note for transmission to Japan, it advised withdrawal as the only reasonable course to adopt in Siberia. The reasons for intervention had now been fulfilled. Lansing wrote that "conditions have now entirely changed." In the first place, the United States had given all the aid and encouragement possible to

[30] Japanese Embassy to Lansing, Dec. 8, 1919, file 861.00/6109, D.S.N.A. The note also suggested that the American government approach the British and French governments on the question of co-operation against the activities of the Red Army.

[31] Morris to Lansing, Jan. 7, 1920, United States, *Foreign Relations, 1920,* III, 486-487.

the Siberian people in their efforts for self-government. Secondly, the army of the Czechoslovaks which had remained a long time in Central Siberia had now moved eastward and reached Eastern Siberia. In the meantime arrangements had been made in Paris for the repatriation of these soldiers, and plans were proceeding for their return to their native land. The advance of the Bolsheviks had caused the Allies to abandon the protection, operation, and control of that part of the Trans-Siberian Railway which lay west of Lake Baikal. Of those branches which lay east of Lake Baikal, the Chinese Eastern was practically all within Chinese territory. Lansing added that the forces operating under the direction of the Russian authorities in control of Trans-Baikal should be numerically sufficient to protect and maintain the operation of that portion of the railroad from Irkutsk to Manchouli. Consequently, it appeared that the proper joint activities of the United States and of Japan in Siberia were at an end. The only practical step left was the withdrawal of troops from Siberia. Any other plan might lead to warlike activity with the Bolsheviks. Lansing added that he would not consult Britain or France on the matter as suggested by Japan, since the arrangement to enter Siberia was made only with the government of Japan.[32] Lansing heartily recommended that Wilson approve the note. Baker had read it and was in thorough agreement. In a simple paragraph Lansing explained the real reason for the note:

The truth of the matter is the simple fact that the Kolchak Government has utterly collapsed; the armies of the Bolsheviki have advanced into Eastern Siberia, where they are reported to be acting with moderation. The people seem to prefer them to the officers of the Kolchak regime. Further, the Bolshevik army is approaching the region where our soldiers are, and contact with them will lead to open hostilities and to many complications. In other words, if we do not withdraw we shall have to wage war against the Bolsheviki.[33]

Lansing thus indicated to Wilson that the real reason for withdrawing American troops was the fear that their continued maintenance in Siberia might lead to conflict with the Bolsheviks. This, however, was not the reason emphasized in the note to Japan. This note stressed the

[32] Lansing to Wilson, Dec. 23, 1919, file 861.00/6107, D.S.N.A.

[33] Lansing to Wilson, Dec. 23, 1919, *Lansing Papers*, II, 392. Breckinridge Long had already told the Russian ambassador that "we could not get any sentiment in this country for fighting the Bolsheviki. . . ." He further called attention to the "fact that each of the anti-Bolshevik forces were fighting the Bolsheviks only a little harder than they were fighting each other" (Memorandum of a Conversation between Long and the Russian Ambassador, Dec. 2, 1919, Long Papers).

fact that American help was no longer needed; the United States had done all it could for the Russians.[34]

Poole made additional suggestions which were embodied in the note. He advised the elimination of any mention that reinforcements sent to Siberia might lead to war with the Bolsheviks. Since the United States had not declared war against them, Poole thought this was a dangerous subject, and therefore did not wish any embarrassing questions raised. After correcting certain errors in Lansing's geography, Poole added a paragraph in which he reluctantly stated that the Railway Service Corps must be withdrawn with American troops. At the same time, a word was included to the effect that the United States was not relinquishing its interest in Eastern Siberia.[35] The note with these changes was sent to Japan on January 9, 1920.[36] On the same day the Japanese War Minister advised the American Embassy that he had received a telegram from General Oi, Japanese commander, stating that General Graves had been instructed to withdraw all American troops from Siberia.[37]

The Japanese Minister for Foreign Affairs was greatly disturbed over this news. He could not account for such sudden action, especially since the State Department had been engaged in conversations with Ambassador Shidehara on a joint Siberian policy and had made no suggestion about the immediate withdrawal of American troops. The Foreign Minister observed that this action put his government in an extremely difficult position.[38] Ambassador Morris was also quite surprised at this news, and immediately informed the State Department that if "General Graves has interpreted his orders correctly, our sudden action, without any previous notice to the Japanese Government, is a stunning blow to Japanese pride as well as to all Liberal and pro-American influence here and will have, I fear, far-reaching effects."[39]

The State Department was thus placed in an embarrassing position,

[34] See unsigned and undated note accompanying Lansing's Memorandum to the President on Dec. 23, 1919, file 861.00/6109, D.S.N.A.

[35] Poole to Polk, Jan. 2, 1920, file 861.00/6115, D.S.N.A.

[36] Lansing to Shidehara, Jan. 9, 1920, United States, *Foreign Relations, 1920*, III, 488-490.

[37] Morris to Lansing, Jan. 9, 1920, United States, *Foreign Relations, 1920*, III, 490. On Dec. 31, General Graves had received orders to prepare for withdrawal but had been instructed to keep these orders secret; he had been informed that the final decision to withdraw had been reached on Jan. 5; that it was to be published in Washington on Jan. 7, and that he was authorized to make it public in Vladivostok on Jan. 8 (Poole to Lansing, Jan. 9, 1920, file 861.00/6126, D.S.N.A.).

[38] Morris to Lansing, Jan. 9, 1920, United States, *Foreign Relations, 1920*, III, 491-492.

[39] Morris to Lansing, Jan. 11, 1920, file 861.00/6113, D.S.N.A.

although the confusion of orders had evidently occurred in the War Department. Baker expressed his regret and informed Lansing that he was telegraphing Graves that American troops would not leave until a substantial portion of the Czechs were afloat. Morris read the American note of withdrawal to the Japanese Foreign Minister on January 12. He hoped that the wording of the note would help to overcome the prevailing feeling among Japanese officials that they had been treated with "scant consideration."[40]

On January 12 Lansing explained to Morris that the orders issued to General Graves had been dual in character and had unfortunately been misinterpreted. Morris was told to explain the error to the Minister for Foreign Affairs and also to inform the public at an opportune time that there had been "no purpose on the part of this government to act otherwise than frankly and with the greatest possible measure of coordination." Since the State Department had assumed that the Japanese *aide memoire* of December 8 required a definite answer, it had been forced to select one of three alternatives; namely, reinforcement, maintenance of the status quo, or withdrawal. Despite his illness, the President had made the final decision. It was then communicated as promptly as possible to the Japanese government.[41]

The premature announcement of withdrawal, coupled with the subsequent statement that the first contingent of American troops would sail on January 12, raised a storm of indignation and resentment in Japan. The United States was criticized bitterly for its alleged double dealing and discourtesy. The imperialistic elements in Japanese public life made the most of the incident to further their views and policies. However, Morris was hopeful that a policy of expedient compromise would prevail. He believed that such a policy would probably include the immediate dispatch of the Takata division to Siberia, and the transfer of troops from the Amur Railway to the Chinese Eastern Railway with such control of operations as could be secured without unduly exciting Russian and Chinese feeling. Morris added that the dispatch of additional troops would be called an "emergency measure," whereas the general policy would be termed "gradual evacuation."[42]

The feeling among the local Chinese officials at Peking was also very bitter on the withdrawal of American troops from Siberia. They contended that if American and Allied contingents were withdrawn,

[40] Morris to Lansing, Jan. 12, 1920, United States, *Foreign Relations, 1920*, III, 494-495.
[41] Lansing to Morris, Jan. 12, 1920, United States, *Foreign Relations, 1920*, III, 493-494.
[42] Morris to Lansing, Jan. 14, 1920, file 861.00/6134, D.S.N.A.

the Japanese should withdraw also. The latter, however, were sending reinforcements.[43]

On January 22, 1920, the Japanese government replied to the American memorandum announcing withdrawal. Japan expressed regret that the United States had not consulted her prior to the decision to withdraw. However, she accepted the American explanation that conditions in the United States had made the decision urgent, leaving no time for the discussion of the question with the Japanese government. Japan was apparently mollified by Secretary Lansing's declaration to Ambassador Shidehara that the American government would have no objection to Japan's continued maintenance of troops in Siberia, or to the sending of reinforcements to the Trans-Siberian and Chinese Eastern Railways.[44] On January 30 the American government formally affirmed Lansing's declaration to Shidehara.[45]

The method of withdrawing American troops from Siberia provided another reason for friction between the State and War Departments. Graves had been given orders to concentrate his troops in Vladivostok. The State Department was opposed to these orders because it feared that the strained relations existing between the Czechs and General Semenov might result in serious difficulty without the Americans there to guard the railway.[46] Unmoved by this plea, Baker replied that the movement was a military necessity recommended by General Graves himself.[47] Acting Secretary Polk then sent Baker a summary of various reports from Siberia which emphasized the resulting serious condition of the Czechs if the American troops were withdrawn.[48] Baker replied with much force:

The number of our troops remaining in Siberia is something like 5,000 and it is obvious that their assistance is not necessary to some 72,000 Czecho-Slovaks who are withdrawing toward Vladivostok. You may re-

[43] Albert W. Pontius (consul general at Mukden) to Tenney, Jan. 21, 1920, file 861.00/6372, D.S.N.A.

[44] Japanese Embassy to Lansing, Jan. 22, 1920, United States, *Foreign Relations, 1920,* III, 497-498.

[45] A leading editorial in a national magazine pointed out that Washington was so hysterical over the Bolshevik menace that it was giving Japan an excellent opportunity for aggrandizing herself ("Japan and Siberia," *New Republic,* XXI, Jan. 14, 1920, 187-188). For a similar view, see Lincoln Colcord, "Japan in Siberia," *Nation,* CX (Jan. 10, 1920), 37-39. The *Nation* had consistently attacked the State Department's policy in Siberia (Oswald Villard, *Fighting Years,* New York, 1939, p. 353).

[46] Lansing to Baker, Jan. 22, 1920, United States, *Foreign Relations, 1920,* III, 496.

[47] Baker to Lansing, Jan. 23, 1920, United States, *Foreign Relations, 1920,* III, 498.

[48] Polk to Baker, Jan. 28, 1920, United States, *Foreign Relations, 1920,* III, 498-501.

call that Mr. Stevens in one of his original cablegrams on this subject, stated in substance that if the small detachments of Americans scattered along the railroad had difficulty in getting out, they could be protected by the Czecho-Slovaks.[49]

The State Department was by no means happy over affairs in Siberia. Polk and MacMurray were particularly concerned over the question of Japan's withdrawal from Siberia. Lansing, however, had no such qualms. He said that from the beginning it had been understood that Japan contemplated no territorial acquisitions in Siberia; that she would not have sent an expedition into Siberia except in cooperation with the United States; and that co-operation was based upon eventual and complete withdrawal. Moreover, Lansing added that every Japanese diplomat with whom he had spoken had assured him that Japan would withdraw completely from Siberia. Therefore, Lansing felt that it was unnecessary to demand assurances from Japan at that time. Polk, however, feared that the withdrawal of American forces might be construed to affect this obligation on the part of Japan. Lansing did not share Polk's fears. MacMurray then raised the question of the Chinese Eastern Railway:

I suggested that the question of the Chinese Eastern Railway was to be distinguished from the case of Siberia; that this involved not a question of territorial acquisitions, but one of control over the railway in Manchuria; and I enquired whether the Secretary would consider it advisable to suggest, in his conversation with the Japanese Ambassador, that the *status quo* should be preserved. The Secretary pointed out, and Mr. Polk concurred, that it would be necessary for Japan to maintain at least temporarily a control over the Chinese Eastern Railway, as the means of communication with their troops in Siberia. I suggested that while such temporary control must of course be taken for granted, it might be possible and advisable to obtain from the Japanese some assurances that ultimately the *status quo ante* would be restored so as in the end to leave unimpaired the existing rights both of the Chinese and others interested. The Secretary said that he proposed to have with the Ambassador a full discussion of the military aspects of the situation, and that in the course of it he would take occasion to ascertain the attitude of the Japanese government on this question.[50]

As a result of these discussions Secretary Lansing sent a note to the Japanese government on January 30, reaffirming his declaration to Shidehara concerning the retention of Japanese troops in Siberia and stating:

[49] Baker to Polk, Feb. 19, 1920, United States, *Foreign Relations, 1920*, III, 503-504.

[50] MacMurray to Poole, Jan. 23, 1920, file 861.00/6735, D.S.N.A.

The Government of the United States desires to record an assurance of its confidence that the Imperial Japanese Government will, in the exercise of the trust devolving upon it, pursue the same policy that was mutually agreed upon when the two Governments determined to cooperate in Siberia,—particularly in connection with the operation of the Siberian Railway system (including therein the Chinese Eastern Railway), the existing rights to which, it is confidently assumed, will in no way be impaired in the consequence of the efforts of the Japanese Government to carry out the purposes which induced the two Governments to send their military forces to Siberia.[51]

Throughout the month of January, 1920, Hara's ministry was under fire on its Siberian policy. The policy was criticized in the Diet as well as in the newspapers. Military authorities were accused of interfering with diplomatic authorities in the conduct of foreign relations. Japanese representatives, as well as a large share of the informed public, registered their opposition to an increase of forces in Siberia and demanded that the government make public its policy there.[52] The Kobe *Japan Chronicle* reported that no expedition had been more unpopular with the Japanese nation. The Tokyo *Ji ji* opposed the reinforcement of troops in Siberia on the grounds that it would make the powers "suspect Japan of territorial ambitions." The Tokyo *Kokumin* added that "Japan would better protect Japanese interests only and leave Russia's rehabilitation to the Russians." The Tokyo *Yamato* differed. It felt that Japan must "make herself responsible for the maintenance of order in eastern Siberia, at least."[53] Ambassador Morris reported that many of the livelier journals advised the dispatch of five thousand additional troops as a temporary measure in order to protect Japanese residents, to preserve Manchuria and Mongolia from being plunged into chaos, and to guard the Koreans from contamination by the Bolsheviks.[54]

On February 3 Japan explained her Siberian policy to the United States. She informed the State Department that geography made her position in Siberia distinct from that of the other European powers. Political conditions in Eastern Siberia not only gravely affected affairs in Korea and Manchuria but also threatened the safety of the lives and property of a large number of Japanese subjects in these regions. This was the sole cause of Japan's inability to withdraw her troops immedi-

[51] Lansing to Morris, Jan. 30, 1920, United States, *Foreign Relations, 1920*, III, 501-502.

[52] Takeuchi, *War and Diplomacy*, pp. 211-212.

[53] *Literary Digest*, LXIV (Jan. 31, 1921), 25.

[54] Morris to Lansing, Jan. 28, 1920, file 861.00/6368, D.S.N.A.

ately. Japan added that it was her sincere desire to withdraw from Siberia as soon as possible after the completion of the Czechoslovak evacuation and as soon as political affairs in the districts bordering on her frontier became sufficiently settled to remove all danger to the regions of Korea and Manchuria.[55]

The Japanese note provoked no change in the State Department's policy of withdrawing from Siberia. American troops remained in Vladivostok until a substantial portion of the Czech troops were afloat. The last contingent of Americans left Vladivostok on April 1, 1920.[56] Few tears were shed over their departure. America's part in the Siberian situation had already been summed up aptly, if somewhat facetiously, by the *Literary Digest* when it remarked that "some might have liked us more if we had intervened less, that some might have disliked us less if we had intervened more, but that, having concluded that we intended to intervene no more nor no less than we actually did, nobody had any use for us at all."[57]

[55] Memorandum of Japanese Government to Department of State, Feb. 3, 1920, file 861.00/6706, D.S.N.A.; Young, *Japan under Taisho Tenno*, p. 179; Major General Tsunekichi Kono, *The Japanese Army* (Tokyo, 1929), p. 29.

[56] U. S. Army War College, *Order of Battle*, p. 389. The small British and French detachments had already been withdrawn in the late summer and early fall of 1919 (Churchill, The *Aftermath*, p. 256; Moulis and Bergonier, *La Guerre entre les allies et la Russie*, p. 131).

[57] *Literary Digest*, LXII (Sept. 6, 1919), 60.

CHAPTER XI

Japan, Sakhalin, and the Maritime Province

THE AMERICAN decision to leave Siberia became the signal for widespread rumors of Japanese intentions in Siberia. The State Department learned that there was fairly good, though not conclusive, evidence available in Warsaw, indicating that Germany and Japan were aligning Poland on their side against Great Britain, France, and the United States in an attempt to effect a virtual control of Russia.[1] On February 19 David B. Macgowan, new consul at Vladivostok, cabled that an official radio from Alexandrovsk, Russian Sakhalin, reported that Japanese warships had been trying to land troops there for the last three days.[2] Stevens reported that the Japanese army was supporting Semenov in every way to delay the movement of the Czechs.[3] The Bolsheviks, on the other hand, were doing everything possible to aid in the movement. Stevens urged the State Department to protest against the obstructive tactics of the Japanese. He added, "They will not admit charge of obstruction but they are accomplished liars."[4]

On February 22 the Bolsheviks signed an armistice with the Czechs.[5] They also attempted to come to terms with the Japanese through peace proposals, reminding them of their common interests in the Far East.[6] These efforts were fruitless. The Japanese continued

[1] Polk to American Legation at Warsaw, Jan. 28, 1920, file 861.00/6258a, D.S.N.A. On Feb. 3 the same rumor was reported with further evidence from Warsaw (Gibson [Warsaw] to Lansing, Feb. 3, 1920, file 861.00/6293, D.S.N.A.).

[2] Macgowan to Lansing, Feb. 19, 1920, file 861.00/6478, D.S.N.A.

[3] Stevens to Lansing, Feb. 18, 1920, file 861.00/6382, D.S.N.A.

[4] Stevens to Lansing, Feb. 20, 1920, file 861.00/6414, D.S.N.A.

[5] Harris to Polk, Feb. 22, 1920, United States, *Foreign Relations, 1920*, III, 564-565.

[6] Minister in Sweden to Lansing, Feb. 26, 1920, United States, *Foreign Relations, 1920*, III, 448.

their obstructing tactics against the Czechs. Stevens reported that the Czechs would probably fight anybody or everybody to get out if such activities continued.[7] Stevens had agreed to remain in Siberia until the complete evacuation of the Czechs had been accomplished, despite the fact that American troops were already being evacuated. The U.S.S. *Albany,* an American cruiser, remained at Vladivostok to safeguard American interests there.[8]

On February 25 the Japanese Cabinet announced its decision to recommend to the Diplomatic Advisory Council the gradual withdrawal of all Japanese troops from Siberia.[9] However, these professed plans were interrupted by two "incidents" which provoked an extension rather than a reduction in the Japanese occupation of Siberia. The first of these incidents resulted in the massacre of an alleged six hundred Japanese residents and soldiers at Nikolaevsk, Siberia, on March 15, 1920. The Russian and Japanese versions of the affair were totally different. Each blamed the other for beginning the attack.[10] News of the massacre was first given out to the press of the world on March 28, 1920. At first the affair excited little comment. Later, however, the Japanese government used the incident to arouse the feelings of its nationals against the Siberians. It was also used as a reason for retaining Japanese forces in Siberia.

Before the Nikolaevsk massacre occurred, the American Military Intelligence in Siberia had been convinced that the Japanese would shortly launch an attack in Eastern Siberia for the purpose of forcibly taking possession of the Maritime Province. This conviction was based on knowledge of thorough preparations at Vladivostok for an attack upon the province.

The United States government was also informed of the possibility of the second "incident" before it actually occurred. On April 1 Frank King, Associated Press correspondent in Vladivostok, told General Graves that he had reliable information that "the Japanese Military Party in a few days would do something in Siberia to which the Civil Party in Japan would be opposed" and that the Russian account of the Nikolaevsk affair was the correct one. General Graves cabled this statement to the United States.[11]

[7] Stevens to Lansing, Feb. 28, 1920, file 861.00/6474, D.S.N.A.
[8] Daniels to Lansing, March 19, 1920, file 861.00/6606, D.S.N.A.
[9] Morris to Acting Secretary of State, Feb. 25, 1920, United States, *Foreign Relations, 1920,* III, 504.
[10] For the Russian and Japanese versions of the incident, see Varneck and Fisher, *Testimony of Kolchak,* pp. 331-364; Young, *Japan Under Taisho Tenno,* pp. 181-187.
[11] Memorandum Prepared by Military Intelligence on Fighting at Nikolaevsk, Nov. 10, 1921, file 861.00/9103, D.S.N.A.

In accordance with King's prediction, the second incident occurred on the night of April 4, 1920. The Japanese captured the city of Vladivostok. Admiral Albert Gleaves, commander-in-chief of the United States Asiatic fleet, reported that the occupation "was evidently done according to a preconceived plan," and without any provocation by the Russians.[12] Japan reported that her actions were defensive; the Russians had begun the attack. Macgowan and Harris had no evidence to indicate that the Russians had even answered the fire. Colonel Winterburn of the United States Army, an eyewitness to the affair, reported that the Japanese capture of Vladivostok was entirely without Russian provocation. He stated that the Japanese had made elaborate plans for the action.[13]

On April 11 Admiral Gleaves submitted a summary of Japanese activities in Siberia. He reported that after reading all naval intelligence reports on the incident, he felt that "beyond question the Japanese occupation of Vladivostok was premeditated and fully arranged for and that it was accompanied by the practically simultaneous occupation of all important places in the Maritime District as far as Habarovsk." It was further apparent that Japan's explanation of the incident was untrue, and designed to "deceive the neutral nations and more particularly the civilian population." Gleaves was convinced that Japan intended to control Eastern Siberia. He felt that in time this action would have far-reaching effects on American prestige in the Far East and would bar the extension of trade and influence in Siberia. He urged the American government to prevent the extension of Japanese influence before the situation becomes "so acute as to lead to war between the two countries." Opposed to halfway measures, the Admiral insisted that any protest by America should be backed by adequate force.[14]

Ambassador Morris substantiated the views of Gleaves, adding that

[12] Gleaves to Office of Naval Operations, April 5, 1920, WA-6. Siberia, Conditions in Vladivostok, Naval Records Collection. The last American troops had departed on April 1.

[13] Memorandum by J. P. Jameson of an Interview with Colonel Winterburn, Nov. 19, 1920, file 861.00/7796, D.S.N.A. At the end of March General Graves had noted that Japanese troops were digging trenches and filling sandbags near Vladivostok, as though in preparation for a strong defense (Graves, *America's Siberian Adventure,* pp. 326-328). On April 10 the Russian ambassador, very much alarmed over what Japan was doing in Vladivostok, rushed to the State Department to find out whether the United States planned to make a protest. Polk told him "that he thought not as we had had an opportunity to make a protest and had let it go by" (Polk, Confidential Diary, April 10, 1920).

[14] Gleaves to Office of Naval Operations, April 11, 1920, Wilson Papers, series II; Daniels to Colby, June 5, 1920, file 861.00/6999, D.S.N.A.

all reports from American as well as other observers giving details of Japanese military activities in Vladivostok alleged a concerted and unprovoked attack by the Japanese followed by a general disarmament of Russian soldiers and the arrest of large numbers of Koreans. There were some indications that the Japanese Foreign Office was not fully informed of the plans of the General Staff and was fearful of international opinion. Morris, however, had received no word either directly or indirectly from government officials.[15]

The diplomatic corps in Tokyo was decidedly interested in the American reaction to the Nikolaevsk massacre. The Russian ambassador could see nothing to criticize in Japan's recent activities since they had resulted "in the death of a few more Bolsheviki."[16] Sir Charles Eliot, the British ambassador, expressed a similar viewpoint. He told Morris that British interest in Siberia was wholly an incident of the war; the creation of the Kolchak government was simply another step in the formation of a new Eastern Front. Since the Armistice made further efforts of that character unnecessary, subsequent British support of Kolchak during 1919 was induced by a sense of honorable obligation not to desert the movement simply because it was no longer useful. The fall of Kolchak discharged this obligation. Great Britain had no further political or national interest in such a remote territory as Siberia. Eliot could therefore see no reason why his government should interfere in the national aspirations of Japan. Differing from all other countries, "the interests of Japan in Siberia were vital and exciting." Furthermore, the threat of Bolshevism was, in his judgment, real. As Japanese citizens and business interests in the Maritime Province were endangered, it seemed to Eliot only natural that Japan should adopt rigorous measures to protect these interests. Morris was concerned over Eliot's views and expressed his anxiety to the State Department.[17]

Accounts from American diplomatic observers in the Far East led Bainbridge Colby, the new Secretary of State, to ask Ambassador Morris whether he believed that the Japanese government, despite its assertions to the contrary, contemplated a permanent occupation of Vladivostok and the surrounding territory. If Morris believed this to be true, Colby felt that the retention of the American consular officials

[15] Morris to Colby, April 13, 1920, file 861.00/6758, D.S.N.A.; Stevens to Colby, April 7, 1920, file 861.00/6707, D.S.N.A.

[16] Morris to Colby, April 13, 1920, file 861.00/6758, D.S.N.A.

[17] Morris to Lansing, April 14, 1920, file 861.00/6762, D.S.N.A. The British government reported that it did not "share the views expressed by Sir Charles Eliot . . ." (Davis to Colby, April 28, 1920, United States, *Foreign Relations, 1920,* I, 687-688).

in Siberia might appear to be a tacit acquiescence to Japan's changed policy.[18] Morris responded:

I regret to say I have never doubted for the past two years that the Japanese General Staff has not only contemplated but has carefully laid plans for the permanent occupation of Vladivostok and the Chinese Eastern Railway should conditions so develop as to render such action practicable. Since the armistice every development has led to the realization of this ambition, cherished by the Japanese military leaders. The increasing disorder and conflict in China, the collapse of anti-Bolshevik movements in Russia, the failure of our Senate to ratify the peace treaty and the consequent postponement of any effective League of Nations and finally our withdrawal from claim on interest in Siberia have all combined to create a situation peculiarly favorable to a policy of aggressive action by Japan. Liberal and enlightened leaders here are opposed to this policy but the trend of world events has been steadily against them and our sudden withdrawal [of] cooperation in Siberia was as I stated at the time a stunning blow. For the moment the military group appear to be in full control and they have lost no time in putting their plans into operation. Such is my personal interpretation of the recent developments in Eastern Siberia. But even if all the information received by the Department appeared to confirm my interpretation of the facts I do not think we are as yet justified in assuming officially that the Japanese Government has changed its previously announced policy. Such an assumption would in my judgment be premature and if acted on too hastily might only serve further to strengthen the military control here, alienate liberal opinion in Japan and make future course even more difficult.[19]

On April 25 the Japanese Foreign Office issued a statement concerning the Nikolaevsk massacre which seemed to lend strength to Morris's statement. The Japanese government had decided to dispatch a contingent of soldiers to Nikolaevsk to protect Japanese residents. Since ice made it impossible to go directly to the district, the contingent was to be sent via Sakhalin. It would remain at Alexandrovsk, Sakhalin, until the freezing season was over, in the meantime protecting the Japanese residents in that locality. This was the first public announcement of Japanese activities in Northern Sakhalin since Macgowan's telegram to the Department from Vladivostok on February 19.[20] The Foreign Office statement regarding Nikolaevsk was followed on May 6 by an announcement from General Oi "that

[18] Colby to Morris, April 20, 1920, file 861.00/6737, D.S.N.A.
[19] Morris to Colby, April 27, 1920, file 861.00/6832, D.S.N.A.
[20] Morris to Colby, April 25, 1920, United States, *Foreign Relations, 1920*, III, 511-512.

with the consent of all the Allied powers the Japanese Government will begin military operations in Siberia to suppress Bolshevism."[21]

The State Department was quite concerned over both these statements, particularly since the Siberian press reported that the Japanese Siberian policy was not independent but had the approval of the Allies. General Oi himself reported that the Japanese occupation of Manchuria and Siberia had been made with the consent of all the Allied powers. Caldwell asserted that the Russians were beginning to believe this news, since no American contradiction was issued.[22] Secretary Colby immediately issued a statement of denial for publication in Vladivostok, Harbin, and Peking.[23]

On June 9 the Japanese Foreign Office reported that the one hundred Japanese residents who had survived the Nikolaevsk massacre had apparently been slaughtered on May 25.[24] The first two weeks in June witnessed a campaign of propaganda in the Japanese press for the purpose of arousing public opinion in connection with the Nikolaevsk affair. The press was full of graphic accounts of the tragedy. People were demanding an investigation of the facts. Many advocated that Japan take over the entire Maritime Province and Northern Sakhalin until a recognized Russian government provided reparation for the incident.[25] In contrast to this view, other elements in Japan attacked the military with the charge that the whole Nikolaevsk business was a "frame-up" created by the Japanese War Office as an "incident" to give the military party another opportunity to emerge with honor, prestige, and the renewed confidence of the public.[26]

On July 3 the Japanese government informed the State Department of the policy it proposed to pursue in regard to the Nikolaevsk affair. Since there was no Russian government to which the Japanese government could protest, it had "no alternative but to seize and occupy certain points in the Province of Sakhalien until a legal government shall have been established in Russia and the present question satisfactorily adjusted." At the same time, the Japanese government reported that since the Czechoslovaks had now departed, it was withdrawing Japanese forces from the region of the Trans-Baikal. However, as the

[21] Stevens to Colby, May 6, 1920, file 861.00/6880, D.S.N.A.

[22] Caldwell to Colby, May 1, 1920, United States, *Foreign Relations, 1920*, III, 512-513; Caldwell to Colby, May 3, 1920, file 861.00/6859, D.S.N.A.

[23] Colby to Morris, May 7, 1920, United States, *Foreign Relations, 1920*, III, 513.

[24] Bell to Colby, June 9, 1920, United States, *Foreign Relations, 1920*, III, 513.

[25] Bell to Colby, June 18, 1920, file 861.00/7044, D.S.N.A.; Bell to Colby, June 26, 1920, file 861.00/7169, D.S.N.A.

[26] Miles M. Sherower, "The Nikolaevsk Massacre," *Nation*, III (Aug. 21, 1920), 211-213.

situation in Vladivostok still constituted a direct menace to Korea, Japanese troops would be maintained in that area as well as at Khabarovsk, which afforded a direct line of communication with the province of Sakhalin.[27]

The State Department expressed its gratification over the contemplated withdrawal of troops from the Trans-Baikal, but reserved opinion on the maintenance of Japanese forces in the vicinity of Khabarovsk and Vladivostok, on the grounds that it had insufficient facts to form a judgment on the military necessity of such an action. The Department, however, was quite frank in its disapproval of the occupation of parts of Northern Sakhalin. While deploring the slaughter at Nikolaevsk, the State Department could see no reason to occupy Northern Sakhalin for crimes in which the people of that area had played no part. Expressing his concern over the Japanese action, Secretary Colby wrote: "I should be lacking in candor if I were to conceal from you the concern with which this government learns of a decision so entirely at variance with the trust which we jointly assumed and have sought to discharge in behalf of the distracted and oppressed people of Siberia." In conclusion, Colby added that the United States government could not "participate in the announced decision of your Government with regard to Sakhalien, nor can it recognize the occupation of said territory by any non-Russian authority."[28]

On August 13 the Japanese government replied to America's protest. It upheld the retention of troops in Vladivostok and Khabarovsk on the grounds that it was a measure of self-defense absolutely necessary not only for the protection of Japanese residents in that area, but also for the preservation of order and security in Korea. Referring to the occupation of Sakhalin, it pointed out that the action was unavoidable since there was no other means of securing redress for the injuries so painfully received. The reply added "that it would be entirely beside the mark if it were construed as an act of territorial aggression."[29]

By the middle of September the Japanese had ordered the immedi-

[27] Japanese Embassy to Department of State, July 3, 1920, United States, *Foreign Relations, 1920*, III, 516-517.

[28] Colby to Japanese Ambassador, July 16, 1920, United States, *Foreign Relations, 1920*, III, 517-519. The State Department did not know that Nikolaevsk had been incorporated into the province of Sakhalin by a Russian imperial decree in 1914 (United States, *Foreign Relations, 1920*, III, 518, 521, 523).

[29] Memorandum of Japanese Government to Department of State, United States, *Foreign Relations, 1920*, III, 522-524.

ate evacuation of their troops from the territory north of Nikolsk. The Japanese press speculated as to whether the action was due to American protests.[30]   Evidently inspired by the Foreign Office, certain Japanese papers reported that since nothing had been heard from the American government in answer to Japan's explanation of the reason for occupying Sakhalin, it might be assumed that America had accepted those explanations.   Yet intercepted messages, presumably sent by the Japanese Minister of War to his military staff in Siberia, stated: "America's desire that we leave Siberia immediately has become serious question which demands caution. . . .   An immature act may destroy our aims hence we must temporarily abandon plan to occupy Siberia and not fortify districts where troops are."[31]

Throughout the winter of 1920 the State Department received regular reports on the activities of the Japanese military in Siberia. C. H. Smith, American representative on the Inter-Allied Railway Committee, was convinced that the Japanese were in Siberia to stay unless the Allies took some action against them. His patience in dealing with them had been tried to the breaking point. He reported that the actions of the Japanese military were "almost beyond belief."[32] Macgowan cabled from Vladivostok that robberies and murders in that city were increasing daily.[33] Admiral Gleaves reported that between October 6 and November 1, 1920, thirteen Japanese transports and ten thousand troops had arrived in Vladivostok.[34] By January, 1921, it appeared that Japan had no intention of leaving Siberia. When Premier Hara was questioned in the Diet concerning the retention of troops in Siberia, he replied that they would be maintained there until tranquillity had been restored.[35] At the same time it appeared that the Japanese military were doing everything possible to prevent the establishment of the desired "tranquillity." To this end, they continued to support Semenov at Chita.

After the collapse of the Kolchak government, Semenov faced

---

[30] The Minister for Foreign Affairs was credited with such a statement in an interview on Sept. 15 (Bell to Colby, Sept. 15, 1920, file 861.00/7367, D.S.N.A.).

[31] Department of State to Ambassador in Great Britain, Sept. 17, 1920, file 861.00/7356. Japanese actions were conformable with the evidence contained in the messages.

[32] Smith to Colby, Oct. 6, 1920, file 861.77/1806, D.S.N.A.

[33] Macgowan to Colby, Oct. 12, 1920, file 861.00/7512, D.S.N.A.

[34] Gleaves to Office of Naval Operations, Nov. 1, 1920, file 861.00/7618, D.S.N.A. The *Japan Chronicle*, a British publication at Kobe, as well as other anti-Japanese critics reported that Japan had the deliberate purpose of holding Eastern Siberia permanently (*Current History, The New York Times*, XII, Sept., 1920, 983-986).

[35] Takeuchi, *War and Diplomacy*, pp. 214-215; Bell to Colby, Jan. 27, 1921, United States, *Foreign Relations, 1921*, II, 701.

competition for the control of Eastern Siberia from at least three other Siberian governments: the Verkneudinsk, the Amur, and the Vladivostok governments. Of these the Vladivostok government was the most stable. Calling itself the Far Eastern Republic, it claimed to include the territories of Trans-Baikal, Amur, Primorskaia, Sakhalin, and Kamchatka. In addition, it claimed the right of way of the Chinese Eastern Railway. The new government proclaimed the calling of a constituent assembly and amnesty to all the soldiers of Kolchak and Semenov, if they laid down their arms. Although it emphasized the necessity of stopping the Red Army in its eastern march, it was opposed to any aid or support by a foreign country, particularly Japan. Furthermore, it desired the immediate withdrawal of all foreign expeditionary forces from Siberia.[36]

On March 22 the Far Eastern Republic made a formal protest to the American government in regard to Japan's continued occupation of Vladivostok. It desired to know whether intervention was at an end, or whether Japanese actions in Siberia were being carried on under the original agreement for intervention made between the United States and Japan. It pointed out that Japan showed no intentions of withdrawal, but on the contrary had begun the occupation of Sakhalin in addition to the Maritime Province. The Far Eastern Republic desired to know "when the United States Government which invited the Japanese government to a military cooperation in the Russian Far East" would declare that intervention was at an end.[37]

The protest from the Far Eastern Republic was followed by the news that Japan was extending her activities in Siberia. On March 23 the Japanese Minister of War announced the temporary military occupation of important districts in Sakhalin. Furthermore, peace and order were to be maintained in the districts of Nikolaevsk, De Castries, Mago, Sophiesk, and other important districts by the temporary estab-

[36] Tenney to Colby, May 18, 1920, Jenkins to Acting Secretary of State, Jan. 21, 1921, United States, *Foreign Relations, 1920*, III, 549-550, 554-561. Six months after it assumed power, the Far Eastern Republic succeeded in eliminating Semenov from the Chita government, and thereafter Chita became the virtual capital of the Far Eastern Republic. Tompkins, *American-Russian Relations in the Far East*, p. 154. The Far Eastern Republic was largely the result of the planning of Alexander Krasnoshchekov, whose experience during the intervention convinced him that the only answer to Japanese imperialism in Siberia was the establishment of a democratic, non-Communist buffer state in Eastern Siberia. He was able to come to an agreement with the Soviet government and the eventual result was the creation of the Far Eastern Republic (Stewart, *White Armies of Russia*, p. 379; White, *The Siberian Intervention*, pp. 368-369).

[37] Far Eastern Republic to United States of America, March 22, 1921, United States, *Foreign Relations, 1921*, II, 739-741.

lishment of a system of civil administration.[38] On March 31, 1921, in view of an attempted *coup d'état* at Vladivostok, Japan disarmed all warring parties and announced that Japanese troops would permit no further fighting in the zone occupied by them.[39]

These declarations, coupled with the protest from the Far Eastern Republic, resulted in the dispatch of another American note of protest to the Japanese government on May 31, 1921. Retracing the history of the joint Japanese-American expedition to Siberia, the note referred to the American expectation that Japanese troops would be withdrawn within a reasonable period after the withdrawal of American troops. The State Department disapproved of Japanese military and civil occupation of strategic Siberian districts. It pointed out that the establishment of civil administration functioning under the authority of military occupation lent to the occupation an appearance of permanence, indicating a further encroachment upon Russian political and administrative rights. Such activities tended to increase rather than allay the unrest and disorder in the occupied regions. The memorandum then asserted that the Nikolaevsk issue was not fundamentally a question of the validity of procedure under international law (i.e., the validity of reprisal) but of the scrupulous fulfilment of the assurances originally given to the Russian people. These assurances were intended to convey to the people of Russia a promise, on the part of Japan and the United States, not to use the joint expedition, *or any incidents which might arise out of it,* as an occasion to occupy territory, even temporarily. The United States then categorically informed Japan that it could neither then nor thereafter recognize as valid any claims or titles arising out of the existing occupation and control, and that it could not acquiesce in any action taken by the government of Japan which might impair existing treaty rights or the political or territorial integrity of Russia.[40]

Replying on July 8, 1921, the Japanese carefully drew a distinction between the joint expedition to Siberia in 1918, and the conditions which had arisen since the American withdrawal. Japan could not withdraw because she had to protect Japanese residents in the area. In addition, the geographic propinquity of the districts of Vladivostok and Nikolsk was bound to affect the security of the Korean frontier.

[38] Bell to Colby, March 23, 1921, United States, *Foreign Relations, 1921,* II, 701-702.

[39] Bell to Colby, April 1, 1921, United States, *Foreign Relations, 1921,* II, 721.

[40] Department of State to Japanese Embassy, May 31, 1921, United States, *Foreign Relations, 1921,* II, 702-704.

The Sakhalin case was entirely different. The horrible massacre at Nikolaevsk gave Japan no alternative but to occupy Sakhalin until the affair could be settled. The note added that Japan had refrained from taking sides in Russian affairs, and was doing everything possible to restore order and stable authority in the Far East. Furthermore, an early and complete withdrawal of Japanese troops from the Maritime Province was being contemplated. The note concluded:

> Nothing is further from the thought of the Japanese Government than to take advantage of helpless conditions in Russia for prosecuting selfish designs. Japan believes that she has shown very sympathetic interest in the efforts of patriotic Russians aspiring to the unity and rehabilitation of their country. The military occupation of the Russian Province of Sakhalin will naturally come to an end as soon as a satisfactory settlement of the question shall have been arranged with an orderly Russian Government.[41]

Early in August, 1921, the Japanese Vice Minister of Foreign Affairs informed the American chargé of Japan's intention to evacuate Vladivostok at the opportune moment. However, withdrawal could not take place until satisfactory guarantees had been obtained regarding the protection of Japanese interests and subjects after the departure of troops.[42] This news was followed on August 22 by a memorandum from the Japanese government announcing that it was conducting negotiations with the Far Eastern Republic. The proposed conference had "essentially in view the conclusion of commercial arrangements, the removal of the existing menace to the security of Japan and to the lives and property of Japanese residents in Eastern Siberia, provision of guarantees for the freedom of industrial undertakings in that region and the prohibition of Bolshevik propaganda over the Siberian border."[43] Japan reported that the negotiations were not calculated to give her "any right or advantage of an exclusive character." The Nikolaevsk affair would not be discussed, but reserved for a later occasion. Japan concluded with the information that if the conference should succeed in settling the immediate issues at hand, the Japanese government would at once proceed to withdraw its troops from the Maritime Province.[44]

[41] Japanese Embassy to Department of State, United States, *Foreign Relations, 1921*, II, 707-710.

[42] Bell to Colby, Aug. 8, 1921, United States, *Foreign Relations, 1921*, II, 713.

[43] It was Stevens's belief that "If Japanese would take their intrigues and troops out of the way the country would begin at once to return to normal conditions; Their continual howl about the Bolsheviks is only dragging herring across the trail" (Stevens to Colby, July 30, 1921, file 861.00/8886, D.S.N.A.).

[44] Shidehara to Hughes, Aug. 22, 1921, United States, *Foreign Relations, 1921*, II,

Japan's notes of July 8 and August 22 required a definite statement of policy from the State Department. Poole believed that these notes indicated what was already understood; namely, that Japan intended to continue its military occupation of the Russian Province of Sakhalin indefinitely as an act of reprisal for the massacre of Japanese at Nikolaevsk, and that she was making troop withdrawal from the Maritime Province the basis for bargaining for concessions. He prepared a suggested memorandum for transmission to the Japanese ambassador in which he briefly surveyed the history of intervention, and then urged "upon the Government of Japan, in the most earnest and friendly manner, that all remaining troops be unconditionally withdrawn from all Russian territory."[45] Poole hoped that Secretary Hughes would see upon reading the note that the United States could not let Japan proceed without serious protest. Although he had limited the memorandum to the moral issue created by Japan's refusal to live up to the promise given at the outset of intervention, Poole urged that the Japanese ambassador be told orally also of the practical expediency of withdrawing Japanese troops unconditionally. The memorandum pointed out that as long as Japanese troops remained on Siberian soil, there would be disorder and discontent in the occupied region. Moreover, in so far as Korea was concerned, any frontier was best protected from within.[46] Although Poole did not believe that the note would bring about the withdrawal of troops from Sakhalin, he thought it might have a generally deterrent effect upon Japanese aggression in Siberia.[47]

Henry P. Fletcher, the Under Secretary of State, read Poole's memorandum but did not believe it would accomplish anything if it were delivered on the eve of the Washington Conference. He advised that a similar memorandum might be offered at the conference itself. This advice was evidently followed, for there is no indication that the original note was ever sent.[48]

On December 20 the National Assembly of the Far Eastern Republic presented another protest concerning Japanese activities in the

713-715. Shortly thereafter the American government ordered Consul Caldwell to go to Chita on special duty as an observer of the negotiations between Japan and the Far Eastern Republic. At his discretion Caldwell was to exert his influence to protect American private interests (Hughes to Bell, Sept. 9, 1921, United States, *Foreign Relations, 1921*, II, 745-746).

[45] Draft of a note by Poole, Sept. 20 (?), 1921, file 861.00/8797, D.S.N.A.

[46] Poole to Hughes, Sept. 16, 1921, file 861.00/9025½, D.S.N.A.

[47] Poole to Hughes, Sept. 21, 1921, file 861.00/8797, D.S.N.A.

[48] Fletcher to Hughes, Sept. 23, 1921, file 861.00/8797, D.S.N.A.

Russian Far East. It averred that the Japanese were aiming to seize their territory and turn it into a Japanese colony. Japan's activities in Siberia since the beginning of intervention were aimed at prolonging civil war, thus creating conditions warranting the continuation of intervention. By ruining the economic life of the Russian Far East, Japan aimed to spread her own. The note also stated that at a recent conference with Japan, she had attempted to obtain the consent of the Far Eastern Republic to the retention of Japanese troops in Siberia. Furthermore, Japan desired the destruction of fortifications in Russian cities and concessions in the territory along the Tartar Straights—all of which meant a loss of Russian sovereignty, and dependence upon Japan politically and economically. Failing to obtain these concessions, the Japanese had rendered assistance to a certain Spiridon Merkulov to launch an attack against the Far Eastern Republic, for which the Japanese supplied munitions.[49] Consul Caldwell substantiated the information in the Far Eastern Republic's memorandum, adding that Japan's demands had become even more insistent since the opening of the Washington Conference. He, too, believed that Japan was responsible for the recent attack in the Maritime Province.[50] Letters from individuals in private capacities in Sakhalin and Siberia indicated that the activity of the Japanese in those areas hardly fell short of conquest and occupation. Poole again advised a strong public protest against the continuance of Japanese troops in Russian territory.[51]

In lieu of sending an independent protest to Japan, the State Department placed the Siberian question upon the agenda of the Washington Conference. However, less than two full sessions were devoted to a discussion of it. At the conference, the United States hoped to secure from Japan certain guarantees in regard to Siberia. Poole listed them in a memorandum to Secretary Hughes:

(1.) An expression of intention to refrain from taking advantage of present conditions in order to impair the rights of the Russian people or Russian territorial (or administrative) integrity in Siberia. (Mention of administrative integrity may have to be omitted since the occupation of Sakhalin constitutes a clear instance of the impairment, thereof.)

(2.) An expression of intention to afford the people of Siberia the fullest and most unembarrassed opportunity for the establishment of effective and stable government.

[49] A. Yazikiloff to Hughes, Dec. 20, 1921, United States, *Foreign Relations, 1921,* II, 717-719.
[50] Warren to Hughes, Dec. 24, 1921, United States, *Foreign Relations, 1921,* II, 719-720.
[51] Poole to Hughes, Dec. 20, 1921, file 861.00/9315, D.S.N.A.

(3.) An expression of intention to maintain, pending the establishment of recognized and stable government, the principle of equal opportunity for the commerce and industry of all nations in Siberia, and to refrain from taking advantage of present conditions in order to seek special rights and privileges which would abridge the rights of the subjects or citizens of friendly states.[52]

Although Japan had already pledged herself at various times to uphold statements similar to those presented in Poole's memorandum, nevertheless, her note of July 8, 1921, had tended to contradict the joint pledges given by the United States and Japan upon entering Siberia.

On the eve of the Washington Conference Japan seemed firmly entrenched in the Maritime Province and Sakhalin. Although she had asserted in her last memorandum of July 8 that she was seriously contemplating plans for an early withdrawal from the Maritime Province, there had in fact been no diminution of the number of Japanese troops in that region. On the contrary, an additional division had been dispatched. This had been ostensibly for the purpose of relieving one of the two divisions already on duty, but there were no signs that the relieved division was returning to Japan. Every indication pointed to the retention of all three divisions.

In Sakhalin the Japanese had taken over the local administration to the most minute detail. There was complete civil and economic, as well as military, domination. The most important petroleum and coal resources of the province were apparently being brought into the exclusive and complete control of the Japanese. The State Department learned that foreigners were excluded from the exploitation of these natural resources. Russians might travel to Sakhalin only with Japanese permission.[53] On January 21, 1922, Macgowan reported confidentially that Japan very shortly intended to proclaim the "temporary" occupation of the Maritime Province and its administration by Japanese officials and courts under the laws of Japan just as Sakhalin was governed. Pretexts were to be created by provoking political disturbances through the medium of a certain Hetman.[54]

---

[52] Poole to Hughes, Jan. 17, 1922, file 861.00/9316, D.S.N.A.

[53] Division of Russian Affairs, Summary Statement of Facts Respecting the Continuance of Japanese Military Forces in Siberia, Jan. 17, 1922, pp. 11-14, file 861.00/9316, D.S.N.A.

[54] Macgowan to Hughes, Jan. 21, 1922, file 861A.00/171, D.S.N.A. K. K. Kawakami, Japanese observer at the Washington Conference, attempted to explain Japan's activities in Siberia to the American public: "I think that nothing is the matter with Japan in Siberia, except that she has appeared upon the scene of international land-grabbing just a little too late. Nothing except that she was sleeping a saintly sleep when the great nations of Christendom were busy practicing the moral code of the dying

On January 23, 1922, Baron Shidehara, the Japanese delegate to the Washington Conference, put Japan's case in Siberia before the Far Eastern Committee of the conference, before any other delegation had an opportunity to bring up the question. Recapitulating the entire history of Allied military action in Siberia and the subsequent withdrawal of all Allied troops but the Japanese, he justified their continued presence in Siberia as a necessity for protecting Japanese residents in the area and the Korean frontier. Furthermore, he added that no part of the Maritime Province was under Japan's military occupation. It was the established policy of the Japanese government not to interfere with the various factions in Siberia. He admitted that Japan had supported Semenov in 1918 at the beginning of intervention, but had discontinued that support when she found that it complicated the internal conditions of Siberia. The Japanese government was considering withdrawal, and would do so after the successful conclusion of negotiations with the Far Eastern Republic. These negotiations were not intended to secure any special advantages for Japan. As soon as adequate provisions for the safety of Japanese residents were acquired, the Japanese planned a complete withdrawal of troops from the Maritime Province. The occupation of Sakhalin would be continued until Japanese differences were settled with an established Russian government. However, the occupation was only a temporary measure. In conclusion, the Baron stated:

The Japanese Delegation is authorized to declare that it is the fixed and settled policy of Japan to respect the territorial integrity of Russia, and to observe the principle of non-intervention in the internal affairs of that country, as well as the principle of equal opportunity for the commerce and industry of all nations in every part of the Russian possessions.[55]

When J. P. Jameson, expert assistant to the Washington Conference, read Baron Shidehara's concluding statement, he commented, "The last paragraph is an excellent statement, but if this has been the policy of Japan, it is strange that by all indications their intentions have actually been the opposite."[56]

---

patriarch, My son, get money—honestly, if you can, but get money! Japan's sin, if sin it be, lies in her eleventh hour entrance into the company of international freebooters, who having divided among themselves all the riches of the world, are now putting forth a Sunday front and preaching morals to the belated Japanese" (Kawakami, *Japan's Pacific Policy*, New York, 1922, pp. 226-227).

[55] *Conference on Limitation of Armaments*, pp. 1394-1400; file 861.00/9239, D.S.N.A. For a sympathetic view of Shidehara's speech, see Kawakami, *Japan's Pacific Policy*, pp. 242-243.

[56] Memorandum of J. P. Jameson, Jan. 23, 1922, file 861.00/9239, D.S.N.A.

In general, Shidehara's statement of the Siberian question was simply a compilation of the various notes which Japan had written in the past on the subject of withdrawal of troops and the Sakhalin Province. On the surface it seemed a reasonable statement of Japan's position in Siberia.

Jameson, who analyzed the Japanese note, made some rather significant comments. He pointed out that, although the Japanese spoke of their purpose in assisting the Czechs to evacuate, they made no mention of the fact that Japanese military authorities had deliberately hindered that evacuation, especially through the Trans-Baikal Province. Moreover, Japan had omitted Sakhalin from the list of the "only" regions left to be evacuated. The Japanese neglected to note that the places where Japanese residents were most endangered and molested had been the places at which Japanese troops were stationed. Furthermore, there was no reason why the Japanese residents should not withdraw. American residents had done so or were permitted to remain only at their own risk. In so far as protecting Korea was concerned, the proper place for that defense was in Korean territory. American reports disproved Japanese claims that she was not in effective military occupation of the Maritime Province and that she was neutral in Siberian affairs. These reports also indicated that Japan still supported Semenov. Despite Shidehara's conciliatory attitude, he had set no definite date for Japan's withdrawal. Japanese actions did not bear out her statement that nothing was further from her thought than to take advantage of the present helplessness of Russia to secure any advantages. The American government had facts which indicated that Japan had made outrageous demands upon representatives of the Far Eastern Republic at Chita, while Japan admitted that she would occupy Sakhalin pending the establishment of responsible Russian authority.[57]

Jameson insisted that American acquiescence to the Japanese statement would put the stamp of American approval upon Japan's past acts in Siberia. He believed that America's failure to protest publicly against Japan's continued presence would confirm Russian suspicions that America was a party to the aggressive action of Japan in Siberia and approved of her continued occupation. Referring to Japan's promise to withdraw, he pointed out that she made such a promise when she first sent troops into Siberia and had been making the same statement for months. Instead of fulfilling it, she had continually made excuses for remaining. Her actions in Korea, Manchuria, and Shan-

[57] Memorandum of J. P. Jameson, Jan. 23, 1922, file 861.00/9239, D.S.N.A.

tung were excellent examples of what might be expected in Siberia. Jameson believed that the present time was the crucial moment for Siberia and that should the powers not oppose Japan's aggressive actions, she would eventually occupy a position in Siberia such as she occupied in South Manchuria, even though eventual annexation did not occur. He added:

> In a word, it will mean the closing of the "open door" of equal opportunity in Siberia. It will mean that the integrity of Russian territory has been violated without a *public* protest of the United States. We cannot escape our responsibility, not only because of our promise to the Russian people on the occasion of our joint military expedition with Japan in Siberia, but also because the United States has assumed the moral trusteeship of Russian rights at this conference.[58]

Jameson was convinced that Japan would continue her aggressive activities in Siberia for many years unless the other powers made a concerted movement to force her to withdraw. Although he knew that the United States would not go to war over the matter, nevertheless, he felt that since the United States had assumed the moral trusteeship over Russian rights, it should make a definite request for the withdrawal of Japanese troops from Siberia. If Japan refused, at least the United States would have made clear to the world that it was "not sanctioning or participating in the betrayal of the Russian people by acquiescing in Japanese aggression in Siberia." He enclosed a draft statement for the proposed resolution.[59] Although the draft was not accepted, Jameson's suggestions were incorporated into the reply which Secretary Hughes delivered to the conference on January 24, 1922.

Secretary Hughes traced the history of the Siberian expedition, carefully indicating Japan's agreement to respect the territorial integrity of Russia and "to immediately withdraw all Japanese troops from Russian territory," as soon as the temporary exigency was over. Hughes observed that after her withdrawal America had continued to be a close observer of events in Eastern Siberia, maintaining extended diplomatic correspondence upon the subject with the Japanese govern-

[58] Jameson to Hughes, Jan. 24, 1922, file 861.00/9240, D.S.N.A.

[59] Jameson to Hughes, Jan. 24, 1922, file 861.00/9240, D.S.N.A. Thomas F. Millard pointed out that the United States would not lose too much if the Siberian question remained unsettled. On the contrary, it might work to her advantage to have the situation continued for several reasons. It kept alive antagonism between Japan and Russia. It was a severe drain on Japanese finances and kept her aggressive tendencies occupied, thus lessening the probability of their finding expression elsewhere. Finally, by exposing to the world Japan's imperialistic designs, it weakened her moral position. For these reasons, America's position versus Japan's would be immeasureably strengthened (Millard, *Conflict of Policies in Asia*, pp. 286-287).

ment. Hughes frankly avowed that "this correspondence has not always disclosed an identity of views between the two Governments." He then reiterated the views of the United States on the continued occupation of the Maritime Province and Sakhalin. Since no agreement could be reached on the matter, Hughes fell back upon the device of "reading into the record" the correspondence and debates that had taken place.[60]

Stevens was very much disappointed by the apparent acquiescence of the conference to Japan's continued occupation of Vladivostok and the Maritime Province. Convinced that there was no possibility of an open door in these circumstances, he added that further discussions concerning the Chinese Eastern Railway would be fruitless as long as Japan controlled the outlet of the Chinese Eastern, the port of Vladivostok. If the conference intended to do no more than to write its protests into the record, Stevens felt that he had no choice but to turn in his resignation.[61] The Far Eastern Republic, on the other hand, expressed its gratitude for the position America had taken in regard to the intervention.[62]

By the summer of 1922 Allied censure, as well as the increasing disapproval of the Japanese people, was having its effect on the plans of the Japanese military party in Siberia. In June, 1922, members of the House of Commons repeatedly requested the British government to ask Japan to evacuate Siberia without further delay.[63] Bitter denunciation of the expedition grew in Japan both within and outside the Diet. On June 24, 1922, Admiral Kato announced the intended evacuation of troops from Siberia at the end of October, 1922.[64] The Japanese government formally announced this decision to the American government on the same day.[65]

Japan's announced withdrawal from Siberia did not mention

[60] *Conference on Limitation of Armaments*, pp. 1404-1412; Mark Sullivan, *The Great Adventure at Washington* (New York, 1922), pp. 241-244; Tompkins, *American-Russian Relations in the Far East*, p. 178.

[61] Stevens to Hughes, Jan. 31, 1922, file 861.77/2588, D.S.N.A. The State Department dissuaded Stevens from resigning.

[62] Poole to Hughes, Feb. 2, 1922, file 861A.00/265, D.S.N.A. The *Peking and Tientsin Times,* one of the leading Chinese journals, also praised Mr. Hughes's declaration on Siberia and applauded America's position (Poole to Hughes, March 10, 1922, file 861A.01/266, D.S.N.A.).

[63] Phillips to George Harvey (ambassador to Great Britain), June 3, 1922, file 861A.01/277a, D.S.N.A.; Great Britain, *House of Commons Debates*, fifth series, CLIV, 685, 1410, 1570.

[64] Takeuchi, *War and Diplomacy*, p. 215.

[65] Japanese chargé d'affaires to Hughes, June 24, 1922, United States, *Foreign Relations, 1922*, II, 853.

withdrawal from Sakhalin Island. Secretary Hughes therefore dispatched a note to Japan which, while indicating America's gratification over Japan's proposed withdrawal from the mainland of Siberia, reminded her that American protests at the Washington Conference against Japanese occupation of Siberian territory included Sakhalin Island to an equal degree.[66] Charles Warren, the American ambassador to Japan, made these views known to Viscount Uchida. The Foreign Office replied with a public statement to the effect that the Japanese government would withdraw all troops from the districts opposite the Island of Sakhalin, but would not terminate its occupation of the island itself until a satisfactory settlement for the Nikolaevsk affair had been obtained.[67]

At a conference which was held between the Japanese and the Far Eastern Republic at Changchun, on September 5, 1922, the latter also protested the Japanese intention to continue the occupation of Northern Sakhalin, repeating the American view that there was no necessary connection between the massacre at Nikolaevsk and the occupation of the adjoining Sakhalin territory. Although quite willing to discuss with Japan the question of compensation for the loss of Japanese lives at Nikolaevsk, the Far Eastern Republic at the same time intended to present large counterclaims based upon the destruction of Russian lives and property by the Japanese elsewhere in Siberia during the military occupation. The Far Eastern Republic appealed to the United States to bring pressure to bear in order to induce Japan to relinquish Sakhalin. The State Department felt that any action on their part would simply arouse Japanese resentment. Therefore, no action was taken.[68]

The Changchun Conference failed primarily because of differences of opinion on Sakhalin. During the conference Japan expressed a wish to buy Sakhalin or lease it for a long time. Failing this, she desired to secure the exclusive privilege of holding concessions in the Russian part of the island. However, the Far Eastern Republic was firm in refusing these demands and announced its desire to pursue the open-door policy if American capital took an active interest in developing Sakhalin.[69]

[66] Hughes to Warren, June 27, 1922, United States, *Foreign Relations, 1922*, II, 854.

[67] Warren to Hughes, July 14, 1922, United States, *Foreign Relations, 1922*, II, 855.

[68] Poole to Phillips, Sept. 25, 1922, United States, *Foreign Relations, 1922*, II, 856-857; Young, *Japan Under Taisho Tenno*, pp. 273-276.

[69] Warren to Hughes, Oct. 26, 1922, file 861A.01/412, D.S.N.A.

Despite the failure of the Changchun Conference, Japan continued her withdrawal from the mainland of Siberia. On October 26 the Secretary of State received news that the last Japanese transport had left Vladivostok.[70] On the same day the forces of the Far Eastern Republic entered the city. On November 3, 1922, the Far Eastern Republic conveyed its thanks to the American government for its "friendly interest" in helping to bring about the Japanese evacuation from the Siberian mainland.[71] On November 17 the Far Eastern Republic voluntarily abolished itself and became an "inseparable and integral part of Soviet Russia."[72] Two years later, on January 20, 1925, after Japan had recognized the Soviet government, an agreement was negotiated settling their outstanding difficulties, and the Japanese army evacuated Northern Sakhalin.[73]

[70] Vice-consul at Vladivostok to Hughes, Oct. 26, 1922, United States, *Foreign Relations, 1922*, III, 864; Leo Pasvolsky, "Russia Takes Over Vladivostok," *Current History*, XVI (Dec. 1922), 499-501.

[71] Poole to Hughes, Nov. 3, 1922, United States, *Foreign Relations, 1922*, II, 866.

[72] Poole to Hughes, Nov. 3, 1922, United States, *Foreign Relations, 1922*, II, 867; New York *Times*, Nov. 18, 1922.

[73] New York *Times*, May 13, 1925; A. L. P. Dennis, "The New Russo-Japanese Treaty Explained," *Current History*, XXI (May, 1925), 240-244; Victor A. Yakhontoff. *Russia and the Soviet Union in the Far East* (New York, 1931), pp. 404-410.

CHAPTER XII

Allied Withdrawal from the Chinese Eastern Railway

THE DECISION to withdraw American troops from Siberia initiated the final phase of America's program to stop Japan from gaining control of the Chinese Eastern Railway. According to the Inter-Allied Railway Agreement of January 15, 1919, the assistance of foreign railway experts in the operation of the Trans-Siberian and Chinese Eastern Railways was to cease upon the withdrawal of the foreign military forces from Siberia. The experiences of recent months in the operation of the railways furnished the State Department with a strong reason for abiding by the terms of the original agreement. It had, therefore, decided upon arrangements for the withdrawal of American railway experts simultaneously with the departure of American military forces.[1]

The projected withdrawal of American troops and railway experts forced the State Department to reconsider its policy in regard to the Chinese Eastern Railway. The Chinese government was considering the possibility of taking over full control of the Chinese Eastern Railway and retaining John F. Stevens and a selected staff to operate it. Financial assistance was necessary to accomplish this, and the American Legation at Peking desired to know whether the project should be encouraged.[2] Morris had already reported the disturbing news that Japan would probably withdraw her troops from the Amur Railway and concentrate them along the line of the Chinese Eastern Railway, establishing as much control over the operation of the railway as could be secured without unduly exciting Russian and Chinese feeling.[3] In

[1] Lansing to Shidehara, Jan. 9, 1920, United States, *Foreign Relations, 1920*, III, 489.

[2] Tenney to Lansing, Jan. 15, 1920, United States, *Foreign Relations, 1920*, I, 679.

[3] Morris to Lansing, Jan. 14, 1920, file 861.00/6134, D.S.N.A.

view of this news from Peking and Tokyo, the American government was faced with an important decision. As Poole pointed out, it would obviously be advantageous for future trade in Manchuria if the Chinese Eastern could be brought under Chinese control and operated by an American. On the other hand, such an action would bring the United States into a sharp conflict of interests with the Japanese and strengthen the Japanese allegation that the United States had not dealt honestly with them. Poole concluded, "Moreover, I do not know where the necessary financial assistance may be drawn. I believe therefore that China should not be encouraged in this enterprise." China was informed accordingly.[4]

Poole believed that the United States should do everything possible to prevent the Japanese from establishing complete control over the Chinese Eastern Railway and thus strengthening their claim to special or vested interests in Northern Manchuria. Poole's views were incorporated into a memorandum and sent to the Japanese ambassador. The memorandum pointed out that the American government was "not disposed to object to any reasonable measures which Japan may decide to take in Eastern Siberia with a view to halting the advance of Bolshevism and bringing about a stable economic and political situation, provided that the measures taken do not prejudice Russia's existing rights in this region proper to the establishment of a competent Russian Government." At the same time, the Japanese ambassador was informed that the "situation in Manchuria must be considered somewhat apart." This was Chinese territory, the railroad having been leased to Russia. The interests of China were directly involved. Thus it was necessary to avoid all measures in the railroad zone which might prejudice the interests of either Russia or China. Moreover, the Inter-Allied Railway Agreement had explicitly stated that the Trans-Siberian and Chinese Eastern Railways would ultimately be returned to the parties in interest without impairing any of the existing rights. Since this was one of the underlying principles of American and Japanese action in Manchuria, Japan might be assured of America's confidence that the Japanese government would not depart from that principle in any way.[5]

On January 20 the State Department learned that Horvat had issued a proclamation announcing his assumption of all the governmental

[4] Poole to Lansing, Jan. 16, 1920, file 861.77/1461, D.S.N.A.; Lansing to Tenney, Jan. 19, 1920, United States, *Foreign Relations, 1920*, I, 680.

[5] Poole to Lansing, Jan. 16, 1920, file 861.77/1461, D.S.N.A.; Department of State to the Japanese Embassy, Jan. 30, 1920, United States, *Foreign Relations, 1920*, III, 501-502.

powers of the Russian people within the jurisdiction of the Chinese Eastern Railway.[6] The Chinese government immediately filed a protest stating that as the Chinese Eastern Railway was in Chinese territory throughout its length and under Chinese territorial sovereignty, no other nation could be permitted to exercise its national sovereignty therein. Furthermore, the powers of General Horvat were simply those of an official of the railway, and as such he was invested with no national sovereign powers whatsover. Finally, the terms of the Chinese Eastern Railway Agreement vested entirely in the Chinese government the duty of protecting the Russian officials of the railway as well as the Chinese and foreign residents of the railway zone.[7]

On February 11 Horvat informed Stevens that the Japanese government had offered the Chinese Eastern Railway a five-year loan of twenty million yen without security—simply receipt of the railway. When Stevens's advice was solicited, he told Horvat "to let it alone," pointing out that if the loan were consummated it would mean Japanese domination. At the same time the Chinese government, in an effort to control the Chinese Eastern Railway, was trying to appoint a majority of its directors. It was also threatening covertly to take charge by force. However, Stevens believed that China was helpless alone.[8] Affairs were made still worse by the activities of the Japanese.

In an effort to create a chaotic situation, thereby justifying their presence, they were supporting Semenov in every way to delay the movement of the Czechs. They were even turning back locomotives which Stevens had sent from Harbin to move the Czechs from Irkutsk.[9] Stevens believed that if the United States did not take steps to stop Japan, it would have "much to regret in the future."[10]

Towards the middle of April, 1920, the members of the Technical Board, except for the Japanese member, drew up a formal resolution protesting against the arbitrary conduct of the Japanese military representatives within the railway zone.[11] Japan was undeterred by this action. She seemed bent upon creating a situation which would give her an excuse to control the Chinese Eastern Railway.[12] She had taken military occupation of important stations on the Chinese Eastern

[6] United States, *Foreign Relations, 1920*, I, 680.

[7] Tenney to Lansing, Jan. 29, 1920, file 861.77/1323, D.S.N.A.

[8] Stevens to Lansing, Feb. 11, 1920, United States, *Foreign Relations, 1920*, I, 680-681.

[9] Stevens to Lansing, Feb. 18, 1920, file 861.00/6382, D.S.N.A.

[10] Stevens to Lansing, Feb. 11, 1920, United States, *Foreign Relations, 1920*, I, 680-681.

[11] Robert T. Pollard, *China's Foreign Relations* (New York, 1933), pp. 157-158.

[12] Jenkins to Colby, April 16, 1920, file 861.77/1469, D.S.N.A.

and had assumed complete control of the Siberian railway from Vladivostok to Nikolsk. According to the Inter-Allied Railway Agreement, the guarding of the Chinese Eastern Railway had been assigned to the Chinese Army, which had faithfully performed its duty. Thus there was no military necessity requiring Japanese intervention. Everything had been moving smoothly until occupation by the Japanese military forces. Although the Japanese justified their occupation by the terms of the Sino-Japanese Military Agreement of May, 1918, the American government believed that the acceptance of the Inter-Allied Railway Agreement of 1919 by the Japanese suspended for the time being any treaty between China and Japan relative to the occupancy of the Chinese Eastern zone by Japanese troops. Furthermore, the State Department believed that Japan should have notified the Allies of her withdrawal from the railway agreement before placing her troops on the Chinese Eastern. The Siberians assumed that the Allies must certainly approve of Japan's recent policy or she would not have ventured to put such a policy in force. Stevens suggested that the Allies, especially the United States, immediately ask Japan to explain her action and define clearly her intentions concerning the Chinese Eastern.[13]

The chaotic situation on the Chinese Eastern Railway grew even worse once the railway became intertwined in the concluding negotiations for the establishment of a new four-power consortium. The purpose of the new consortium was to make loans to China for economic reconstruction and improved communications. Negotiations for its organization were begun in June, 1918, but were delayed for two years largely as a result of Japan's attempt to get the other three powers, Great Britain, France, and the United States, to exclude the areas of Mongolia and Manchuria from the activities of the consortium.[14]

In February, 1920, the British government approached the United States with an oral proposal that control of the Inter-Allied Board be continued, that operation of the Chinese Eastern Railway be confined to the Chinese, and that finances be arranged not by the Japanese but by the consortium. Although the British proposal was a welcome change from her earlier unco-operative attitude toward Siberian affairs,

---

[13] Stevens to Colby, April 18, 1920, file 861.77/1470, D.S.N.A.

[14] The negotiations were finally concluded in Oct., 1920. Frederic V. Field, *American Participation in the China Consortiums* (Chicago, 1931), pp. 142-166; M. J. Bau, *The Foreign Relations of China* (New York, 1921), pp. 389-415.

the American government made no response to her inquiry.[15]   Later in February the British again urged upon the United States the importance of taking steps "to prevent the control of the Chinese Eastern Railway passing exclusively into the hands of any single power."   The British attached the "greatest importance" to the continued exercise of the functions of the Allied Technical Board at Harbin, and desired them to remain at their posts as long as possible.   Therefore, they hoped that the United States would not withdraw the American representatives from the board.[16]

A few weeks later the British Foreign Office announced its intention to retain General Beckett, the British representative on the Technical Board, in his position as long as Stevens remained in Harbin. They desired to know when Stevens would be withdrawn.   The State Department was unable to set a definite date.   The original plan had been to keep Stevens in Harbin until the Czechs had been evacuated.   However, a general strike on the railway made it impossible to ascertain when that evacuation would be completed.[17]

The British continued their inquiries.   In April they tentatively suggested the advisability of reiterating the principle of trusteeship and arranging that China undertake to administer the trust as next in interest to Russia.   This could be done with the assistance of the foreign technical experts.   Again, the American government made no formal reply.[18]

While the British government was prodding the State Department to action from one quarter, the Chinese government was prodding it from another quarter.   On March 1, 1920, the Chinese government informed Charles Tenney that it was assuming full responsibility for the protection of the Chinese Eastern Railway and for the maintenance of peace and order in the railway zone.[19]   The Chinese Foreign Office formally urged the retention of Stevens in his post on the Chinese Eastern Railway.   At the same time they urged Thomas Lamont, American representative for the consortium, then in China, to place the railway under the protection of the consortium.   A loan was requested.   The manager of the Russo-Asiatic Bank added his

[15] Davis to Colby, April 28, 1920, United States, *Foreign Relations, 1920,* I, 687-688.

[16] Lindsay (British chargé) to Lansing, Feb. 24, 1920, United States, *Foreign Relations, 1920,* I, 681.

[17] Polk to Lindsay, March 17, 1920, United States, *Foreign Relations, 1920,* I, 683; Weigh, *Russo-Chinese Diplomacy,* pp. 235-236.

[18] Colby to Davis, April 26, 1920, Davis to Colby, April 28, 1920, United States, *Foreign Relations, 1920,* I, 685-687, 687-688.

[19] Tenney to Colby, March 24, 1920, file 861.77/1485, D.S.N.A.

support to this request.[20] Since the State Department considered it unwise to bring into the consortium discussion of any issue which might start a controversy, they reserved the Chinese suggestions for future consideration.[21]

By the middle of May the American government was still in the process of deciding its future policy in regard to the Chinese Eastern Railway. C. H. Smith recommended that the Railway Agreement remain in effect until the Japanese withdrew. The Russian Embassy proposed that the railway be internationalized through an international committee with provision for its financing by one of the powers, by banking interests, or by joint action of the powers, the purpose being to return the railway eventually, with existing rights unimpaired, to those who held an interest in it. Great Britain had expressed a desire to see the continued participation by Americans in the Inter-Allied Board and Committee. She was evidently very anxious to prevent Japan from obtaining control of the railway. Her alternative suggestions covered three possibilities: namely, that the Inter-Allied Agreement be continued on the Chinese Eastern Railway, that a mandate for the railway be given to China, or that the railway be financed by the consortium.

At this time the State Department was also considering a proposal to place the railway in the hands of the Inter-Allied Committee as it was then constituted. The committee could transfer the duties of the Technical Board to China under a mandate, and the technical operation of the road could be managed either by the Chinese government or by a new board chosen by that government, with provision for review by the Inter-Allied Committee. The Military Committee would be discontinued.[22] The Department was troubled by one complication. The Inter-Allied Railway Agreement had provided that representation in its committees and boards would be held by those who had armed troops in Siberia. This seemed to indicate the exclusion of the British, French, and Americans, whose troops had been withdrawn. Thus the Japanese would be in a dominant position, since Chinese and Russian participation was quite ineffective. Furthermore, the Department had already announced in its note to Japan of January 9, 1920, that when the Czech evacuation was completed, both American railway experts and forces would be withdrawn.[23]

[20] United States, *Foreign Relations, 1920,* I, 434.

[21] Colby to Tenney, April 21, 1920, United States, *Foreign Relations, 1920,* I, 532.

[22] Colby to Bell, May 17, 1920, United States, *Foreign Relations, 1920,* I, 690-691.

[23] United States, *Foreign Relations, 1920,* I, 690-691.

The former British High Commissioner in Siberia, now ambassador to Japan, was well acquainted with the arrangements made when the agreement regarding the railways was put into operation. His interpretation of the agreement was quite different from that of the United States. He had always understood that representation on the committees and boards should be given to the powers which had armed forces in Siberia at the time of the making of the agreement, and that such representation should continue as long as these bodies were in existence. Furthermore, he believed withdrawal of troops by a power implied no obligation to withdraw the railway representatives. He gathered that his government shared his views since the representation of Great Britain on the Inter-Allied Board, the Technical Board, and the committees was continuing indefinitely. Eliot had considered the various plans for the future operation of the railway and reported his belief that Japan would probably object to continuing the railway under the arrangement in force, with financing by the consortium. Furthermore, Japan would also oppose giving China a mandate to the railway. Eliot advised the continuation of the Technical Board and Inter-Allied committees as they then existed with financial arrangements assumed either by the consortium or jointly by the powers.[24]

Early in the spring of 1920 John Davis, the American ambassador in Great Britain, began a series of informal conversations with the British Foreign Office, at their request, in regard to the Chinese Eastern Railway. They proceeded on the assumption that since a consortium agreement had been reached, it now could be utilized in determining future policy toward the Chinese Eastern Railway. The British Foreign Office held the following views in which they believed the French would concur: namely, that Russia should be considered first in interest and China second; that the Allied and Associated powers were under a moral obligation to act as Russia's trustee in maintaining the status quo ante; that the Inter-Allied Railway Agreement, with its organs, the Inter-Allied Railway Committee and the Inter-Allied Technical Board, be continued; that British, French, and American participation be continued to insure success in bringing Japan into the consortium without reservations; and that, as Japan had just grounds for keeping troops in Siberia because of the Bolshevik menace, Chinese and Japanese military forces should jointly protect the line. The British Foreign Office believed that under these provisions the consortium might properly finance the line. Such a scheme would

[24] Bell to Colby, May 22, 1920, United States, *Foreign Relations, 1920*, I, 693.

control Japan, stabilize China, limit the Bolshevik menace, and publicly proclaim the first step of the consortium to be of broad international value. The Foreign Office also pointed out that as the British banking group was delayed in completing financial arrangements for the consortium, the American and Japanese might be asked to carry the preliminary advance.[25]

The American government was quite gratified with the British views although it had several suggestions to make.[26] It agreed to joint Japanese-Chinese military protection only as a practical necessity, and as a temporary expedient in view of the apparent military exigency. The American government emphasized this point as Japanese forces had been placed upon the Chinese Eastern in disregard of the allocation of that line to Chinese protection by the agreement of the Allied commanders at Vladivostok in April, 1919. Furthermore, while the American government considered that financing by the consortium would be satisfactory in principle, it feared that such a suggestion might be misconstrued by Japan. Therefore it desired postponement of this suggestion until Lamont's return from the Far East.[27] In the meantime, the negotiations between the United States and Britain were kept absolutely confidential.[28]

While the British and Americans negotiated, the Japanese were apparently proceeding with their own plans in regard to the Chinese Eastern Railway. Intercepted messages revealed that they had ordered nine hundred bandits to points on the Chinese Eastern Railway with definite instructions to enter into a series of actions which would discredit the Chinese army and its ability to protect the railroad, and thereby, as Stevens reported, give the Japanese the opportunity to seize the railway.[29] These messages also revealed that the Japanese had decided to take over the guarding of the Maritime Province because of the increasing bandit raids, which they themselves had instigated. Japan had so informed China in an ultimatum.[30] The British were evidently

[25] Davis to Colby, May 22, 1920, United States, *Foreign Relations, 1920*, I, 691-692.

[26] Davis to Colby, May 28, 1920, file 861.77/1545, D.S.N.A.

[27] Colby to Davis, May 27, 1920, United States, *Foreign Relations, 1920*, I, 693-694.

[28] Colby to Bell, June 19, 1920, United States, *Foreign Relations, 1920*, I, 695.

[29] Stevens to Colby, June 2, 1920, file 861.00/6967, D.S.N.A. Dr. C. S. Wang, president of the Chinese Eastern Railway, confirmed the reports that the Japanese were arming the bandits along the zone of the Chinese Eastern Railway and thereby causing the existing disturbances (Memorandum of an Interview between Dr. C. S. Wang and Mr. A. B. Ruddock, Sept. 5, 1921, file 861.77/2271, D.S.N.A.).

[30] Stevens to Colby, June 9, 1920, file 861.77/1558, D.S.N.A. These bandit raids continued, presumably under Japanese instigation. Macgowan reported that "Japanese

in receipt of similar information, as Lindsay, counselor to the British Embassy, came to the State Department and casually mentioned that his government was much interested in an early decision on the question of financing the railway, as "they had received disquieting intimations of proposed action by Japan in reference to the Chinese Eastern Railway." The British government had conveyed its fears to the Japanese government, indicating that "while they were not disposed to credit these reports, they desired to express to Japan the hope that as an Ally Japan would take no step affecting the *status quo* of this railway without previously conferring fully with the British Government."[31]

In the meantime Lamont had returned from China. He reported a long conversation with Stevens, who had carefully described the activities of the Japanese in their steady and rapid strides to get control of the entire region and block the rest of the world from the immense possibilities of trade with Siberia. Stevens had said:

> You may think it curious, that just for this one hour conference, I have come seven hundred miles from Harbin, to and fro, to see you but I just felt it my duty to leave no stone unturned to bring the situation before the leading men of affairs of America so they may know the menace to American interest for the future that is going on.. Something perhaps that does not concern me very much, because I am getting to be an old man, or even you twenty years younger, but does very much concern our sons and our grandsons and the whole future of America.[32]

Lamont urged the advisability of financing the Chinese Eastern through the consortium. The Chinese too had been insistent on this point.[33] Although the Japanese government did not like the idea, the Cabinet had agreed to consider it.[34] Uchida, the Japanese Foreign Minister, was having a bad time with the Diet and feared that if the consortium arrangement went through, it would be said that "his policy had begun with the Nikolaevsk massacre and ended with his handling over the Chinese Eastern Railway to the Consortium." In

---

aim to show what disorders follow their evacuation" (Macgowan to Department of State, Oct. 4, 1920, file 861.00/7467, D.S.N.A.).

[31] Memorandum of a Conversation between MacMurray and Lindsay, June 15, 1920, file 861.77/1569, D.S.N.A.

[32] Report of a Conference with Stevens by T. W. Lamont, June 19, 1920, file 861.77/1574, D.S.N.A.

[33] Norman Davis (Acting Secretary of State) to Bell, June 30, 1920, United States, *Foreign Relations, 1920,* I, 699.

[34] Bell to Colby, June 22, 1920, United States, *Foreign Relations, 1920,* I, 696.

a few weeks Uchida thought it might be advisable to discuss the point in the Diet, but he considered it inadvisable at present.[35]

Since the Japanese seemed averse to including the Chinese Eastern in the consortium plans, the State Department proposed another plan. This provided that the Technical Board and the Inter-Allied Committee be consolidated as a new committee of international character composed of representatives from China, Japan, France, Great Britain, Russia, and the United States. Similar to a committee in bankruptcy, it would be given authority to perform all the duties necessary for carrying out the trust except that it could not borrow funds for the Chinese Eastern without authorization by the governments concerned. The American plan would place the railroad administration upon a business footing, excluding the military and political features which were inherent in the original organization set up by the Railway Agreement.[36]

The British were not enthusiastic about the plan. They thought it was simply an involved way of doing that which the consortium was best able to do. Apparently Great Britain was willing to take a strong stand in favor of the original plan. She felt that although local Japanese conditions were to be regretted, they could not be allowed completely to break up the plan. The British suggested that if the original plan did not bring the desired results, the Japanese government might be requested to offer a substitute.[37]

In the meantime Japan was attempting to precipitate China into a civil war as a pretext for occupying North Manchuria. It appeared to Stevens that she was succeeding. Semenov was proposing to establish himself on the Chinese Eastern Railway to keep order. Stevens wrote that the Inter-Allied Railway Agreement was a farce, respected by no one. He added, "I have no support from the military of any nation in the enforcement of any order or instruction." Stevens could not understand why the powers could not agree on a policy toward the railway, and suggested that the delay was due to the work of "a certain people playing for time until they stack cards here when their real plans will become clear to everyone."[38]

The State Department informed Stevens that he was in error.

[35] Bell to Colby, June 30, 1920, United States, *Foreign Relations, 1920,* I, 699.

[36] Norman Davis to John Davis (ambassador to Great Britain), June 30, 1920, United States, *Foreign Relations, 1920,* I, 698-699.

[37] John Davis to Colby, July 8, 1920, United States, *Foreign Relations, 1920,* I, 700.

[38] Stevens to Colby, July 15, 1920, file 861.77/1609, D.S.N.A.; Stevens to Colby, July 19, 1920, United States, *Foreign Relations, 1920,* I, 701-702.

The delay in reaching an agreement was due to Anglo-American negotiations. The Secretary of State added:

The Department has proposed to Great Britain that the British join with us in an effort to have Japanese troops entirely withdrawn from the railway, to have the system of operation and control reorganized in such a way as to give you the authority which is necessary, and to secure at once for necessary expenses an appropriation of $10,000,000. Great Britain is apparently ready, from evidence we have, to join vigorously with us in such a program.[39]

The negotiations over the Chinese Eastern Railroad continued. Ambassador Morris, now in Washington, began a series of conferences with Alston, the British minister to China, who had come to Washington, en route to England for a vacation. The two men had an informal conference with the Secretary and Under Secretary of State. They agreed on the necessity for international control of the railway, the necessity for entrusting the protection of the railroad to China, and the difficulty of financing the railway through the consortium.[40] These conferences were reported in Japan, where they occupied an important place in the newspapers, "creating a sensation." Editorials revealed a feeling of alarm lest such conferences result in an understanding between Great Britain and America to restrain Japan's freedom of movement on the Asiatic mainland. The view was also expressed that the reported conference was a prelude to America's launching upon a strong Far Eastern policy.[41]

By the end of August negotiations for financing the Chinese Eastern Railway through the consortium had come to a standstill. France reported its disinclination to go ahead with the idea in view of Japan's disapproval.[42] In reality, she had been conducting private negotiations to put control of the railway in the hands of the Russo-Asiatic Bank, which was owned by French interests. France was thus seeking to get a permanent hold on the line and increase her prestige in the Far East.[43] Great Britain still favored the consortium idea and expressed her willingness to join in any plan having as its object international control. Nevertheless, she hesitated to exert any real pressure.

[39] Colby to Stevens, July 29, 1920, United States, Foreign Relations, 1920, I, 703-704.

[40] Colby to John Davis, Aug. 5, 1920, United States, Foreign Relations, 1920, I, 704-705.

[41] Bell to Colby, Aug. 3, 1920, file 861.00/7204, D.S.N.A.

[42] John Davis to Colby, Aug. 1, 1920, United States, Foreign Relations, 1920, I, 706.

[43] Colby to Stevens, Aug. 31, 1920, file 861.77/1689A, D.S.N.A.

She felt that Japan was justified in maintaining troops on some parts of the railway in view of the dangerous situation caused by the Bolsheviks. Moreover, she felt that if Japan were allowed a share in guarding the railway, negotiations on other matters might be made less difficult.[44] Japan was bitterly opposed to any new international arrangement and did not approve of an international loan. However, she had no objection to continuing the arrangements then in practice, and devising a policy of financial assistance for urgent needs.

Meanwhile Russian representatives in Paris and Tokyo alleged that the Chinese government was taking every possible means of infringing Russian treaty rights, with the intention of eventually taking over complete control of the Chinese Eastern Railway. The Russian ambassador in Tokyo was earnestly requesting Japanese assistance to prevent this and was asking for an immediate loan of two million yen. The State Department felt it was only Stevens's continued presence at Harbin that prevented the Japanese military from taking over complete control of the railway.[45]

The Chinese goverment maneuvered to oust the Japanese as well as the Russians from the line of the Chinese Eastern. On August 7 the Chinese government sent a formal protest to Japan. It announced its earnest intention to keep out the Bolsheviks. Since China desired to assume entire responsibility in dealing with this measure, she requested that Japan withdraw her soldiers from the Chinese Eastern Railway.

The Japanese reply on August 18 announced the withdrawal of Japanese troops west of Harbin. However, Japanese soldiers would be retained south and east of Harbin, in order to keep out the Bolsheviks. This would place no obstacle in the way of China's providing the railway guards in accordance with the agreement of April, 1919, among the Allies.[46]

In the meantime China had begun independent negotiations concerning the Chinese Eastern Railway. On October 2, 1920, the Minister of Communications signed an agreement with the Russo-Asiatic Bank providing for the joint management of the railway. The agreement provided for an increase in the number of Chinese on the staff

[44] Colby to Stevens, Aug. 31, 1920, file 861.77/1689a, D.S.N.A.; J. B. Wright (chargé in Britain) to Colby, Aug. 18, 1920, United States, *Foreign Relations, 1920*, I, 708-709.

[45] Stevens to Colby, Aug. 13, 1920, file 861.00/7243, D.S.N.A.; Colby to Stevens, Aug. 31, 1920, file 861.77/1689a, D.S.N.A.

[46] Charles Crane (minister in China) to Colby, Sept. 24, 1920, United States, *Foreign Relations, 1920*, I, 710-711.

for joint administration of the railway. The railway was to be administered purely as a commercial concern, with the Chinese government assuming temporary executive control of the railway on behalf of the Russian government until definite arrangements could be reached with a united Russian government recognized by China.[47] Upon representation from the American government, the Chinese government informed the State Department that this arrangement contemplated nothing contradictory to the Inter-Allied Agreement.[48]

The agreement between China and the Russo-Asiatic Bank caused Japan to increase her efforts to incite the Chinese bandits to disorder along the railway zone. On October 20 the Japanese government dispatched a note of explanation to the United States. The note stated that in view of increasing activities of disorder by Korean malcontents in Chentao, the Japanese government had approached the Peking government and the provincial authorities at Mukden and Kirin with a proposition for joint efforts in the suppression of these movements. The Chinese government had refused to co-operate and had organized an independent expedition to cope with the difficulty. This was unsuccessful and served only to increase the activities of the recalcitrant Koreans who had since joined the Chinese bandits and Russian Bolsheviks. They had grown more truculent than ever. In order to protect Japanese life and property, it had become necessary to send reinforcements to Chentao for purposes of self-defense, especially in view of a recent Hunchun raid, which had been responsible for the burning of the Japanese consulate. Therefore, the Japanese government was continuing with the expedition in view of the menacing conditions in that area. The note concluded: "It need hardly be added that the present expedition being merely undertaken as a temporary measure to meet the requirements of the critical situation in Chentao, the troops des-

[47] Crane to Colby, Oct. 12, 1920, United States, *Foreign Relations, 1920,* I, 722; Quarterly Report of the Legation in China for the Period of Oct. 1 to Dec. 31, 1920, United States, *Foreign Relations, 1920,* I, 495-497. Weigh, *Russo-Chinese Diplomacy,* pp. 238-240; *China Year Book* (1923), p. 660. Weigh points out that the agreement "was unquestionably a long step forward towards the vindication of China's sovereign rights, but, from the legal point of view, it was a great blunder on the part of the Chinese government. Prior to the conclusion of this agreement the Bolsheviks had already made their overtures returning the Chinese Eastern Railway to the Chinese people 'without any compensation whatsoever.' What China should have done was to recognize the Soviet declaration as sincere and take over the whole Chinese Eastern Railway. But this was not what she did. She permitted the enterprise in which she alone had a paramount interest to fall into the hands of an international body of control. To aggravate the situation, she entered into an agreement with a third party, the Russo-Asiatic Bank . . ." (Weigh, *Russo-Chinese Diplomacy,* pp. 239-240).

[48] Bell to Colby, Nov. 5, 1920, United States, *Foreign Relations, 1920,* I. 725.

patched are to be promptly withdrawn as soon as the danger is removed and peace restored in the province."[49]

As the year 1920 drew to a close, affairs along the Chinese Eastern did not improve. When, on December 14, 1920, the Chinese government requested the withdrawal of Japanese troops from the Chinese Eastern Railway zone, Japan declined, stating that "Bolshevik activities rendered it inadvisable at the present time to withdraw."[50]

Back in Washington, the British ambassador was continuing his conversations with the State Department in regard to the Chinese Eastern Railway. Stevens, who was then in Washington, discussed the problem with him. They agreed on three major points; namely, the enlargement of the Technical Board to increase the efficiency of railway administration, the financial reorganization of the railway by the consortium, and the immediate payment of all debts due the railway. While the British did not desire to initiate such proposals as the first two, they intimated that they would support them if they were advanced by the United States.[51]

In accordance with these discussions, the State Department drafted a memorandum to meet the new conditions on the Chinese Eastern. The memorandum's stated object was to provide a more economical operation of the Chinese Eastern Railway, to place the line on a sound financial basis, to restore normal traffic conditions, to provide a proper trusteeship for Russian interests, and to stabilize the situation in the Far East. The method recommended was an amendment of the Inter-Allied Agreement of January, 1919. This contemplated the abolition of the Inter-Allied Committee and the placement of the Chinese Eastern Railway under the joint control of the United States, England, France, Japan, and China. Supervision was to be vested exclusively in a Technical Board, which would include the representatives of England, France, United States, Japan, Russia, and China. The board was to be solely responsible for the economic administration of the affairs of the railway. In addition to possessing the powers of the present Technical Board, the new board was to have full control over the receipts and disbursements of the company's revenues, and the

[49] Japanese Embassy to Department of State, Oct. 20, 1920, file 861.00/7978, D.S.N.A. Both C. H. Smith and Stevens reported that the Japanese were instigating these bandit raids. Their views were substantiated by the American Naval Intelligence (Colby to Crane, Nov. 6, 1920, file 861.00/7617, D.S.N.A.; Crane to Colby, Nov. 11, 1920, file 861.00/7655, D.S.N.A.).

[50] Crane to Acting Secretary of State, Jan. 5, 1921, United States, *Foreign Relations, 1920*, I, 727.

[51] Crane to Acting Secretary of State, Jan. 5, 1921, United States, *Foreign Relations 1920*, I, 726.

power to fix all the tariffs and control all questions relating to personnel. The president of the Technical Board was to be the responsible head. No political activity was to be permitted. The memorandum also raised the question of debts. "Certain powers" owed the railway six million dollars. If this debt were paid, and an additional six million were added to the credit of the Technical Board, sufficient capital would then be available. In submitting its plan, the American government expressed confidence that the interested governments "would be willing that Mr. John F. Stevens who has so ably filled the position of President of the Inter-Allied Technical Board since its inception, shall be selected as the President" of the new Technical Board.[52]

While the State Department awaited a reply from the British government, conditions along the Chinese Eastern were moving from a state of confusion to one of complete chaos. B. O. Johnson, acting president of the Technical Board in Stevens's absence, reported that the Chinese directors were forcing the railway to make illegal payments. Railway creditors were pressing the railway so that the Chinese directors were trying to arrange loans from Chinese banks. If unsuccessful, they would probably turn for help to the Japanese banks. Johnson felt that the Technical Board could not withstand the combination of Japanese and Chinese intrigue much longer.[53] Stevens's reply to this appeal was "You must hold the situation despite intrigue."[54]

Johnson found this advice difficult to follow, particularly as the Chinese military had begun adopting an extremely aggressive attitude with reference to the Chinese Eastern Railway. They had a heavy concentration of troops in North Manchuria, and disregarding the Technical Board, they had assumed control of train movements.[55]

Throughout the year 1921 the State Department had been receiving

[52] Memorandum by the Department of State, Jan. 21, 1921, United States, *Foreign Relations, 1921*, I, 564-566. The memorandum was dispatched to Great Britain on March 24 (Hughes to Geddes, British ambassador, March 24, 1921, United States, *Foreign Relations, 1921*, I, 573).

[53] Johnson to Hughes, March 14, 1921, United States, *Foreign Relations, 1921*, I, 572.

[54] Hughes to Johnson, March 24, 1921, United States, *Foreign Relations, 1921*, I, 573.

[55] Johnson to Hughes, May 4, 1921, United States, *Foreign Relations, 1921*, I, 580; Bell to Colby, May 7, 1921, file 861.77/2061, D.S.N.A. Minister Crane was instructed to call the attention of the Chinese government to this violation of the Railway Agreement. In presenting his protest, he was to attempt to secure the co-operation of his British, French, and Japanese colleagues (Hughes to Crane, May 17, 1921, United States, *Foreign Relations, 1921*, I, 583).

intercepted secret messages exchanged between various Japanese officials in China, Siberia, and Tokyo. A careful examination of their contents had led to the belief that they were "undoubtedly authentic." The intercepted telegrams revealed that the Japanese military intended to begin hostilities in Manchuria and Siberia, and contemplated the seizure of control of the Chinese Eastern Railway in the near future. The Japanese were collecting evidence of China's illegal acts along the railway zone as a justification for assuming control.[56] Confronted with this news, the State Department desired an immediate decision concerning the future control of the Chinese Eastern Railway.

When on May 14 the British government replied to the American proposal of March 24, 1921, it announced its belief that both Japan and China would be strongly opposed to any plan which tended to increase the international control of the Railway. The British note concluded that although "His Majesty's Government would welcome the introduction of this scheme if it could be brought into force . . . they are inclined to doubt whether, practically speaking, it could be so enforced in existing circumstances." However, if the United States took the lead in proposing such a scheme to the other interested powers, the British agreed to follow.[57]

Upon receiving this note, Hughes wrote to Fletcher:

Until a few months ago the British seemed to be inclined to cooperate cordially with us, but in the last few months they have seemed rather to be pulling away. The significance of the Chinese Eastern situation is such that I think we ought to be somewhat persistent in bringing them to co-operate with us if possible.[58]

To the British government Hughes expressed his sincere regret at the position taken on the matter, adding that "it seems to disappoint the hopes of cooperation, in this important phase of the situation in the Far East. . . ."[59]

The British attitude left the Department in an unfortunate position. Any formal action on the part of the United States seemed doomed to failure. The Department believed that the British note "actively and undoubtedly" reflected the disinclination of the Japanese to strengthen the control of the Technical Committee under Stevens.

[56] Memorandum by Division of Far Eastern Affairs, May 11, 1921, file 861.00/8610, D.S.N.A.; Memorandum by J. P. Jameson, May 26, 1921, file 861.00/7777, D.S.N.A.

[57] H. G. Chilton (British chargé) to Hughes, May 14, 1921, United States, *Foreign Relations, 1921*, I, 580-581.

[58] Hughes to Fletcher, April 15, 1921, file 861.77/2054, D.S.N.A.

[59] Hughes to Chilton, May 20, 1921, United States, *Foreign Relations, 1921*, I, 583.

Moreover, there was undoubtedly some basis for the belief that the Chinese were somewhat jealous of the powers of the Technical Board and would therefore hesitate to take a strong position in support of the American suggestion. No co-operation could be expected from the French government, whose sole concern in the matter was to protect the immediate monetary interests of the French financial group which controlled the Russo-Asiatic Bank, which in turn owned the Chinese Eastern Railway. The attitude of the French, throughout, had been entirely unsympathetic. The State Department suspected that the French were conniving with the Japanese to create a situation in which "Japan would have a color of justification for taking possession of the railway making a financial adjustment with the French interests concerned." The chief of the Far Eastern Division sadly stated his views:

Under these circumstances, we have felt—and Mr. Stevens agrees with us—that we can not hopefully undertake any international action; and that to attempt any such action would not only subject us to the probability of a rebuff, but bring into question the basis of authority now exercised by the Technical Board. Mr. Stevens is planning to stop in Tokyo on his way back to Manchuria, and urge upon his Japanese collaborators that they move their government to view with favor an increase of the powers of his Board. This is a somewhat forlorn hope, with nothing but the prestige of Mr. Stevens to justify it. But it is really the only hope we now have for bettering our position. We are frankly very close to being defeated in this matter; and the only apparent hope of eventual success is that Stevens can "limp along," as he puts it, until such time as it may be possible for us to exert upon the other powers concerned—especially Great Britain and Japan—sufficient pressure to bring them to accept our views of the matter.[60]

When Stevens reached Japan, he was received with high honors. He discussed the Chinese Eastern Railway situation with the Minister of Railways and the Minister of Foreign Affairs. He told them that the American government was extremely anxious to preserve normal conditions along the Chinese Eastern Railway in co-operation with the Allies, using the Technical Board for the purpose. He suggested the possibility of increasing the powers of the Technical Board to include complete control of finances and personnel. Stevens stated that America's purpose was to preserve the open door, to aid Russia, and to stabilize conditions. His suggestions were favorably received in principle by the Japanese government. Stevens pointed out that the United States was ready to co-operate in any reasonable and just plan which Japan might desire.

[60] MacMurray to Hughes, May 25, 1921, file 861.77/2426, D.S.N.A.

Upon the conclusion of his discussions in Japan, Stevens urged the State Department to continue the negotiations in a vigorous manner. He added that, in view of the negative attitude of the British government, the only alternative was direct negotiation with Japan.[61] Bell, the American chargé in Japan, agreed with Stevens.[62]

On August 2 the State Department instructed Bell to suggest to the Japanese government the reorganization of the supervision of the Chinese Eastern Railway on the basis of the plan proposed to Britain on March 24, 1921.[63] The British government agreed to support the proposal through their ambassador in Tokyo.[64]

The Chinese government was not informed of the American proposal. However, it had already begun independent negotiations for the issue of bonds by the Chinese Eastern Railway to an amount of approximately twenty-five million taels, to be secured by railway property. This was done without consulting the Inter-Allied Technical Board, which was charged with the administration of the technical and economic management of the railways. Since this was a violation of the Railway Agreement, the State Department protested to the Chinese government. As a result, the bond issue was dropped.[65]

The Chinese Foreign Minister seemed apprehensive about the plans of the American government concerning the Chinese Eastern Railway. He requested a written statement of American views from A. B. Ruddock, American chargé in China.[66] Apparently the Japanese had informed the Chinese government of the recent American note to Japan concerning expansion of the Railway Agreement. Thus, China felt that the United States was taking action regarding the Chinese Eastern Railway, while keeping her in ignorance. The State Department pointed out orally to the Chinese minister that the object of the United States regarding the railway was to continue the preservation of Chinese and Russian rights by keeping the railway running and providing for its efficient operation. The Chinese minister was informed that he need feel no apprehension that any ideas of the United States regarding the railway would be detrimental to Chinese

[61] Bell to Hughes, June 24, 1921, United States, *Foreign Relations, 1921*, I, 588-589.
[62] Bell to Hughes, June 27, 1921, file 861.77/2167, D.S.N.A.
[63] Hughes to Bell, Aug. 2, 1921, United States, *Foreign Relations, 1921*, I, 596.
[64] Wellesley to Hughes, Aug. 16, 1921, file 861.77/2233, D.S.N.A.
[65] Hughes to Chinese Legation, July 14, 1921, United States, *Foreign Relations, 1921*, I, 595; Memorandum of a Conversation between MacMurray and the Chinese Counselor (Tung Kwai), July 10, 1921, file 861.77/2171, D.S.N.A.
[66] Ruddock to Hughes, Aug. 6, 1921, United States, *Foreign Relations, 1921*, I, 598.

rights in any way.[67]   Although the Chinese government was informed of the interview, it continued to harbor suspicions of the Technical Board.   On September 1, 1921, Stevens reported that the Chinese Minister of Communications and other officials had decided to prevent financial aid to the railway by any power except China and to destroy the effectiveness of the Technical Board in every way.[68]

In the meantime the proposed financial negotiations for the Chinese Eastern had reached what appeared to be a dead end.   Strangely enough, the negotiations had been halted by the American group of the consortium.   On June 21, 1921, the British government had reported that Japan had signified her readiness to join the other interested governments in a loan to the Chinese Eastern Railway.   Although China's attitude was unknown, Britain felt that there were reasons to believe that the prospects of a loan by the consortium were ripening.[69]

Gratified by this news, the American government prepared to join with the other interested powers in arranging such a loan to the Chinese Eastern Railway.[70]   The United States communicated the British memorandum concerning a consortium loan to J. P. Morgan, who was quite surprised at this news since it represented a decided change in the Japanese attitude.   He replied:

We feel that for the long future it would be altogether appropriate for the Consortium, provided China finally determines that it wished the Consortium to function, to undertake a financial operation covering the Chinese Eastern Railway; but until such time, and until the financial position of the railway itself makes a better exhibit, we think there is little immediate possibility of offering in the United States a loan to this railway.   The American Group, in offering any Far Eastern loan to American investors, must exercise the greatest caution and assure itself that such a loan shall be based upon sound operation and adequate security.   In these two respects unfortunately at the present time the Chinese Eastern Railway does not come up to specifications.   It is true that in a situation of this kind Japanese bankers are sometimes able to proceed, but only under a guaranty on the part of their government which the American Group would deem entirely unfitting to suggest to the American Government.[71]

[67] MacMurray to Hughes, Aug. 10, 1921, United States, *Foreign Relations, 1921*, I, 599-600.

[68] Stevens to Hughes, Sept. 1, 1921, file 861.77/2218, D.S.N.A.

[69] Geddes to Hughes, June 21, 1921, United States, *Foreign Relations, 1921*, I, 587-588.

[70] Hughes to Geddes, June 28, 1921, United States, *Foreign Relations, 1921*, 589-590.

[71] Morgan to Hughes, Aug. 2, 1921, United States, *Foreign Relations, 1921*, I, 595-596.

Hughes regretted deeply the decision of the American group. He had hoped that the consortium would provide an opportunity to put the Chinese Eastern upon a sound basis. He was even more regretful in view of the British interest. Explaining his disappointment to Morgan, Hughes wrote: "The international importance of the Chinese Eastern Railway is quite obvious, and I had hoped that through adequate financial support it might be made an important instrumentality of our 'open door' policy."[72]

On October 29, 1921, the Japanese government replied to the American proposal for the reorganization of the Inter-Allied Railroad Board. The Japanese considered so radical a change as that proposed unnecessary and inadmissible. They submitted a counterproposal, which provided that direct control of the railway be given to the board of directors of the railway. The Technical Board should give technical and financial assistance only in case of need.[73]

Stevens refused to consider the Japanese plan, which he regarded "not worthy even of discussion."[74] As Stevens saw the problem, it was necessary to preserve the integrity of the Chinese Eastern Railway if the open door was to be established successfully. Japanese control of the Chinese Eastern, of the Ussuri Railway, or of the port of Vladivostok would bring unfair commercial discrimination. On the other hand, under Chinese control, the Chinese Eastern would promptly become a victim of fatal inefficiency and graft. Therefore, for the present, he felt that international control was essential.[75]

It was quite plain that Japan was opposed to the effective international control and operation which Stevens advocated. Both the Far Eastern Republic and China were also opposed to internationalization. Through informal conversations with the members of the Chinese delegation at the Washington Conference, the State Department had found a great fear in the Chinese mind of the internationalization of railroads in China generally.[76]

The alternatives to an international receivership were either that the railway come into effective Japanese control directly or through a nominal Chinese control, or that the Far Eastern Republic assert and exercise the legal rights of Russia with respect to the railway. Poole believed that if a suitable international receivership proved unattain-

[72] Hughes to Morgan, Aug. 8, 1921, United States, *Foreign Relations, 1921,* I, 598.
[73] Warren to Hughes, United States, *Foreign Relations, 1921,* I, 608-610.
[74] Poole to Hughes, Dec. 3, 1921, file 861.77/2465, D.S.N.A.
[75] Poole to Hughes, Dec. 3, 1921, file 861.77/2465, D.S.N.A.
[76] Poole to Hughes, Nov. 30, 1921, file 861.77/2447, D.S.N.A.

able, the second alternative was worthy of careful consideration. Furthermore, a suggestion to the effect that the United States would be prepared to co-operate with the Far Eastern Republic in the operation of the railway might move Japan to consent to a continuance and strengthening of the existing agreement. It appeared, however, from recent telegrams that there was much misunderstanding both in China and the Far Eastern Republic as to the motives of the United States with respect to the Chinese Eastern Railway. For this reason Poole felt that it was desirable to give the utmost publicity to any proposals which might be made regarding the railway.[77]

Although the French government had expressed its thorough accord with the plan for international control of the Chinese Eastern Railway, it felt that the Russo-Asiatic Bank, which the French government controlled, should be appointed as the financial agent of the railway as heretofore. Stevens did not object to such an arrangement. He felt that the choice of a bank of any other nationality would be certain to create misunderstanding.[78]

American financial circles also seemed to favor the idea of international control as revealed by a letter to Hughes from Lamont. Lamont wrote:

> But now is the time it would appear, to put our feet down and work out some solution, even though it might not be a final one. It would hardly be within the province of the International Consortium actually to undertake the management of the Chinese Eastern Railway, as all the members of the Peking Cabinet last year desired us to do. Railway management is hardly within the function of bankers. But as for the financing of the system upon any sound basis, that could readily be put within the purview of the Consortium. The British are anxious to have it done; the French also, I am confident would fall in line and then the Japanese would be obliged to.[79]

Hughes determined to make a final effort to get Chinese assent to a plan for international control. This would be particularly difficult, as Dr. Hawkling Yen, member of the Chinese delegation to the Washington Conference, had revealed China's abhorrence to "internationalization." Yen was convinced that international control was unacceptable to Chinese public opinion.[80] Hughes decided to try a new avenue of approach. He instructed Jacob G. Schurman, American minister in

[77] Poole to Hughes, Dec. 2, 1921, file 861.77/2465, D.S.N.A.
[78] Hughes to Harvey, Nov. 2, 1921, file 861.77/2282, D.S.N.A.
[79] Lamont to Hughes, Dec. 16, 1921, file 861.77/2466, D.S.N.A.
[80] Poole to Hughes, Nov. 30, 1921, file 861.77/2447, D.S.N.A.

China, to have an informal and confidential talk about the Chinese Eastern Railway with Chang Tso-lin, War Lord of Manchuria. He was to point out the following facts:

The interest of the United States is to maintain the railway as a free avenue of commerce. China and the United States are therefore equally concerned that the railway should not fall into Japanese possession or effective financial control. If the railway were confided to China at this time as a trustee for Russia, financial control by Japan would certainly ensue probably through the purchase by the South Manchuria Railway of the new issue of bonds which would be necessary. . . . Under existing circumstances and until the situation in China is more stable the railway can be secured against international aggression only by instituting a temporary international conservancy the purpose of which would be to preserve the integrity of the railway and existing rights therein and return it as soon as practicable to those in interest.[81]

Hughes felt that if Chang were sufficiently impressed with the Japanese danger and the possibility of a later conflict with a recuperated and dissatisfied Russia, he might lend his support to a temporary plan of international control.[82]

In accordance with his instructions, Schurman had a long talk with Chang concerning a temporary international guardianship such as might be undertaken by the Inter-Allied Technical Board. The suggestion was not well received by Chang. He observed that it was not for him but for the Chinese government to handle the subject. Later he said that the fear of American predominance in the Chinese Eastern aroused the apprehensions of the Japanese. The general prejudice of the Chinese against any proposal for internationalization was clearly shared by Chang. Schurman found that the various Chinese official circles entertained this sentiment very strongly as did also the Prime Minister and the Minister of Communications.[83]

The Chinese Minister for Foreign Affairs desired that China's position be understood by the powers. The Chinese government preferred that the Chinese Eastern be made a state railway. If this could not be done, they desired its present status to be maintained. He said that the Chinese people were unanimous in their opposition to international control, and that in no case was such control desired by the government. Furthermore, he did not see why the Washington Con-

[81] Hughes to Schurman, Dec. 24, 1921, file 861.77/2364a, D.S.N.A.
[82] Hughes to Schurman, Dec. 24, 1921, file 861.77/2364a, D.S.N.A.
[83] Schurman to Hughes, Jan. 1, 1922, United States, *Foreign Relations, 1922*, I, 877-878.

ference should even consider the Chinese Eastern Railway, particularly as the conference had no Russian representatives. When Schurman told the Minister that the railway would need money to rehabilitate itself financially, the Foreign Minister replied that China expected to raise money by floating railway bonds in the international market and that this could be done independently of the consortium.[84]

China's definite stand on international control was soon adopted by the other interested powers at the Washington Conference. During the course of further discussions, it transpired that both France and Japan, and Great Britain as well, felt that it was neither admissable nor practicable to exercise anything but a general supervision over the railway. It was plain that neither France nor Japan would ever consent to an extension of technical control. This created a deadlock between Stevens and the powers. In these circumstances the American government was forced to yield its desire for detailed technical control.[85] The best that could be obtained was the following resolution, adopted at the thirtieth meeting of the Committee on Pacific and Far Eastern Questions on February 2, 1922:

Resolved, That the preservation of the Chinese Eastern Railway for those in interest requires that better protection be given to the Railway and the persons engaged in its operation and use; a more careful selection of personnel to secure efficiency of service, and a more economical use of funds to prevent waste of the property. That the subject should be dealt with through the regular diplomatic channels.[86]

At the same meeting a second resolution was adopted by all powers other than China:

The powers, other than China, in agreeing to the resolution regarding the Chinese Eastern Railway, reserve the right to insist hereafter upon the responsibility of China for the performance or the nonperformance of the obligations towards the foreign stockholders, bondholders, and creditors of the Chinese Eastern Railway Company, which the powers deem to result from the contracts under which the railroad was built and the action of China thereunder and the obligations which they deem to be in the nature of a trust resulting from the exercise of power by the Chinese Government over the possession and administration of the railroad.[87]

[84] Schurman to Hughes, Jan. 7, 1922, United States, *Foreign Relations, 1922,* I, 878.

[85] Poole to Hughes, Jan. 20, 1922, file 861.77/2446, D.S.N.A.

[86] Hughes to Schurman, Feb. 3, 1922, United States, *Foreign Relations, 1922,* I, 883; *Conference on Limitation of Armaments,* p. 316; Weigh, *Russo-Chinese Diplomacy,* pp. 241-243.

[87] *Conference on Limitation of Armaments,* p. 318; Weigh, *Russo-Chinese Diplomacy,*

From Harbin, Jenkins reported that the Chinese had organized a society to carry on a campaign against international control of the Chinese Eastern Railway. Street demonstrations had taken place. The movement was believed to be instigated by the authorities.[88]

During the next month developments respecting the Chinese Eastern Railway followed two courses. The American and British ministers at Peking reiterated to the Chinese Minister of Foreign Affairs in a personal interview the suggestions made to the Chinese delegation at Washington, namely, that China undertake to improve conditions of public order in the railway zone by organizing a special railway guard, and that China take the initiative in the diplomatic discussions recommended by the conference by inviting the powers to aid her in maintaining the railway. When the Chinese Minister for Foreign Affairs telegraphed the Chinese minister at Washington asking what the United States really wanted, the minister replied that they were only offering friendly advice.

Matsudaira, of the Japanese delegation, had informed Poole before leaving for Japan that he intended to seek the authority of his superiors in Tokyo to take up the question of the Chinese Eastern Railway with the American Embassy there, in an attempt to obtain preliminary Japanese-American accord. The American ambassador to Japan was informed of this and instructed to maintain a purely receptive attitude.[89] China continued to exhibit a reluctance to discuss any new plans regarding the railway. In a conversation with Dr. C. C. Wang, the new president of the railway, Minister Schurman gained the impression that the chief reason for Chinese reluctance to seek co-operation was their desire to remain free from entering into political, territorial, or other arrangements as to their rights in the Chinese Eastern, which might jeopardize informal discussions with the Russians looking to an agreement.[90]

Chinese reluctance to discuss the Chinese Eastern situation was reinforced by a new move on the part of Britain. The British Foreign Office announced that since Great Britain had virtually no commercial interest in the Chinese Eastern Railway, it seemed a luxury to maintain a British member on the Technical Board. Therefore it was felt

p. 243. See also C. C. Wang, "The Chinese Eastern Railway," *Annals of the American Academy of Political and Social Science*, CXXII (Nov., 1925), 67.

[88] Jenkins to Hughes, Feb. 6, 1922, United States, *Foreign Relations, 1922*, I, 884.

[89] Poole to Hughes, March 9, 1922, file 861.77/2543, D.S.N.A.

[90] Schurman to Hughes, March 25, 1922, United States, *Foreign Relations, 1922*, I, 889-891.

that the expenses of the Technical Board should be met by the Chinese government.[91] The American government reported that it would regard the withdrawal of the British member of the Technical Board as most unfortunate, especially as Stevens was then returning to Harbin, and in view of the intimations that the Japanese government intended soon to initiate discussions of future policy regarding the railway.[92]

In the meantime organized demonstrations in China were demanding the withdrawal of the Technical Board, and leading newspapers in North Manchuria were arguing that the objects for which the board was created no longer existed. Various organizations and patriotic societies in certain North Manchurian cities had forwarded circular telegrams to the Peking government demanding that the Technical Board be abolished.[93] Stevens reported that the financial situation of the railroad was chaotic and that the Technical Board was being ignored in every way by the Board of Directors. He predicted the collapse of the railway under the present system of management.[94] At the same time, Warren reported that when Uchida was told of existing conditions on the railway he replied that he had no plan to propose to remedy the situation.[95]

Under these conditions Hughes had just about decided that any further expenditure of American funds in connection with the Chinese Eastern and Trans-Siberian Railways was inadvisable. On July 17, in view of Japan's announced purpose to withdraw her troops and the consequent automatic termination of the Railway Agreement, the Secretary of State discussed with the Japanese and British governments, in a preliminary and confidential manner, the question of ending the Inter-Allied Committee and Technical Board, and of confirming the attitude of the powers toward the Chinese Eastern Railway as outlined at the Washington Conference.[96]

The American government then directed a note to the nations which had participated in the Inter-Allied Agreement. The note sug-

[91] Schurman to Hughes, March 28, 1922, United States, *Foreign Relations, 1922*, I, 892.

[92] Hughes to Harvey, April 8, 1922, United States, *Foreign Relations, 1922*, I, 892.

[93] Memorandum by Douglas Jenkins of the Division of Russian Affairs, May 1, 1922, United States, *Foreign Relations, 1922*, I, 892-894.

[94] Stevens to Hughes, May 25, 1922, United States, *Foreign Relations, 1922*, I, 896.

[95] Warren to Hughes, June 6, 1922, United States, *Foreign Relations, 1922*, I, 897.

[96] Hughes to Hanson, July 17, 1922, United States, *Foreign Relations, 1922*, I, 905.

gested that upon the abolition of the Technical Board the Allies adopt the following policy in regard to the Chinese Eastern Railway:

That those powers should confirm the resolutions above quoted relating to China's responsibility; that they should, so far as there may be occasion, reserve all rights with respect to advances in money or material made in aid of the railway; that they reaffirm their concern in the preservation of the railway, its efficient operation and its maintenance as a free avenue of commerce open to the citizens of all countries without favor or discrimination, that they inform the Chinese Government that they purpose to continue to observe carefully the administration and operation of the railway and the manner in which China discharges the responsibilities which she has assumed; and that they apprise the Chinese Government at the same time of their entire good will and readiness to assist or cooperate at any time in any practicable way with a view to conserving the railway property and assuring efficient operation in the interest of all concerned.[97]

All the participating nations agreed to the resolution. Thus the affairs of the board were brought to a conclusion.[98] The final meeting of the Technical Board was held on November 1, 1922. On March 15, 1923, John F. Stevens filed his final report. He was quite aware of the fact that it read like the "Lamentations of Jeremiah," but he pointed out that it could not be otherwise. He himself was amazed at his moderation. If it had been intended for the exclusive use of the State Department, it would have necessitated the use of asbestos paper.[99]

[97] Hughes to Harvey, July 17, 1922, United States, *Foreign Relations, 1922,* I, 905-906.

[98] Warren to Hughes, Aug. 9, 1922, Harvey to Hughes, Aug. 24, 1922, Myron T. Herrick (ambassador to France) to Hughes, Oct. 13, 1922, United States, *Foreign Relations, 1922,* I, 909-910, 913, 919.

[99] Stevens to Hughes, March 16, 1923, file 861.77/3064, D.S.N.A.

CHAPTER XIII

Conclusion

THE TERMINATION of the Inter-Allied Railway Agreement of
1919 marked the end of Allied intervention in Siberia. A complex and confused phase of American foreign policy in the Far East
was thus brought to a close. Throughout the intervention the United
States had been engaged in a lone struggle against the intrigues of
Great Britain, France, and Japan. Each nation had its own motives
for participating in the expedition. The British and French desired
to set up an Eastern Front in the belief that this was a necessary step
in the winning of the war. Early in 1918 they were even willing to
negotiate with the Bolsheviks in order to secure renewed warfare
against the Central Powers. At the same time both the British and the
French supported various revolutionary groups in Russia and Siberia
in the hope of enlisting their aid against the Central Powers. After
the Armistice was declared, the British and the French were unwilling to desert the Russian friends who had aided them in Siberia.
They professed a conviction that the Bolsheviks were a German-
inspired government; and this belief, in conjunction with their hatred
of the principles and practices for which the Bolsheviks stood, led them
to a continued support of the anti-Bolsheviks after the war was over.[1]

[1] Winston Churchill later said, "As it was, enough foreign troops entered Russia to
incur all the objections which were patent against intervention, but not enough to break
the then gimcrack structure of the Soviet power. When we observe the amazing ex-
ploits of the Czech Army Corps, it seems certain that a resolute effort by a compara-
tively small number of trustworthy American or Japanese troops would have enabled
Moscow to be occupied by National Russian and Allied forces even before the German
collapse took place. Divided counsels and cross-purposes among the Allies, American
mistrust of Japan, and the personal opposition of President Wilson, reduced Allied intervention in Russia during the war to exactly the point where it did the utmost harm
and gained the least advantage" (Churchill, *The Aftermath,* p. 285). At the end of
1919 Lloyd George, referring to Allied intervention, said he did not wish to criticize
any of his Allies, but "if there has been a failure it is not our failure" (*Literary Digest,*
LXIII, Dec. 27, 1919, 20).

When public opinion demanded the withdrawal of Allied troops from Russia, Britain and France urged Japan to continue the fight against the Bolsheviks in Siberia.[2]

Japan's motives were inspired primarily by the military elements who desired first and last to take over political, military, and economic control of Eastern Siberia and the Chinese Eastern Railway. Although opposed to this scheme, the civilian elements were too weak to thwart it. Thus the Japanese military party supported such Russian leaders as Kalmikov and Semenov, in the hope of fomenting discord in Siberia, thereby providing a pretext for increased military occupation of the region. Japanese policy was to divide and rule.[3]

American motives were far more complex. Wilson resisted Allied pressure for intervention in Siberia until July, 1918. His suspicions of Japan led him to believe that lone Japanese intervention would probably result in the alienation of Russian territory and the closing of the open door in Siberia and North Manchuria. Moreover, he believed that such an intervention was unneutral and undemocratic. In this respect he followed a Russian policy which was consistent with his own deepest convictions as enumerated in the Fourteen Points. He demanded for Russia a free and unembarrassed opportunity to determine her own political development and national policy, and assurance to her of a "sincere welcome into the society of free nations under institutions of her own choosing." In March, 1918, as a result of overwhelming pressure from his Allies, Wilson agreed reluctantly to permit Japanese intervention in Siberia without American participation. However, when confronted with the view that by such a policy he would lose the moral leadership of the world, Wilson returned to his original position.

In July, 1918, in the face of new and compelling circumstances, Wilson changed his mind. He not only agreed to intervention, but took the lead in inviting the Japanese to a joint intervention in Siberia. His avowed reasons were to "rescue" the Czechs and to aid the Russian people in any efforts at self-government they might desire. The Czechs, however, were quite capable of taking care of themselves as indicated by their amazing military successes before the Allies arrived. Furthermore, Wilson's second objective was subject to confused and

---

[2] The American government also informed Japan that it was "not disposed to object to any reasonable measures which Japan may decide to take in Eastern Siberia with a view to halting the advance of Bolshevism . . . ." (Department of State to the Japanese Embassy, Jan. 30, 1920, United States, *Foreign Relations, 1920*, III, 501-502).

[3] D. B. Macgowan to Secretary of State, Sept. 12, 1921, file 861.77/2279, D.S.N.A.; John Weeks to Secretary of State, Oct. 7, 1921, file 861.00/9040.

varied interpretation, since he failed to say what Russians the American troops were to aid in their efforts to acquire self-government.

Wilson's basic and unpublicized reason for intervention was to restrain Japan from imperialistic adventures and to preserve the open door in Siberia and North Manchuria. Although on the surface his policy appeared to be contradictory, actually it was quite consistent. He agreed to intervention in July, 1918, for the very same reasons that he had opposed it in the early part of the year. When it became evident that, despite his opposition, his Allies were ready to sanction Japan's lone entry into Siberia, and Japan herself was preparing to embark upon an independent expedition under the auspices of the Sino-Japanese Military Agreements of May, 1918, Wilson invited Japan to participate in a joint expedition to Siberia. He did so, however, not because he believed in the expedition, but because he thought he could control it in the interests of Russia, China, and the United States. He believed that the Czech troops in Siberia provided the nucleus of an Allied army and would thereby make unnecessary the sending of large numbers of Japanese troops. A further reason for Wilson's decision was his belief that he could no longer thwart the unanimous desires of his Allies.

Once Wilson yielded on the major decision to intervene, the British, French, and Japanese attempted to use the intervention for their own purposes. Wilson had not desired the participation of either Great Britain or France. He had opposed the secret support and encouragement given to factions in various parts of Russia.[4] Wilson soon realized that the joint expedition which he had sponsored was rapidly being turned into an unneutral intervention in the internal affairs of another nation. He deplored this result and attempted, within the limits of diplomacy, to restrain the independent operations of his Allies.

After the Armistice was declared, the avowed reasons for intervention were no longer adequate. Yet for two reasons American troops continued to remain in Siberia. For all practical purposes American evacuation would have left Japan in virtual control of North Manchuria and Eastern Siberia. Moreover, Britain, France, and Japan were opposed to withdrawal. President Wilson did not wish to jeopardize his program at the Peace Conference by independent action. Thus, in order to block Japan and to further his League, Wilson followed a policy which appeared to be totally at variance not only with the principles which he had enunciated concerning Russia, but also with the principles of his proposed League. As time went on, these clashes between what Wilson said and what he did made the

[4] Lansing to Polk, Aug. 3, 1918, Lansing Papers.

American position in Siberia even more difficult. Wilson found it impossible to keep American troops in Siberia without actively aiding Kolchak. Whatever may be said concerning America's neutrality in Siberia in 1918, there is little doubt that in 1919 the State Department actively supported and aided Kolchak despite the fact that Wilson himself admitted that the American people did not believe in Kolchak.[5] Wilson's justification for this policy was his belief that it preserved the open door in Siberia and Manchuria, preserved Russia's territorial integrity, and aided him in establishing his League of Nations. The Bolsheviks themselves conceded America's justification in following such a policy, when in 1933, after being shown certain documents concerning America's policy, they agreed to drop all claims against America for her part in the Siberian intervention.[6] As Cordell Hull pointed out, "These latter documents made clear to Litvinov that American forces had not been in Siberia to wrest territory from Russia, but to ensure the withdrawal of the Japanese, who had a far larger force in Siberia with the intent to occupy it permanently."[7]

It would seem to be notable, however, that throughout the intervention the American public was permitted to believe that the United States went into Siberia to combat Bolshevism. It was difficult for the State Department to refute this belief while the United States was at war. Japan was an ally, and it was not considered diplomatic to question publicly the motives of one's allies, especially when a fear existed that Japan might possibly join the Central Powers. Even after the war was over, the popular feeling persisted that intervention was solely to defeat the Bolsheviks.[8] This sentiment was intensified by the actions of the underlings in the State Department who assumed control of America's policy in Siberia upon Wilson's illness, and who themselves favored Kolchak and wanted him to receive the greatest aid possible.

[5] General Graves believed that "no well-informed man can deny Kolchak was held in power by the moral and material assistance given him by the foreign governments having military forces in Siberia" (Arthur Bullard's extracts from General Graves's Final Report, Bullard to Secretary of State, Sept. 21, 1920, file 861.00/7354, D.S.N.A.). Graves thought intervention a fundamental error, "an inexcusable departure from the generally accepted practice of nations in their dealings with other nations . . ." (Graves, *America's Siberian Adventure*, p. 354).

[6] N. W. Graham, "Russian-American Relations, 1917-1933: An Interpretation"; *American Political Science Review*, XXVIII (June, 1934), 408-409.

[7] Cordell Hull, *Memoirs*, (2 vols.; New York, 1948), I, 299.

[8] When General Graves reported that "ninety-eight per cent of the people in Siberia are Bolsheviki" and that "they are working for peace and the good of the country and in my opinion they are trying to be fair and just to the people," Colby brought the "impropriety" of these remarks to the attention of Secretary Baker (Colby to Baker, April 20, 1920, file 861.00/6862, D.S.N.A.).

Since the attitude of the State Department had long since ceased
to be neutral, why did the United States withdraw its troops in 1920?
Why were they not maintained and reinforced? The answer would
appear to be that the Department feared an actual conflict with the
Bolsheviks. For this reason Japanese troops were left in occupation of
Eastern Siberia and partial occupation of the Trans-Siberian Railway.
Although the State Department gave tentative approval to Japan's
decision to remain in Siberia to combat Bolshevism, it continued to
protest for the next two and a half years against her occupation of
Eastern Siberia, the Chinese Eastern Railway, and the southern half
of Sakhalin.[9]

The positive results of intervention were due largely to American
participation. The United States prevented Japan from going into
Russia alone, with a free hand. To some extent the United States
restrained Japan from absorbing Eastern Siberia and the Chinese
Eastern Railway. Upon entering Siberia, the United States extracted
promises from Japan guaranteeing Russia's territorial integrity and
promising Japanese withdrawal. America refused to support Allied
demands for the re-creation of an Eastern Front, which in effect would
have amounted to major operations against the Soviet government.
At various times the United States prevented political action against
the Soviet government. After America's withdrawal from Siberia,
this country kept up a steady stream of protests to Japan concerning
her continued presence on Russian territory and consolidated world
opinion against the Japanese activities in Siberia at the Washington
Conference. Thus, America's participation in Allied intervention did
provide a moderating influence which tended to curb the more extreme
ideas of the Allies.[10]

[9] Professor Norton has pointed out that "if America could have invited Japan to leave
Siberia, and that invitation had been accepted with as great alacrity as the one to enter,
the story of Allied intervention in the Far East would not have been the sorry tragedy
it is . . . . Her action, and that of the other Allies, in merely withdrawing their troops
and leaving Japan to make the explanations, placed the seal of approval on the continued intervention of the Japanese, and threw upon them a large share of the responsibility for the subsequent events" (Norton, *Far Eastern Republic,* pp. 107-109).

[10] Secretary Baker stated: "If the Siberian Expedition was in fact unjustified and if it
really failed to accomplish substantially helpful results, this much is true of it—it was
justified by conditions as they appeared to be at the time, it [the United States] refrained
from militaristic adventures of its own, it restrained such adventures on the part of
others, and it created a situation which made necessary the withdrawal of all Allied
forces from Siberian soil when it was withdrawn, thus making impossible territorial
conquests and acquisitions on Russian soil by other nations whose interests in the Far
East might easily have induced them to take over pacification, and ultimately for
permanent colonial administration, vast areas of Russia's Far East" (Baker, Foreword in
Graves, *America's Siberian Adventure,* pp. xi-xii).

Appendix

The Secretary of State to the Allied Ambassadors
AIDE-MEMOIRE

The whole heart of the people of the United States is in the winning of this war. The controlling purpose of the Government of the United States is to do everything that is necessary and effective to win it. It wishes to cooperate in every practicable way with the Allied Governments, and to cooperate ungrudgingly; for it has no ends of its own to serve and believes that the war can be won only by common counsel and intimate concert of action. It has sought to study every proposed policy or action in which its cooperation has been asked in this spirit, and states the following conclusions in the confidence that, if it finds itself obliged to decline participation in any undertaking or course of action, it will be understood that it does so only because it deems itself precluded from participating by imperative considerations either of policy or of fact.

In full agreement with the Allied Governments and upon the unanimous advice of the Supreme War Council, the Government of the United States adopted, upon its entrance into the war, a plan for taking part in the fighting on the western front into which all its resources of men and material were to be put, and put as rapidly as possible, and it has carried out that plan with energy and success, pressing its execution more and more rapidly forward and literally putting into it the entire energy and executive force of the nation. This was its response, its very willing and hearty response, to what was the unhesitating judgment alike of its own military advisers and of the advisers of the Allied Governments. It is now considering, at the suggestion of the Supreme War Council, the possibility of making very considerable additions even to this immense program which, if they should prove feasible at all, will tax the industrial processes of the United States and the shipping facilities of the whole group of associated nations to the utmost. It has thus concentrated all its plans and all its resources upon this single absolutely necessary object.

In such circumstances it feels it to be its duty to say that it cannot, so

long as the military situation on the western front remains critical, consent
to break or slacken the force of its present effort by diverting any part
of its military force to other points or objectives. The United States is at
a great distance from the field of action on the western front; it is at a
much greater distance from any other field of action. The instrumentali-
ties by which it is to handle its armies and its stores have at great cost
and with great difficulty been created in France. They do not exist elsewhere. It is practicable for her to do a great deal in France; it is not
practicable for her to do anything of importance or on a large scale upon
any other field. The American Government, therefore, very respectfully
requests its associates to accept its deliberate judgment that it should not
dissipate its force by attemping important operations elsewhere.

It regards the Italian front as closely coordinated with the western
front, however, and is willing to divert a portion of its military forces from
France to Italy if it is the judgment and wish of the Supreme Command
that it should do so. It wishes to defer to the decision of the Commander
in Chief in this matter, as it would wish to defer in all others, particularly
because it considers these two fronts so closely related as to be practically
but separate parts of a single line and because it would be necessary that
any American troops sent to Italy should be subtracted from the number
used in France and be actually transported across French territory from the
ports now used by the armies of the United States.

It is the clear and fixed judgment of the Government of the United
States, arrived at after repeated and very searching reconsiderations of the
whole situation in Russia, that military intervention there would add to
the present sad confusion in Russia rather than cure it, injure her rather
than help her, and that it would be of no advantage in the prosecution of
our main design, to win the war against Germany. It can not, therefore,
take part in such intervention or sanction it in principle. Military intervention would, in its judgment, even supposing it to be efficacious in its
immediate avowed object of delivering an attack upon Germany from the
east, be merely a method of making use of Russia, not a method of serving
her. Her people could not profit by it, if they profited by it at all, in time
to save them from their present distresses, and their substance would be
used to maintain foreign armies, not to reconstitute their own. Military
action is admissible in Russia, as the Government of the United States
sees the circumstances, only to help the Czecho-Slovaks consolidate their
forces and get into successful cooperation with their Slavic kinsmen and
to steady any efforts at self-government or self-defense in which the Russians
themselves may be willing to accept assistance. Whether from Vladivostok
or from Murmansk and Archangel, the only legitimate object for which
American or Allied troops can be employed, it submits, is to guard military
stores which may subsequently be needed by Russian forces and to render
such aid as may be acceptable to the Russians in the organization of their
own self-defense. For helping the Czecho-Slovaks there is immediate

necessity and sufficient justification. Recent developments have made it evident that that is in the interest of what the Russian people themselves desire, and the Government of the United States is glad to contribute the small force at its disposal for that purpose. It yields, also, to the judgment of the Supreme Command in the matter of establishing a small force at Murmansk, to guard the military stores at Kola, and to make it safe for Russian forces to come together in organized bodies in the north. But it owes it to frank counsel to say that it can go no further than these modest and experimental plans. It is not in a position, and has no expectation of being in a position, to take part in organized intervention in adequate force from either Vladivostok or Murmansk and Archangel. It feels that it ought to add, also, that it will feel at liberty to use the few troops it can spare only for the purposes here stated and shall feel obliged to withdraw those forces, in order to add them to the forces at the western front, if the plans in whose execution it is now intended that they should cooperate should develop into others inconsistent with the policy to which the Government of the United States feels constrained to restrict itself.

At the same time the Government of the United States wishes to say with the utmost cordiality and good will that none of the conclusions here stated is meant to wear the least color of criticism of what the other governments associated against Germany may think it wise to undertake. It wishes in no way to embarrass their choices of policy. All that is intended here is a perfectly frank and definite statement of the policy which the United States feels obliged to adopt for herself and in the use of her own military forces. The Government of the United States does not wish it to be understood that in so restricting its own activities it is seeking, even by implication, to set limits to the action or to define the policies of its associates.

It hopes to carry out the plans for safeguarding the rear of the Czecho-Slovaks operating from Vladivostok in a way that will place it and keep it in close cooperation with a small military force like its own from Japan, and if necessary from the other Allies, and that will assure it of the cordial accord of all the Allied powers; and it proposes to ask all associated in this course of action to unite in assuring the people of Russia in the most public and solemn manner that none of the governments uniting in action either in Siberia or in northern Russia contemplates any interference of any kind with the political sovereignty of Russia, any intervention in her internal affairs, or any impairment of her territorial integrity either now or hereafter, but that each of the associated powers has the single object of affording such aid as shall be acceptable, and only such aid as shall be acceptable, to the Russian people in their endeavor to regain control of their own affairs, their own territory, and their own destiny.

It is the hope and purpose of the Government of the United States to take advantage of the earliest opportunity to send to Siberia a commission of merchants, agricultural experts, labor advisers, Red Cross representatives, and agents of the Young Men's Christian Association accustomed to organizing the best methods of spreading useful information and rendering educational help of a modest sort, in order in some systematic manner to relieve the immediate economic necessities of the people there in every way for which opportunity may open. The execution of this plan will follow and will not be permitted to embarrass the military assistance rendered in the rear of the westward-moving forces of the Czecho-Slovaks.*

WASHINGTON, July 17, 1918.

* United States, *Foreign Relations, 1918, Russia*, II, 287-290.

Glossary of Names

Alston, Right Honorable Sir Beilby Francis, British deputy high commissioner, Siberia, 1918-1919; minister to Tokyo, 1919-1920; minister to China, 1920-1922.

Atherton, Ray, secretary of embassy, assigned to Tokyo, September 6, 1917—March 14, 1919; assigned to Peking, July 30, 1919.

Auchincloss, Gordon, assistant counselor to the Department of State, June 11, 1917; secretary of the American War Mission to England and France, November, 1917; secretary to Colonel Edward M. House during negotiations of Armistice, Paris, November, 1918, and during Peace Conference, Paris, 1919.

Baker, Newton D., Secretary of War, March 7, 1916—March 4, 1921.

Bakhmetev, Boris A., Assistant Minister of Trade and Industry in the Provisional government; ambassador to Washington, May, 1917—June 30, 1922.

Balfour, Arthur J., British Secretary of State for Foreign Affairs, 1916-1919; plenipotentiary at the Paris Peace Conference.

Barclay, Colville A., counselor of the British Embassy at Washington, 1918; chargé d'affaires *ad interim*.

Barrows, Lieutenant Colonel David P., Chief Intelligence Officer, Department of Philippines and A.E.F. to Siberia, 1918-1919.

Bell, Edward, assigned as counselor of the Embassy at Tokyo, December 11, 1919; assigned as expert assistant, Conference on the Limitation of Armament, November 3, 1921.

Beneš, Dr. Eduard, General Secretary of the Czechoslovak National Council in Paris, 1917; Minister of Foreign Affairs of Czechoslovak Republic, 1918-1935; Premier, 1921-1922.

Benson, Admiral William S., Chief of Naval Operations, May 11, 1915—September 25, 1919; naval advisor to Commission to Negotiate Peace.

Bertie, Lord (Francis Leveson Bertie), British ambassador to Paris, 1905-1918.

Bliss, General Tasker H., Chief of Staff, September 22—December 31, 1917; member of the Allied Conference, 1917; member of the Supreme War Council in France; member of the American Commission to Negotiate Peace.

Buckler, W. H., appointed special assistant in the American Embassy at London, December 19, 1914—1918; attached to American Commission to Negotiate Peace, Paris, June-December, 1919.

Bullard, Arthur, Director of the Russian Division of the Committee on Public Information, Moscow, June, 1917; transferred to Vladivostok, Siberia, September, 1918—January, 1919; appointed special assistant to Department of State for work in Russian Division, December, 1919; Chief of Russian Division, November, 1920—March, 1921.

Bullitt, William C., appointed a temporary clerk in the Department of State, January 1, 1918; attached to the American Commission to Negotiate Peace, November 30, 1918; special mission to Russia, 1919.

Caldwell, John K., consul at Vladivostok, August 1, 1914; assigned to Kobe, July 1, 1920; appointed Japanese secretary of Embassy at Tokyo, July 1, 1921.

Cecil, Lord Robert, British Assistant Secretary of State for Foreign Affairs, 1918.

Chang Tso-lin, War Lord of Manchuria, 1911-1928.

Chicherin, George V., Acting Soviet Commissar for Foreign Affairs, March 13, 1918; Commissar for Foreign Affairs, May 30, 1918—1930.

Chilton, Sir Henry G., secretary of British Embassy at Washington, 1918; counselor of Embassy at Washington, 1921.

Churchill, Right Honorable Winston, British Secretary of State for War and Air, 1918-1921.

Clemenceau, Georges E. B., French Premier and Minister for War, November 16, 1917—January 20, 1920.

Clerk, George R., private secretary to British Acting Secretary of State for Foreign Affairs, 1919.

Colby, Bainbridge, member of the American Mission to Inter-Allied Conference at Paris, November, 1917; Secretary of State, March 22, 1920—March 4, 1921.

Crane, Charles R., appointed envoy extraordinary on special mission to Russia, August 11, 1917; envoy extraordinary and minister plenipotentiary to China, March 22, 1920; retired June, 1921.

Daniels, Josephus, Secretary of the Navy, March 5, 1913—March 6, 1921.

Davis, John W., American ambassador to Great Britain, November 21, 1918—March, 1921.

Davis, Norman H., financial adviser to President Wilson and American Commission to Negotiate Peace; Under Secretary of State, June 15, 1920—March 7, 1921.

Debuchi, Katsuji, Japanese chargé d'affaires in the United States, 1918-1920.

Deniken, General Anton I., assistant to Chief of Staff of the Russian Army, April—June, 1917; June—September, 1917, successively commander of the western and southwestern fronts; after the November revolution took part in the Don in the formation of the Volunteer Army; became commander-in-chief of the anti-Bolshevik forces in South Russia, 1918-1919.

Drummond, Sir Eric, private secretary to British Foreign Secretary, 1915-1919; Secretary-General to League of Nations, 1919-1933.

Drysdale, Major Walter S., American military attaché at Peking, December 28, 1917—October, 1921 (on detached service at Harbin, Manchuria, and at Irkutsk and Vladivostok, Siberia).

Eichelberger, Lieutenant Colonel Robert L., assistant chief of staff, Operations Division Siberia and chief intelligence officer, A.E.F., 1918-1920.

Eliot, Sir Charles, British high commissioner in Siberia, 1918-1919; ambassador to Japan, 1920-1926.

Emerson, Colonel George, in command of the Russian Railway Service Corps in Siberia, October 15, 1917—January 1, 1920.

Fisher, Harold H., vice chairman of the Hoover War Library, 1924-1944; chairman since 1944.

Fletcher, Henry P., appointed Under Secretary of State, March 7, 1921; appointed a member of the Advisory Committee to the American Commissioners to the Conference on the Limitation of Armament, November 2, 1921.

Foch, Ferdinand, Marshal of France and Generalissimo of the Allied armies, 1918.

Francis, David Rowland, ambassador to Russia, March 6, 1916—May, 1921.

Frazier, Arthur Hugh, counselor of Embassy at Paris, June 11, 1918; on detail in diplomatic liaison office, Supreme War Council, November, 1917—November, 1918.

Geddes, Sir Auckland (Lord), president of British Board of Trade, 1919-1920; ambassador to the United States, 1920-1924.

Gleaves, Admiral Albert, commander-in-chief of the United States Asiatic Fleet, September 1, 1919—1921.

Goto, Baron Shimpei, Japanese Minister of the Interior, October, 1916—April, 1918; Minister of Foreign Affairs, April—September, 1918.

Graves, Major General William S., commander of the American expeditionary forces in Siberia, 1918-1920.

Grew, Joseph E., acting chief of Western European Division, Department of State, March 14, 1918—October 15, 1918.

Hara, Takashi, Japanese Prime Minister, September 30, 1918-1921; leader of the Seiyukai party; first commoner to become Prime Minister and the first to form a party cabinet in accordance with the principles of parliamentary government.

Harris, Ernest L., American consul general at Irkutsk, May 8, 1918, to October 15, 1920.

Harvey, George, American ambassador to Great Britain, April 16, 1921 to November, 1923.

Heid, August, representative of the War Trade Board at Vladivostok.

Horvat, Lieutenant-General Dmitri L., appointed general manager of the Chinese Eastern Railway and chief administrator of the zone in 1903; attempted to establish an all-Russian, anti-Bolshevik government in July, 1918; served as Kolçhak's high plenipotentiary in the Far East; forced to resign as manager of the railroad in late 1920.

House, Colonel Edward M., appointed representative of the United States government in the Supreme War Council at Versailles, December 1, 1917; designated by the President on October 17, 1918, to act for the United States in the negotiation of the Armistice with the Central Powers; member of American Commission to Negotiate Peace, 1918-1919.

Hughes, Charles Evans, appointed American Secretary of State, March 5, 1921; commissioned by the President October 24, 1921, commissioner plenipotentiary, with the rank of ambassador extraordinary, to serve as a member of the commission to represent the United States at the Conference on the Limitation of Armament, Washington.

Ishii, Viscount Kikujiro, negotiated in 1917 the Lansing-Ishii agreement with the United States; Japanese ambassador to the United States, 1918-1919.

Ivanov-Rinov, General Pavel Pavlovich, appointed by Kolchak as commander of Russian troops in Eastern Siberia.

Jameson, Jay P., detailed for special duty in Russia and Siberia, May 1, 1918; detailed to Department of State June 12, 1920; expert assistant, Conference on the Limitation of Armament, November 3, 1921; resigned March 15, 1922.

Janin, General Maurice, supreme commander of the Czechoslovak Army in Siberia.

Jenkins, Douglas, detailed to Harbin, August 16, 1918; appointed consul at Harbin, September 6, 1919; detailed to Department of State, December 23, 1921.

Johnson, B. O., acting president of the Inter-Allied Technical Board supervising the Chinese Eastern and Siberian Railways, 1922.

Judson, General William V., with the Root Mission to Russia, 1917; remained in Russia as military attaché and chief of American Military Mission to Russia until spring, 1918.

Jusserand, Jean Adrien Antoine Jules, French ambassador to the United States, 1902-1925.

Kalmikov, Ivan, ataman of the Ussuri Cossacks.

Kato, Viscount Takaakira, Japanese Minister for Foreign Affairs, 1914-1916; organizer and leader of the Kenseikai party.

Kato, Tsunetado, Japanese special representative in Siberia, appointed in 1918 to take charge of the diplomatic side of the expedition.

Kerensky, Alexander F., Minister of Justice in Provisional government, March—May, 1917; Minister of War and of Marine, May to July, 1917; Prime Minister, July-October, 1917.

Kerr, Phillip, secretary to Lloyd George at the Paris Peace Conference.

Knight, Admiral Austin M., commander-in-chief of the United States Asiatic fleet, April, 1917, to December 9, 1918.

Knox, General Alfred W., British military attaché in Petrograd, 1911-1918; chief of the British Military Mission in Siberia, 1918-1920.

Kolchak, Admiral Alexsander V., commander of the Black Sea Fleet; after the November revolution a leader of anti-Soviet forces in Siberia; Minister of War and Navy of the All-Russian Directory; on November 18, 1918, at Omsk, proclaimed Supreme Governor of Russia.

Koo, Vi Kyuin Wellington, appointed Chinese minister at Washington, 1915; delegate to the Paris Peace Conference, 1919; minister to Great Britain, 1920; delegate at the Washington Conference, 1921-1922.

Kudashev, Prince Nikolai A., Russian ambassador to China, 1916-1918.

Lamont, Thomas W., member of J. P. Morgan and Company, Bankers, 1911-1940; chairman of American Group International Consortium for Assistance of China.

Lansing, Robert, Secretary of State, June 23, 1915—February 13, 1920; member of the American Commission to Negotiate Peace, 1918-1919.

Lenin, Vladimir I., President of the Soviet of People's Commissars, November 8, 1917-1924.

Lindsay, Ronald Charles, counselor of British Embassy at Washington, 1919-1920.

Litvinov, Maxim M., accredited Soviet diplomatic agent to Great Britain, 1918; member of People's Commissariat for Foreign Affairs, 1918-1921.

Lloyd George, David, British Prime Minister, December 1916—1922.

Lockhart, R. H. Bruce, British acting consul general at Moscow, 1914-1917; head of Special British Mission to Bolshevik government, 1918.

Long, Breckinridge, Third Assistant Secretary of State, 1917-1920.

Macchi di Cellere, Count Vincenzo, Italian ambassador to the United States, 1913-1921.

McCormick, Vance C., chairman of the War Trade Board, 1917-1919; adviser to American Commission to Negotiate Peace, 1919.

Macgowan, David B., consul at Moscow, on special detail at Vladivostok, June, 1918—July 1, 1920.

MacMurray, John Van A., assigned as counselor of the Embassy at Tokyo, November 10, 1917; chargé at Peking, July 1—November 30, 1918; reassigned to Tokyo October 15, 1918; assigned to Department of State for duty in the Division of Far Eastern Affairs, July 23, 1919; appointed chief, Division of Far Eastern Affairs, August 20, 1919; expert assistant, Conference on the Limitation of Armament, November 3, 1921.

March, General Peyton C., Chief of Staff, May, 1918—1921.

Masaryk, Thomas G., President of the Czechoslovak National Council, 1918; first President of the Czechoslovak Republic, November, 1918; re-elected 1920, 1927, and 1934.

Matsudaira, Tsuneo, member of Inter-Allied Railway Commission in Siberia, 1919; director of the European and American Departments of Japanese Foreign Affairs, 1920.

Miles, Basil, special assistant to the ambassador at Petrograd with rank of minister plenipotentiary, January 4, 1917; ordered temporarily for duty in the Department of State in connection with Russian affairs, October 16, 1917; in charge of Russian Affairs, Department of State, 1917-1919; executive secretary, Washington Conference on Limitation of Armament, 1921-1922, and secretary of the American delegation.

Morris, Roland S., American ambassador to Japan, August 1, 1917—March, 1921.

Moser, Charles K., American consul at Harbin, June 24, 1919—September 5, 1919.

Motono, Viscount Ichiro, Japanese Minister of Foreign Affairs, November, 1916—April, 1918.

Nabokov, Constantin, Russian chargé d'affaires in London, 1917-1919.

Niessel, General Henri Albert, director of French Military Mission in Russia, 1917-1918, and Poland, 1919-1920.

Noulens, Joseph, French ambassador to Russia, July 1917—1919.

Oi, General Narimoto, commander of Japanese forces in Siberia, 1919-1921.

Otani, General Kikuzo, commander of the Japanese expeditionary forces in Siberia; senior officer of the Allied forces in Siberia, August 9, 1918—1919.

Page, Walter Hines, American ambassador to Great Britain, April 21, 1913—November, 1918.

Phillips, William, Assistant Secretary of State, January 24, 1917—March 3, 1920.

Pichon, Stephen, French Minister of Foreign Affairs, November 16, 1917—January 20, 1920; plenipotentiary at the Paris Peace Conference.

Polk, Frank L., counselor for the Department of State, 1915-1919; Acting Secretary of State, December 4, 1918—July 18, 1919; plenipotentiary at the Paris Peace Conference, July 28—December 9, 1919; Under-Secretary of State, 1919-1920.

Poole, DeWitt C., detailed for duty in the Consulate General at Moscow, July 17, 1917; detailed to Archangel as special assistant to the ambassador, October 5, 1918; detailed to Department of State as chief of the Division of Russian Affairs, October 1, 1919—March, 1920; unassigned, March to October, 1920; designated acting chief of the Division of Russian Affairs, April 27, 1921; expert assistant, Conference on the Limitation of Armament, November 3, 1921; designated chief of the Division of Russian Affairs, December 20, 1921.

Reading, Marquess of (Rufus Daniel Isaacs), British special envoy to the United States, 1917; high commissioner and special ambassador to the United States, 1918.

Reinsch, Paul S., American minister to China, August 15, 1913—1919.

Robins, Lieutenant Colonel Raymond, head of the American Red Cross Commission to Russia, December, 1917—May, 1918.

Rodgers, Admiral William L., commander-in-chief of the United States Asiatic Fleet, 1918-1919.

Root, Elihu, ambassador extraordinary at the head of the special United States diplomatic mission to Russia in the spring of 1917.

Ruddock, A. B., American chargé d'affaires at Peking, February 26, 1920 to December 4, 1922.

Sazanov, Sergei D., Minister of Foreign Affairs in Kolchak government.

Schurman, Jacob G., American minister to China, 1921-1925.

Scidmore, George H., consul general at Yokohama, November 24, 1913—November 27, 1922.

Semenov, Captain Gregorii, ataman of the Far Eastern Cossacks.

Sharp, William G., American ambassador to France, June 19, 1914—April, 1919.

Shidehara, Baron Kijuro, Japanese ambassador to the United States, 1919-1922.

Sisson, Edgar, associate chairman of the Committee on Public Information, Washington, D. C., May 13, 1917—April 1, 1919.

Slaughter, Major Homer H., American military representative and liaison officer to Kolchak forces until December 20, 1919; at Headquarters, A.E.F., Siberia, and with Ataman Semenov, to January 1, 1920; at Vladivostok with Headquarters, A.E.F., Siberia, to April 1, 1920.

Smith, Charles H., American representative on the Inter-Allied Railway Committee for the supervision of the Chinese Eastern and Siberian Railways.

Sookine, John, attached to the Russian Embassy at Washington; later Acting Minister of Foreign Affairs of the Kolchak government.

Spencer, Willing, secretary of Embassy at Peking, December 29, 1917; at Tokyo, June 19, 1918; reassigned to Peking, October 15, 1918—March 5, 1920.

Spring-Rice, Sir Cecil Arthur, British ambassador to the United States, 1913—January, 1918.

Steffens, Lincoln, American editor and author.

Stevens, John F., chairman of the Advisory Commission of Railway Experts to Russia, 1917-1918; president of the Inter-Allied Technical Board supervising the Chinese Eastern and Siberian Railways, 1919-1923.

Summers, Maddin, consul general at Moscow, April 21, 1917—May 4, 1918.

Tanaka, General Baron Giichi, assistant chief of the Japanese General Staff,

October, 1915—September, 1918; Minister of War, September, 1918—1921.

Tchaikovsky, Nicholas V., President of the North Russian government (Archangel).

Tenney, Charles, secretary of Legation at Peking, May 1, 1914—June 26, 1919; counselor of Legation, July 21, 1919—February 28, 1921.

Terauchi, Count Masakata, Japanese Prime Minister, October 9, 1916—September 29, 1918.

Tereschenko, M. I., Minister of Finance in Provisional government, March-May, 1917; Minister of Foreign Affairs, May-October, 1917.

Trotsky, L. D., chairman of the Petrograd Soviet of Workman's and Soldiers' Deputies, October 8, 1917; Soviet Commissar for Foreign Affairs, November 8, 1917—March 13, 1918; Commissar for War and Navy, March 30, 1918—1925.

Uchida, Viscount Yasuya, Japanese Minister of Foreign Affairs, September, 1918—September, 1923.

Wang, C. C., representative on Inter-Allied Technical Board for control of Siberian Railways, 1920-1922; director-general of the Chinese Eastern Railway, 1922-1924.

Warren, Charles B., ambassador to Japan, June 29, 1921—March, 1923.

Willard, Daniel, appointed chairman of the Advisory Commission of the Council of National Defense, March, 1917; appointed Chairman of the War Industries Board, November 17, 1917.

Williams, E. T., chief of the Division of Far Eastern Affairs, Department of State, December 31, 1913—September, 1918.

Wilson, General Sir Henry H., chief of the British military representatives on Supreme War Council; chief of Imperial General Staff, 1918-1922.

Wiseman, Sir William, chief adviser on American affairs to British Delegation, Paris, 1918-1919.

Wright, J. Butler, counselor of the Embassy at Petrograd, October 2, 1916; assigned to Department of State, May 14, 1918; counselor of the Embassy at London, September 19, 1918; assigned to Department of State for duty in connection with the Conference on the Limitation of Armament; designated expert assistant, Conference on the Limitation of Armament, November 3, 1921.

Yen, Hawkling L., chief secretary to the Chinese Delegation, Conference on the Limitation of Armament, 1921.

Selected Bibliography

I. MANUSCRIPT SOURCES: OFFICIAL AND PRIVATE PAPERS

Official

Department of State, National Archives, 1917-1922
The decimal files contain the official diplomatic records of Allied intervention in Siberia. They constitute the most valuable single source on the subject. The most useful files on intervention were 861.00, "Political Conditions in Russia," and 861.77, "The Trans-Siberian and Chinese Eastern Railways." Files 763.72SU, "Proceedings of the Supreme War Council," and 793.94, "Relations Between China and Japan," were also helpful.

Naval Records Collections in the Office of Naval Records and Library, National Archives, 1917-1920
Files covering intervention are WA-6, "Russian Situation," and WA-6, "Siberia, Conditions in Vladivostok." Uneven in value. Much of this material is still restricted.

Records of the Adjutant General's Office, War Records Collection, National Archives, 1917-1919
Only selected documents in file 370.22, "Russian Expedition," are available to the scholar. The major portion of the material on the Siberian intervention is restricted.

World War I Records of the Supreme War Council, Old Records Section, Department of War, National Archives, 1918-1919
Incomplete. Helpful in revealing Allied motives for intervention.

Private

Auchincloss, Gordon. Diary in Division of Manuscripts, Yale University Library
Particularly helpful on events leading to intervention. Reveals changing attitudes of Colonel House and President Wilson on the subject.

Baker, Newton D. Collection in the custody of Baker, Hostetler, and Patterson, Inc., Cleveland, Ohio

Useful. The papers clearly indicate Baker's constant disapproval of the whole Siberian venture. Many of his more important letters on the subject are duplicated in the Wilson Papers.

Bliss, Tasker H. Collection in Division of Manuscripts, Library of Congress

The most important source on the changing attitudes of the Supreme War Council toward the Siberian expedition. Paris Peace Conference Diary is also helpful.

House, Edward M. Collection in Division of Manuscripts, Yale University Library

Many of the important documents covering the Siberian intervention in this collection are reproduced in Seymour, *Intimate Papers of Colonel House.*

Lansing, Robert. Collection in Division of Manuscripts, Library of Congress

Useful. Lansing's views are more clearly revealed in the diplomatic correspondence in the State Department Archives.

Long, Breckinridge. Collection in Division of Manuscripts, Library of Congress

Very important, particularly on the negotiations surrounding the Trans-Siberian and Chinese Eastern Railways.

Polk, Frank L. Collection in Division of Manuscripts, Yale University Library

Few of these letters bear upon the Siberian intervention.

Polk, Frank L. Confidential Diary in Division of Manuscripts, Yale University Library

Valuable. Indicates the changing views of individual members of the State Department and the President as a Siberian policy is formulated and carried out. The Diary is especially useful for the negotiations concerning the delegation of the High Command in Siberia to Japan.

Railway Service Corps Papers. Collection in Hoover War Library, Stanford University

These include lengthy memoranda on the activities of the Railway Service Corps by leading members of the group, such as John F. Stevens, George H. Emerson, and B. O. Johnson.

Wilson, Woodrow. Collection in Division of Manuscripts, Library of Congress

The papers are chronologically arranged in two files, Wilson's private papers and the White House files. The private papers are indispensable for a study of the Siberian intervention.

Wiseman, Sir William. Collection in Division of Manuscripts, Yale University Library·

Valuable. Clearly reveals the intense British pressure placed upon American statesmen for acquiescence to intervention, and later for an expansion of the expedition. The papers further indicate that many delicate negotiations concerning Siberian policy were conducted through the unofficial channels of Sir William Wiseman and Colonel House rather than through the State Department and the British Foreign Office.

II. PRINTED SOURCES

Official Documents

The German-Bolshevik Conspiracy. (War Information Series, No. 20.) Washington, October, 1918.
Selected excerpts from the so-called "Sisson Documents."

Great Britain. *Parliamentary Debates, House of Commons,* Fifth Series, 1918-1919. Vols. CIII-CXXIII.

United States Army War College. *Order of Battle of the United States Land Forces in the World War, American Expeditionary Forces in the World War.* Washington, 1937.
Gives explicit information on the make-up of the American expeditionary force in Siberia as well as on its activities throughout its stay in Siberia.

United States Congress. *Congressional Record, Proceedings and Debates,* 1918-1920. (Sixty-fifth and sixty-sixth Congresses.) Washington, 1918-1920.

United States Department of State. *Papers Relating to the Foreign Relations of the United States, 1917.* Washington, 1926.

United States Department of State. *Papers Relating to the Foreign Relations of the United States, 1917, Supplement 2, The World War.* Washington, 1932. 2 vols.

United States Department of State. *Papers Relating to the Foreign Relations of the United States, 1918, Russia.* Washington, 1931-1932. 3 vols.
Well-organized. Volume I covers political affairs and diplomatic relations. Volume II, entitled *Disintegration and Intervention,* is devoted to papers dealing with the anti-Bolshevik movements in Siberia and Manchuria, Murmansk, Archangel, and elsewhere, and Allied reaction to them. Volume III, entitled *Economic Relations,* deals chiefly with loans to the Provisional Government, assistance in railway transportation, and Soviet repudiation of loans.

United States Department of State. *Papers Relating to the Foreign Relations of the United States, 1919. The Paris Peace Conference.* Washington, 1942. Vols. I-IX, XI.

United States Department of State. *Papers Relating to the Foreign Relations of the United States, 1919, Russia.* Washington, 1937.
Covers the Siberian intervention in 1919. Vital, although not as well-organized as the 1918 volumes on Russia.

United States Department of State. *Papers Relating to the Foreign Relations of the United States, 1920.* Washington, 1936. 3 vols.

Selected documents in these volumes cover Allied withdrawal from Siberia, Japanese expansion in the Maritime Province and Sakhalin, and negotiations over the Chinese Eastern Railway.

United States Department of State. *Papers Relating to the Foreign Relations of the United States, 1921.* Washington, 1936. 2 vols.

United States Department of State. *Papers Relating to the Foreign Relations of the United States, 1922.* Washington, 1938. 2 vols.

United States Department of State. *Papers Relating to the Foreign Relations of the United States. The Lansing Papers, 1914-1920.* Washington, 1940. 2 vols.

Volume II contains selected documents from the Secretary's correspondence on Siberia. Very helpful.

United States Senate Document No. 60, Sixty-sixth Congress, Second Session. *American Troops in Siberia.* Washington, 1919.

Official statement of American policy in Siberia.

United States Senate Document No. 61, Sixty-sixth Congress, First Session. *Brewing and Liquor Interests and German and Bolshevik Propaganda.* Washington, 1919.

United States Senate Document No. 126, Sixty-seventh Congress, Second Session. *Conference on the Limitation of Armaments, Washington, November 12, 1921-February 6, 1922.* Washington, 1922.

Contains an official account of the Conference proceedings in regard to Siberia and the Chinese Eastern Railway.

Official Documents Unofficially Published

Bullitt, William C. *Bullitt Mission to Russia; Testimony Before the Committee on Foreign Relations, United States.* New York, 1919.

Bullitt's own story of his mission to Russia in 1919.

Bunyan, James. *Intervention, Civil War, and Communism in Russia. April-December 1918.* Baltimore, 1936.

An excellent selection of official and unofficial documents, confidential reports, decrees, proclamations, speeches, resolutions, and military decrees arranged in chronological order. One of the best published sources on the subject.

Bunyan, James, and H. H. Fisher. *The Bolshevik Revolution, 1917-1918. Documents and Materials.* Stanford, 1934.

An excellent selection of documents, well edited and well arranged.

Correspondance diplomatique se rapportant aux relations entre la république Russe et les puissances de l'entente, 1918. Moscow, 1919.

This correspondence is particularly concerned with the Czech revolt in the latter part of May, 1918.

Cumming, C. K., and W. W. Pettit, eds. *Russian-American Relations, March 1917-March 1920, Documents and Papers.* New York, 1920.

Includes some of the most important documents on the Siberian intervention.

Degras, Jane, ed. *Soviet Documents on Foreign Policy.* London, 1951. 2 vols.

MacMurray, J. V. A., ed. *Treaties and Agreements with and concerning China, 1849-1919.* New York, 1921. 2 vols.
Useful. Volume II covers the period from 1914 to 1919.

Varneck, Elena, and H. H. Fisher. *The Testimony of Kolchak and Other Siberian Materials.* Stanford, 1935.
Well edited with excellent explanatory and supplementary notes and a valuable bibliography. The first half of the book covers the testimony of Admiral Kolchak at his trial before the extraordinary investigating commission, January to February, 1920. Also useful were the materials on the Nikolaevsk massacre and the Vladivostok incident, April 4-5, 1920.

Letters, Diaries, Memoirs, Addresses, etc.

Ackerman, Carl W. *Trailing the Bolsheviki: Twelve Thousand Miles with the Allies in Siberia.* New York, 1919.
A journalistic account of Siberian affairs during the civil war. Not always accurate.

Baker, Ray Stannard. *Woodrow Wilson. Life and Letters.* New York, 1939. 8 vols.
Volumes VII and VIII include entries on the Siberian intervention. Useful, although the shortness of the entries and the lack of exact dates is tantalizing.

Baker, Ray Stannard, and William E. Dodd. *The Public Papers of Woodrow Wilson.* New York, 1927. 3 vols.

Barrows, David P. "Japan as Our Ally in Siberia," *Asia,* XIX (Sept., 1919), 927-931.
Personal observations by a member of the American Military Intelligence in Siberia in 1918.

Beneš, Eduard. *My War Memoirs;* trans. Paul Selver. London, 1928.

Buchanan, Sir George. *My Mission to Russia and Other Diplomatic Memories.* London, 1923. 2 vols.

Callwell, Major General Sir C. E. *Field-Marshal Sir Henry Wilson, His Life and Diaries.* London, 1927. 2 vols.
Frankly antagonistic toward President Wilson and American policy in Siberia.

Channing, C. G. F. *Siberia's Untouched Treasure, Its Future Role in the World.* New York, 1923.
Chapters XI to XX cover the author's experiences as a member of the American expeditionary force in Siberia.

Churchill, Winston. *The Aftermath.* New York, 1929.
Chapters V and XII contain an account of intervention in Siberia and elsewhere. Churchill was the British Secretary of War and an advocate of maximum intervention.

Dawson, Warrington, ed. *War Memoirs of William G. Sharp.* London, 1931.
  Contains personal observations of the French official and unofficial attitude toward the Siberian intervention. Sharp was ambassador to France during the war years.

Dwinger, Eric. *Between White and Red.* New York, 1932.
  Experiences of a German war prisoner who took part in the fighting against the Bolsheviks in 1919 and in the retreat of the Kolchak army.

Francis, David R. *Russia from the American Embassy. April 1916-November, 1918.* New York, 1921.
  An account of the ambassador's experiences in Russia taken from his notes, interviews, letters, and impressions. Strongly anti-Bolshevik.

Graves, William Sydney. *America's Siberian Adventure 1918-1920.* New York, 1931.
  The story of the American expeditionary force in Siberia by its commander. One of the most illuminating accounts on the subject.

Grondijs, Ludovic H. *La Guerre en Russie et en Siberie.* Paris, 1922.
  Useful account by a Dutch war correspondent sympathizing with the Allies.

Harper, Samuel N. *The Russia I Believe In: The Memoirs of Samuel N. Harper, 1902-1941.* Chicago, 1945.

Hill, George A. *Go Spy the Land.* London, 1932.
  The adventures of a British secret service man in Russia.

Hodges, Phelps. *Britmis. A Great Adventure of the War. Being an Account of Allied Intervention in Siberia and an Escape Across the Gobi to Peking.* London, 1931.
  By a member of the British Military Mission in Siberia.

Hull, Cordell. *Memoirs.* New York, 1948. 2 vols.
  Chapter XXII of Volume II touches briefly on Allied intervention in Siberia and its results.

Ishii, Kikujiro. *Diplomatic Commentaries.* Baltimore, 1936.
  Illustrates the psychology of a leading Japanese diplomat and statesman during an expansive period in Japanese history.

Janin, Maurice. *Ma mission en Siberie, 1918-1920.* Paris, 1933.
  Personal account by the French commander of the Czech forces in Siberia. Based on his diary.

Kindall, Sylvian G. *American Soldiers in Siberia.* New York, 1945.
  Personal account of the author's experiences as a member of the American expeditionary force in Siberia. Strongly anti-Japanese.

Lansing, Robert. *War Memoirs.* Indianapolis, 1935.
  Personal narrative covering the foreign affairs of the United States from June, 1915, through 1917.

Lennox, Lady Algernon Gordon. *Diary of Lord Bertie of Thame, 1914-1918.* London, 1924. 2 vols.

Contains illuminating commentaries on Allied and American policy in Siberia by the British ambassador to France during the war years.

Lloyd George, David. *Memoirs of the Peace Conference*. New Haven, 1939. 2 vols.
Chapter VII of Volume I covers Lloyd George's account of the negotiations concerning Russia and Siberia at the Peace Conference.

Lloyd George, David. *War Memoirs*. Boston, 1933-1937. 6 vols.
Volume V and VI contain sections on Britain's early reactions to the Bolshevik revolution, and the Siberian intervention.

Lockhart, R. H. Bruce. *British Agent*. New York, 1933.
Memoirs of the British unofficial agent in Moscow in the period when the Allies were vacillating between intervention and nonintervention. Contains the narrative of his negotiations with Lenin and Trotsky and others in regard to securing a renewal of the Russian war effort against Germany.

March, Peyton C. *The Nation at War*. New York, 1932.
War memoirs of the American Chief of Staff. Chapter IX deals with Siberia. Presents some enlightening military views on the subject of intervention in Siberia.

Masaryk, Thomas G. *The Making of a State: Memories and Observations*. New York, 1927.
By the founder and unifier of the Czechoslovak Republic. Chapters V and VI relate especially to the activities of the Czechoslovak legions in Russia.

Nabokov, Constantin. *The Ordeal of a Diplomat*. London, 1921.
By the Russian chargé d'affaires in Great Britain from January 12, 1917, to September 9, 1919.

Noulens, Joseph. *Mon ambassade en Russie soviétique, 1917-1919*. Paris, 1933. 2 vols.
Memoirs of the French ambassador to Russia covering the period from June, 1917, to December, 1918. Noulens was an early and staunch advocate of maximum intervention.

Pares, Sir Bernard. *My Russian Memoirs*. London, 1931.

Pershing, John J. *My Experiences in the World War*. New York, 1931. 2 vols.
Makes only brief mention of the Siberian expedition.

Reinsch, Paul S. *An American Diplomat in China*. New York, 1922.

Repington, Charles à Court. *The First World War, 1914-1918: Personal Experiences*. Boston and New York, 1920. 2 vols.

Sadoul, Jacques. *Notes sur le révolution bolchévique, octobre, 1917-janvier, 1919*. Paris, 1926.
Contains valuable material on the early history of intervention, particularly on the Czechoslovak question.

Seymour, Charles, ed. *The Intimate Papers of Colonel House*. Boston, 1926-1928. 4 vols.

Based upon House's journal, correspondence, and other documents. Volume III is particularly valuable.

Sisson, Edgar. *One Hundred Red Days.* New Haven, 1931.

A highly personal account of a crucial period. Relates the acquisition of certain documents purporting to show a German-Bolshevik conspiracy.

Smirnov, M. I. "Admiral Kolchak," *The Slavonic and East European Review* (London), XI (January, 1933), 373-387.

A summary of Kolchak's career by his former Chief of Staff and a member of his Omsk government.

Smith, Charles H. "What Happened in Siberia," *Asia,* XXII (May, 1922), 373-378, 402-403.

By the American member of the Inter-Allied Railway Committee established in January, 1919.

Smith, Charles H. "Four Years of Mistakes in Siberia," *Asia,* XXII (June, 1922), 479-483.

Smith, Charles H. "The Smoke-Screen between Siberia and Washington," *Asia,* XXII (August, 1922), 639-644.

Strongly anti-Japanese.

Sorokin, Pitirim. *Leaves from a Russian Diary.* New York, 1924.

Steffens, Lincoln. *Autobiography.* New York, 1931.

Steffens, Lincoln. *Letters.* New York, 1938. 2 vols.

Contains several enlightening letters on American policy toward Russia.

Villard, Oswald Garrison. *Fighting Years; Memoirs of a Liberal Editor.* New York, 1934.

Autobiography of the editor of the *Nation,* and a constant opponent of Wilson's policy in Siberia.

Ward, John. *With the Die-Hards in Siberia.* London, 1920.

Memoirs of a British Colonel in Siberia, a sympathizer and supporter of Kolchak. Bitterly opposed to American policy in Siberia.

III. SECONDARY WORKS

General Accounts and Special Studies

Baerlein, Henry. *March of the Seventy Thousand.* London, 1926.

A history of the Czech movement in Siberia.

Bailey, Thomas A. *America Faces Russia: Russian-American Relations from Early Times to Our Day.* New York, 1950.

A public-opinion study primarily concerned with diplomatic problems.

Bailey, Thomas A. *Theodore Roosevelt and the Japanese-American Crises.* Stanford, 1934.

Baker, Ray Stannard. *Woodrow Wilson and World Settlement.* New York, 1922. 3 vols.

Bau, J. M. *The Foreign Relations of China: A History and a Survey.* New York, 1922.

Bienstock, Gregory. *The Struggle for the Pacific*. New York, 1937.

Bisson, T. A. *America's Far Eastern Policy*. New York, 1945.

Bock, Benjamin. "The Origins of Inter-Allied Intervention in Eastern Asia, 1919-1920." Unpublished doctoral dissertation, Stanford University, 1940.

Buell, Raymond Leslie. *The Washington Conference*. New York, 1922. Contains only brief mention of the Siberian and Chinese Eastern problems.

Chamberlin, William Henry. *The Russian Revolution 1917-1921*. New York, 1935. 2 vols. Scholarly and relatively impartial. Makes extensive use of Russian sources.

The China Yearbook. London, New York, Peking, Tientsin, Shanghai, 1921-1924. Issues for 1921-1922, 1923, and 1924 contain considerable information on Sino-Soviet relations and events in Manchuria and Mongolia.

Clyde, Paul H. *The Far East. A History of the Impact of the West on Eastern Asia*. New York, 1948. Chapter XXIII contains the best brief account of the Siberian intervention.

Clyde, Paul H. *International Rivalries in Manchuria, 1689-1922*. Columbus, 1922. A monographic survey. Chapter XII treats the period 1915-1922.

Coates, W. P., and Zelda K. Coates. *Armed Intervention in Russia 1918-1922*. London, 1935. Deals primarily with Great Britain's role in armed intervention. Attempts to justify Russia's claims for damages due to Allied intervention.

Coates, W. P., and Zelda K. Coates. *A History of Anglo-Soviet Relations*. London, 1943.

Dennett, Tyler. *Roosevelt and the Russo-Japanese War*. New York, 1925. A study of American foreign policy in Eastern Asia, 1902-1905, based primarily upon the private papers of Theodore Roosevelt.

Dennis, Alfred L. P. *The Foreign Policies of Soviet Russia*. New York, 1924. A history of the international relations of Soviet Russia from the November revolution to the end of 1923. Based largely on newspaper sources. Helpful.

Dugdale, Blanche E. *Arthur James Balfour, First Earl of Balfour*. New York, 1937. Makes use of material gathered by Lord Balfour for an autobiography. Volume II covers the Siberian intervention.

Dulles, Foster Rhea. *Forty Years of American-Japanese Relations*. New York, 1937.

Dulles, Foster Rhea. *The Road to Teheran: The Story of Russia and America 1781-1943*. Princeton, 1944.

Field, Frederick V. *American Participation in the China Consortiums.*
    Chicago, 1931.
    The best single account on the subject.
Fischer, Louis. *The Soviets in World Affairs: A History of Relations be-
    tween the Soviet Union and the Rest of the World.* London, 1930.
    2 vols.
    The first volume contains sections dealing with Russo-Asiatic affairs
    during the civil war.
Griswold, A. Whitney. *The Far Eastern Policy of the United States.*
    New York, 1938.
    Well-documented and very readable. Particularly helpful in fitting
    the Siberian expedition into the larger picture of America's traditional
    Far Eastern Policy.
Hagedorn, Herman. *The Magnate: William Boyce Thompson and His
    Times, 1869-1930.* New York, 1935.
    A biography of the head of the American Red Cross in Russia in 1917.
    Useful.
Hard, William. *Raymond Robins' Own Story.* New York, 1920.
    Robins was the head of the American Red Cross in Russia in 1918.
Ichihashi, Yamato. *The Washington Conference and After: A Historical
    Survey.* Stanford, 1928.
The Japan Yearbook. Tokyo, 1919-1924.
    Contains official statements regarding intervention.
Jessup, Philip. *Elihu Root.* New York, 1938. 2 vols.
Kawakami, K. K. *Japan's Pacific Policy.* New York, 1922.
    Chapter XXXIII attempts to explain Japan's Siberian policy.
Kono, Tsunekichi. *The Japanese Army.* Tokyo, 1929.
LaFargue, Thomas E. *China and the World War.* Stanford, 1937.
    Authoritative and comprehensive. Essential to a knowledge of Ameri-
    can policy in the Far East following World War I.
Lengyel, Emil. *Siberia.* New York, 1943.
    Popular account. Contains vivid descriptions of the major Siberian
    leaders during the civil war.
Li, Tien-yi. *Woodrow Wilson's China Policy, 1913-1917.* New York,
    1952.
Lobanov-Rostovsky, Prince A. *Russia and Asia.* New York, 1933.
    A historical survey of relations between Russia and Asia with chapters
    on the revolution and the civil war.
Manning, Clarence A. *The Siberian Fiasco.* New York, 1952.
Millard, Thomas F. *Conflict of Policies in Asia.* London, 1924.
    A survey of the foreign policies and interests of the nations principally
    concerned in the Far East. Strongly anti-Japanese.
Millard, Thomas F. *Democracy and the Eastern Question.* New York,
    1919.

Mock, James R., and Cedric Larson. *Words That Won the War: The Story of the Committee on Public Information 1917-1919*. Princeton, 1939.

Moore, Frederick F. *Siberia Today*. New York, 1919.
Journalistic account. Strongly anti-Bolshevik.

Mordacq, Jean Jules Henri. *Le Ministère Clemenceau, journal d'un témoin*. Paris, 1931. 4 vols.

Norton, H. K. *Far Eastern Republic of Siberia*. New York, 1927.
Brief account of revolution, civil war, and intervention in Siberia, and in greater detail, the establishment of the Far Eastern Republic.

Palmer, Frederick. *Bliss, Peacemaker. The Life and Letters of General Tasker Howard Bliss*. New York, 1934.

Palmer, Frederick. *Newton D. Baker, America at War*. New York, 1931. 2 vols.

Pelzel, Sophia Rogoski. *American Intervention in Siberia, 1918-1920*. Philadelphia, 1946.
Doctoral dissertation in political science.

Pollard, Robert T. *China's Foreign Relations 1917-1931*. New York, 1933.
Chapters V, VI, and IX deal with Chinese relations with the Whites and the Soviets.

Price, Ernest Batson. *The Russo-Japanese Treaties of 1907-1916 Concerning Manchuria and Mongolia*. Baltimore, 1933.

Ross, E. A. *The Russian Soviet Republic*. New York, 1923.

Schuman, Frederick L. *American Policy Toward Russia Since 1917*. New York, 1928.
A careful and critical analysis.

Sokolsky, George E. *The Story of the Chinese Eastern Railway*. Shanghai, 1929.

Spargo, John. *Russia as an American Problem*. New York, 1920.

Stewart, George. *The White Armies of Russia; a Chronicle of Counter-Revolution and Allied Intervention*. New York, 1933.
One of the best accounts on the subject. An attempt to weave together all aspects of intervention in Russia.

Strakhovsky, Leonid I. *Intervention at Archangel: Story of Allied Intervention and Russian Counter-Revolution in North Russia, 1918-1920*. Princeton, 1944.
A carefully prepared and documented study of the administration of a foreign territory under military occupation.

Strakhovsky, Leonid I. *The Origins of American Intervention in North Russia, 1918*. Princeton, 1937.
Documented. The author played an active part in many of the events described.

Sullivan, Mark. *The Great Adventure: The Story of the Conference*. New York, 1922.

Takeuchi, Tatsuji. *War and Diplomacy in the Japanese Empire.* New York, 1935.
   Chapter XVIII covers the Siberian expedition. Clearly reveals the conflict between the military and civilian authorities in regard to the problem. An excellent summary based upon Japanese sources.
Tompkins, Pauline. *American-Russian Relations in the Far East.* New York, 1949.
   Valuable. Contains several chapters on the Siberian intervention. The author concludes that Wilson's decision to intervene in Siberia was "right and inevitable."
Tupper, Eleanor, and George E. McReynolds. *Japan in American Public Opinion.* New York, 1937.
   A diplomatic history based largely upon newspapers, congressional debates, and expressed opinions of representative men and women.
Weigh, Ken Shen. *Russo-Chinese Diplomacy.* Shanghai, 1928.
Wheeler-Bennett, John. *Brest-Litovsk, The Forgotten Peace, March, 1918.* London, 1938.
White, John Albert. *The Siberian Intervention.* Princeton, 1950.
   An excellent survey, carefully annotated and based upon American, Japanese, and Russian sources. Primarily concerned with the events following the departure of American troops from Siberia. Attempts to cover all phases of the intervention.
Williams, William A. *American-Russian Relations, 1781-1947.* New York, 1952.
Young, A. Morgan. *Japan Under Taisho Tenno.* London, 1928.
Young, C. Walter. *Japan's Special Position in Manchuria.* Baltimore, 1931.

Articles

Adachi, Kinnosuke. "Concerning Japan and Siberia," *Asia,* XXIII (August, 1918), 637-639.
"America and Japan; The Swing of the Pendulum." *Far Eastern Review,* XVII (May, 1921), 332-335.
"American Policy in Russia," *New Republic,* XVIII (February 8, 1918), 37-39.
"China's Effort to Recover Control over the Chinese Eastern Railway," *Far Eastern Review,* XVI (September, 1920), 605-606.
Colcord, Lincoln. "Japan in Siberia," *Nation,* CX (January 10, 1920), 36-39.
"The Crime against Russia," *Nation,* CIX (August 2, 1919), 136.
Deane, Frederick. "The Chinese Eastern Railway," *Foreign Affairs,* III (September 15, 1924), 147-152.
Dennis, A. L. P. "The New Russo-Japanese Treaty Explained," *Current History,* XXI (May, 1925), 240-244.

Fleming, Jackson. "A Counter-Thrust for Russia: World Democracy Must Strike Germany in Asia," *Asia,* XVIII (July, 1918), 537-541.

Gilbreath, Oliver. "The Sick Man of Siberia: The Story of the Trans-Siberian Railroad," *Asia,* XIX (June, 1919), 546-552.

Graham, M. W. "Russian-American Relations, 1917-1933: An Interpretation," *American Political Science Review,* XXVIII (June, 1934), 401-409.

Graves, Sidney C. "Japanese Aggression in Siberia," *Current History,* XIV (May, 1921), 239-245.

"Japan and Siberia," *New Republic,* XXI (January 14, 1920), 187-188.

"Justice to Russia," *Nation,* CVIII (January, 1919), 6-7.

Keith, Orrin. "Re-birth of Industry and Commerce in Eastern Siberia," *Far Eastern Review,* XVIII (February, 1922), 127-129.

Kennan, George. "Can We Help Russia?" *Outlook,* CXIX (May 22, 1918), 141.

Mason, Gregory. "Japan and Bolshevism," *Outlook,* CXIX (June 12, 1918), 259-261.

Mason, Gregory. "Japan, Germany, Russia and the Allies: An Authorized Interview with Count Masakata Terauchi, Premier of Japan," *Outlook,* CXIX (May 1, 1918), 18-22.

Mason, Gregory. "Shall We Send an Army to Russia," *Outlook,* CXVII (October 24, 1917), 292-297.

Pasvolsky, Leo. "Russia Takes Over Vladivostok," *Current History,* XVI (December, 1922), 499-501.

Peffer, Nathaniel. "Japan's Absorption of Siberia," *Nation,* CXII (October 5, 1921), 367-369.

"President Masaryk on Intervention," *New Republic,* XIX (July 23, 1919), 377.

Reinsch, Paul S. "Manchuria, Mongolia, and Siberia," *Nation,* CXIV (May 3, 1922), 523-525.

Sherower, Miles M. "Japanese Imperialism," *Nation,* CXII (February 2, 1921), 175-177.

Sherower, Miles M. "The Nikolaevsk Massacre," *Nation,* CXI (August 21, 1920), 211-213.

Wang, C. C. "The Chinese Eastern Railway," *Annals of the American Academy of Political and Social Science,* CXXII (November, 1925), 67-75.

Wilton, Robert. "The Rush for Siberia: Causes of the Present Crisis in the Pacific," *Fortnightly Review,* CX (November 1, 1925), 782-805.

Zippin, Max. "The Far East Gets a Respite," *Nation,* CXI (August 2, 1920), 210-211.

Newspapers and Periodicals

American Political Science Review.

Annals of the American Academy of Political and Social Science.

Asia.
Current History.
Current Opinion.
Far Eastern Review (Shanghai).
Foreign Affairs.
Fortnightly Review (London).
Literary Digest.
London *Times.*
Nation.
New Republic.
New York *Times.*
Outlook.
Pacific Affairs.
Slavonic and East European Review (London).

Index

and Czech role in Siberia, 59 n. 94
and high command in Siberia, 76, 89, 90
and withdrawal of American troops from
    Siberia, 178, 178 n. 37, 179, 180
attitude toward Bolsheviks, 90, 122,
    122 n. 13, 233 n. 8
characteristics of, 89
criticized by
    General Knox, 123
    Omsk government, 127
    State Department, 124-125
interpretation of American policy in
    Siberia, 104, 122 n. 13, 124
relations with
    Cossacks, 121, 126-127
    Japanese military in Siberia, 101-102
role of, in intervention, 3, 120-121
views on
    Austro-German war prisoners, 46 n.
        36, 47
    intervention, 233 n. 5
    Omsk government, 102, 152, 157 n.
        29, 158, 233 n. 5
    Vladivostok incident, 185, 186 n. 13
Great Britain
attitude toward
    General Graves, 123
    joint Japanese-American expedition to
        Siberia, 71-73
motives for intervention in Siberia, 230-
    231
negotiations for
    Consortium of 1920, 207, 211, 214,
        222
    Inter-Allied Railway Agreement, 1919,
        109-110, 112-113, 116, 117 n. 42
policy toward
    Chinese Eastern Railway, 208-209,
        210-214, 217-220, 226-227, 228
    Czechs in Siberia, 54, 58, 100, 101
    Russia, 141, 147
    Siberia, 73-75, 86, 91-95, 105, 183,
        232
proposals for intervention, 23-25, 29-30,
    37, 38, 41-42, 43, 64
reaction to Wilson's *aide memoire*, 78,
    79
relations with
    Bolsheviks, 10-12, 42-43, 230-231
    Japan, 4, 105 n. 63
    Kolchak government, 123, 149, 150,
        151, 153, 158, 161
    Semenov, 15, 120, 126
sends troops to Siberia, 39, 73

views on withdrawal of American troops
    from Siberia, 171
Grew, Joseph E.
    and use of Czechs in Siberia, 56, 65
Guins, Georgii K.
    and use of Czechs in Siberia, 58

Hara, Takashi
    relations with Japanese General Staff,
        106
    Siberian policy, 81, 174-175, 182, 191
Harris, Ernest L., 45, 88 n. 81, 127, 163
    n. 47, 186
    and Japanese expansion in Siberia, 112 n.
        26
    policy toward Omsk government, 118,
        121, 149, 150-151, 152, 162, 163,
        164-165
    views on intervention, 61 n. 99
Hay, John, 4
Heid, August, 162, 164
Hicks, Captain W. L., 46, 47
Horvat, General Dmitri L.
    description of, 14 n. 50, 102, 119
    policy in Chinese Eastern Railway zone,
        14-15, 107-108, 111, 205, 206
    relations with Japan, 15, 75, 75 n. 29,
        101-102
House, Colonel Edward M.
    and expansion of Siberian expedition,
        71 n. 12, 92
    attitude toward Bolsheviks, 19, 141
    distrust of Japan, 7, 36
    policy toward Russia, 7, 146, 147, 147
        n. 55
    proposals for intervention, 62, 63
    views on intervention, 31-33, 38, 42 n.
        16
Hughes, Charles Evans, 195, 196
    and Japanese withdrawal from Siberia,
        202
    policy toward Chinese Eastern Railway,
        219, 223-225, 228
    reviews Siberian policy at Washington
        Conference, 200-201
Hull, Cordell, 233

Inagaki, General S., 18
Inter-Allied Railway Agreement, 1919,
    159, 168
    effect on American policy, 117
    interpretation of, 166, 169-171, 173, 207,
        209, 210, 213, 216
    negotiations for, 108-110, 112, 116